SECOND E

WYOMING BACKROADS

An Off-Highway Guide to Wyoming's Best Backcountry Drives, 4WD Routes, and ATV Trails

Marc Smith

Open Space Publications

Casper, Wyoming

Direct all inquiries to:
Open Space Publications, LLC
PO Box 50133
Casper, WY 82605-0133

www.OpenSpacePublications.com

ISBN: 978-0-9740900-9-2

Printed in the United States of America. Second Edition

All photos by author unless otherwise credited.
Cover photos by Marc Smith, Brent Fuchs, Kathy Fuchs.
Edited by Judith Savala-Wright.
Cover design by Julie Cornia of Black Dog Design.

Caution

Backcountry travel and outdoor recreation are potentially dangerous activities that pose risks. The author and publisher assume no responsibility or liability for any damages, losses, accidents, inconveniences, or injuries incurred from using this book. It is the reader's responsibility to be aware of all risks and take the necessary precautions to mitigate those risks.

While the author has made a considerable attempt to make this book as accurate as possible, errors may exist. Remember that roads, trails, facilities, field conditions, signs, and maps are constantly changing. Laws, regulations, and land ownership are also prone to change.

This guidebook does **not**:
- Direct you through every junction or fork that you'll encounter. Keep track of where you are and do not hesitate to turn back if you become uncomfortable with the route. Roads rarely improve the farther you drive.
- Replace your responsibility to do your own research and check legal requirements. Before you shift into gear, be sure you know that your vehicle is allowed on the route and that the route is open to your use.
- Offer the level of detail that some drivers may want for backcountry navigation. The maps included in this guidebook are only intended for general reference. They should be used in conjunction with detailed maps, such as those that are published or distributed by the land management agency.

Wyoming Regions

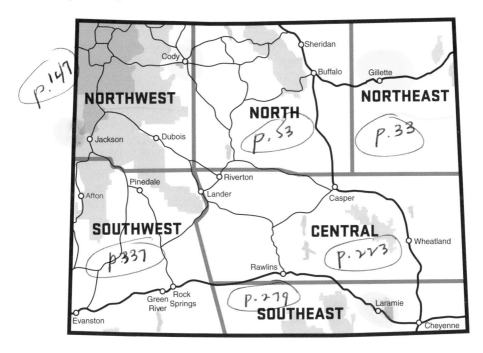

Map Legend

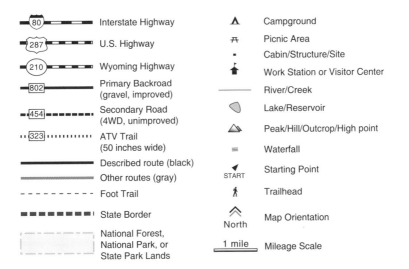

80 Interstate Highway	▲ Campground
287 U.S. Highway	⊼ Picnic Area
210 Wyoming Highway	▪ Cabin/Structure/Site
802 Primary Backroad (gravel, improved)	⛫ Work Station or Visitor Center
454 Secondary Road (4WD, unimproved)	—— River/Creek
323 ATV Trail (50 inches wide)	◗ Lake/Reservoir
—— Described route (black)	◮ Peak/Hill/Outcrop/High point
—— Other routes (gray)	≡ Waterfall
– – – Foot Trail	◀ START Starting Point
▬▬▬ State Border	🜚 Trailhead
⌟ ⌝ National Forest, National Park, or State Park Lands	⌃⌃ North Map Orientation
	1 mile Mileage Scale

Abbreviations and Acronyms

The following abbreviations and acronyms are used throughout this book:

FR	Forest Road; these roads are located within a National Forest and managed by the USDA Forest Service.
FT	Forest Trail; these are designated ATV trails located within a National Forest and managed by the USDA Forest Service. These routes are limited to vehicles that are 50 inches or less in width.
CR	County Road; these roads are managed by the county. Road numbers often change when you cross a county line.
BLMR	BLM Road; these roads are managed by the Bureau of Land Management.
HWY	Highway (both Federal and State).
I	Interstate Highway.
Two track	A primitive, overgrown road where only two parallel tire tracks are visible.
ORV	Off-Road Vehicle (same as OHV).
OHV	Off-Highway Vehicle (same as ORV).
4WD	Four wheel drive. This term is often used to describe a route that requires, or has the potential to require, a 4WD vehicle.
4x4	Four wheel drive vehicle. A stock 4x4 refers to a factory-equipped four wheel drive vehicle without modifications (such as oversized tires and lift kit).
ATV	All Terrain Vehicle.

Contents

Preface

I'll never forget my first trip across Wyoming as I headed toward Yellowstone. Just a grade school kid, I was thrilled to spot antelope on the high plains, though I stopped counting them after 150. I found Yellowstone to be absolutely captivating, but this was a family vacation and as the youngest member, I didn't get to do many of the things that I wanted. I vowed that I would go back someday to finish my exploring. That part I've fulfilled. What I didn't anticipate is that by this time I'd have traversed tens of thousands of miles across the rest of Wyoming—that the desire to keep exploring would be insatiable.

These adventures led me to write several other books: Hiking Wyoming's Medicine Bow National Forest, The Wyoming Camping Guide, and Black Hills Camping. However, when a bookstore manager asked me to write a Wyoming four-wheeling book, I quickly declined and explained that I wasn't an off-roader—at least not like the ones portrayed on the cover of magazines. Little did either of us know at the time that he had just planted the seed.

Over the next few weeks, my mind was astir with the idea. I finally concluded that not only would I write the book, but that I was already well on my way. After all, it's impossible to travel throughout Wyoming in pursuit of hiking trails and campgrounds without getting mud on the fenders and a few scars on the skid plates. Research for the previous books had put over 100,000 miles on my odometer (thank goodness gas was cheap back then). To finish this book, I'd end up using a Yamaha Rhino and Polaris RZR. Using these capable vehicles changed everything. I was suddenly able to access areas that were previously beyond my reach. I discovered a whole new Wyoming and it renewed my appreciation for this unique state, as well as the Rocky Mountain West.

Unfortunately, I saw some disheartening things along the way—senseless vandalism, blatant violations, pollution, resource damage, and once, a group of out-of-control ATV riders who used a campground road as a racetrack, and then yelled obscenities to everyone who rightfully opposed. Those individuals were particularly harassing to a family who were on a camping vacation, and I wouldn't be surprised if it ruined a trip they may have spent years saving for and planning. These injustices put enough doubt in me to suspend the book project several times. I had to ask whether a guide like this would lead people to the outdoors to enjoy and help protect them or destroy them.

Ultimately, I was inspired by what I saw off the beaten path. There was a family on ATVs in the Medicine Bow who were carrying bags of trash, ensuring that they left the forest cleaner than they had found it. There was an elderly gentleman—no longer capable of backpacking—who motored himself to a faraway lake and spent a fantastic night camping with moose as his guests. I was awestruck by the genuine western hospitality of people from places like Worland, Wheatland, Dubois, and Lander. Once on the fringe of the Bighorns, I was stopped by a group of local ranchers who asked me to get off of the Rhino. I nervously complied, only to learn that each one wanted to sit on it and ask some questions. We stood on the road trading laughs for the good part of an hour and they enthusiastically welcomed me to their part of the state. And the off-roading community itself, folks from all different states, proved to be a generous, tight-knit family of complete strangers who are willing to help each other. Be assured that if you have a problem on a backroad, you'll get free and unconditional roadside assistance from this group of backcountry enthusiasts.

When the dust settled, I found that this book project was much more difficult than anything I had imagined. Both the first and second editions took years longer than expected, but I have the book that I initially envisioned when I walked out of that bookstore—a utilitarian guide that will help you plan your outings and will lead you to new adventures. To do that, I've taken an approach that I believe works well for this state. The people who live in or frequent Wyoming are an independent, capable, and self-reliant bunch. With that known, this book will not guide you from GPS coordinate to GPS coordinate. You also won't find a level of detail so great that it extinguishes your curiosity. Rather, you'll get route information that sets your expectations and keeps you on track, while allowing you to have some discovery of your own. You'll happen upon some unmentioned treasures and at least a few scenic overlooks that will surprise you. Keep your camera ready.

So with that, I encourage you to venture into the wilds of Wyoming with an attitude of stewardship and responsibility. Value the land you traverse and stay on the designated routes to encourage others to do the same. If you find someone in need, offer assistance. Show respect to those who would rather not listen to an engine by giving them space. Be prepared, stay safe, and have a blast out there!

Acknowledgements

I doubt many books are completed as solo projects and this certainly was not one of them. I must first acknowledge Julie, my patient wife, who occupied the passenger seat on nearly every route. She rode without complaint on many hot and dusty 13-hour days. She is a good transcriber and outdoor cook. So, Julie, thanks for the companionship and for keeping the train on the tracks while I toiled away at this thing. Thanks also to my kids, who have taught me how to slow down to see the world from a less hectic pace.

Mike Hambleton, thanks for riding with me through the Red Desert and the Black Hills—great times! I'm also filled with gratitude for my parents, who have an endless supply of support. When my transmission failed on the first day of what was my final push to get the research done, they handed over the keys to their unblemished truck. I had quite a time with that rig and nearly didn't get it out of the Wind River Range. Many of those stories will remain untold. So Mom and Dad, thank you. Your simple act of trust saved me two seasons.

I'd like to thank the handful of Forest Service employees from the Ashley, Black Hills, Bighorn, Bridger-Teton, Medicine Bow, and Shoshone who provided assistance. Three individuals in particular deserve recognition: Marcia Rose-Ritchie, Michelle Buzalsky, and Clint Kyhl. Other individuals who provided invaluable information or assistance include Steve Rafuse, Steven King, Ryan Twomney, Jeff Namesnik, Wesley Gooch, Beth Boddiger, Logan Heath, and Charles and Vyrla Prior—many thanks to each of you for your contributions.

There were numerous others, nameless folks, who shared information for a few minutes before spinning off out of sight. Hopefully, you'll read this some day and recognize yourself. And finally, a humongous thank you to Julie Cornia and Judith Wright who helped me pull everything into one piece. I very much appreciate the expertise and patience the two of you have.

INTRODUCTION

The paved road only gets you so far. To truly experience what Wyoming has to offer, you have to go further and turn off the pavement. The backroads of Wyoming lead to amazing places. There are deep canyons, sand dunes, ancient sketches on colorful sandstone cliffs, lonely fishing lakes, vast open spaces, soaring mountains, dark forests, high deserts, and even a few moonscapes. You'll discover historical remnants of the westward migration, sweeping vistas along the nation's Continental Divide, and the most diverse and complete wildlife habitats in the Rocky Mountain West. This driving guide will lead you on these adventures, so load up, shift into gear, and let's go!

Wyoming: A Crash Course

As the tenth largest state in the union, Wyoming encompasses a lot of ground. Its rectangular shape covers 97,818 square miles, nearly half of which is owned by the federal government and made public. These lands are varied and diverse. There are gentle grasslands like those found in the northeast corner where the elevation drops as low as 3,099 feet. Across the rest of the state, which has an average elevation of 6,700 feet (the second highest state in the country), the terrain is a mix of prairies, deserts, mountain ranges, badlands, and huge intermountain basins. At the ceiling, there is Gannett Peak, a pinnacle of granite and ice in the Wind River Range that stands at 13,804 feet.

Wyoming's major mountain ranges—the Absaroka, Bear Lodge, Beartooth, Bighorn, Laramie, Medicine Bow, Salt River, Wind River, and Wyoming—are vital not only to the state but also to distant regions. The snow that falls in these highlands feeds mighty rivers, such as the Yellowstone, Green, and Platte. The waters from these drainages fill many reservoirs across the state, which are heavily used for municipality supplies, recreation, hydroelectricity, and irrigation.

The mountains, in conjunction with the expanses that surround them, provide habitat to a very long list of animals. Many of these species are to be expected, like moose, elk, deer, pronghorn antelope, black bears, bighorn sheep, mountain lions, and raptors. Yet others that find refuge in Wyoming have long been eradicated from much of the middle and lower continent. Among the notable ones are grizzly bears, wolves, bison, wolverines, and black-footed ferrets.

Wyoming has a semi-arid climate. With the exception of the highest mountains, the majority of the state receives less than 20 inches of annual precipitation. This is evident in the sprawling rangelands and high deserts where vegetation is sparse. In fact, there are still many places where the tracks of the Oregon Trail—a primary route of the western migration—have yet to be overgrown.

During eras such as the Jurassic Period and Eocene Epoch, Wyoming was a very different place. Fossil records show that the state was a warm and moist subtropical wonder complete with palm trees and crocodiles. Wyoming's rich fossil beds have produced dinosaur exhibits that are on display in museums worldwide and discoveries are still being made today. One recent find, the world's largest Columbian mammoth, is on display at the Tate Geological Museum in Casper.

Unsurprisingly, Wyoming is rich with fossil fuels such as coal, natural gas, and oil, as well as other minerals such as trona and uranium. On a nationwide scale, Wyoming ranks among the top producers of these natural resources. As a windy state, Wyoming is also positioned to be a leader in wind-powered renewable energy. The state already has numerous wind farms in operation and more are on the way.

Aside from energy production, tourism and outdoor recreation are key drivers of Wyoming's economy. Chief among the destinations are Yellowstone and Grand Teton National Parks, both of which hold international fame. Supplementing these gems, Wyoming has eight national forests, a pair of national monuments and national recreation areas, a dozen state parks, and nearly two dozen historic sites.

The backroads of Wyoming are a commonality across the state's various industries and special areas. For those who work on the land like ranchers, guides, miners, researchers, land managers, and drillers, backroads are a part of the daily commute. For others, like hunters, anglers, photographers, hikers, wildlife enthusiasts, sightseers, and weekend warriors, backroads offer access to the places they love. However they're utilized, these roads are an integral part of Wyoming.

Trip Preparation

Before you leave for a trip off the pavement, prepare and pack for the worst. You'll fare much better if something goes wrong.

Contacts

Line up your emergency contacts before you leave home. Make sure that any relative or friend who may need to come to your assistance will be available to do so. If you're going into an area where you don't know anyone, you can turn to the phone directory. Do a quick Internet search to find a local towing company or two for the area, giving preference to those that offer off-road vehicle recoveries if you're going to be on secondary roads. I keep a statewide list in the glove box so that if the need arises, I already know whom I'm going to call and what services they provide.

Second, tell someone where you are going (being as specific as possible), what your intentions are, and when you expect to return. Don't ignore this safety precaution even if you're traveling with several other parties. I have encountered groups who had all of their vehicles stuck in the same place and there was nobody left to go for help.

Current Area Information

Once you know where you are going, follow up with the managing agency to check current conditions and regulations. Routes that indicate they'll be open on a map are sometimes found locked and gated—a simple phone call can you save you considerable time and expense. Conversely, remember that an open gate doesn't mean the road is passable. People have been stranded when they foolishly assumed that the absence of a locked gate implied safe conditions.

Last, check the weather forecast for the area and consider how elevation will impact a weather front. The storm that produces sprinkles of rain 30 miles away in the basin may bring a vicious blizzard to the high country.

Maintenance

Driving a poorly maintained vehicle around town carries little risk. If you break down, help is imminent. Driving the same poorly maintained vehicle into the backcountry is irresponsible and unsafe. Before you head out, give your vehicle a thorough inspection. Ensure the fluids are at appropriate levels. Check the belts for cracks and wear and consider carrying an extra serpentine belt or accessory belts, depending on your vehicle. Make sure your tires don't have any flaws and don't forget to check the spare. If you have oversized tires, be sure your spare is the same size as the rest of the tires on your vehicle. An undersized spare is of little use off-road.

Recovery Kit

What you take with you may determine how you get back. Acting on a bit of a premonition as I was pulling out of the driveway before a weeklong trip, I paused to grab a set of tire plugs and a portable air compressor from the garage. The next day I was four-wheeling a distant portion of the Wind Rivers around sunset when I got a flat tire. Then I discovered that the spare tire was also flat! I aired up the spare and put it on, plugged and inflated the flat, and was back on my way in the dark. Had I not been prepared, I likely would have had to hike to a main road the next day to find someone who could take me (and my tires) to town and back, which would have been a nearly 100-mile round-trip. That's a lot to ask of a stranger.

You should always carry a well-equipped recovery kit and secure it to the vehicle or ATV so that it can't move while driving. Suggested items include:

- Gloves.
- Basic toolkit.
- Fire extinguisher.
- Flashlight.
- First-aid kit.
- Hatchet or saw.
- Tire puncture repair kit.
- Tire pressure gauge.
- Booster cables or pre-charged battery jumper.
- D-ring shackle for securing a recovery strap to a hitch receiver.
- Short shovel or extendable snow shovel in snowy conditions.
- Zip ties and duct tape for emergency repairs.
- Extra automotive fluids and parts, as necessary.
- Portable air compressor, such as the type that plugs into a 12V outlet, or a portable compressed air tank. Serious off-roaders opt for an on-board compressor (and even welder).
- Recovery (tow) strap. Choose a strap that has loops on the ends and a 20,000-pound rating or higher. Avoid straps with metal hooks on the end. These can become deadly missiles if the strap snaps or comes off its anchor.

An example of a recovery kit

- Tire chains (set of four) if you'll be driving backroads during the offseason.
- Extra water and food. Military-style packages, such as MREs (Meals Ready to Eat), are small and have a long shelf life.
- Electric winch if you're a serious off-roader who often drives in difficult conditions, but this is overkill for most drivers.
- Camping gear or at least some extra clothes and emergency supplies.
- Off-road jack, which can be operated outside of the vehicle rather than under it. The versatile Hi-Lift Jack is a popular favorite. Aside from raising a single wheel, you can also use this jack to lift your vehicle from a bumper or as a manual winch—jack accessories may be required depending on your vehicle. Also consider carrying a short, thick board, which can be used as a base plate for the jack. This board can also be used to build a ramp or to place under your tire to improve traction in snow or mud.

Your Off-Highway Vehicle

Most backroads, such as county gravel roads, can be negotiated with any vehicle when driven carefully. But if you're going to venture off the main paths, or if conditions deteriorate, you'll need a vehicle that is capable to get you back to the pavement. Consider these factors:

Ground Clearance

When driving backroads, ground clearance—the distance between the ground and the lowest component on the undercarriage of your vehicle—is more important than having four-wheel drive. It's this clearance that will get you over rocks, potholes, dips, and other obstacles. Most stock 4x4 SUVs and pickup trucks have between 7-9 inches of clearance, which is sufficient for many secondary roads. But for the tougher routes, especially the rocky ones in the mountains, you'll want a vehicle that stands 10 inches or higher off the ground. In Wyoming, 12 full inches of ground clearance (common for ATVs) will get you almost anywhere that you want to go. With a few exceptions, full-sized vehicles in this upper range have been modified with a lift and oversized tires.

Tires

Despite their rough-and-tough marketing, many manufacturers equip their 4x4s with passenger-rated street tires. If you're headed off the highway, there may be no better upgrade for a stock vehicle than to get a durable set of light truck (LT) all-terrain (AT) tires. With a good set of all-terrains, you'll be surprised at what you can traverse without 4WD. These tires have more aggressive tread patterns and thicker 2-ply or 3-ply sidewalls that can withstand the abuses of rough terrain. This is a good tire choice if your vehicle doubles as your daily driver.

Mud-terrain tires have large lugs with extra spacing that improve traction by preventing mud build-up. These are excellent tires for mud and rock, but they can be annoyingly noisy, wear poorly, and don't perform as well on ice or wet pavement.

Airing down your tires to a lower PSI can also increase tire traction over certain terrains. However, airing down your tires too much can cause the tire to separate from your wheel, so use caution and consult the tire manufacturer or local tire shop before trying this. You will also need a way to re-inflate your tires when you return to a more solid driving surface.

Four Wheel Drive

Four wheel drive (4WD), or a variant of it such as all-wheel drive (AWD), adds considerable capability to your vehicle. In the simplest of terms, this system sends power to all four wheels of your vehicle to drastically improve traction and off-road performance.

Auto manufacturers offer a multitude of 4WD systems and technologies. Manual systems are engaged by pushing a button, turning a knob, pulling a lever, or physically "locking the hubs" on the front wheels. Vehicles that have what is known as "on-demand 4WD" engage the system automatically when a computer determines that a wheel has lost traction. Regardless of the system with which your vehicle is equipped, it's imperative that you get familiar with it before you find yourself in a situation where you need it. Be sure you know how to engage the system and understand its limitations— some vehicles require that you be stopped while others can be shifted while driving under a specific speed. Many 4x4s now come with a separate off-road driving guide that fully explains the 4WD system as well as recommended driving tips.

When to use 4WD is a personal preference, given that you are driving a vehicle that allows you to engage and disengage the system. Some drivers shift into 4WD as soon as they turn off the pavement and onto a gravel road. I personally use it only if I need to get through, or out of, a particularly tricky section or in very low-traction environments. Using it in this manner helps assure that you won't exceed your abilities. If you drive until you're about to get stuck, you can use 4WD to help you get out. If you use 4WD until you get stuck, you're really stuck.

Off-Highway Driving

If you're new to off-highway driving, consider reading a book dedicated to the subject, joining a club, or going with a more experienced driver. Here are general guidelines for tackling the most common challenges that you may find off the paved road.

Log Crossing

Encountering logs across the roadway is very common and it's becoming even more prevalent as the pine bark beetle epidemic has killed millions of trees that are now falling. If your vehicle has suitable clearance, you may be able to simply drive over the log. This is sometimes made easier if approached at an angle. You can also try using a strap to pull or drag the log from the roadway. As a last resort, you can attempt to build a ramp over the log by using other logs or rocks. This approach certainly has its risks. Some drivers carry chainsaws to help clear blocked roadways.

Water Crossing

Water crossings, or fords, are mostly a concern during late spring and early summer when creeks run deep and swift. By late summer or fall, most creeks are flowing low, if at all. As a general rule, creeks run shallower in the early morning than they do during the afternoon when the heat of the day accelerates snow melting. The depth that you can ford depends on your vehicle. In general, you want your air intake to be about a foot above the water. Also be conscious of where the vehicle's electrical components are located.

Before crossing a stream or flooded area, get out and check the depth. Streams are almost always deeper than they appear from behind the wheel. Also, check the far bank and make sure you'll be able to climb out of the stream with compromised traction—these banks are sometimes eroded and quite steep. Once you are in the water, maintain a steady speed to avoid splashing, spinning, and stalling.

Mud

In general, you should refrain from driving a road that is muddy enough that you're creating ruts. In some areas, wet roads are considered closed until they are dry enough to drive without causing damage. Of course, you don't have that choice when the road you're already on suddenly deteriorates into a slippery hazard. A frozen road (typical in the early morning during spring or the hunting season) can become muddy during the day as the ground thaws. Likewise, a short afternoon thunderstorm can render a good road completely impassable. In the case of the latter, you'll find that roads tend to improve quickly in Wyoming's sunny, dry climate. If you can wait a couple of hours, you'll often be happily on your way.

When driving through mud, maintain a steady speed and don't let up unless you lose your forward progress. If you start losing traction, try turning the steering wheel back and forth, which sometimes gives the tires new grip. If you lose momentum and start to sink, don't punch the throttle or you'll risk getting buried and making the recovery more difficult. If you get stuck, try rocking the vehicle back and forth or airing down the tires. If all that proves unsuccessful, it'll be time to start digging or find someone who can pull you out.

Sand

Sand in Wyoming? You bet. The largest active sand dunes in North America are found in this state, and sandy beaches can be found around the reservoirs. Even if you're not looking to drive in sand, it's sometimes unavoidable as Wyoming's wind blows it across roadways. When driving on sand, use enough throttle to maintain forward momentum, but not so much that the wheels slip. If you're not moving forward, stop immediately and try something different so you don't bury the rig. For the best traction, reduce the air pressure in your tires to between 8-12 PSI (this does not apply to ATV tires). Just be sure to air them back up upon returning to a solid driving surface.

If you get stuck in sand, try lightening your load (especially if you have passengers) or try to back out of it. You may need to dig sand away from the wheels, and put something like a board under the wheels (you may need to jack the wheel up) to start moving again. Also, remember that wet sand provides better traction than dry sand.

Rock

Unless it's obvious that you have enough ground clearance to pass over a rock, don't try to straddle it. Straddling rocks is a sure way to damage undercarriage components such as differentials, exhaust pipes, and the suspension. Instead, drive the tire on top of the rock. Driving on rocks lifts the vehicle and increases ground clearance. Though it seems risky to beginners, experienced backcountry drivers know that the lugged surface of an all-terrain tire is designed for this kind of abuse. The sidewalls are more vulnerable to damage—protect them as much as possible.

When tackling large rocks and boulders, use a low gear and proceed slowly. Crawl the tire up the rock and ease down the other side (be sure that the frame of your vehicle is high enough to clear the rock on the descent). A controlled descent cannot be overstressed—coming off a rock too fast or too hard is an invitation for a bad day. In particularly tricky sections, step outside (or send a passenger) to choose the best line across the rocks. It's also good practice to keep your thumbs on the outside of the steering wheel in case the wheel suddenly spins.

The sound and sensation of your rig grating against a rock is atrocious. When this happens, stop and check to see what is making contact—hopefully it's a skid plate. Back off and choose another line or build a ramp to help you over the obstacle. If you build a ramp, remember to dismantle it after you are clear of the obstacle. The next driver may welcome the challenge.

Ruts and Ravines

If you can do so safely and without causing resource damage, straddle deep ruts to avoid high centering your vehicle. If you're the one carving ruts, save the road for another day.

Ravines are best handled by driving into them at an angle so that only one wheel is committed at a time. Be sure that the clearance between your bumpers and wheels—the departure angles—is great enough that you can climb into and out of the depression.

Washboard

This term refers to the continuous series of bumps and dips (like small speed bumps) on unpaved roads that are created by the repetitive oscillating motion of modern suspensions. Drive too slow and you'll bounce yourself silly. Drive too fast and you can lose control. Try to find a moderate speed that minimizes the severity of the bumps.

Steep Grades

When ascending a steep grade, use a lower gear (and preferably 4WD Low) and keep momentum without spinning the wheels. If you lose power or traction and can't continue, you'll want to hit the brakes and shift into reverse as quickly as you can to back straight down the hill—this keeps you in control and prevents the vehicle from slipping sideways. Under no circumstances should you try to turn around on the side of a hill, which can cause you to roll. Keep the vehicle going either straight up or straight down.

When descending a steep grade, again shift into a lower gear to allow engine compression to slow your vehicle. If you get sideways on a hill, immediately steer downhill and ride it out, even if that's not where you want to go. It's better to be at the bottom with the tires on the ground than at the bottom with the tires in the air. This is also a good time to mention that everything in your rig should be securely fastened down so it can't become airborne in the event of a rollover.

Snow and Ice

The key to driving in snow and ice is to reduce your speed. Driving too fast for conditions is one of the most commonly cited reasons for winter accidents. Remember that 4WD improves forward traction, not braking traction. Driving a 4WD vehicle in snowy conditions doesn't make you invincible. In fact, it can make you overconfident, which leads to a higher chance of an accident. You can see for yourself, and statistical numbers tend to agree, that most of the vehicles that end up in the ditch on a slippery day are 4x4s.

Here are some points to keep in mind when driving on snow and ice. Drive lightly (no heavy throttling or braking) and use smooth steering movements. If you are skidding, immediately let off of the accelerator and resist the temptation to stomp the brake. Then, steer the front wheels in the direction that the vehicle is sliding (if you're skidding left, turn the wheels to the left) and gently accelerate to regain traction on the front tires. Be prepared for the vehicle to swing back the other direction. If this happens, gently counter the skid by again turning the front wheels in the direction of the skid. Go lightly with these steering motions or you can overcorrect and make the situation worse.

The most fatal obstacle when four-wheeling, in terms of getting stuck, has got to be snowdrifts. These mounds of snow look benign, especially when encountered in May, June, and even July. But they're not. Over the course of researching this book, I pulled out four vehicles that were stuck and got stuck once myself. In four out of five of these cases, the vehicles were stuck in snowdrifts. By the time you encounter a snowdrift in the spring or summer, it's consolidated and dense (not powder) and the bottom of it is icy, which makes traction even more difficult.

Getting Unstuck

Getting stuck or stranded can be a dreadful ordeal, especially when traveling alone. It happens in lousy road conditions (snowdrifts, mud, sand) and just as easily in perfect road conditions (bad fuel pump, split hose, transmission failure).

The moment that you realize you are getting stuck due to terrain, let off of the accelerator so you don't further sink the vehicle. Get out and assess the problem. If you're not going anywhere, it's time to make a change.

First, make sure you've employed all of your vehicle's features, such as 4WD and 4WD LOW. If you have the option to lock your rear or center differential, do it. Consider reducing your tire pressure to gain better traction, but only if you have a way to air back up once you are back on your way.

A common recovery technique is to rock the vehicle back and forth by quickly shifting between a forward gear and reverse, slowly building up enough momentum to overcome whatever entraps you. Failing this, you'll probably have to start digging. Clear out the space around your tires as well as below the vehicle's axles, differentials, and other low-hanging components. And while you're busy with the shovel, dig out enough room in front of the vehicle (or behind if you're going in reverse) so that you won't get stuck immediately after you break free. Another option is to jack up the vehicle, or at least one wheel, and then place solid material (like rocks) under the wheel before lowering the vehicle. This works well if you have to build a ramp to get up and over an obstacle.

Resist the temptation to use manpower to free your vehicle. Having a couple of folks pushing from behind may work to move a sedan from an icy intersection in town, but it's outright dangerous to place people behind a rig on a rugged backroad. Don't make a bad situation dire.

If you have to be pulled out, or you're pulling someone else out, secure the recovery strap to a solid anchor on the vehicle's frame. Frame-mounted tow-hooks, D-ring shackles, and hitch receivers work well. Do not connect to axles, receiver balls, or suspension components. When both vehicles are connected, shift them into appropriate gears, take up slack on the recovery strap, and steadily pull the vehicle out—avoid yanking!

ATV Safety

Simply stated, ATVs are dangerous. According to the Consumer Product Safety Commission, there are 700 to 1,000 ATV-caused deaths each year. More alarming yet is the number of emergency room visits that are caused by ATVs each year, which number upwards to 150,000. You can reduce your chance of serious injury or death by following these common-sense rules and precautions:

- Wear safety gear, particularly a helmet and eye protection. Long pants and boots are also recommended.
- Limit each ATV to one rider, unless your ATV is specifically designed for a passenger.
- Choose an ATV size and engine that are reasonable for your size. This is a particular concern with children, as ATV engines get larger and more powerful.

- Avoid alcohol and drug use, just as you would when operating a full-sized vehicle.
- Limit your time driving on paved surfaces. Many an accident has occurred when ATVs were driven on streets and highways—ATVs and their knobby tires perform poorly on these surfaces.
- Recognize when you are exceeding your skill and comfort level and return to safer terrain.

Learn more about being safe on ATVs at: http://www.atvsafety.org/

Sharing the Routes

While driving the routes included in this book, you'll likely encounter hikers, bikers, and horseback riders. Here are a few guidelines to minimize conflicts and build goodwill:

- Always yield to non-motorized users. You should also yield to motorized users who are traveling uphill. On narrow routes, you may have to back up to a wider section in order to yield.
- When you approach a party on foot, pass courteously. Consider that they may have spent an entire day hiking a segment that takes you just half an hour to drive.
- When approaching oncoming horses, pull to the side and shut off your engine until they are a reasonable distance past you. If you are approaching them from behind, going the same direction, give the riders a chance to respond—they'll often signal you when they prefer you to pass.

Protecting the Routes

Driving in a responsible manner that protects natural resources is crucial to maintain motorized access to remote places. Irresponsible acts like driving off the road or trail, destructive mud-bogging, and destroying vegetation and property lead to closures. By doing your part, you encourage others to do the same. Here are some key rules that will help protect off-road privileges:

- Stay on designated roads and trails. Avoid creating new tracks or furthering the damage of existing tracks that leave the trail to go around obstacles. Take extra precautions when driving in riparian areas to minimize your impact.
- Stay off routes that are wet or muddy and respect seasonal closures. If it's not possible to continue without causing damage, such as ruts, choose another route or another day.
- Remember that ATVs should not be driven within designated recreational areas such as campgrounds and picnic areas unless it's for ingress and egress for a paid site. If you're camping outside a developed campground, please be respectful to other visitors, especially paying customers, by minimizing your presence and staying out of the fee area.

Litter and resource damage like this leads to closures

- Leave historical artifacts, fossils, and ruins (such as cabins and mining equipment) as you found them. It's unlawful to remove or excavate objects that are more than 50 years old.
- Pack out your trash. Even better, take an extra trash bag and leave the area better than you found it. Motorized access is jeopardized whenever a land manager encounters litter or junk.
- To reduce the risk of spreading invasive species, try to avoid carrying dirt and mud to other areas. Clean off what you can.
- Leave gates as you find them.
- Observe wildlife from a distance. In Wyoming, it's illegal to harass these animals.
- Maintain your vehicle. Most vehicle fluids are toxic to vegetation and wildlife. Even a small fluid leak can negatively impact the environment.

Wilderness Areas

The Wilderness Act of 1964 laid the foundation for permanently protecting designated areas of public land from mechanized use, development, and resource extraction. These areas include designated wilderness areas on Forest Service lands and wilderness study areas (WSA), which are usually found on BLM lands. Wilderness areas are open to public use, but motorized or mechanized devices and machines (including chainsaws, bicycles, and game carts) are not permitted. Wheelchairs are exempt when used as intended. Wilderness study areas, which are lands that are being evaluated for wilderness designation, often limit motorized use to existing, designated roads. These study areas are not all managed the same way—rules can vary.

Currently, Wyoming has fifteen designated wilderness areas, most of which are located in the western half of the state. Many of the state's best four-wheeling routes lead to a wilderness boundary. Please respect these boundaries by parking your vehicle and proceeding into the area on foot or by pack animal. Violating this law can result in a fine of up to $5,000 and/or six months in jail.

Laws and Requirements

The various laws that govern off-road vehicle use are often misinterpreted due to inconsistent presentation and the complication of dealing with numerous jurisdictions at the federal, state, and county levels. To further add complexity, these laws change, as does enforcement. Even the "experts" have differing interpretations, making it difficult to get clarity. While an earnest attempt has been made here to accurately explain the rules you'll need to know, please take personal responsibility by reading the regulations yourself. You'll find them printed on many maps and brochures as well as online at http://wyotrails.state.wy.us/.

To best understand Wyoming's laws, you'll first need to know the language. An ORV (or OHV) refers to an off-road recreational vehicle such as an ATV or dirt bike. An MPV is a multipurpose vehicle, such as a side-by-side ATV (like the Yamaha Rhino) or a dune buggy, though the term is sometimes used to describe a street-legal ORV. Technical definitions of these vehicles are available on the state website: http://legisweb.state.wy.us/. Search this site for MPV to find the definitions and specifications.

The main difference between these two types of machines is their size and weight, which affect where you can take them. For example, many MPVs cannot be driven on designated ATV trails because those routes are restricted to vehicles that are 50 inches or less in width. Aside from this difference, the distinction between an ORV and MPV is mostly irrelevant. To simplify the following information, only the term ORV is used. Full-sized vehicles are exempt from this subject.

Permits and Licenses

The Wyoming State ORV program allows you to drive an ORV that is not street legal on "enrolled" roads and trails without an MPV (motorcycle) license plate. Instead of a license plate, you simply purchase and display a Wyoming ORV Permit, which costs just $15 dollars at the time of this writing. This permit, a sticker, is valid for the calendar year and is widely available from selling agents, such as dealerships and sporting good outlets, as well as online at: http://wyotrails.state.wy.us/.

If you have a street-legal ORV with a license plate, you can drive all the same roads (and more) without buying a permit. However, to drive on a designated trail that is enrolled in the program, you must have an ORV permit.

Simply stated, you will need to buy an ORV permit if your machine does not have a license plate or if you want to drive on a designated trail. To avoid confusion or misunderstanding, many drivers opt to get both the ORV permit and a license plate, essentially allowing them to go wherever they need to go. These guidelines apply to both residents and non-residents.

Route Type	ORV Permit	License Plate	Driver's License	Proof of Insurance
Enrolled Road (State lands, BLM roads and most Forest Service roads)	✔ or	✔	✔	✔ (if plated)
Non-Enrolled Road (Highways, many county roads, some Forest Service roads)		✔	✔	✔
Designated Trail (50") (Forest Service ATV trails)	✔			
Prohibited Routes (National Park roads, Interstates)	No ORV use allowed			

Where to Ride

Where you can ride your ORV depends on who manages the roads and whether or not they utilize the state's ORV program. All BLM and most Forest Service roads are enrolled in the program, as are those located on Wyoming Game and Fish Habitat Management Areas, State Trust Lands, and State Parks. Of course, local exceptions exist and some roads (such as a county road that passes through a National Forest) may not be enrolled.

In general, county roads are not enrolled in the state program and can only be driven with a street-legal ORV that has a license plate. (A handful of counties do have roads that are enrolled in the program, so check with the local county Sheriff.) You cannot drive an ORV in a national park or on an Interstate.

The state offers detailed maps that show enrolled roads and trails for Wyoming's National Forests and BLM districts. You can order these for free at http://wyotrails.state.wy.us/ or download and print them from: http://wyotrails.state.wy.us/Maps. If you cannot determine if a particular route is enrolled or not, contact the land management agency.

Driver Requirements

To drive on roads, you need a driver's license or driver's permit as well as proof of liability insurance. A helmet is strongly recommended, but is only required for motorcycle (not ATV) operaters and passengers under 18 years old. No driver's license is required to drive on a designated trail that is enrolled in the ORV program.

Equipment Requirements

An ORV with the ORV permit must be equipped with brake lights, tail lights, and headlights if you'll be driving half an hour before sunrise or a half an hour after sunset. A spark-arresting muffler is required. A street-legal ORV with a license plate must be equipped with a horn, rear reflectors, four tires, muffler, brakes, brake lights, tail lights, headlights, and driver-side mirror. The number of lights—one in the middle or two on each side—depends on the width of your vehicle. Exact specifications and information for making your ORV street legal with an MPV license plate can be found at this website: http://www.dot.state.wy.us/.

How to Use this Guide

The routes in this guide are separated into six regional chapters. The boundaries were drawn in a manner that minimizes the division of major mountain ranges or basins. These boundaries also contain routes to a single region. This prevents a long route from being described in more than one chapter. Each regional chapter is subdivided into separate areas of similar geography. Each area is described by these sections:

Overview

This overview describes the area's local features such as terrain and wildlife.

Land Ownership

This section describes the area's land ownership so you can be vigilant in areas with private property. Local management offices are also listed.

Roads and Trails

This section summarizes the area's motorized routes, from the main thoroughfares like Interstates and highways to the most primitive tracks. You'll learn about general road conditions and characteristics so you know what to expect, regardless of the individual route you choose to drive.

Seasons and Conditions

This section familiarizes you with the area's climate and weather, which determines the driving season and impacts road conditions.

Fuel

Driving the backroads of Wyoming takes you far from towns and fueling stations. This section tells you where to find historically reliable service stations so you're not wasting time and fuel driving to a place that offers no services. Obviously, this type of information changes so keep that in mind.

Maps

The maps in this book will suffice for general navigation, but you are strongly encouraged to supplement them with the maps suggested in this section. To research this book, I used an average of five maps for each route. This is because maps of the same area have different purposes. For example, one may indicate land ownership while another shows topographical features.

Be aware, though, that modern-day maps are still fraught with errors and inconsistencies. In the worst case, I compared nine different maps for the same area and found all but one to be in error. Fortunately, these mistakes tend to be insignificant and shouldn't cause much inconvenience, if they're noticed at all.

The most common maps, including those described below, are available across Wyoming as well as online at: http://plicmapcenter.org/.

- **Statewide:** Two excellent statewide maps include the DeLorme Wyoming Atlas & Gazetteer and the Wyoming Road & Recreation Atlas published by Benchmark Maps. Every driver should have at least one of these publications. Both maps have their strengths and weaknesses. I have found that the Gazetteer does a better job of denoting land ownership and identifying the faintest of tracks. However, I favor the Benchmark map for it's superb presentation and extensive marking of named points. The smaller (and very affordable) Recreational Map of Wyoming published by GTR Mapping (www.gtrmapping.com) is also a personal favorite.

- **Forest Service:** Each National Forest includes a large Forest-wide map that shows land ownership, roads, trails, and geographic features. Some include travel management regulations and general area information, but most don't show topography. For about $10 each, these maps are affordable and extremely useful. If available, choose the plastic version over a paper one for long-term durability.

  The Forest Service—in conjunction with the Wyoming ORV Program—also offers a free ORV map that shows the status of motorized roads and trails. Another free map is the MVUM, or Motor Vehicle Use Map, which shows all of the open roads and trails that are available for motorized use. The MVUM only displays routes (no land features) so it should be supplemented with another map. Both of these maps can be downloaded for free from Forest Service websites. Be aware that there are often inconsistencies between the three types of Forest maps.

- **BLM:** The Bureau of Land Management offers 56 maps (1:100K scale) that cover the entire state. These show land ownership, topography, roads, and other geographic features. These are especially useful when navigating BLM lands that are interspersed with private property.

Routes

Each route is numbered to facilitate identification on maps. They are generally numbered from east to west, with north presiding over south. Descriptions include the information shown below.

Route Type

Each route is classified into one of these three categories:

- **Backcountry Drive:** These routes follow major trunk roads that usually receive maintenance at least once per year, such as county roads, non-paved National Park roads, and arterial Forest Service and BLM roads. When driven in good conditions, these roads can be negotiated with most vehicles, including low-clearance sedans. However, you won't know when the road was last maintained and if adverse weather has deteriorated it. For this reason, it's suggested that you drive a more durable vehicle such as a pickup truck or SUV. Also, consider that many of the side trips off of these main backroads require a 4x4 vehicle. You can also ride your ATV on many of these routes, though regulations vary between the county, state, and federal levels. Having a street-legal machine with a MPV license plate is your best option if you want to use an ATV for backcountry drives.

- **4WD Route:** These routes utilize secondary roads of varying quality depending on location and seasonal conditions. Some are simply dirt roads that are not maintained. In other places, secondary roads are "two tracks" (overgrown path with two parallel tire tracks) or a rocky creek bottom that bears little resemblance to a road. Many 4WD routes can be negotiated in a stock 4x4 that has no modifications. For tougher trails, particularly those in the mountains, you'll want a 4x4 that has higher ground clearance and more aggressive tire tread than what is typically found on stock vehicles. Most of these 4WD routes can also be driven with an ATV (if it has a license plate or Wyoming ORV permit), though there are a few exceptions.

- **ATV Trail:** These routes are intended for ATV use, such as an ORV park or a designated ATV trail that is only open to vehicles 50 inches or less in width. Many of these routes were former 4WD roads or foot trails, so you'll see a wide variance between widths and difficulties. Designated ATV trails require a Wyoming ORV permit for your machine, even if it has a license plate.

You'll notice that there are no difficulty ratings for these routes. The decision to exclude ratings was based on experiences that proved just how subjective and potentially dangerous they can be. In place of a rating system, read the description before you drive the road to make the determination of how challenging it is. Also, take into account variables such as weather, current road conditions, your driving experience, and your vehicle's capabilities.

Location

This section gives you a general idea where the drive is located, such as "North of Cody." Prominent, well-known towns were selected as the reference points, so they may not necessarily be the nearest town.

Roads/Trails

This section lists all of a route's roads or trails by their number, if applicable. Be aware that road numbers change when you enter a different jurisdiction, such as crossing a county line or entering a National Forest.

Distance

Route mileages are shown for one-way trips, unless it is a loop. Where it is not practical to list all of the possible combinations of routes, such as a network of logging spurs, the total mileage is given for all routes combined. Be aware that distances in this book will most certainly vary from your own odometer. There are many variables that affect mileage readings, such as backing up to get a better glimpse of a moose or using slightly undersized or oversized tires.

When relying on the mileages in this book, allow a margin of error of about a mile. For example, if you are expecting to reach a junction at mile 46, you should be watching for it between miles 45-47 (a mile before and a mile past). A considerable effort has been made to provide accurate mileages. Field recordings were compared to USGS 1:24,000 topographic maps as well as Google Earth.

Management

This section lists the route's primary landowners or land managers. This is typically a federal government agency such as the USDA Forest Service, Bureau of Land Management, or the National Park Service. You may also cross land owned or managed by the Bureau of Reclamation, the State of Wyoming, a county, or private citizen or organization. Contact information for these entities can be found in an appendix at the back of this book.

Considerable attempts were made to provide trespass-free routes that are either located entirely on public land or have obvious public access. Some popular roads and trails were excluded where public access was not entirely verifiable. Remember that land ownership or access changes. A road open last year may be closed this year and you can't always rely on private property signs—they fade and get vandalized. Ultimately, you bear the responsibility of ensuring that you have permission to drive where you do. If in doubt, return to known public land or contact the owner for permission to cross their land. Private property rights are taken seriously in Wyoming and some landowners consider trespassing a major wrongdoing.

Starting Coordinates

Starting coordinates (in the Degrees - Decimal Minutes format found on most paper maps) are provided for each route. These coordinates also correspond with the START point shown on the maps in this book. Take note that the coordinates may not be as precise as you expect. Variances between GPS receivers, satellite reception, and mapping software can plot the coordinates a short distance from the intended point. Commonly, this difference is only a few yards but you may encounter a few that are off by a quarter mile.

Overview

The overview provides a brief summary of the route, which may include a description of the trip's scenery, typical conditions, recommendations, and other information such as local history.

Start

This section provides directions to a route's starting point, which is shown as START on the map. Other starting points may also be included if the route can be accessed by more than one location. Directions start from the edge—often the city limit—of a nearby town or city. Be aware that mileage reported on your odometer may vary slightly.

Description

This section describes the route to be driven and is based on mileage. The description includes route directions as well as information relating to road conditions, landmarks, terrain, highlights, cautions, and local flora and fauna.

NORTHEAST

Northeastern Wyoming is on the fringe of America's Great Plains. It is here that the expansive belt of open prairie begins to curl up toward the Rocky Mountains to create a transition zone that is rich with natural resources. North America's largest coal mine is found on the edge of these plains, as are many significant oil and gas fields. It's also home to Wyoming's only national grassland, the Thunder Basin. But the area is best known for what the Lakota Sioux called Paha Sapa, meaning "hills that are black."

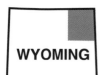

Northeast Areas

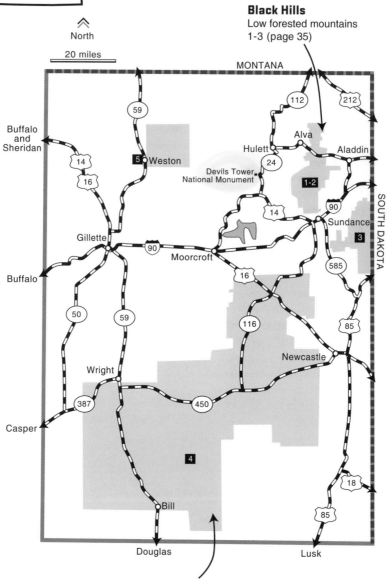

Black Hills
Low forested mountains
1-3 (page 35)

North

20 miles

MONTANA

59

Buffalo
and
Sheridan

14

16

5 Weston

112

212

Alva

Hulett

Aladdin

24

Devils Tower,
National Monument

1-2

14

90

Sundance

Gillette

90

Moorcroft

3

Buffalo

16

SOUTH DAKOTA

50

59

116

585

Wright

85

Newcastle

387

450

Casper

4

18

Bill

85

Douglas

Lusk

Thunder Basin National Grassland
Praries and buttes
4-5 (page 46)

Black Hills

The Black Hills of southwestern South Dakota and northeastern Wyoming comprise the only mountainous terrain found on the Great Plains. While South Dakota's share of these mountains boasts national fame, the tiny remnants that are located in Wyoming go virtually unnoticed, aside from the nearby landmark, Devils Tower. But these mountains hold a unique beauty. You'll find enchanting forests with clear spring-fed brooks in the draws and scenic overlooks on the summits. This woodland is a beneficial wildlife habitat for northeast Wyoming. Common game animals include both mule deer and whitetail deer. The area is also prized for its wild turkeys.

Land Ownership

The lion's share of the Black Hills are managed by the Black Hills National Forest, but this public land has considerable amounts of private land within its boundaries. Forest Service offices are located in Sundance and Newcastle.

Roads and Trails

Wyoming's Black Hills are easily reached by I-90. Several highways—HWY 14 and 24 to the north and HWY 585 and 85 to the south—further make this an accessible area. Maintained gravel roads through the Black Hills National Forest are plentiful and they offer some of Wyoming's best backcountry touring. The 4WD roads and ATV trails tend to be easily driven with few obstacles or tricky sections. They make good routes for beginners or those looking to push their stock 4x4 a little further off the beaten path. Perhaps the biggest challenge is navigation, particularly on ATV trails. Tall grass and brush can obscure trail signs, especially the thin green-brown composite markers.

Seasons and Conditions

The lowest elevations in Wyoming are found in this corner of the state. Most of the prairie is around 4,000 feet. Even the mountainous terrain of the Black Hills claims few points over 6,000 feet. You'll find that this lowland offers less snowpack, warmer temperatures, and an earlier spring than the rest of Wyoming. For most major backroads in the Black Hills, this allows for a driving season that begins in May and extends through the fall season. Late June and late September are particularly beautiful times to explore the Black Hills. To avoid resource damage, only drive roads that are dry. Some roads are explicitly signed that they are only open in dry conditions.

Fuel

Service stations are plentiful along I-90 as well as in the town of Newcastle.

Maps

For the most detail, obtain or download the Black Hills National Forest map, Black Hills ORV map, and the Motor Vehicle Use Map (MVUM).

1: Bear Lodge Mountains
Tour of the northern Black Hills

| **☒ Backcountry Drive** | **☐ 4WD Route** | **☐ ATV Trail** |
| Most vehicles | 4x4 vehicle or ORV | ORV less than 50" wide |

Location/Map	North of Sundance; Page 37
Roads	FR 838, FR 843, FR 830, FR 832
Distance	30 miles
Managing Agency	USDA Forest Service—Black Hills National Forest
Starting Coordinates	N44° 23.70' W104° 25.05'

Overview: This drive tours the Bear Lodge Mountains in Wyoming's Black Hills National Forest. The route traverses the crest of this small range while passing a lookout tower, impressive aspen stands, and Cook Lake. Though there are many intersections and roads, you can easily stay on course by generally maintaining a northern bearing. While traveling through the mountains, keep watch for wildlife such as whitetail and mule deer, blue heron, and wild turkeys.

Start: From Sundance, take HWY 14 west for 2 miles and turn north onto FR 838. To reach the northern point from the town of Aladdin, drive west on HWY 24 for 9.5 miles.

Description: From HWY 14, begin the drive by heading north on paved FR 838. The road soon enters the Black Hills National Forest and immediately begins to climb. Reuter Campground is passed at 2.5 miles and Warren Peak Lookout at 7 miles. This fire tower, and a few nearby radio towers, are perched on the top of Warren Peaks, a ridge of short, treeless summits with an elevation around 6,650 feet. The pavement ends here at the highest point in these mountains, and the road changes to an easily traveled dirt and gravel surface.

The road descends to the trees and reaches an intersection at 9 miles. Stay left on FR 838 and continue north. This next stretch takes you through a thick stand of aspen trees that shades the roadway. There are other "aspen alleys" in Wyoming, but those in the Black Hills are among the most impressive.

Continuing north, the road reaches FR 843. Turn right at the junction here and follow the road east for nearly 2 miles to another intersection. Turn left and drive northward along Beaver Creek. After a few miles, watch for a sign marking the Cook Lake Recreation Area, one of the few lakes in Wyoming's Black Hills. A short detour to the lake is a must. Fishing, paddling, camping, and picnicking are popular at the recreation site. There are also a couple of hiking trails that can be used to explore the area around the lake.

After returning from Cook Lake, find FR 830, the course that continues north. This road makes a few curves as it travels north to a three-way

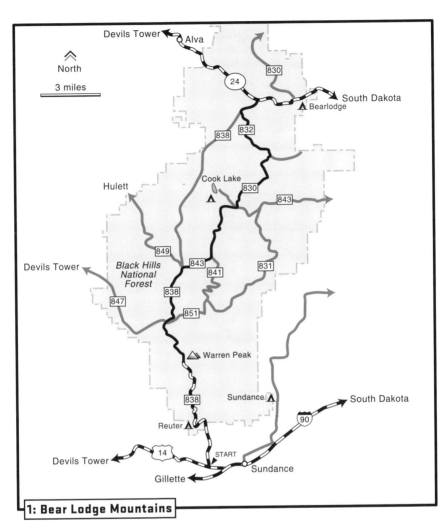

1: Bear Lodge Mountains

intersection with FR 832. Once again, turn left to maintain your northern bearing at the junction. The route here follows Fawn Creek through a ravine as it descends toward a confluence with Beaver Creek at roughly 29 miles. Bear right at the nearby intersection and continue a little over a mile on FR 838 to end the drive.

From the highway, you can turn left to reach Devils Tower (24 miles away) or turn right to follow HWY 24 and HWY 11 back toward Sundance. However, if you want to explore more of the Black Hills, follow the highway east for a couple of miles and turn north on FR 830 (across the road from Bearlodge Campground). This gravel road travels along a crest and passes numerous springs on the left side and overlooks of the plains on the right. The maintained road ends after 11 miles, but a rougher 4WD road continues north to exit the national forest.

Cook Lake in Wyoming's Black Hills National Forest

2: Bear Lodge ATV Trails
Miles of interconnected routes

☐ **Backcountry Drive**
Most vehicles

☐ **4WD Route**
4x4 vehicle or ORV

☒ **ATV Trail**
ORV less than 50" wide

Location/Map	North of Sundance; Page 39
Trails	FT 1101-1107, FT 1041-1044, FT 1201-1204, FT 1281-1283
Distance	40+ miles
Managing Agency	USDA Forest Service—Black Hills National Forest
Starting Coordinates	Ogden Trailhead: N44° 27.75' W104° 24.73' North end of FT 1281: N44° 34.70' W104° 23.21' Bearlodge Pit: N44° 35.90' W104° 20.51' Blacktail Motorized Trailhead: N44° 34.71' W104° 29.07'

Overview: Some of Wyoming's most unique ATV trails are located in the Bear Lodge Mountains in the northern Black Hills. These trails cover terrain that is very different from the state's other mountain areas; you'll find lush forests of waist-high grass, thick brushy understory, evergreens, and deciduous trees such as aspen, birch, and oak. The tread, while predominantly dirt, is ever-changing. You can bounce over crumbly rock, spin through soft sand, and splash through muddy puddles all along the same short stretch of trail.

Overall, the Bear Lodge trails offer easy riding with relatively smooth driving surfaces. The most difficult obstacles you're likely to encounter are

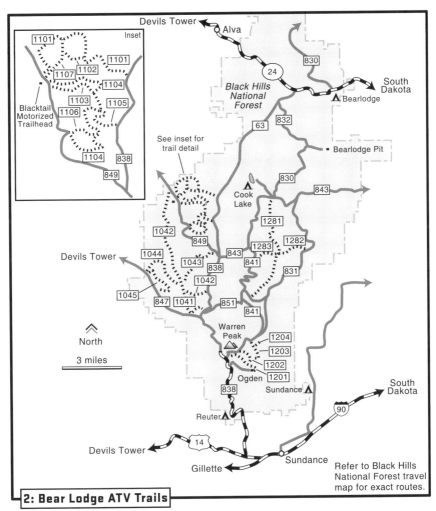

2: Bear Lodge ATV Trails

the numerous gates, stiles, and bridges that enforce the 50" vehicle width. Many of these trails start by driving around a locked gate where the official ATV path has been carved out of an adjacent berm. This doesn't pose a problem for most ATVs, but it is very difficult for longer units to make the turn, especially trail-width side by sides.

These trails are open from May 15 to December 15, except for the Ogden routes near Warren Peak, which are open from August 15 to December 15. A Wyoming ORV permit is required.

Start: To reach the Ogden Trailhead from Sundance, take HWY 14 west for 2 miles and turn right onto FR 838. Drive north for 6.2 miles to FR 839. Turn right and follow this road for 2.3 miles to the parking area.

To reach the middle trails and the Bearlodge Pit, take HWY 14 west from Sundance for 2 miles and turn right onto FR 838. Drive north for 12.7 miles. Turn right onto FR 843 and drive 5.3 miles to a five-way junction where you'll find ample parking at the northern end of FT 1281. To reach the Bearlodge Pit from this spot, follow FR 830 northward for 2.8 miles and then continue straight along FR 830.8 for less than a mile to reach the pit.

The Blacktail Motorized Trailhead provides the best starting point for the bulk of the interconnected trails on the west side of the mountain range. (While there are many access points for these trails, most of them have limited or no parking.) To reach the trailhead from Sundance, take HWY 14 west for 2 miles and turn right onto FR 838. Drive north for 12.7 miles to a junction. Turn left here onto FR 849 and drive 4.5 miles to the trailhead. Once you're unloaded at the parking lot, you can use FR 849 to reach the trail segment that you want.

Description (Ogden Trails): The four segments of FT 1201, 1202, 1203, and 1204 create a trail network of roughly 7 miles. At 6,000 feet, these trails cover the area's higher terrain near the Warren Peak fire lookout tower. The two-track paths pass through light pine forests on south-facing slopes and denser, diverse forests on north-facing slopes. By utilizing other forest roads (FR 831, FR 841, FR 851), you can reach additional ATV trails to the north. Take note that FR 838 (the paved road from the highway) is only open to street-legal, licensed vehicles.

Description (FT 1281): With elevations of nearly 5,800 feet, this terrific 6.5-mile trail runs along one of the highest crests in the Bear Lodge Mountains. From the northern end (which has good parking), the trail switchbacks higher over a patchy rock and gravel surface. This is a pretty stretch that passes through a thick, diverse forest. Atop the rim, the trail runs through a lighter apsen and pine forest with occasional overlooks to the west. The gravel tread is replaced with pockets of sand and fine dirt, which make for a very dusty ride. The southern end of the trail connects to FR 831, but there are two connector trails that you can use to enter or exit the main route. The first, FT 1283, connects to FR 841 to the west and fords Beaver Creek. The second, FT 1282, connects to FR 831 to the east. Both routes include moderate elevation change. Take note that FR 843 is only open to street-legal, licensed vehicles.

Description (Bearlodge Pit): This small gravel pit is an open ORV area where you can take your machine for a spin. While it's less than a tenth of a mile in either direction, it serves as a good place to have a good time, especially for beginners.

Description (Blacktail Trails): Immediately north of the trailhead, you'll find a figure-8 loop comprised of FT 1101, 1102, and 1107. These are easy and quick-to-drive loops on the edge of the national forest. You'll find two-track trails that pass through tall grass with a few mud puddles and very short rocky patches. Watch for short sign posts to find your turns.

Just to the south of the trailhead, FT 1103 through FT 1106 can be used to form a nice 6+ mile loop. These fun and scenic trails tunnel through very dense vegetation, weaving through a wetter area of these mountains. Many of the turns are on blind curves, so use caution, especially on weekends when there are more riders.

The trail network south of the trailhead includes FT 1041 through FT 1045. This roughly 15-mile collection is quite possibly the most interesting trail network in this area. When you're not kicking up a cloud of red dust from the clay-based soils, you'll be cutting through grassy meadows or crossing flat rock slabs. The main north-south route here, FT 1042, travels through a heavy forest along the Hershey Creek drainage with occasional drop-offs. The riparian area here is rich with wildlife such as deer and blue heron.

Forest Trail 1104 in the Bear Lodge Mountains

3: Grand Canyon
Curvy route in the southern Black Hills

☒ **Backcountry Drive**	☐ **4WD Route**	☐ **ATV Trail**
Most vehicles	4x4 vehicle or ORV	ORV less than 50" wide

Location/Map	Southeast of Sundance; Page 43
Roads	CR 129, FR 863, FR 875, FR 106
Distance	44 miles
Managing Agency	USDA Forest Service—Black Hills National Forest
Starting Coordinates	N44° 32.52' W104° 4.86'

Overview: Edged up against the South Dakota border, this easy drive follows a curvy route that climbs 3,000 feet from grassy plains into a pine forest. The trip features a popular Wyoming Game and Fish public access area, a National Historic Site, plentiful whitetail deer, and a short canyon that was probably named for its age rather than its magnitude. Take note that unlicensed ORVs cannot be used on sections of this drive that are outside of the national forest.

Start: From Sundance, take I-90 east for 18 miles to Beulah (Exit 205). To reach the south end from Newcastle, drive north on HWY 85 for 30 miles.

Forest Road 863 in the Black Hills' Grand Canyon

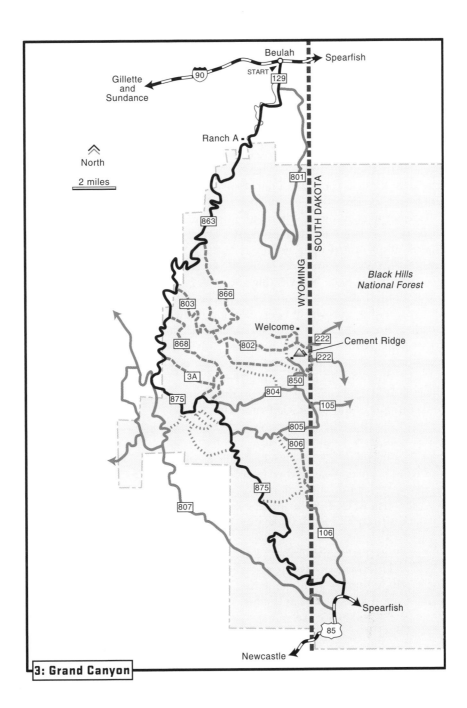

Beulah

Spearfish

Gillette
and
Sundance

90

START

129

Ranch A

801

North

2 miles

863

SOUTH DAKOTA

WYOMING

Black Hills
National Forest

866

803

Welcome

222

Cement Ridge

868

802

222

3A

850

875

804

105

805

806

875

807

106

875

Spearfish

85

Newcastle

3: Grand Canyon

Description: Begin this backcountry tour from I-90 by heading south on CR 129, which is shown on some maps as Grand Canyon Road (FR 863). Follow the road across open prairie, staying right at an unsigned fork. After a few miles, the route follows Sand Creek through a short canyon. As the road bends to the west, you'll discover Sand Creek Public Access Area, which is managed by the Wyoming Game and Fish Department. This beautiful, mile-long hideaway is a terrific place to spend an afternoon or weekend. With grassy meadows, shade trees, and a small creek that is said to hold between five and six thousand trout per mile, this area is no secret to local campers. The area is also said to have a fair share of rattlesnakes, so be alert if you get out to explore on foot.

Continuing southward, the road passes numerous private residences. As impressive as some of these properties are, it's the huge lodge at Ranch A that is sure to catch your attention. The log home was built in 1932 as a summer home for newspaper publisher Moses Annenburg. Today the ranch is owned by the State of Wyoming and is a National Historic Site.

At 6 miles, the smooth roadway crosses into the Black Hills National Forest where it narrows and curves along the west edge of the Sand Creek Roadless Area. This is a pretty stretch as you follow spring-fed Sand Creek between short rock cliffs and timbered hills of ponderosa pine. This is the beginning of the so-called Grand Canyon.

At 19.5 miles, a rough two-track (FR 868) splits off to the left and heads through Williams Gulch. To stay on the main course, stay right at the fork and continue along Grand Canyon Road (FR 863).

From the fork, the roadway weaves back and forth across the national forest boundary a number of times while passing other major roads. Just past 23 miles, FR 863 reaches an intersection with FR 807. Stay left, drive south less than a mile, and then bear left again onto FR 875. This gravel road heads back east into the national forest. After several miles, the road passes the other end of FR 868 (the route coming through Williams Gulch) and FR 804 at the mouth of Rattlesnake Canyon.

> You can reach the Cement Ridge Lookout by bearing left onto FR 804 and following it east for over 4 miles. Then, drive north 2 miles on FR 850, a bumpy 2-mile lane that leads to the tower and its impressive overlook. The lookout is a historical fire tower standing at 6,674 feet. The Civilian Conservation Corps built the fifteen-foot stone and wood structure in 1941. It's still used for fire detection during the summer months making it only one of a few such lookouts that are still staffed in the country. An interpretive center is located in the base of the tower. During the off-season, you'll find the upper deck locked and boarded. A nearby pit toilet and picnic table make this an ideal picnic spot. Consider returning to the main route by taking FR 805 west through Wagon Canyon.

SIDE
TRIP

Cement Ridge Lookout

Up to this point, the curvy route has careened to the south, east, west, and even back to the north. Though still full of curves, FR 875 now maintains a general southeast direction as it travels through the remainder of the Grand Canyon. Don't expect higher rock walls along this stretch, though. Most of the trip's remaining distance rolls over hills covered with pine and aspen trees. At times the road cuts through grassy creek bottoms as it passes by Jones Spring, Willow Spring, and then O'Brien Spring.

At 41 miles, you cross into South Dakota and soon reach a junction with FR 106. Turn right and drive a short distance to HWY 85. To reach Newcastle, turn right onto the highway and drive 30 miles. This beautiful paved stretch is itself a very scenic drive.

Other Nearby Drives

4WD Routes and ATV Trails—This area has many miles of scenic 4WD routes that are suitable for stock 4x4 vehicles. Roads such as FR 866 (Idol Gulch), FR 803 (Surprise Gulch), and FR 868 (Williams Gulch) are good choices. You can also tie in with roads within South Dakota to reach Spearfish Canyon. One area of interest is Welcome, a ghost town near Mineral Hill just north of the Cement Ridge Lookout. This site has nearly a dozen collapsed mines and aging mining equipment, though much of it has been badly looted.

The ATV trails in this area are short and overgrown. They can be hard to find and follow, especially where signs are obscured or the trails intersect logging roads. The best is FT 1681, which runs 5.3 miles between Grand Canyon Road (FR 875) and Wagon Canyon Road (FR 805). Keep watch for wire gates.

Thunder Basin National Grassland

Wyoming's sole designated grassland, the Thunder Basin National Grassland, is located in the minerals-rich Powder River Basin. With grassy plains, escarpments, badlands, and pine-dotted hills, the grassland's terrain is more complex and diverse than many expect.

For the energy industry, the Thunder Basin is a wellspring. In the past, bentonite, trona, and uranium have been mined here. Today, oil, gas, and coal are the mainstays. Active oil and gas wells number in the hundreds. Coal mines number in the single digits, but they include impressively productive operations such as the Black Thunder, which claims to be the largest surface coal mine on the continent.

The grassland serves as an important habitat for wildlife as well as a resource for the production of domestic cattle and sheep. Roaming among the prairie's more common animals like fox and coyote are some unexpected inhabitants like mountain lions and bobcats. Ungulates such as deer and elk can be found here, but it's pronghorn antelope that you're likely to spy across the range. The Forest Service has identified 220 species of birds that benefit from the grassland, including cranes, owls, hawks, and bald eagles. Prairie dog colonies occupy over 10,000 acres of the land and are critical to a plan that seeks to reintroduce black-footed ferrets.

Land Ownership

The Thunder Basin is managed by the Forest Service, primarily from an office in Douglas. Though it's a large tract of public land, the grassland has a patchwork of land ownership that is heavily fractioned by private holdings and mineral leases. Watch for private property signs and stay on the road to respect public easements. A grassland travel map is essential for distinguishing routes that are open to the public.

Roads and Trails

Three highways access the main grassland—HWY 450 to the north, HWY 16 to the northeast, and HWY 59 to the west. Within the grassland, you'll find wide gravel roads that accommodate service trucks that come and go from production mines and fields. For four wheeling, there are many primitive two-track roads in the Thunder Basin, but many are short and dead-end. Designated ATV trails can be found in Weston Hills (north of Gillette) as well as in the Fiddleback area.

Seasons and Conditions

The driving season in the Thunder Basin National Grassland is generous as some roads are accessible nearly all year long. However, be aware that high winds in the winter and early spring are common and can cause roads to be closed with snowdrifts. During the peak summer months, scorching temperatures and thunderstorms with hail and tornadoes are possibilities.

Late spring, fall, and mild summer days are preferable times to drive here. Many secondary roads have seasonal restrictions—refer to a Thunder Basin National Grassland Motor Use Vehicle Map (MVUM) for exact dates.

Fuel

The Thunder Basin is remote and a trip between fueling stops can measure 200 miles or more. You'll want to top your tank in Newcastle, Douglas, Wright, or Gillette.

Maps

The DeLorme Wyoming Atlas & Gazetteer and Wyoming Road & Recreation Atlas published by Benchmark Maps are good references for the main trunk roads. However, the most accurate resource showing routes and land ownership is the Thunder Basin National Grassland map. If you're interested in primitive roads and ATV trails, be sure to also obtain the Motor Vehicle Use Map (MVUM).

4: Fiddleback

Loop through a national grassland

☒ **Backcountry Drive**
   Most vehicles

☐ **4WD Route**
   4x4 vehicle or ORV

☐ **ATV Trail**
   ORV less than 50" wide

Location/Map	Northeast of Douglas; Page 49
Roads	CR 38, FR 933, FR 942
Distance	46 miles
Managing Agency	USDA Forest Service—Thunder Basin National Grassland
Starting Coordinates	N43° 13.95' W105° 15.58'

Overview: This backcountry drive explores the area of the Thunder Basin National Grassland known as the Fiddleback. Gravel backroads lead you into the Cheyenne River Valley where you'll see the scenic Rochelle Hills before exiting through the Red Hills. Though the route hits many of the grassland's scenic areas, it passes a multitude of side roads that also beg to be traveled. A high clearance vehicle is suggested for this route because there is a pair of shallow fords.

Start: From Douglas, head north on HWY 59 for 36 miles to the small settlement of Bill. If coming from Gillette, drive 77 miles south on HWY 59.

Description: From Bill—a tiny community named after four early settlers who shared the same name—drive east on Dull Center Road (CR 38). This gravel road turns north after 3 miles, east at 6 miles, and then north again just after 9 miles. The stretch passes through sheep and cattle rangeland with

Fiddleback area of the Thunder Basin National Grassland

an occasional windmill and oil pump. The Cow Creek Buttes can be seen to the east.

At mile 13, you pass Tin Can Lake on the right side of the road, though the term "lake" is a bit generous—all I found was a dusty, dry basin filled with sheep. Shortly after, the flat terrain changes to badlands colored with red and white hues.

Turn left at 22 miles and follow FR 933 as it dips to the Cheyenne River near the Fiddleback Ranch. The Cheyenne River originates here in the grassland and flows east nearly 300 miles before emptying into the Missouri River. The river—at its infancy at this point—is easily crossed on a ground-level concrete bridge, though a shallow ford may be necessary during times of high water. Less than a mile past the river, bear left at the next junction onto FR 942.

SIDE TRIP
A right turn at this intersection (staying on FR 933) puts you on course to reach Rochelle Hills, an area of lightly timbered mounts that comprise one of the most scenic areas of the grassland. The road heads 9 miles to the base of the hills but ends where a rockslide obliterated a half-mile section of the route. The Forest Service has no plans to reconstruct the roadway.

Continuing west, the road passes through a prairie dog field as it parallels Antelope Creek, a small drainage that is intermittently lined with cottonwoods. The lane soon crosses the stream on another low concrete slab, and again, a shallow ford may be required.

At 31 miles, Phillips Road (FR 973) turns north toward a slope covered with ponderosa pines and eventually reaches a mining area. Stay left on FR 942 and continue west past escarpments that reach upwards to 5,000 feet. Maintaining a steady ascent, the route climbs to overlook a basin of badlands and scoria outcrops. The Laramie Range is visible to the far south from this vantage point.

Before reaching HWY 59, watch for long stretches of train cars on the railroad. Union Pacific and Burlington Northern Sante Fe lines transport coal away from numerous mines found in this grassland, including some of the world's largest. Approximately 25% of the nation's annual coal production is mined from the Powder River Basin and the volume that is moved along this railway is astounding.

Upon reaching HWY 59, it's a 14-mile drive south on the highway to return to Bill and complete the loop. If returning to Gillette, turn north instead and drive 63 miles.

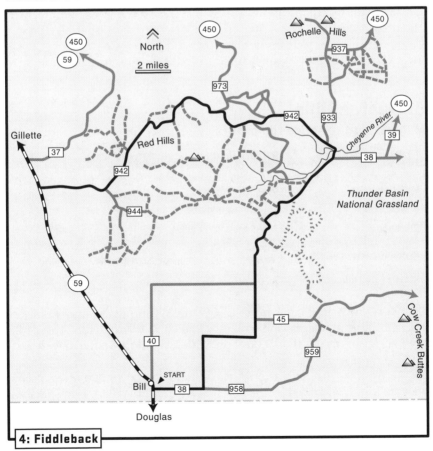

4: Fiddleback

Other Nearby Drives

Fiddleback—There are over a dozen miles of ATV trails in the Fiddleback area of the grassland near a pair of pipelines. These old converted roads (FT 1350, 1351, 1352, 1353, 1357, and 1358) form a small network of four loops. The southern loop, FT 1351, is only open July through November. To reach the trails from Bill, follow CR 38 to the northeast for over 16 miles to turnoffs on the right.

Spring Creek Unit—An isolated "satellite" section of the grassland is found north of Gillette near the town of Weston. To get there, drive north on HWY 14 for 4 miles and turn east on HWY 59. Drive 25.5 miles to a pullout with information boards. On the west side of HWY 59, you'll find ATV trails in the Weston Hills Recreation Area (route #5). On the east side of the highway, head east on Heald Road (CR 49) or turn north onto Rocky Point Road (CR 85). These main roads will lead you to short, crisscrossing tracks that explore this broken terrain near the Montana border.

Rochelle Hills—Perhaps the most popular area in the grassland, Rochelle Hills has numerous tracks that cross the terrain near sparsely forested escarpments. Numerous trunk roads including Piney Creek Road (CR 17) and Lynch Road (CR 7A) can be used to access the hills from HWY 450.

5: Weston Hills
Rugged routes above the prairie

☐ Backcountry Drive Most vehicles	☒ 4WD Route 4x4 vehicle or ORV	☒ ATV Trail ORV less than 50" wide

Location/Map	North of Gillette; Page 51
Roads/Trails	FR 1246, various trails
Distance	20+ miles of trails and roads
Managing Agency	BLM—Buffalo Field Office, USDA Forest Service—Thunder Basin National Grassland
Starting Coordinates	N44° 38.20' W105° 20.18'

Overview: The prairie lands north of Gillette, Wyoming rise into a series of rugged ridges, drainages, and badlands known as Weston Hills. These hills crest at elevations less than 5,000 feet, with tops that are covered with grass and light timber.

The Weston Hills Recreation Area includes roughly 9,000 acres of land that are jointly managed by the Forest Service and the BLM. Lying adjacent to an isolated parcel of the Thunder Basin National Grassland called the Spring Creek Unit, the hills help sustain healthy populations of mule deer and antelope. Turkeys and elk also live here, though they are less likely to be seen. In addition to ORV use, hunting, hiking, and horseback riding are common at Weston Hills. Camping is also permitted and you'll find dispersed campsites throughout the recreation area.

According to the BLM, Weston Hills includes 7 miles of 4WD roads and ATV trails. That may only include routes on BLM lands because I rode twice that number before I had seen the entire area. You can easily rack up a few dozen miles on the odometer before you tire of riding. Take note that maps of this area may not accurately represent what actually exists—there were at least two trails shown on the Forest Service map that I could not find on the ground. Motorized travel is limited to roads and trails that are marked with white arrows. Some routes are closed from September 15 to October 20 (before and during hunting season). A Wyoming ORV permit is required for the ATV trails.

Start: From the west side of Gillette, drive north on HWY 14 for 4 miles and turn east on HWY 59. Drive 25.5 miles to a pullout with information boards. Large parking areas are located on both sides of the highway. Additional parking can be found farther west as you drive into the recreation area.

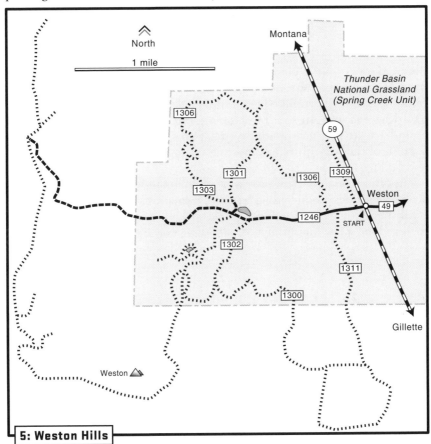

Eastern side of Weston Hills

Description: From the entrance at the highway, the main road (FR 1246) heads west into the recreation area and climbs to the top of a crest in just 3 miles. You can then run the length of the crest to the north for over a mile to a dead end, or turn south to loop around Weston, the hills' high point at 4,563 feet. This nearly 8-mile circuit cuts through the most vegetated portion of the recreation area, passing through grassy slopes of sagebrush and ponderosa pine.

The central portion of the recreation area contains shorter loops that travel across rugged terrain including badland formations speckled with junipers. While these routes are not difficult, you will find some tricky sections, steep inclines, and a few intermittent streams that may have water.

NORTH

The Bighorn Mountains dominate northern Wyoming by creating a long arc from central Wyoming to Montana. Topping out at 13,167 feet on Cloud Peak, the mass towers spectacularly over the surrounding lowlands. The grand scenery of these mountains stretches much farther than its boundaries—you'll find that they enrich much of this region.

West of the mighty range lies the arid Bighorn Basin, an expanse of rugged relief that has little vegetation. Adorned by colorful badlands and snowcapped peaks on the surrounding skyline, the basin typifies Wyoming's varied and diverse landscapes.

WYOMING

North Areas

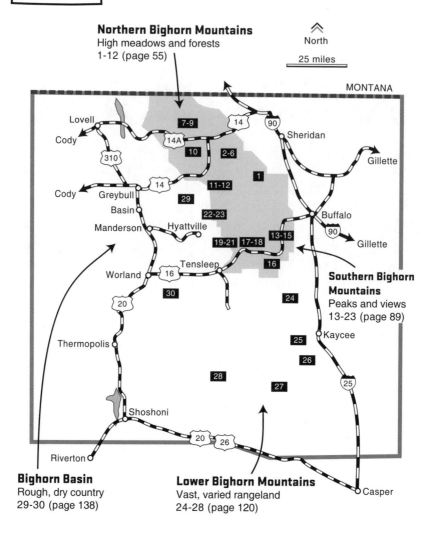

Northern Bighorn Mountains
High meadows and forests
1-12 (page 55)

North

25 miles

MONTANA

Lovell
Cody
310
Cody
Greybull
Basin
Manderson
Hyattville
Worland
Tensleep
Thermopolis
Shoshoni
Riverton

7-9   14   90   Sheridan
14A
10   2-6   Gillette
1
14   11-12   Buffalo
29   90
22-23   Gillette
19-21 17-18 13-15
16

Southern Bighorn Mountains
Peaks and views
13-23 (page 89)

16
30
20
24
25   Kaycee
26
28   27   25

Casper

Bighorn Basin
Rough, dry country
29-30 (page 138)

Lower Bighorn Mountains
Vast, varied rangeland
24-28 (page 120)

Northern Bighorn Mountains

The northern Bighorn Mountains—namely the northern half of the Bighorn National Forest—rise steeply from the lower basins to form a gentle crest comprised of rolling, grassy terrain with small, dense stands of spruce and fir. Many of the high points are simply gentle, rounded knolls that you would expect to find anywhere except in the high mountains of Wyoming. But the illusion that this is a common woodland is shattered by the biting chill of the air, snowdrifts that linger into July, and intimate views of granite peaks in the nearby Cloud Peak Wilderness.

Among the abundance of recreational opportunities that the Bighorns offer, wildlife viewing is near the top of the list. The mountains are known to hold moose, elk, deer, bighorn sheep, black bear, mountain lions, and wild turkeys. Wolves—migrants from Yellowstone National Park some 100 miles to the west—have also been found here, though it's still unknown whether they have established a local, sustainable population.

Land Ownership

The Bighorn National Forest encompasses nearly all of the northern Bighorn Mountains. Trespassing onto private property is rarely a concern as private residences and resorts are well signed. Local Forest Service offices are located in Buffalo and Sheridan. There is also a visitor center on the west side of the range along HWY 14 at Shell Falls.

Roads and Trails

The flanks of the northern Bighorn Mountains are quite steep and any drive to the high country involves an aggressive incline. Two highways, HWY 14 (Bighorn Scenic Byway) and HWY 14 ALT (Medicine Wheel Passage), provide paved access across the mountains and through deep canyons on the range's west side.

The Bighorn National Forest offers an extensive layout of ever-changing backroads and motorized trails. This is especially true in the northern half of the range where you'll enjoy long routes that often interconnect to create loops and full-day excursions. The major trunk roads are wide, graveled, and very well maintained. The four-wheel drive roads are greatly varied; some permit easy passage for the less daring driver while others rank among the toughest in the state. The northern Bighorns also offer many miles of ATV trails that are diverse enough to appeal to casual riders as well as those looking for a technical challenge.

Seasons and Conditions

The routes in this area are mountainous with elevations as high as 10,000 feet. Even with the intensity of the sun at high altitude, you'll encounter snowdrifts well into the summer months. Most roads are passable by the middle of June and certainly by July, but mud can be expected throughout the driving season. September and October usually offer good driving conditions, but a cold front will often bring snow with it. I've seen it snow in every month of the year in the Bighorns; be prepared for it.

Fuel

Service stations are available in nearly all of the surrounding communities. On the eastern front, you can fill up in Buffalo, Story, Sheridan, Ranchester, or Dayton. On the west side, make your stops in Ten Sleep, Worland, Basin, Greybull, or Lovell. There is also a station near Burgess Junction where HWY 14 splits with HWY 14 ALT.

Maps

The Bighorn National Forest map, the ORV map, and the Motor Vehicle Use Map (MVUM) are excellent references for the Bighorn Mountains.

1: Penrose Park
Long trails to faraway reservoirs

☐ **Backcountry Drive**
Most vehicles

☐ **4WD Route**
4x4 vehicle or ORV

☒ **ATV Trail**
ORV less than 50" wide

Location/Map	West of Sheridan; Page 57
Roads/Trails	FR 320, FT 33, FT 38, FT 82
Distance	55 miles of roads and trails
Managing Agency	USDA Forest Service—Bighorn National Forest
Starting Coordinates	N44° 34.09' W106° 55.69'

Overview: This extensive layout of ATV trails in the northeastern Bighorn Mountains provides access to a number of scenic reservoirs such as Kearney Lake Reservoir, Willow Park Reservoir, and Cloud Peak Reservoir. This is not the typical "in and out" trail system. Since it takes several back-aching hours of riding to reach many of the destinations, backcountry camping is commonplace. If you get a late start, you'll surely be driving in the dark.

Trail surfaces vary greatly throughout the area as well as from year to year. There are stretches of dirt that are easy to traverse. Many segments are much tougher, with steep, rocky, or uneven patches that can tumble your machine. Some segments, such as FT 38 to Kearney Lake, are so narrow and rocky that they are better suited for single-track use. Due to the challenging terrain, the trails here are for skilled riders (accidents and fatalities have happened). This is not the place to learn how to handle a 600-pound quad. Caution and good judgment are paramount. Traffic can be heavy on the narrow paths and passing is difficult (sometimes impossible) especially near the beginning.

These routes have differing seasonal restrictions, but all of them are open by June 16. A Wyoming ORV permit is required for the trails.

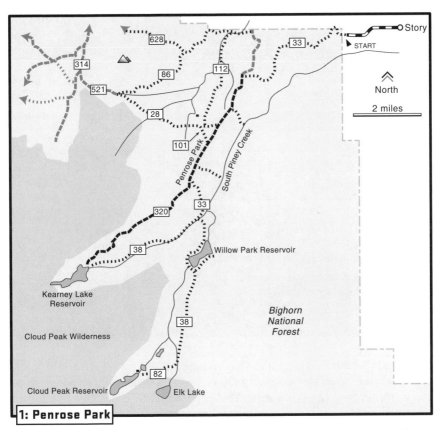

1: Penrose Park

Start: From Sheridan, drive south on HWY 87 for 14 miles. Bear right at the fork near Banner and drive 2.5 miles to Story. You can also reach Story from Buffalo or Sheridan by taking I-90 to Exit 44. From Story, take HWY 194 west for 2.6 miles to unsigned Penrose Lane. This narrow road is found just before a playground near a curve in the road. Follow the road past private residences to the trailhead's one-way entrance. It can be difficult to get turned around if you miss the entrance. This is a decent-sized parking lot, but it easily fills up when there are vehicles with trailers.

Description: From the trailhead at an elevation of 5,400 feet, the trail begins with a long ascent of the mountain range's eastern front. The initial climb—the first 2 miles—begins with a steep grade through shrubs to reach a light ponderosa pine forest that has been scarred from a past fire. This is a very narrow segment of the trail with a drop-off on one side. Proceed cautiously, being mindful of oncoming traffic that may be encountered.

After a slight reprieve around 3 miles, there is more uphill driving to do until the trail joins FR 320 at mile 6. Turn left onto this 4WD road and follow it south 1.5 miles into Penrose Park. Aside from some occasional breaks and overlooks, much of the trail to this point has been confined to the timber

Cloud Peak Reservoir —Steve Rafuse photo

where views have been limited. This changes in the vast, 3-mile long park. Here, you'll find an awe-inspiring vista of some of the Bighorn Mountains' most impressive craggy summits. This is perhaps the best place to stop for an extended rest before proceeding to one of the area's backcountry lakes.

Two ATV trails, FT 028 and FT 101, are passed on the west side of Penrose Park by mile 9. These trails traverse a mostly timbered expanse and connect to 4WD roads in the Little Goose area. Combined, the Penrose Park trails and the roads around Little Goose Creek number more than 100 miles.

More options are found to the south along the road that bisects Penrose Park. For the preferred and most direct route to Kearney Lake Reservoir, continue along the same path for another 5 miles. To reach other destinations, take FT 033, located near the south end of the park. From the beginning of this trail (which transitions into FT 38 and FT 82), you can reach Willow Park Reservoir at 3.5 miles or stunning Cloud Peak Reservoir at 10 miles. Plan on taking up to five hours to reach Cloud Peak Reservoir from the trailhead.

All of these destinations require uphill travel as they are at elevations 500 to 1,700 feet above Penrose Park. Depending on the time of season, a number of creeks may be crossed along the way, but the largest of these (Kearny Creek and South Piney Creek) are bridged.

A slew of foot trails can also be used to further explore this remarkable country, especially around Cloud Peak Reservoir. The subalpine lakes that can be reached with about a mile of hiking include Frying Pan Lake, Elk Lake, Flatiron Lake, and Gem Lake. All of these have their own lure, but Elk Lake in particular has an incredible backdrop of jagged mountain peaks.

2: Red Grade

The Bighorn's back door

☒ **Backcountry Drive**
Most vehicles

☐ **4WD Route**
4x4 vehicle or ORV

☐ **ATV Trail**
ORV less than 50" wide

Location/Map	West of Sheridan; Page 60
Roads	FR 26
Distance	35 miles
Managing Agency	USDA Forest Service—Bighorn National Forest
Starting Coordinates	N44° 38.34' W107° 4.18'

Overview: Red Grade Road—sometimes referred to as Big Goose—is among northern Wyoming's best backcountry drives. Perhaps no other backroad captures the transition between the plains and the high country like this one. Beginning the drive from Sheridan, you will more than double your elevation within 20 miles. Then, as you enter the high country, you'll find rushing creeks, evergreen forests, and roadside history.

Trailers and RVs are not advised along the steep and narrow eastern half of this route (I did this once, and never again.) Trailer parking is available at the east end of the road. Take note that the eastern half of this route is not open to unlicensed ATVs. However, plated, street-legal ATVs are allowed, and the east half has become a popular access point for the Penrose Park and Little Goose ATV trails.

The road is open to motorized use from April 1 to December 14, but it's best to drive it between June and October.

Start: To make the uphill drive described here, head south from Sheridan on HWY 87 for 4 miles and turn right onto HWY 335. Continue along HWY 335 for 10 miles to the point where the road turns into FR 26. There are three large parking lots here where you can unload street-legal ATVs.

To make a downhill drive, or to access the upper sections of this road that are suitable for trailers and RVs, drive north from Sheridan on I-90 and take Exit 9 to HWY 14. Travel west on HWY 14 for 37 miles and turn left onto FR 26.

Description: Your first stop may very well be on your way to Red Grade Road. Just south of the town of Big Horn, among the beautiful, grassy rolling knolls is the Bradford Brinton Memorial Ranch. This historical site features a ranch house and a western art collection.

From the end of HWY 335, you can see where Red Grade Road ascends the east face of the Bighorn Mountains until getting engulfed by the Bighorn National Forest. These first few miles of the county road are very steep with a 13% grade. It's an exhilarating climb with a drop-off made more pronounced because the trees have burned. Since loose gravel and steep

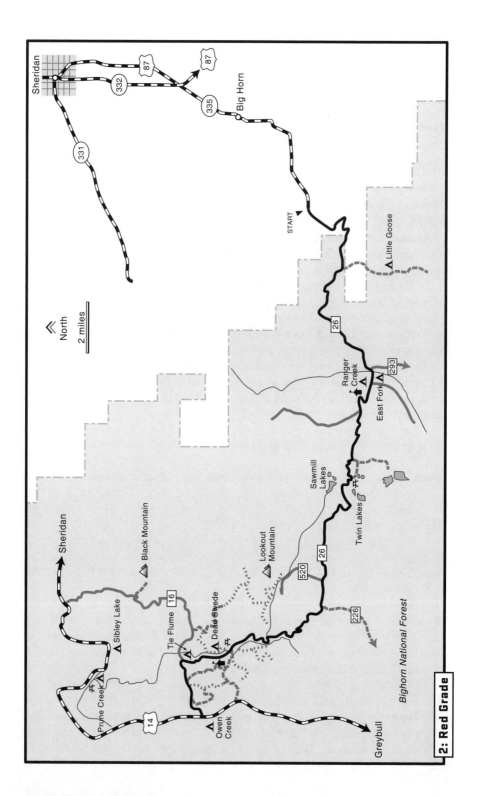

2: Red Grade

inclines aren't conducive to stop-and-go driving, you'll find yourself trying not to lose momentum on your uphill advance.

Inside the Bighorn National Forest, stunning views begin to be revealed as you enter an area named Poverty Flat. The road becomes somewhat more level here, offering you a chance to survey your surroundings. Look to the south for Blacktooth Mountain (13,014 feet) and Mt. Woolsey (12,978 feet), two of the Bighorns more jagged crags.

Around 5 miles, you'll pass a 4WD road leading to Little Goose Campground, a primitive tent camp and one of Wyoming's least accessible. Continue along FR 26 for another 5 miles to enter Big Goose Park.

SIDE TRIP At Big Goose Park, take FR 293 south for 2.6 miles to reach Park Reservoir where dispersed camping is common. It's a bumpy road that gets much worse past the lake where it heads to Cross Creek, a no-frills Forest Service campground.

Within Big Goose Park, FR 26 becomes wider and smoother making the remaining distance easier to drive. Big Goose Ranger Station, Ranger Creek Campground, and East Fork Campground are all developed sites found on the west side of the park.

By 17 miles, the road enters an area pocketed with lakes and marshes. Virtually none of these are visible from the roadway, but many are accessible by following short foot trails or secondary roads. Three of the more common stops include Sawmill Lakes to the north, and Duck Pond and Twin Lakes to the south.

The road now climbs to its indiscernible high point at Sawmill Pass (9,350 feet), a small park. An interpretive sign a short distance farther describes stage routes that once passed through the area. There were three separate courses, but their use was terminated after a railroad was built to Cody.

Continuing west through the forest, several primitive roads are passed including Lookout Mountain Road (FR 520) and FR 226, which heads to Woodchuck Pass. These very worthwhile side roads afford striking views of the Bighorn's high country. Woodchuck Pass itself (2 miles to the south) is worth every bounce along the 4WD road that is required to reach it.

Another interpretive site is found near mile 26 along the East Fork of the South Tongue River. Here, you'll find a splash dam, a wooden structure built in 1905 that was used to dam the river. When enough water was held back, the water was released for the purpose of flushing logs and railroad ties downstream to processing facilities near Dayton. There are reports that the ties reached 80 miles per hour as they were washed downhill.

From the splash dam, the route takes a northern bearing while curving through the evergreen forest. After passing Graves Creek and Mohawk Creek, the road reaches Woodrock Guard Station and Dead Swede Campground. Another roadside stop is found less than 2 miles farther where a sign on the east side of the road marks a devastated swath of ground. On June 25,

Splash dam along Red Grade Road

1991, a microburst blew down over 1,100 acres of trees along an 8-mile path between HWY 14 and Black Mountain Lookout. The windstorm only lasted 15 minutes.

From the blowdown site, the road continues north a short distance to reach Tie Flume Campground at the junction with Black Mountain Road (FR 16). Turn left and drive through broad high meadows to reach the end of this backcountry drive at HWY 14.

ALTERNATE ROUTE If you're headed back to Sheridan, you can turn right at the last junction and head east on FR 16. This wide gravel lane is easily driven, save for some washboard and potholes. The road begins by crossing over the South Tongue River where you'll find nice picnic sites along a primitive track that parallels the river's west bank. Further east, several 4WD tracks and ATV trails lead into the pine forest on the south side of the road. The main course turns northward near Black Mountain (with a fire lookout tower on top) and then connects to HWY 14 after 9 miles.

3: Little Goose
A rugged loop with many side trips

☐ **Backcountry Drive**
Most vehicles

☒ **4WD Route**
4x4 vehicle or ORV

☐ **ATV Trail**
ORV less than 50" wide

Location/Map	West of Sheridan; Page 64
Roads	FR 293, FR 289, FR 290, FR 314
Distance	22 miles
Managing Agency	USDA Forest Service—Bighorn National Forest
Starting Coordinates	N44° 36.17' W107° 12.25'

Overview: The Little Goose area of the Bighorns has a great assortment of four-wheeling roads and ATV trails. With roughly 40 miles of roads and another dozen miles of designated ATV trails, it's an area you can explore all day without backtracking. The trip described here is a 22-mile tour that visits Park Reservoir and Bighorn Reservoir. Much of this route is fairly easily traveled on an ATV. If driving a full-sized vehicle, you'll want to have above-average ground clearance and skid plates for the steep, rocky stretches. There are also a number of fords that are often 12 inches or deeper.

Part of this loop incorporates a stretch of FR 26 that is closed to unlicensed ATVs that only have an ORV permit, but licensed ATVs are allowed. There are alternative roads (FR 309 and FR 316) that can be used if you are only driving with an ORV permit. The route is open to motorized use from April 1 through December 14, but it's best to drive it between June and October.

Start: From Sheridan, drive north on I-90 and take Exit 9 to HWY 14. Drive west on HWY 14 for 37 miles, bearing left at Burgess Junction. Turn east onto FR 26 and follow this road 23 miles to FR 293 on the right. A small area at the beginning of the road can be used for ATV unloading. Better spots can be found at Park Reservoir, 2 miles to the south.

Description: Starting from the junction of FR 26 and FR 293, drive south on the maintained road for 2.6 miles to reach Park Reservoir. This is a bumpy and rocky stretch but it is easily driven in any vehicle. Park Reservoir is one of the Bighorn Mountains' larger lakes and it's popular with anglers and campers, particularly along the northern shoreline. Continue following FR 293 along the reservoir and through a meadow to reach a junction near the Spear-O-Wigwam Ranch.

SIDE TRIP

If you bear right at the fork, you'll soon ford Cross Creek near a primitive campground of the same name. From here, the road continues southward for another 2.5 miles and is degraded by mud holes, dips, a shallow ford of Lightner Creek, and some large rocks. The road ends at Coffeen Park, a wilderness trailhead. Stock 4x4s can make the drive, but it's a slow go.

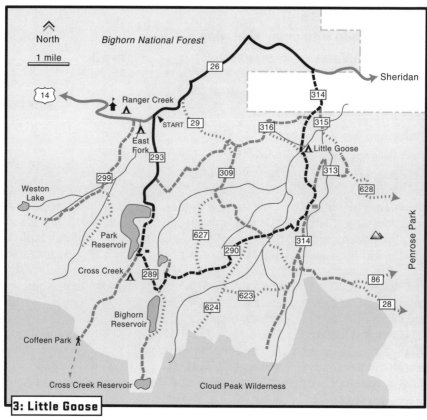

3: Little Goose

From Spear-O-Wigwam, bear left onto FR 289. This road proceeds up a rocky, steep incline for a mile and a half to reach Bighorn Reservoir. The road bears left immediately before the reservoir, but it's possible to drive along the northern shoreline. It's a beautiful lake crowned with 11,000-foot peaks from the Cloud Peak Wilderness.

SIDE TRIP Motorized access is restricted around the west side of Bighorn Reservoir, but an ATV trail follows the east shoreline and continues 2.5 miles farther to Cross Creek Reservoir—a smaller body of water that is enveloped on three sides by the Cloud Peak Wilderness.

Many stock 4x4 drivers call it a day when they reach Bighorn Reservoir. The road you now follow to the northeast, FR 290, is a rougher track that is narrower and rockier.

SIDE TRIP Just over a half mile from Bighorn Reservoir, watch for a 1.3-mile spur (FR 291) that leads to Martin Reservoir.

The Little Goose area of the Bighorn National Forest

As you advance eastward on FR 290, several well-marked ATV trails can be found: one to the north that connects to FR 309 and a pair to the south that ends near the Cloud Peak Wilderness boundary. You'll also find FR 309, which branches off to the north at Granite Park.

SIDE TRIP

FR 309 is a decent road (and alternative return route to Park Reservoir) that passes Lamburger Rock, a distinctive outcropping near some summer cabins. FR 309 repeatedly intersects a a few short ATV trails.

There is a ford (a foot deep in early July) of the West Fork of Little Goose Creek at the east end of Granite Park. Past this, the road soon reaches FR 314 at 11 miles, the trip's halfway point. A right turn at this junction would take you south where you could tie into the extensive ATV trail system at Penrose Park. Instead, turn left at the junction and follow this dirt road northward across beautiful open country. Watch for a sign for Little Goose Falls, a pretty cascade can be reached by foot or from a short, off-camber ATV trail.

SIDE TRIP

Located just north of Little Goose Falls, FR 313 is a 2.2-mile spur that leads to Kenny Wood Park after crossing the East Fork of Little Goose Creek. Two segments of FT 628, an ATV trail, are accessible from this road. The first segment makes a steep, switchbacking ascent toward Little Goose Peak (9,378 feet) before it ties in with ATV trails farther east. The second segment is found at the end of the road. This short 1.2-mile trail leads north toward an old cow camp where it makes two fords before connecting to FR 315.

Two miles north of the falls, the road descends to Little Goose Campground, another remote, primitive tent camp. However, a high ford of Little Goose Creek is required to reach the camp. I found the creek to be 20 inches deep in early July, but a hiker I encountered said the waters had nearly reached the windows of his pickup truck just a couple weeks earlier.

From the campground, the road clambers out of the Little Goose drainage just to drop into the Tepee Creek drainage. Here again is another ford, albeit shallower, and another climb out as the road passes through private property with a smattering of summer residences. Traction can be poor on these washed-out inclines.

Stay on the main road—a public access route—and ignore the multitude of unsigned junctions to ultimately reach Red Grade Road (FR 26). You can now return to the starting point by turning left on FR 26. However, this section of road is closed to ATVs that only have an ORV permit. As an alternative, you can take FR 316 and FR 309 to return to the starting point.

4: Woodchuck Pass
A high country loop

☐ **Backcountry Drive** Most vehicles	☒ **4WD Route** 4x4 vehicle or ORV	☐ **ATV Trail** ORV less than 50" wide

Location/Map	West of Sheridan; Page 68
Roads	FR 226, FR 277, FR 278
Distance	17.5 miles
Managing Agency	USDA Forest Service—Bighorn National Forest
Starting Coordinates	N44° 37.79' W107° 24.50'

Overview: This route climbs to beautiful Woodchuck Pass and then makes a loop through the Bighorn Mountains' grassy high country. The trip includes a few fords, occasional rocky areas with embedded boulders, and steep inclines, but is not an overly difficult route when driven in dry conditions. (At the time of this writing, a section of FR 226 was closed at Willett Creek, but the Forest Service plans on re-routing this crossing.) These roads are open to motorized use from April 1 through December 14, but it's best to drive it between June and October.

Start: From Sheridan, drive north on I-90 and take Exit 9 to HWY 14. Drive west on HWY 14 for 37 miles. Turn east onto FR 26 and follow this road 11 miles to FR 226 on the right. There is a good parking area for ATV unloading on the other side of the road. Additional entry points can be found on FR 17 near the Forest Service's Shell Creek Workstation and from an ATV trail located at Antelope Butte Ski Area off HWY 14.

Forest Road 278 near Woodchuck Pass

Description: Starting from FR 26 and heading south on FR 226, the drive begins with an immediate ford of the East Fork of the South Tongue River. This is an easy crossing (6 inches deep in July) as concrete blocks line the river bottom. The road is easily traveled along this first stretch and soon reaches FR 268 in less than a mile.

SIDE TRIP Be sure to drive up this short and steep side road (FR 268) to see Calvin Lake. It's just a quarter mile to a small parking area where a short foot trail leads to the rocky lakeshore.

At 2.2 miles, the road gains the splendid scenery of Woodchuck Pass at 9,612 feet. There may be no better place to pull out your camera than here. From the top of the windy pass, the bumpy road negotiates around a large granite crest to reach a junction with FR 278. Stay left at the junction.

The road now turns south and descends to a crossing of Willett Creek. Past the marshy banks of this creek, continue through a coniferous woodland and make another two fords within the next three miles. The ensuing climb out of this drainage includes a difficult spot that is steep and rutted.

The junction with FR 277 comes near the trip's halfway point. A left turn puts you on a moderately steep and rocky descent toward Ranger Creek Campground, 2 miles farther. Bear right and drive uphill to regain the spectacular views from the bottom of a valley floor. The driving is now easy, when dry, as the road cuts north through a sprawling wildflower-laden park below Antelope Butte (9,935 feet).

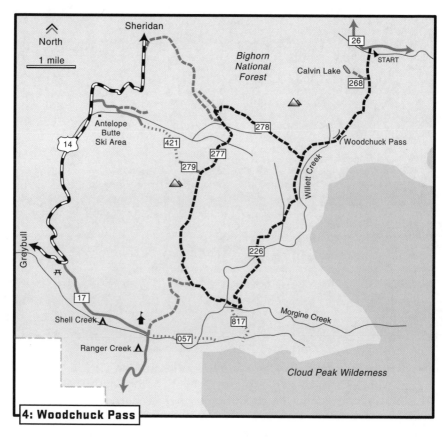

4: Woodchuck Pass

An ATV trail that leads to HWY 14 via FR 279 is passed at the north end of Antelope Butte. Almost 2 miles further, FR 277 splits off to the left and also heads toward HWY 14. Bear right onto FR 278 and follow the rockier path uphill to the granite-crowned crest. Watch for FR 226 to return to Woodchuck Pass and complete the drive.

5: South Tongue River
Follow a scenic river

☐ **Backcountry Drive**
Most vehicles

☐ **4WD Route**
4x4 vehicle or ORV

☒ **ATV Trail**
ORV less than 50" wide

Location/Map	West of Sheridan; Page 70
Roads/Trails	FR 193, FT 430, FR 214211
Distance	6.1 miles
Managing Agency	USDA Forest Service—Bighorn National Forest
Starting Coordinates	N44° 46.73' W107° 28.60'

Overview: This trail follows the west bank of the South Tongue River through lush meadows and dark evergreen forests. This is a diverse route as some stretches present easy riding along an old road, while other sections are found with more rock and mud. The trail is open from May 16 to November 15. A Wyoming ORV permit is required.

Start: From Sheridan, drive north on I-90 and take Exit 9 to HWY 14. Drive west on HWY 14 for almost 30 miles to the large parking lot on the left near Pine Island Picnic Area. This is the best place to unload ATVs as the trailhead itself is very small.

To start the trail from the south, drive north from Sheridan on I- 90 and take Exit 9. Travel west on HWY 14 for 37 miles. Turn left onto FR 26 and drive 2.5 miles to a secondary road (marked as FR 214211 or FR 578 depending on the map) on the left. This road leads to several parking spots and the southern end of the trail in a quarter mile.

Description: Starting from the north end at HWY 14, follow FR 193 for 1.7 miles past some private cabins. The road ends at a small trailhead. The trail itself is a continuation of the access road, which initially retains much of its tame condition, save for some ruts and mud-prone spots.

Two miles from the highway, the trail breaks into Shutts Flats, a photogenic clearing along the South Tongue River. The trail stays along the meadow's treeline for the first half mile, but then draws close to the river as the park narrows. Fishing opportunities abound along this beautiful stretch.

South Tongue River along Forest Trail 430

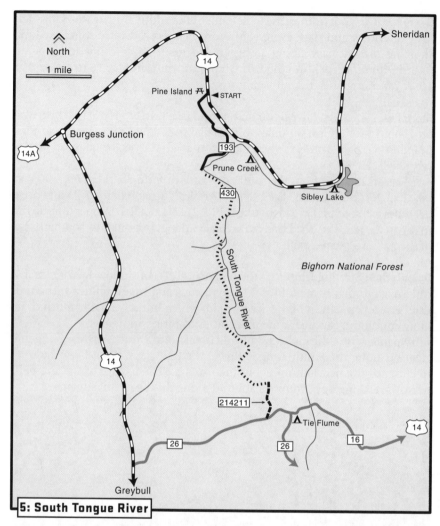

5: South Tongue River

At 3.3 miles, the trail leaves the openness of the vale and enters the evergreen forest, beginning with a ford of Sheeley Creek. This crossing precedes a ford of Owen Creek, reached just a tenth of a mile farther. Depending on the time of year, you may also splash through three intermittent streams along this stretch.

For the next mile, the trail parallels an increasingly-rapid river while climbing through the heavily-wooded drainage. The tread here is filled with occasional large rocks, unforgiving roots, and plenty of muddy potholes. You'll also cross a number of narrow wooden bridges over smaller draws.

As the trail approaches its southern end, you'll leave the South Tongue River completely and begin to climb a moderately steep slope. From the top, another half mile of gentler riding takes you to FR 214211, a short spur that connects to FR 26.

6: Black Mountain
Climb to a fire lookout tower

☐ **Backcountry Drive**
Most vehicles

❎ **4WD Route**
4x4 vehicle or ORV

❎ **ATV Trail**
ORV less than 50" wide

Location/Map	West of Sheridan; Page 71
Roads/Trails	FR 222, FT 011
Distance	2 miles (last mile is an ATV/hiking trail)
Managing Agency	USDA Forest Service—Bighorn National Forest
Starting Coordinates	N44° 44.65' W107° 23.92'

Overview: Black Mountain (9,489 feet) is a prominent pinnacle that caps the east face of the Bighorn Mountains. Its summit offers a high overlook that the Forest Service long utilized as a fire lookout. Though the tower is no longer in service, you can still climb to it and enjoy the vantage point.

How close you drive to the lookout depends on your capabilities. From FR 16, a high-clearance vehicle can get you to a trailhead on the southwest side of the mountain. From there, a very rocky and challenging ATV trail continues closer to the summit, though it's more suitable for hiking than driving. Near the end, a short hiking path weaves through the rocks to gain the summit. A Wyoming ORV permit is required for the ATV trail.

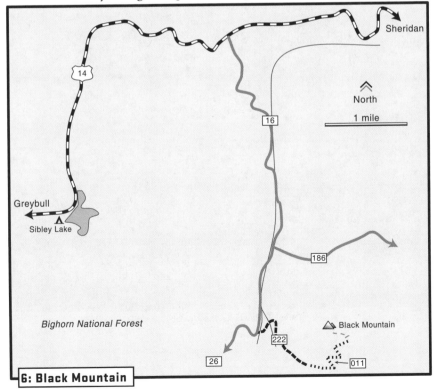

Start: From Sheridan, drive north on I-90 and take Exit 9 to HWY 14. Drive west on HWY 14 for just over 23 miles to reach Black Mountain Road (FR 16). Drive south on the gravel road for 3.5 miles and turn left onto FR 222.

Description: From FR 16, follow FR 222 uphill for about a mile to the Black Mountain Trailhead. The road has two fords (both are usually shallow) and a couple of short, rocky stretches.

At the trailhead, a rugged ATV trail, FT 011, continues uphill. Though ATVs are allowed, the steep, narrow path has so many large rocks that most people leave their machines at the trailhead and continue to the top on foot. Regardless of how you get there, the last part of the trail requires a short hike to reach the boarded fire lookout tower, which was built in 1929. The view from the top of Black Mountain is unforgettable. You can see many miles across the Bighorn Mountains and eastern plains.

Forest Trail 011 on Black Mountain

7: Dayton Gulch
A cross section tour of the northern Bighorns

☒ **Backcountry Drive**
   Most vehicles

☐ **4WD Route**
   4x4 vehicle or ORV

☐ **ATV Trail**
   ORV less than 50" wide

Location/Map	West of Sheridan; Page 73
Roads/Trails	FR 15
Distance	25 miles
Managing Agency	USDA Forest Service—Bighorn National Forest
Starting Coordinates	N44° 46.18' W107° 31.35'

Overview: Dayton Gulch Road (FR 15) traverses the rolling subalpine terrain that characterizes the northern reaches of the Bighorn National Forest. You'll find sprawling meadows, rounded hills dotted with dense conifer stands, summertime snowdrifts, and animals such as moose foraging in the creeks. The road is open to motorized use from April 1 to December 14, but it's best driven between July and October.

Start: From Sheridan, travel north on I-90 and take Exit 9 to HWY 14. Drive west on HWY 14 for 32 miles, bearing right onto HWY 14 ALT. The eastern end of the road is located just past Burgess Junction. The western end of the road can be accessed 20 miles farther west on HWY 14 ALT.

Description: The road begins by departing the highway to the north near Burgess Junction. You soon pass North Tongue Campground and then cross over the North Tongue River.

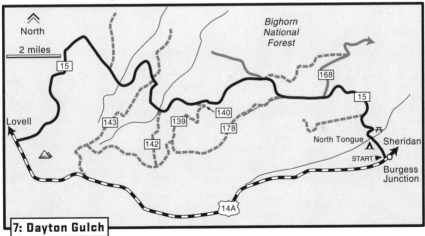

SIDE TRIP After the bridge, take the short spur on the right to reach Burgess Picnic Area, a remarkable recreation area shrouded by towering rocks. The boulder-choked North Tongue River flows through the site.

The road continues to the north to a view of Twin Buttes, dolomite outcroppings that stand over the surrounding countryside. These structures are thought to have weathered millions of years of wind and water erosion. A short distance later at 3 miles, the road assumes a western bearing and soon enters the timber. Stay left at the fork with FR 168 and follow Fool Creek across sagebrush-robed terrain to reach Schuler Park by mile 8.

SIDE TRIP FR 168, leads to Freeze Out Point (8,305 feet), a high perch where you can get a bird's eye view of the northeastern corner of the Bighorn National Forest. A 4x4 vehicle, or vehicle with decent clearance, is needed to attain the high point. There are numerous 4WD roads around the point that can also be driven (route #8).

Shortly after 11 miles, you reach a highlight of the drive, Burgess Overlook at 9,008 feet. From the pullout, you can look across miles of grassy slopes that are pocketed with dark conifer stands. From this high point, the road falls into the Lake Creek drainage where you cross over a pretty, oxbow-curved stream.

Climbing sharply out of the verdant creek bottom, FR 15 works its way into the Dayton Gulch area in which the road is named. Much of this stretch is timbered, so views of the gulch are largely hidden. What you will see,

Lake Creek along Forest Road 15

however, are glimpses of the upper hillsides that hold snowdrifts well into midsummer.

A fork of the Little Bighorn River is crossed at 23 miles just as the roadway breaks into the open. In front is Little Bald Mountain (9,907 feet), appropriately named for its treeless summit. From here, the road wraps two miles around the flank of the tall mountain before returning to the highway.

8: Northern Routes
Off the beaten path in the northern mountains

☐ Backcountry Drive Most vehicles	☒ 4WD Route 4x4 vehicle or ORV	☒ ATV Trail ORV less than 50" wide

Location/Map	West of Sheridan; Page 77
Roads/Trails	Freeze Out Point: FR 199, FR 180, FR 182, FR 181, FR 198, FR 201 Riley Point: FR 150 Dry Fork Ridge: FR 149, FT 201
Distance	21+ miles
Managing Agency	USDA Forest Service—Bighorn National Forest
Starting Coordinates	Freeze Out Point: N44° 52.03' W107° 27.73' Riley Point and Dry Fork Ridge: N44° 50.24' W107° 30.21'

Overview: The northern edge of the Bighorn National Forest has many secondary roads and ATV trails that cross the mountains near the Montana border. These three routes—Freeze Out Point, Riley Point, and Dry Fork Ridge—are among the best options for exploring this wide-open high country. Characterized by grassy draws, sunny slopes, and occasional stands of light timber, the ever-changing terrain makes for fun and scenic touring. There are many miles of peripheral routes that can also be driven. These routes have varying seasonal restrictions, but all of them are open between June 16 and November 15. A Wyoming ORV permit is required for the ATV trails.

Start: From Sheridan, travel north on I-90 and take Exit 9 to HWY 14. Drive west on HWY 14 for 32 miles, bearing right onto HWY 14 ALT. Turn onto FR 15 located just past Burgess Junction. Drive north on FR 15 for 5.5 miles and bear right onto FR 168. Follow this road 5.3 miles to reach Riley Point and Dry Fork Ridge or drive nearly 9 miles to the end of the road for Freeze Out Point, which is the best place to park.

Description (Freeze Out Point): This 9.5-mile loop is suitable for stock 4x4s. ATV riders can incorporate several connecting trails for a longer outing.

From the parking area, follow rocky FR 199 up a slight grade for about a mile. A separate spur leads to the summit of Freeze Out Point at 8,305 feet. From this overlook, you can survey the surrounding forest, the eastern plains of Wyoming, and the dirt route that you'll soon be driving.

From the high point, descend back to the main track and follow it eastward to a junction. Turn left and drive north a short distance to reach a second junction. Turn right here onto FR 182 and head east across the dusty eastern flank of the Bighorn Mountains.

SIDE
TRIP

Staying left on FR 180 takes you 1.2 miles to the Yonkee Cow Camp site. The rugged 4-mile Freeze Out ATV Trail (FT 008) also branches off this road and descends steeply off the mountain to CR 140.

As you travel east on FR 182, you pass through a sparse forest comprised of spruce and limber pine. The rugged Smith Creek Trail (FT 085) diverts off to the left and travels several miles to private property. As you continue east, use caution when approaching fence lines as there are numerous wire gates along the way.

The road forks at the far end of the loop. A left turn here would take you into the Amsden Creek Wildlife Habitat Management Area. Instead, turn right (west) and follow the route through several shallow draws with intermittent streams.

The 1.8-mile Horse Creek ATV trail (FT 159) is passed to the south before the next junction is reached. There, the road to the right is FR 199 (again), which goes around the east side of Freeze Out Point. Stay left and follow FR 198 through the Sheep Creek drainage. The last junction is reached after 8 miles. You can turn north to return to the starting point or continue west on FR 201 to slightly extend your trip or to access other 4WD roads in the area.

Grassy backroad on the loop around Freeze Out Point

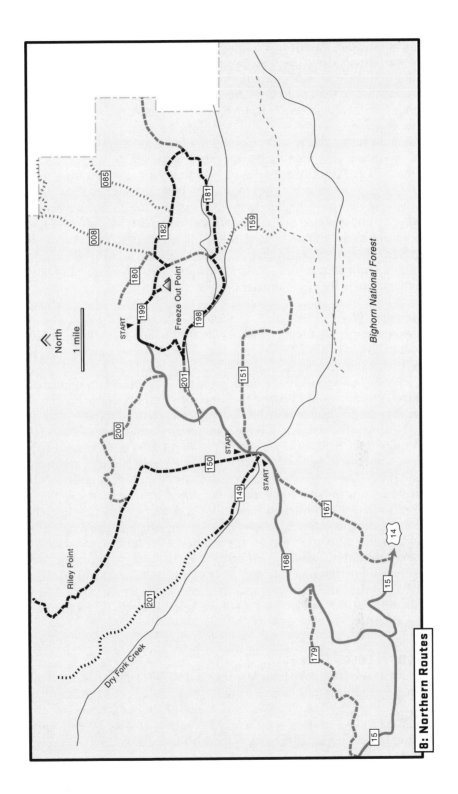

085
008
181
159
182
180
Freeze Out Point
199
198
START
North
1 mile
201
151
200
150
START
149
START
167
168
14
15
201
Riley Point
Dry Fork Creek
179
15
15

Bighorn National Forest

Description (Riley Point): This 6-mile road (FR 150) climbs Dry Fork Ridge and traverses its crest. The ridge is among the highest in this corner of the national forest, making for a scenic drive with sweeping views of the Bighorn Mountains. The road begins at 7,500 feet, but climbs steeply to 8,500 feet within 2 miles. The ascent is relatively easy and rock free, aside from some loose gravel.

Nearing the top of Dry Fork Ridge, the road passes intriguing rock outcrops that are mixed into light limber pine and sagebrush ground cover. Some of the trees are stripped bare from a past fire. Further off on the southern horizon, you can see the rugged tops of the Bighorn's higher peaks.

The road reaches its highest point of 8,548 feet at 2.25 miles. A half mile farther, FR 200 is passed on the right. This rutted track leads down to Sawmill Flats near Freeze Out Point. Bear left at this junction to stay on the ridgeline.

The road now passes in and out of dark timber until it reaches Riley Point at 5 miles. From this scenic 8,536-foot perch, the road curves to the northeast where it ends in the trees.

Description (Dry Fork Ridge): This 6-mile route travels through Dry Fork Canyon, roughly paralleling Dry Fork Creek. The first 1.7 miles are open to all motorized vehicles, but the remaining distance is only open to ATVs with a Wyoming ORV permit.

From the main trunk road (FR 168), the 4WD road (FR 149) immediately begins descending 600 vertical feet into the Dry Fork drainage. The road here cambers sharply to one side, leaving you driving on a tilt.

Where the road begins to level off, it fords Dry Fork Creek twice and then turns into the Dry Fork Cow Camp ATV Trail (FT 201) at 1.7 miles. Looking across Dry Fork Ridge to the north, there are nearly a dozen ravines that come down from the crest—many lined with aspen trees. Most of these draws have tiny intermittent streams that flow across the road.

By 2 miles, the trail leaves Dry Fork Creek and begins traveling above the drainage. The trail now follows easy, rolling terrain below the ridge that stands nearly 2,000 feet higher. A profusion of wildflowers and fields of lupine reward those who make it here during the summer green-up.

Three miles farther, a short spur forks off the main route and leads to an overlook point. The trail ends shortly thereafter at an old cow camp and cabin along Miller Creek. There are three foot trails here that lead in every other direction.

Other Nearby Drives

Amsden Creek Wildlife Habitat Management Area—This scenic area offers primitive campsites and access to the Tongue River below towering rock walls. To reach the lower canyon from the north end of Dayton, drive west on CR 92 for 2.3 miles to a fork. Stay left and drive over 2 more miles to reach the a parking lot at the end of the road.

Twin Buttes Roads—Three short 4WD routes are located in the Twin Buttes area along FR 15 and FR 168. The first of these is Freeze Out Road (FR 167), an open 3-mile route that fords Hay Creek and Fool Creek as it passes the buttes. The second road is Fool Creek Ridge Road (FR 179), a 4-mile connector that travels through both meadows and forest. The third road, Skull Ridge (FR 151), begins by fording Camp Creek and then makes a steep 2-mile ascent. It ends at 3.5 miles at the base of a rocky cap.

9: Little Bald Mountain
Tracks across an alpine landscape

☐ **Backcountry Drive**
  Most vehicles

☒ **4WD Route**
  4x4 vehicle or ORV

☐ **ATV Trail**
  ORV less than 50" wide

Location/Map	West of Sheridan; Page 79
Roads	FR 139, FR 140, FR 142, FR 143, FR 178
Distance	20+ miles
Managing Agency	USDA Forest Service—Bighorn National Forest
Starting Coordinates	N44° 48.12' W107° 36.19'

Overview: These roads create a 4WD network that converges on the high slopes east of Little Bald Mountain. With elevations above 9,000 feet, you'll traverse bald summits covered only by grasses and a mix of subalpine and alpine flora. On the horizons you'll survey gentle rolling forests, craggy mountain peaks, and the vast Bighorn Basin.

Driving across the roof of the mountain range here is not only spectacular, but also potentially dangerous—don't do it when summer afternoon thunderstorms are threatening. During good weather, you'll find the routes

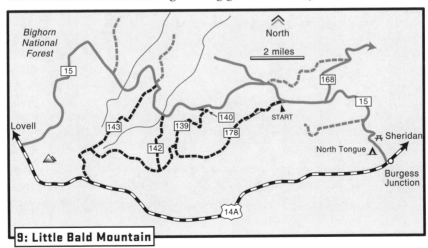

to be relatively easy to negotiate with only occasional rough sections. However, deep mud holes can be a problem. Domestic sheep grazing is also common at the higher elevations—drive cautiously through herds.

The roads are open to motorized use from April 1 to December 14, but deep snows usually reduce the driving season to a period between July and October.

Start: From Sheridan, travel north on I-90 and take Exit 9 to HWY 14. Drive west on HWY 14 for 32 miles, bearing right onto HWY 14 ALT. Turn onto FR 15 located just past Burgess Junction. Take FR 15 to one of the access roads located at 7.5 miles, 11 miles, 13.2 miles, and 15 miles.

Description: The longest road in this network is FR 178. It begins by fording Fool Creek, and then continues along the stream as it climbs to junctions with the other roads between 5 and 7 miles. The highest point of 9,930 feet is reached 2 miles before this road ends at HWY 14 ALT. Completing this 11.5-mile route end to end offers tremendous perspectives of the region.

The shorter peripheral roads here include FR 139, FR 140, FR 142, and FR 143. These are all similar routes that climb under a forest canopy until they reach timberline and connect with FR 178. Since FR 142 (the middle road) parallels and crosses Ice Creek a number of times, it can get wet and sloppy. Remember, too, that snowdrifts last into early summer at these elevations.

High slopes near Little Bald Mountain

Other Nearby Drives

Medicine Wheel National Archaeological Site—FR 12 is a steep road that leads 1.7 miles to a small visitor center near the Medicine Wheel. A 1.3-mile walk is then required to reach the wheel, but the on-site Forest Service staff might accommodate you if you cannot make the trek. The Medicine Wheel is a mysterious circular structure built between 300 and 800 years ago. From a central rock cairn in the middle, there are 28 spokes that extend to an outer rim with smaller, peripheral cairns. The wheel is still held sacred by many American Indian tribes. To reach the site from Sheridan, travel north on I-90 and take Exit 9 to HWY 14. Drive west on HWY 14 for 32 miles, bearing right on HWY 14 ALT. Continue west on HWY 14 ALT for a little over 21 miles to the turnoff on the right. This is about 32 miles east of Lovell.

Porcupine Area—FR 14 is a good trunk road in the northwest corner of the Bighorn National Forest near Porcupine Campground and Work Center. Best driven from July through early October, it provides access to other side roads and two remarkable waterfall hikes. To reach FR 14 from Sheridan, travel north on I-90 and take Exit 9 to HWY 14. Drive west on HWY 14 for 32 miles, bearing right on HWY 14 ALT. Continue west on HWY 14 ALT roughly 19 miles and turn right onto the gravel road.

Less than a mile after turning off the highway, you'll pass FR 125, which leads to the Little Bighorn River (see below). At 3 miles, FR 11 splits off on the right and cuts north across the rolling, treeless mountains toward Montana. It climbs the range while passing rock outcrops along the way. The good portion of this road ends after 6.5 miles near Sheep Mountain, but you can take one of the nearby ATV trails or primitive roads (FR 110 or FR 111) to further explore the hinterlands of the range.

Following FR 14 further to the west, you'll reach the trailhead for Porcupine Falls at 7.5 miles. From the trailhead, it's a steep half-mile hike to reach the 200-foot cascade of Porcupine Falls, which spill into a gorgeous pool. Continuing another 2.3 miles farther will take you to the end of FR 14 at Bucking Mule Falls Trailhead. From here, you can hike 2.5 miles to an astounding overlook of the 500-foot waterfall.

Little Bighorn River—One of my favorite drives in Wyoming is FR 125 (accessed from FR 14 less than a mile from HWY 14 ALT). Follow this good road for 1.2 miles to reach a bumpy side road (FR 123) that passes the historic site of Bald Mountain City. Only a few log foundations and metal scraps remain at this once massive prospectors' settlement from the 1890s.

Continuing northward on FR 125, the 8-mile road passes through dark timber before turning into a narrow and sometimes-rough 4WD lane that descends along the beautiful Little Bighorn River. Ruts and a few steep, rocky inclines make this a rough ride for stock vehicles, but the gorgeous valley views are worth it. You'll reach an old abandoned automobile a half mile before the road ends at a cow camp and hiking trail. Watch for moose!

10: Hunt Mountain
Traverse the backbone of the Bighorns

☐ **Backcountry Drive**
  Most vehicles

☒ **4WD Route**
  4x4 vehicle or ORV

☐ **ATV Trail**
  ORV less than 50" wide

Location/Map	West of Sheridan; Page 83
Roads	FR 10
Distance	22 miles
Managing Agency	USDA Forest Service—Bighorn National Forest
Starting Coordinates	N44° 38.64' W107° 30.20'

Overview: Hunt Mountain Road (FR 10) is one of the most scenic routes that you can take in the northern Bighorn Mountains. The rough lane travels across the backbone of the range at elevations between 9,000 and 10,000 feet to give you a commanding view of the region. It offers access to many miles of secondary 4WD roads and ATV trails. While much of the road is easily driven in dry conditions, it is rated here as a 4WD route due to its tire-grabbing ruts and the potential for deep, inhibiting mud and snowdrifts.

Start: From Sheridan, travel north on I-90 and take Exit 9 to HWY 14. To start from the eastern end of the road, as described here, travel west on HWY 14 for 41.5 miles, bearing left at Burgess Junction. To reach the western end

Rock outcrops along Hunt Mountain Road

of the road, stay right at Burgess Junction and take HWY 14 ALT for a little over 13 miles. Both ends have ample room for ATV unloading.

Description: From HWY 14 at Granite Pass, the maintained road assumes a gentle climb along Prospect Creek. Fascinating rock columns to the south create a distinctive landmark. As the road climbs above the forest of spruce and fir, sagebrush and grass begin to comprise the groundcover. A brief glimpse of peaks on the western horizon is seen at 1.5 miles, but the best views belong to the gorgeous mountains to the southeast.

At 3 miles, the roadway roughens as the gravel surface gives way to dirt, which gets ridiculously rutted in places. A mile farther, a pair of tracks lead off opposite sides of the road. The shorter, FR 217, swings past Prospect Mountain (9,774) to the south. The other, FR 220, leads northeast to Owen Creek Campground along HWY 14.

Just past the junction, the road passes Willey Creek and then skirts the edges of several tiny timber stands. On clear days, the distinct caps of the Absaroka Range near Yellowstone become visible by mile 6. This mountain range is a full 100 miles to the west.

As the road continues across the open highland, the unique rock outcroppings and sprawling meadows that characterize the northern Bighorn Mountains begin to be revealed. Also common to this area, even on hot summer days, are snowdrifts on the slopes. These drifts, along with springs, feed the numerous drainages that are found on both sides of the road. Creeks on the right (north) side of the road drain into the Tongue River. Those on the left (south) side of the road flow into Shell Creek.

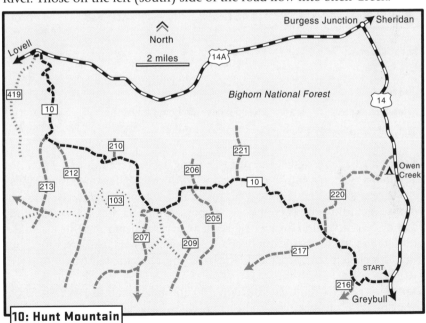

10: Hunt Mountain

At 10 miles, take the opportunity to look behind you at the magnificent display of mountain peaks—it's a stunning view. The road soon passes several more 4WD tracks including FR 221, FR 205, FR 206, and FR 209. Each of these "roads" is best described as a pair of ruts—or numerous pairs of ruts—that are carved into the grassy slopes. One path that better resembles a road is FR 207, which is reached before mile 13.

SIDE TRIP FR 207 is a 4WD road that travels 5 miles to Sunlight Mesa at the edge of the Bighorn National Forest. The road also provides access to over a dozen miles of ATV and single-track trails, some of which tackle steep terrain as they drop toward the desert basin from the high mountains.

The road now crosses the broad edge of Hunt Mountain at 10,000 feet while passing small creeks and more 4WD tracks, FR 212 and FR 213. Both of these roads descend toward Red Canyon Creek. You can spot this drainage if you look for the large timbered seam below the roadway.

As FR 10 nears its end, it travels next to some intriguing limestone outcroppings that stand dramatically against a smooth carpet of grass and wildflowers. These geologic formations beg to be explored further on foot. From here, the road improves back to a gravel surface as it twists and descends to HWY 14 ALT.

11: Medicine Lodge
Scenic drive to a remote recreation area

☒ **Backcountry Drive** Most vehicles	☐ **4WD Route** 4x4 vehicle or ORV	☐ **ATV Trail** ORV less than 50" wide

Location/Map	West of Sheridan; Page 86
Roads	FR 17
Distance	25 miles
Managing Agency	USDA Forest Service—Bighorn National Forest
Starting Coordinates	N44° 34.13' W107° 32.11'

Overview: This route makes a terrific trip along the western side of the Bighorn Mountains where you'll find expansive wildflower-laden meadows, dense forests, and a sense of remote wilderness. You may also see a wide range of wildlife including elk, deer, moose, coyotes, and porcupines. The road ends at a popular recreation area where there are campgrounds, trailheads, and a quartet of lakes. The drive can be made in any vehicle in dry conditions, but high clearance is recommended. The road opens for the season on June 16.

Start: From Sheridan, drive north on I-90 and take Exit 9 to HWY 14. Drive west on HWY 14 for 49 miles, bearing left at Burgess Junction. If traveling from Shell, head east on HWY 14 for 16 miles.

Description: As soon as you turn onto FR 17, you'll pass entrances to a dispersed camping area and the Cabin Creek Picnic Area. The road then skirts the head of Shell Canyon and descends past Shell Creek Campground.

A mile farther, FR 17 passes Shell Creek Ranger Station and then bisects Ranger Creek Campground. The Ranger Creek area is always a crowded place thanks in part to the popular creek, hiking trails, a 4WD route (FR 277), and a motorcycle trail that leads to the Cloud Peak Wilderness.

After the campground, the Ranger Creek Guest Ranch is soon passed on the left but is well concealed by trees. The road now bends its way uphill along a rocky surface through a forest of aspen, spruce, and fir. These are tight turns that are made tighter when there is oncoming traffic. The climb ends when the road emerges from the trees at the edge of the Bighorn National Forest. Here, you'll pass Snowshoe Pass and Snowshoe Lodge (a privately-operated guest lodge), which stands out against a sagebrush landscape.

Now crossing into open mountain country, the road leaves the national forest and enters private property—public access is permitted along the roadway. The next 3 miles are not maintained and they are often found rutted when dry, and very muddy when wet. The reward for enduring this stretch of bad road is paid upon your return to public land where there is a terrific overlook from the top of a hill. From this panoramic viewpoint, you can see the road as it snakes southward across the countryside.

From the high point, the road narrows for a steep descent. The Old Main Trail, which is open to motorcycles, is found at the bottom of the hill as is a lesser road (FR 271) that leads to Shell Reservoir (route #12).

Afternoon clouds cast shadows over Forest Road 17

Continuing south, the road continues through expansive meadows while passing a number of small streams including Jack Creek, Johnny Creek, North Trapper Creek, South Trapper Creek, and Mills Creek. It's near this last drainage where you'll find the junction for Alkali Road (FR 338), a rough backway that leads to the small community of Hyattville, 23 miles to the southwest. Stay on FR 17 and steer east of Spanish Point at 15 miles.

The drive now takes you through an alternation of timber and a pair of beautiful meadows. These parks are often found carpeted with colorful wildflowers like silvery lupine, hairy arnica, and primrose.

Past the meadows, the road enters dark timber and takes an east-bearing course. You'll soon pass a small sign marking the Lower Medicine Lodge Trail on the right, though no parking exists for this foot trail. The road

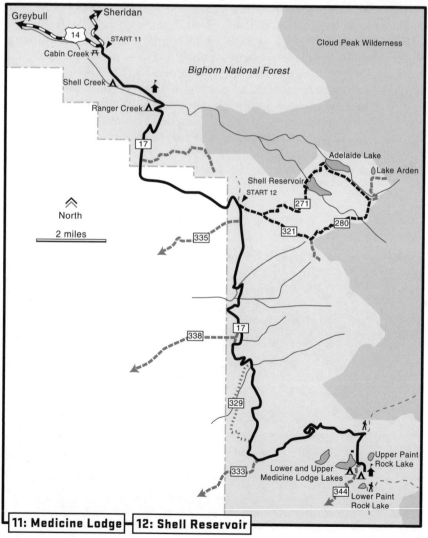

surface then roughens slightly as it reaches Medicine Lodge Creek. There are stunning views of the peaks here above the drainage, which is also where you'll find the Edelman Trail (trailhead parking is just ahead on the right).

Resuming its southward course, the road passes Paintrock Lodge (a privately-owned retreat) on the right before reaching the shores of Upper Medicine Lodge Lake. A campground and primitive boat ramp are found here, as is a foot trail that leads to Lower Medicine Lodge Lake. There is also a primitive 4WD road (FR 344) that begins from the campground—it's a scenic alternative route out of this remote area (route #22).

Around the next bend is a foot trail leading to Upper Paint Rock Lake. The road then passes Paint Rock Lakes Guard Station, a trailhead, and another campground along the shore of Lower Paint Rock Lake.

Together, the campgrounds, trailheads, and four lakes provide plenty of recreational opportunities. There is blissful solitude here for a couple short weeks in late June—a time when the ground is still soggy from the spring thaw. Once July arrives, so do the crowds.

12: Shell Reservoir
A scenic lake loop

☐ **Backcountry Drive** Most vehicles	☒ **4WD Route** 4x4 vehicle or ORV	☐ **ATV Trail** ORV less than 50" wide

Location/Map	West of Sheridan; Page 86
Roads	FR 271, FR 280, FR 321
Distance	11.8 miles
Managing Agency	USDA Forest Service—Bighorn National Forest
Starting Coordinates	N44° 30.33' W107° 27.24'

Overview: This trip makes a loop through open mountain country on the western side of the Bighorn National Forest. Along the way you'll pass a reservoir, a pair of lakes, and grand mountain scenery. The route opens for the summer season on June 16.

Start: From Sheridan, drive north on I-90 and take Exit 9 to HWY 14. Drive west on HWY 14 for 49 miles, bearing left at Burgess Junction. If traveling from Shell, head east on HWY 14 for 16 miles. Turn onto FR 17 and drive nearly 10 miles to FR 271 at the bottom of a hill.

Description: The first 2 miles of this drive are passable in any vehicle as the dirt path crosses the grassy western slopes of the Bighorn Mountains. At mile 2, a number of switchbacks begin to sweep down a timbered mountainside. From this point, the road becomes pocketed with rocks and deep potholes. It's still an easy road to drive, but you might bounce yourself crazy. Shell Reservoir, filling a low basin along the trip's lowest point at 8,997 feet, is visible from the switchbacks.

At the reservoir, after 3 miles, you'll find dispersed campsites and an outhouse. The main road now crosses the northern outlet of the reservoir. This isn't an issue when driven late in the season, such as in August or September, but it can be tricky when the reservoir is at higher levels. One group of ATV riders described their outing: "It was a great ride, except for where we had to drive through the edge of that reservoir—that was pretty bad!"

The road then travels over the reservoir's dam and approaches a steep rock slab near a gate. Maneuver up the rock and follow the course less than a mile farther to reach Adelaide Lake. From here, the dirt course turns southwest and traverses a meadow that is peppered with glacially-deposited boulders. Still, it's easy going as the roadway climbs through the increasingly wet drainage. Front-on views of the Bighorn's granite summits are found along this two-mile stretch.

Near the end of the drainage, the road reaches a junction just past Mud Lake, a small pond. Turn south onto FR 280 and follow this lesser path across more rugged terrain as it parallels the wilderness boundary. A separate road at the junction, FR 270, swings by Mud Lake, heads north toward Arden Lake, and ends at the Cloud Peak Wilderness boundary.

Headed south on FR 280, the road drops into a marshy, boulder-laden drainage where it fords Buckley Creek and three forks of Shell Creek.

Between 8 and 10 miles, the road makes a 500-foot climb to surmount a bald, windswept saddle at nearly 10,000 feet. From this high point, take FR 321, the main course leading to the northwest. This road descends a grassy slope for less than 2 miles to complete the loop.

Looking eastward near Adelaide Lake

Southern Bighorn Mountains

Shadowed by more popular natural attractions in the state, the Bighorn Mountains are often overlooked. But when you're in northern Wyoming, it's impossible to ignore the cloud-reaching domes and crags that fill the skyline. These granite summits are located in the Cloud Peak Wilderness, which occupies much of the southern half the Bighorn National Forest. This area includes some of the nation's most awesome and unspoiled backcountry.

Surrounding the rugged peaks are timbered slopes covered in a predominately lodgepole pine forest. Where trees don't grow, wildflowers often do and the Bighorn Mountains' meadows are usually filled with them during the summer months. As you travel through this varied habitat, watch for moose, deer, elk, and wild turkeys. Marmots are also frequently sighted among rock outcrops.

Land Ownership

The Bighorn National Forest encompasses nearly this entire portion of the Bighorn Mountains. You will find only a smattering of private residences and resorts. Most of these are located along HWY 16 and in the Hazelton area near CR 3. Forest Service offices are in Greybull and Buffalo.

Roads and Trails

The southern Bighorns are accessed by HWY 16, known as the Cloud Peak Skyway. From the highway, there is a plenitude of well-maintained gravel roads that branch throughout the Bighorn National Forest. With closer proximity to the Bighorn's high peaks, the four-wheel drive roads found here are much rockier than the roads found farther north. Overall, you'll find shorter, more rugged drives that often end at trailheads on the Cloud Peak Wilderness boundary. There are also a number of ATV trails. Though short, they often connect to roads making long rides possible.

Seasons and Conditions

Many of the roads in this area can be driven by Memorial Day weekend. Waiting a few weeks into June will ensure drier conditions and safer creek crossings. In most years, you can expect good access through October though winter will be settling in to the area's higher routes. It does snow every month of the year in these mountains and surprise storms often bring surprising accumulations.

Fuel

Service stations are available in nearly all the towns that surround the Bighorn Mountains. On the east side of the mountains, you can fill up in Buffalo, Story, Ranchester, Dayton, Sheridan, and Kaycee. On the west side, make your stops in Ten Sleep, Worland, Basin, and Greybull.

Maps

The Bighorn National Forest map, the free ORV map and Motor Vehicle Use Map (MVUM) are all excellent references for the Bighorn Mountains.

13: Hunter Mesa
Gain a panoramic overlook

☒ **Backcountry Drive** Most vehicles	☒ **4WD Route** 4x4 vehicle or ORV	☐ **ATV Trail** ORV less than 50" wide

Location/Map	West of Buffalo; Page 90
Roads	FR 19, FR 390
Distance	5 miles (last 2.5 miles may require 4WD)
Managing Agency	USDA Forest Service—Bighorn National Forest
Starting Coordinates	N44° 18.92' W106° 56.32'

Overview: This short, but beautiful road receives heavy use as it undercuts Hunter Mesa to reach a popular wilderness trailhead and horse camp near a scenic overlook. From here, a rougher road traverses the top of a mesa for grand views of the Bighorn Mountains. Four-wheel drive is not typically necessary for the second half, but you will want decent ground clearance. The second portion of this road opens for the summer season on June 16.

Start: From Buffalo, head west on HWY 16 for 12 miles to the turnoff for FR 19 on the right.

Description: From the highway, follow the well-maintained gravel road a short distance to the North Fork Picnic Area. This is a great place to park along the rushing North Clear Creek.

From the picnic area, continue past a Forest Service workstation while keeping watch for moose and wild turkeys. After a few blind curves around

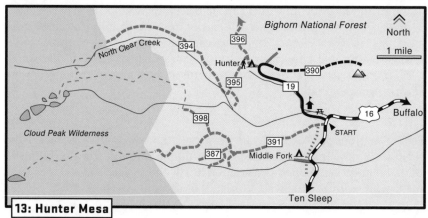

13: Hunter Mesa

towering rock outcrops, the road reaches the southern slope of Hunter Mesa. Continue along the narrow road as it parallels Hunter Creek. Hunter Trailhead/Campground is soon found on the left. Bear right at the fork and follow the road uphill a short distance to a small pullout overlooking rugged 12,000-foot peaks. Paradise Ranch, a guest ranch, is found just down the hill from the overlook.

If you're in a 4x4 or high clearance vehicle, you can continue the second half of this drive on FR 390, which heads east. This easy-to-negotiate road begins with a short, rocky climb to a gate. From here, a two-track path heads east across the top of a lupine and daisy-ridden mesa. At 8,000 feet, the views from the top of this bald ridge are hard to beat.

Further east, you'll pass a number of communication antennas and a building. There is also a Big Game Range Study Plot where two enclosures— one for wildlife, one for livestock—are used to study the affects these animals have on the range. The road ends at a large rock outcropping.

The view from Hunter Mesa

Other Nearby Drives

French Creek Swamps—At 7 miles in length, FR 396 is one of the longer 4WD roads in the area. The first half-mile includes a ford of French Creek, which can be deep and swift during late spring. At 1 mile, the road enters a sprawling meadow known as the French Creek Swamps. From here, the road makes a hard turn back to the east and descends through the wet meadows and pine forests of the eastern Bighorn Mountains. It passes five foot trails along the way and ends at a sixth just a couple miles south of Firebox Park.

To reach the road from Buffalo, head west on HWY 16 for 12 miles. Turn right onto FR 19 and drive 2.4 miles to FR 396 near Hunter Trailhead/ Campground. ATV unloading is best done at the trailhead.

Soldier Park—FR 395 and FR 394 create a 4.5-mile 4WD route to Soldier Park. This is the access point for Seven Brother Lakes, a scenic string of subalpine lakes in the Cloud Peak Wilderness. The road passes through a burn area where the lack of trees yield great mountain views, though younger trees are slowly filling in. This route receives heavy use from hikers and horsemen alike, so be ready to power down and share the road.

The road begins in a thick pine forest. A few short, steep climbs over rough cobble gets you to a bridged crossing of Clear Creek at 2 miles. Less than a mile further, you'll pass the roadside gravesites of a civil engineer and a Swedish tie-hack. What soon follows is Soldier Park, a big meadow with three roads leading through and around it—take the middle one.

The far end of Soldier Park is as far as most 4WD drivers go as the road now becomes much rockier as it climbs gently through the evergreen forest. While navigable, there are enough large rocks in the roadway that you'll have to pay attention to what you're doing. This section of the road is also more likely to be found muddy. The road ends near willow-lined North Clear Creek, which is also the wilderness boundary. No motorized vehicles or bicycles are allowed past this point. To reach the Seven Brothers Lakes from here, hike 2 miles to the first lake or over 3 miles to the last.

This route opens for the summer season on June 21. To reach the road from Buffalo, head west on HWY 16 for 12 miles. Turn right onto FR 19 and drive 2.4 miles to FR 396 near Hunter Trailhead/Campground. Take this road a short distance to reach FR 395 on the left.

Schoolhouse Park—This scenic 5-mile 4WD route follows FR 391 toward the Bighorn Mountains' imposing high peaks while cutting through an area that was swept by fire in 1988. Many drivers stop at Webber Park after 3 miles where the road gets more difficult and is sometimes blocked by downed trees. The road ends at the Cloud Peak Wilderness boundary. From here, it's a 4-mile uphill hike to reach Lake Angeline, a high alpine lake at the base of a cirque. The road opens for the summer season on June 21.

To reach the road from Buffalo, head west on HWY 16 for just over 12 miles and turn right. ATV parking area if located at the top of the first hill.

14: Parallel Highway 16 Trail
Connector trail to trailheads, campgrounds, and picnic areas

☐ **Backcountry Drive**
Most vehicles

☐ **4WD Route**
4x4 vehicle or ORV

☒ **ATV Trail**
ORV less than 50" wide

Location/Map	West of Buffalo; Page 94
Trails	FT 117, FT 187, FT 222
Distance	6 miles
Managing Agency	USDA Forest Service—Bighorn National Forest
Starting Coordinates	N44° 18.92' W106° 56.32'

Overview: The southeastern portion of the Bighorn National Forest is full of recreation sites. Here, you'll find Tie Hack Reservoir, three picnic areas, five developed campgrounds, both developed and primitive trailheads, and several roads that are popular for dispersed camping. However, nearly all of these are found on their own access road. This route, officially named the HWY 16 Parallel Trail, connects these individual roads so that you can effectively reach the various recreation sites on an ATV.

Most sections of this trail present casual, easy riding along a dirt path. There are, of course, a few areas that include steeper slopes, rocks, roots, and a ford. You'll find the trail to be more developed than most with bridges, cattle guards, and good signage. Remember that some recreation sites are fee

A high point on Forest Trail 117

areas. In particular, you should stay out of the campgrounds unless you are entering or exiting a paid campsite. The trail is open from May 16 to the last day of big game hunting season. A Wyoming ORV permit is required.

Start: From Buffalo, head west on HWY 16 for just over 12 miles. Turn off the highway and then head up FR 391. A parking area for ATV unloading is found at the top of the hill. To reach the southern parking area, continue along HWY 16 for another 6 miles to a scenic overlook pullout on the left.

Description: From the northern parking area, drive back down the hill (toward the highway) to reach FT 117 where it heads south. The trail reaches Middle Fork Campground by the first mile. Anglers will find a small parking area here for Middle Clear Creek.

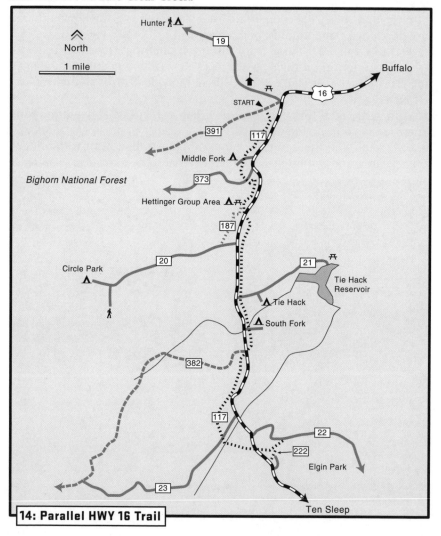

14: Parallel HWY 16 Trail

Southbound, the trail climbs out of the drainage where you'll find good views of the southern Bighorn's large granite domes and peaks. The trail splits after passing the Hettinger Group Area (group picnic and campground site). The right trail (FT 187) leads to Circle Park Road. Bear left to stay on FT 117 and cross HWY 16. On the other side of the highway, the trail resumes its southern advance along Hound Creek in an aspen stand that is frequented by moose. The trail stays on the east side of the highway for most of the next 2 miles as it passes access roads for Tie Hack Reservoir, Tie Hack Campground, and South Fork Campground.

Immediately after the South Fork Campground road, the trail drops down to cross South Clear Creek over a large bridge. A short distance farther, it crosses back to the west side of HWY 16 at FR 382, which leads to the Cloud Peak Wilderness. Continue south over rougher terrain to reach Sourdough Road (FR 23) and a ford of Sourdough Creek. From here, the trail climbs out of the drainage, crosses HWY 16 for the last time, and joins FT 222. Bear right to reach the southern parking area or turn left to drive into Elgin Park where there are several miles of easy backroads to explore.

Other Nearby Drives

Circle Park—The short 2-mile drive to Circle Park Campground and Trailhead on FR 20 is a good choice if you're looking for moose. The willow-lined banks of Circle Park Creek provide good habitat for these large ungulates and sightings are common. To reach the road from Buffalo, go west on HWY 16 for 14 miles and turn right.

Elgin Park—Elgin Park is a wildflower-laden park on the southeastern side of the Bighorn National Forest. Dispersed camping, hiking, four-wheeling, and horseback riding are all common in this area. Be prepared to meet others on the road and give horseback riders plenty of space.

A 3.5-mile gravel backroad (FR 22) loops through Elgin Park, offering a quick drive through the sprawling meadow. For those looking to get further off the beaten path, there are more than a dozen peripheral routes (20+ miles of roads and trails) that extend into slightly rougher terrain. The main loop road has no seasonal restrictions but the lesser routes that sprout from it open for the summer season on June 16.

To reach Elgin Park from Buffalo, head west on HWY 16 for 17.2 miles to reach the northern end of FR 22 or 19.4 miles to reach the southern end. A parking area for ATV unloading can be reached in between the two ends at mile 18—watch for the scenic overlook sign along the highway.

Trigger Lake—A rugged 4WD road, FR 382 takes you to the edge of the Cloud Peak Wilderness where a foot trail continues west to reach the Sherd Lake Loop Trail. This hiking loop accesses dozens of backcountry creeks and lakes, including Trigger Lake, which requires a 1.5-mile hike from the end of the road. To reach the beginning of the road from Buffalo, head west on

HWY 16 for 16 miles to the turnoff on the right. Parking for ATV unloading is very limited.

Aside from Lynx Park (reached at 1.2 miles), FR 382 is a mostly timbered route with lodgepole pine that is regenerating from the 1943 Duck Creek Fire. The road consists of numerous rocky sections that are probably too much for the standard family SUV. Inadequate ground clearance has caused some of the rocks to become scarred and I found somebody's exhaust pipe at one particularly rough spot.

At 3 miles, the road reaches a junction. Stay straight to reach the wilderness trailhead, or bear left to climb a steep rocky lane (FS 611). It's a narrow passage with little room to negotiate. When it levels off, you can bear left to a dead end on FR 611 or turn right onto FR 612 to connect to Sourdough Road to the south. A number of these secondary roads are not signed.

Sourdough Creek—Sourdough Road (FR 23) is known for its historical flash dam—a wooden structure that was used to control creek flows in order to flush ties downstream to the railroad. The area is now very popular for dispersed camping. The 4.5-mile road travels through a willow-filled drainage and then dead-ends after ascending a forested knoll. It's a beautiful and easy drive that can be made in any vehicle. To access this road from Buffalo, head west on HWY 16 for 16.8 miles to reach the turnoff.

15: Crazy Woman Canyon
Popular drive through a photogenic canyon

☒ **Backcountry Drive**	☐ **4WD Route**	☐ **ATV Trail**
Most vehicles	4x4 vehicle or ORV	ORV less than 50" wide

Location/Map	Southwest of Buffalo; Page 98
Roads	FR 33, CR 14
Distance	13.3 miles
Managing Agency	USDA Forest Service—Bighorn National Forest
Starting Coordinates	N44° 9.75' W106° 55.06'

Overview: Nobody knows how Crazy Woman Canyon got its name, but there are several theories. One speaks of a woman who lost her mind after her village was attacked and she was left deserted. Another version describes a woman who went crazy after witnessing the slaughter of her family by a Sioux tribe. Other accounts are similar and involve women who went crazy from clashes between whites and American Indians.

Whatever the origin of the name, the canyon today is very well known for its scenery and the road that is used to explore it. The original roadway dates back to the 1930s when it was built by the Civilian Conservation Corps. In 1997, floodwaters from Crazy Woman Creek obliterated the road and it had to be reconstructed.

This drive weaves through the tight canyon while descending nearly 3,000 feet to the grassy plains east of the mountain range. The grade is steep, about 8% within the canyon, and the narrow road has a good number of dips, potholes, washouts, and embedded rocks. The route can be driven in most vehicles, but trailers, RVs, and low-clearance sedans are not recommended. The road opens for the summer season on June 21.

Squeezing through Crazy Woman Canyon

Start: From Buffalo, head west on HWY 16 for 25 miles to reach the turnoff for Crazy Woman Canyon Road (FR 33) on the left.

Description: Starting from HWY 16, Crazy Woman Canyon Road heads east for a half mile where it crosses a mountain park. A moderate descent begins once the road enters the forest. Here, you'll find rock outcroppings that are intermixed with evergreen trees, willows, and berry shrubs.

At 2 miles, the single lane crosses Crazy Woman Creek. The rushing creek holds rainbow, brook, and brown trout. Fishing and dispersed camping are popular along the narrow road and if you plan on stopping, you'll have to find one of the few precious spots where you can turn out and park.

As you drive downhill, and a low gear is needed to save your brakes, you'll find places where the forest gives way to steep talus slopes that sweep down toward the roadway. The most scenic stretch of Crazy Woman Canyon—and the most photographed—comes in mile 4 where the road closely follows the creek between massive boulders and rock faces with blackened tops. If you can, park your vehicle and experience this section on foot.

The road soon leaves the Bighorn National Forest and passes Crazy Woman Ranch on the left. Drive a short distance past the confines of the forest and then look back at the canyon. Here, beautiful red and white rock spires cover the eastern flank of Crazy Woman Mountain.

The gravel road now traverses rolling ranch land as it heads east. There are two major forks along this stretch; bear left at both to stay on the main route.

The drive ends at HWY 196 after 13 miles. Turn north on the highway and drive 10 miles to return to Buffalo, or turn south to head toward Kaycee and Casper. There are two well-signed side roads that provide access to I-25 before you reach Kaycee.

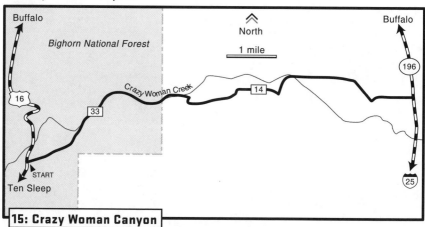

15: Crazy Woman Canyon

Other Nearby Drives

Pole Creek Road—This is an 11-mile drive on FR 31 that connects to HWY 16 at both ends. The well-maintained gravel road travels through a young pine forest and is easily traveled in any vehicle.

Starting from the north end and traveling south, the road offers periodic glimpses of the taller summits in the area such as Bighorn Peak (12,324 feet) and Darton Peak (12,275 feet). You can also spot the fire lookout tower atop Sheep Mountain, a 9,610-foot mountain on the western horizon. The road draws within a mile of the lookout tower before it crosses Pole Creek and turns southward. Purple lupines are found along the roadway's sunnier stretches. Watch for moose and elk.

To reach the road from Buffalo, head west on HWY 16 for 19.5 miles to the turnoff on the right. The southern end of the road can be reached by driving 9 miles farther on the highway.

Muddy Creek—Over a dozen miles of roads can be driven to explore the Muddy Creek area that straddles the eastern Bighorn National Forest boundary. The entrance road is good, but it quickly degrades into several easy 4WD tracks. The area consists of high meadows that are punctuated with rock domes and evergreen stands.

To reach the area from Buffalo, drive west on HWY 16 for 25.2 miles to the turnoff on the left. From here, the road passes Muddy Guard Cabin, a small log structure built in the 1930s that the Forest Service now rents to the public. Past this, there is a foot-deep ford where FR 473 turns east and becomes rougher. Further yet, you'll cross over state-owned land before reaching a spectacular overlook of the range. The road then drops into the forest and switchbacks into Dry Muddy Canyon, where it ends at 6 miles.

Doyle—A few miles of short ATV trails are located east of Doyle Campground. These old roads undercut a patchy forest near the southern boundary of the Bighorn National Forest. To reach the trails from Buffalo, drive west on HWY 16 for 26 miles and turn south on Hazelton Road (CR 3). Then drive 6 miles to the campground turnoff and follow the road east to the trails.

Billy Creek Road—FR 466 is a popular destination for dispersed camping and leisurely ATV riding. The road begins by crossing high mountain meadows that offer good views of Hazelton Peak, Hazelton Pyramid, and eye-catching escarpments. There are several side spurs that lead into the trees, but none of these travel very far. The road passes through an assortment of Forest Service, State, BLM, and private land with summer cabins. A parking area for the BLM Poison Creek Trail—an indistinct hiking path—is found at mile 7. The road ends soon after at a turnaround. To access the Billy Creek Road from Buffalo, head west on HWY 16 for 26.3 miles and turn left onto Hazelton Road. Drive .75 mile and turn left onto FR 466.

Poison Creek—A nondescript 7.5-mile 4WD route, FR 484 travels through the Poison Creek area below a triad of peaks: Hesse Mountain, Hazelton Pyramid, and Hazelton Peak. The road splits several times within the first mile. The first two splits are FR 481 and FR 485, both of which head east and can be used to reach Hazelton Road (CR 3). The third fork, FR 486, travels west where it turns into an ATV trail before connecting to HWY 16. The main route continues to the south over a good surface. However, this surface becomes narrower and prone to large mud puddles as it nears its terminus near a large rock outcropping. Some maps incorrectly show this road connecting to Hazelton Road near Doyle Campground. To reach the road from Buffalo, head west on HWY 16 for 28.6 miles to the turnoff on the left. There are a few primitive campsites near the beginning where you can park to unload ATVs.

Sheep Mountain Lookout—The 5.5-mile Sheep Mountain Road (FR 28) makes a bumpy but easy drive to reach an unstaffed fire lookout tower that was built in 1950. Perched atop 9,610-foot Sheep Mountain, the tower offers generous views of the surrounding forest and higher mountain peaks. Parts of the drive travel through a burned-out forest and a harvested cutting area. While the road can be driven in any passenger car, the rocky surface makes it better suited for pickups and SUVs. There is also a patchwork of intersecting four-wheel drive roads and ATV trails that extend across Sheep Mountain and the southern flanks of the Loaf Mountain massif. These routes mostly travel through a pine forest and make fun rides. To reach FR 28 from Buffalo, head west on HWY 16 for 30.6 miles and turn right.

Powder River Road—Located just below 9,666-foot Powder River Pass, FR 29 heads south next to the headwaters of the river. The decent gravel road forks at the beginning where FR 448 goes east 2.5 miles over Munkres Pass. Bear right at this junction and stay on FR 29 to travel through mature stands of fir, spruce, as well as areas of younger regrowth. The road ends short of 5 miles at a turnaround along the river. To reach FR 29 from Buffalo, head west on HWY 16 for 33.3 miles to the turnoff on the left.

High Park Lookout—The short 1.4-mile drive on FR 429 is too short and sweet to ignore. An uphill half-mile hike is required to reach the lookout tower at 9,477 feet, but there are worthwhile views even if you never step out of your vehicle. This easy road is open to motorized use on May 1, but plan on June to avoid snow. If you're looking to explore this area further, continue south on FR 434 for another few miles through High Park, a broad meadow carpeted in grass and sagebrush. The route descends into a beautiful forest, but there are open places where you can spot the expansive Bighorn Basin. The road ends at a gate near an old cabin ruin. To reach this road from Buffalo, head west on HWY 16 for 41 miles to reach the turnoff on the left. If traveling from Ten Sleep, drive east on HWY 16 for 22 miles.

16: Canyon Creek

A loop over a high crest

☐ **Backcountry Drive**
Most vehicles

☒ **4WD Route**
4x4 vehicle or ORV

☐ **ATV Trail**
ORV less than 50" wide

Location/Map	Southwest of Buffalo; Page 101
Roads	FR 25, FR 420, FR 421, FR 436, FR 452
Distance	14 miles
Managing Agency	USDA Forest Service—Bighorn National Forest
Starting Coordinates	N44° 9.62' W107° 7.70'

Overview: There are 22 miles of roads that traverse the Canyon Creek and Canyon Park area south of Powder River Pass. This route makes a 14-mile loop by first descending into the forest and then returning along the backbone of a scenic ridge. There are several optional side routes that can increase the overall mileage. If you only have time to drive one route in this area, this is the one to choose. While not that challenging, it's one of the most rewarding and access is quick and easy off HWY 16. The route is open to motorized use on April 1, but waiting later into June is advised.

Start: From Buffalo, head west on HWY 16 for 37.2 miles to reach the turnoff on the left for FR 25. Plenty of parking is available for ATV unloading.

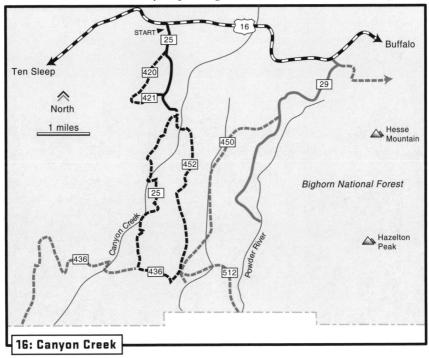

16: Canyon Creek

Description: From the highway, head south on gravel FR 25. The first rugged track, a 2.2-mile 4WD side loop comprised of FR 420 and FR 421, is reached within the first half mile. Turn west onto this lesser path and follow it downhill into the trees. This loop returns to FR 25 where you turn right and continue south to a signed fork. At the split, stay right and continue south on FR 25. The road narrows as it descends through the timber. After 7 miles, FR 25 ends at FR 436. A west (right) turn here takes you toward a cow camp and the national forest boundary. To continue the loop, turn left and drive east.

From here, FR 436 begins a good 440-foot climb to reach the top of an open ridge where several roads converge. Turn left onto FR 452 and follow it northward to traverse Canyon Park, a treeless crest that reveals an impressive panorama. Along the way you'll see the Cloud Peak Wilderness on the northern horizon and a series of summits near Hazelton to the east. On a clear day, you can see as far as the Wind River Mountains to the southwest.

SIDE
TRIP

Another road found at the top of the hill is FR 450, which heads 4 miles to FR 29. This track is deeply rutted in places and is popular with ATV riders. It travels through mountain meadows and fords Webb Creek (6 inches deep in July).

As you drive north, you'll soon see FR 25 down below on the left and FR 450 on the right. Just before rejoining FR 25, the road fords Canyon Creek, which flows 8 inches deep in early July. The area around the creek is often packed with dispersed campers. Past the ford, the road feeds back into FR 25, which is then easily driven a couple miles north to return to HWY 16.

Riding through the Canyon Creek high country

17: East Tensleep Lake
Rugged road or ATV trail to a high lake

☐ **Backcountry Drive**
Most vehicles

☒ **4WD Route**
4x4 vehicle or ORV

☒ **ATV Trail**
ORV less than 50" wide

Location/Map	Southwest of Buffalo; Page 105
Roads/Trails	FR 430, FT 100
Distance	5 miles on FR 430 or 2.3 miles on FT 100
Managing Agency	USDA Forest Service—Bighorn National Forest
Starting Coordinates	4WD Road: N44° 10.72' W107° 12.94' ATV Trail: N44° 12.18' W107° 12.41'

Overview: East Tensleep Lake is one of the few lakes accessible by a motorized vehicle in the southern Bighorn National Forest. At 55 acres in size, the lake is among the largest in the area and it makes an excellent destination for trout fishing, camping, or just escaping the more heavily-visited sites.

The rugged road (FR 430) that leads to the lake can be handled by most 4x4s when driven with skill and care, but it's a rough go. Deep mud and ruts can make the first half a challenge, but it's the rocky ascent near the end that encourages most 4WD drivers to park and hike the remaining mile to the lake. The road is open to motorized use on May 1, but mid-June is advised. If driving an ATV, you can combine this route with the ATV trail to create a nice loop.

The Lake Creek Trail (FT 100) connects Sitting Bull Campground—one of the Bighorn's most popular campgrounds—to East Tensleep Lake. It's a shorter route to the lake than the road, but it's steeper and involves a ford of Lake Creek. A Wyoming ORV permit is required.

Start: From Buffalo, head west on HWY 16 for 43 miles to reach the turnoff on the right near Meadowlark Lake. If traveling from Ten Sleep, drive east on HWY 16 for 20 miles. There is a large but sloped parking area at the beginning of the 4WD road.

To reach the ATV trail, continue west on the highway for another quarter mile to the turnoff for Sitting Bull Campground. Follow FR 432 to the campground's entrance where a 4WD road begins near the campground's fee board. Follow this track north through Sitting Bull Park to reach a gate and a small unloading area where parking is limited.

Description (4WD Road): The road leading to East Tensleep Lake begins in the timber, but climbs a rocky incline to reach a meadow that reveals the range's high country. East Tensleep Creek flows through this two-mile long park and a wooden stock bridge can be found at its southern end.

Traveling through the park can be unwieldy depending on conditions. After two days of heavy rain, I encountered long stretches of mud that were

Forest Road 430 to East Tensleep Lake

more than a foot deep—a good reason to wait for drier weather. A foot trail leading to Maybelle Lake (1.8 miles northeast of the road) is passed at the far end of the meadow before mile 4. This is where many people park to either hike the rest of the way to East Tensleep Lake or Maybelle Lake.

From this point, the route turns to the northwest to re-enter the timber where it begins a rock-laden ascent of several hundred vertical feet. This last mile is rough and the tight rocky path in the trees will have you crawling along at a snail's pace. As you approach the lake, watch for FT 100 off on the left. Stay right to reach the end of the road at a glacial moraine near a small lakelet. A foot path here leads through the trees and up the moraine to reach the shore of East Tensleep Lake. The skyline is crowned with 11,000-foot peaks, which are part of the Cloud Peak Wilderness that envelops the lake on three sides.

Description (ATV Trail): From the gate on the north end of Sitting Bull Park, the ATV path begins by crossing lightly timbered terrain. Most of the rocks have been pushed aside, so the predominately dirt trail is easily driven. Near 1 mile, the route reaches a ford of Lake Creek, a sometimes fast moving and narrow creek. The water depth depends greatly on the year; I've seen it as deep as 18 inches in early July to just a few inches deep in a drought year.

From the creek, the trail tackles a steeper and rockier grade as it approaches the high lake. At 2.3 miles, the path reaches FR 430. Turn left and drive to the end of the road. Park your machine here and hike over the rocky moraine to find East Tensleep Lake at 9,795 feet.

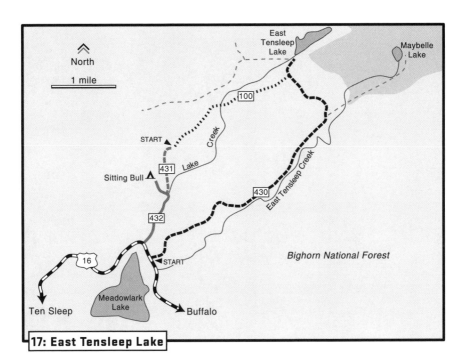

17: East Tensleep Lake

18: West Tensleep Lake
A popular recreation corridor

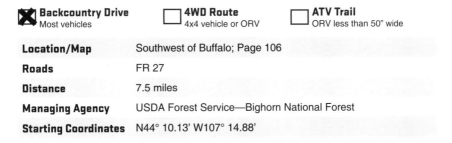

☒ **Backcountry Drive**
Most vehicles

☐ **4WD Route**
4x4 vehicle or ORV

☐ **ATV Trail**
ORV less than 50" wide

Location/Map	Southwest of Buffalo; Page 106
Roads	FR 27
Distance	7.5 miles
Managing Agency	USDA Forest Service—Bighorn National Forest
Starting Coordinates	N44° 10.13' W107° 14.88'

Overview: This drive leads you to West Tensleep Lake where you'll find campgrounds, a picnic area, and a popular trailhead for the Cloud Peak Wilderness. At elevations around 9,000 feet, the weather at the lake is volatile—I found it snowing here during one visit on July 4th. The road is open to motorized use on May 1, but waiting a few more weeks is advised. Take note that the Forest Service plans on constructing new campgrounds and trails along this corridor (and closing some of the existing ones); this area may end up looking much different than how it is described here.

Start: From Buffalo, head west on HWY 16 for 45.5 miles to reach the turnoff on the right. If traveling from Ten Sleep, drive east on HWY 16 for 17.5 miles.

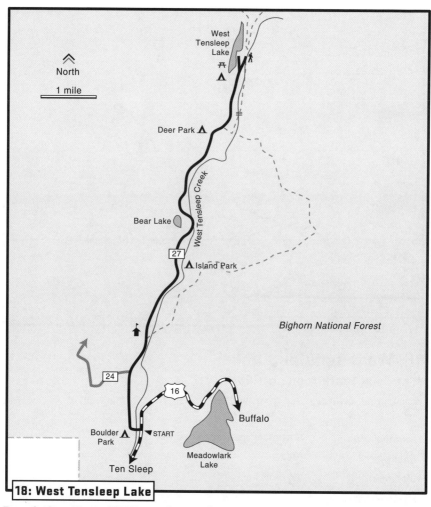

North

1 mile

West Tensleep Lake

Deer Park

West Tensleep Creek

Bear Lake

27

Island Park

Bighorn National Forest

24

16

Buffalo

Boulder Park

START

Meadowlark Lake

Ten Sleep

18: West Tensleep Lake

Description: From HWY 16, the road crosses over West Tensleep Creek. A large stream choked with boulders, it drains the higher alpine areas above the lake of the same name. Follow the curve after the bridge and begin driving north on the washboarded, gravel road.

In the first 2 miles, the road passes a handful of summer cabins, FR 24 headed to Battle Park, and the Tyrell Work Center (a Forest Service complex). As you travel north through the mixed evergreen forest, you'll pass a number of landmarks and recreation sites including Island Park Campground at 3 miles, tiny Bear Lake at 4.4 miles, and Deer Park Campground at 6.2 miles. All of this resides at the bottom of the long forested valley that was once covered by the Bighorn's longest glacier. Lateral moraines—the ridges that parallel the roadway—were formed by the glacier's downhill passage.

The road splits near the end at 7.3 miles. Bear left at the fork for West Tensleep Lake Campground or stay right for the picnic area and trailhead.

West Tensleep Lake

While West Tensleep Lake can be viewed from both areas, the best option is to drive to the trailhead where you'll find a foot trail that runs along the lake's east shoreline.

West Tensleep Lake Trailhead is a popular entry point into the Cloud Peak Wilderness. Trails that head north from the lake all enter the wilderness area within a couple miles. Popular destinations include Lake Helen at 4.9 miles, Lake Marion at 6.2 miles, and well-known Mistymoon Lake at 7.2 miles. There is also a separate trail that leads to Mirror Lake at 3.3 miles and Lost Twin Lakes at 6.1 miles. A much shorter option that is often overlooked is a path that leads to Tensleep Falls. Look for the trail on the southeast side of the trailhead. It's less than a mile to the falls.

19: Battle Park
Western flank of the Bighorn National Forest

☒ **Backcountry Drive**
Most vehicles

☐ **4WD Route**
4x4 vehicle or ORV

☐ **ATV Trail**
ORV less than 50" wide

Location/Map	Southwest of Buffalo; Page 110
Roads	FR 24
Distance	15 miles
Managing Agency	USDA Forest Service—Bighorn National Forest
Starting Coordinates	N44° 11.0' W107° 15.2'

Overview: This drive travels along the pretty western slope of the Bighorn Mountains and ends in Battle Park where there is a wilderness trailhead. This is mostly open terrain that allows for good views of the surrounding countryside. You'll find numerous secondary roads along the way that can add options to your trip.

While most cars can handle the road in good weather, there are rough patches that are best handled with a truck or SUV. You'll also want to be cautious along the narrow stretches and blind curves as trailer traffic is common along the route. The road is open to motorized use on May 1, but waiting until June is advised.

Start: From Buffalo, head west on HWY 16 for 45.5 miles to reach the turnoff for FR 27 on the right. If traveling from Ten Sleep, drive east on HWY 16 for 17.5 miles. Follow FR 27 for 1.2 miles to a fork and bear left onto FR 24.

Description: The road immediately begins by climbing a timbered ridge. The road is usually at its worst during this initial ascent—rocky, potholed, and bumpy. At 1 mile, there is a parking area at the top of the hill where FR 413 heads south. The road improves from here to a smoother surface, but there are still a few rough patches throughout the remainder of the drive.

Bending to the north, FR 24 travels across rolling slopes covered with sagebrush and small stands of aspen and pine. There are several side roads that are passed as you travel north. Among the more notable ones are FR 412 and FR 410 on the left and FR 411 on the right. At mile 5, you'll find FR 408,

Forest Road 24 to Battle Park

a west-bearing road that connects to Hyattville Road (BLMR 1117)—this can be taken all the way to the little town of Hyattville.

The road continues northward by weaving between wooded areas. Nearing mile 7, you'll descend to the lowest point of the drive at Soldier Creek—a pretty segment of the drive. Soldier Creek Camp (a pair of old cabins) is passed as the road parallels the creek for over a mile until crossing it. Sandhill cranes can sometimes be spotted along this riparian area. Above the creek, the long ridge capping the horizon to the west is Buck Mountain.

The remainder of the road now travels through mostly timbered settings except for a reprieve through Bellyache Flats at 11 miles. Soon after, there is an ATV trail on the right that leads to Lily Lake. There are three ways to reach this high lake, but at 2 miles in length, this trail is the shortest route.

The road ends at over 9,000 feet at the edge of Battle Park. The meadow is favored for its primitive campsites, but it also offers non-motorized access to remote wilderness destinations like Lake Solitude and Mistymoon Lake. While the trail headed north is only open to foot and hoof traffic, there is an ATV trail here that accesses the 15-mile network of trails to the southwest.

20: Bald Ridge
Traverse a glacial moraine

☐ **Backcountry Drive** Most vehicles	☒ **4WD Route** 4x4 vehicle or ORV	☐ **ATV Trail** ORV less than 50" wide

Location/Map	Southwest of Buffalo; Page 110
Roads	FR 411
Distance	8.2 miles
Managing Agency	USDA Forest Service—Bighorn National Forest
Starting Coordinates	N44° 11.23' W107° 16.30'

Overview: Bald Ridge is a lateral moraine formed by the West Tensleep Glacier, which was the Bighorn's longest glacier that carved out a slender valley. The east face of the 500-foot high ridge rises abruptly but it has a gentle western slope. This drive takes you across the treeless crest of this ridge, where you'll find excellent views of the area's high country. The road is not difficult and is often handled easily in dry weather. Though it's open to motorized use on May 1, you'll want to wait until summer to make the trip.

Start: From Buffalo, head west on HWY 16 for 45.5 miles to reach the turnoff for FR 27 on the right. If traveling from Ten Sleep, drive east on HWY 16 for 17.5 miles. Follow FR 27 for 1.2 miles to a fork and bear left onto FR 24. Follow this road 1.7 miles and turn right onto FR 411. There are numerous places along FR 24 where you can park and unload ATVs.

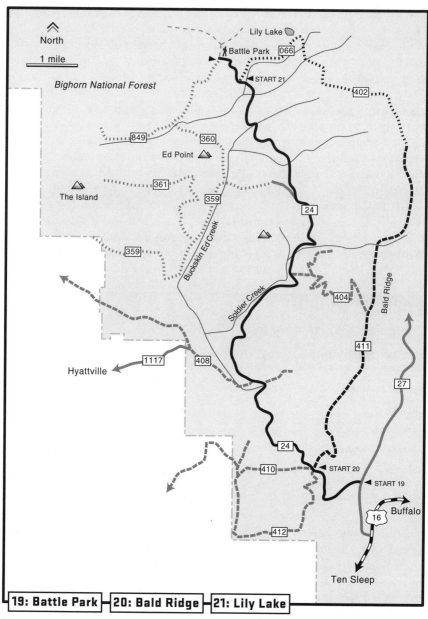

North

1 mile

Bighorn National Forest

Lily Lake

Battle Park

066

START 21

402

849

360

Ed Point

361

359

The Island

359

Buckskin Ed Creek

24

Soldier Creek

Bald Ridge

404

411

27

Hyattville

1117

408

24

410

START 20

START 19

412

16

Buffalo

Ten Sleep

19: Battle Park ┤**20: Bald Ridge** ┤**21: Lily Lake** ├

Description: From FR 24, FR 411 begins by snaking its way up a sagebrush-covered hill. It's an easily traveled start for most 4x4s, though I did watch a pickup with a truck camper swaying like a pendulum on a failed attempt to negotiate the narrow road.

Just before 2 miles, the road reaches the west rim of Brokenback Mountain (9,335 feet). The 500 feet of elevation gained to reach this point is all that is needed to reveal a terrific panorama of the Bighorn Mountains' high

Forest Road 411 on Bald Ridge

country. Here, a nearly 20-mile long chain of rocky summits connects the eastern and northern horizons. From this point, the dirt road continues north through Warner Draw as it gains on Bald Ridge.

An intersection with FR 404 is reached near mile 4. This is a 3-mile route that heads west to FR 24. Stay straight here to continue the northward advance across the exposed crest. At 5 miles, the road crosses a fork of Soldier Creek and then turns to the east to begin climbing a timbered hill. This ascent doesn't abate until mile 7 when you reach the top of Bald Ridge, high above West Tensleep Lake.

The road ends just over a mile farther at the primitive Bald Ridge Trailhead. Here, you'll find a foot trail that heads into the Cloud Peak Wilderness to Lake Helen as well as an ATV trail that leads to Lily Lake and Battle Park.

21: Lily Lake
Forested trail to a subalpine lake

☐ **Backcountry Drive**
Most vehicles

☐ **4WD Route**
4x4 vehicle or ORV

☒ **ATV Trail**
ORV less than 50" wide

Location/Map	West of Buffalo; Page 110
Trails	FT 66, FT 402
Distance	5.5 miles
Managing Agency	USDA Forest Service—Bighorn National Forest
Starting Coordinates	N44° 17.83' W107° 17.93'

ATV trail near Lily Lake

Overview: This ATV trail takes you through a gorgeous area of the Bighorn Mountains where you'll pass a gem of a lake before turning southward and connecting to a 4WD road. Combining the trail with the area's other roads can give you a full day's worth of exploring or at least make a long loop. The road is open to motorized use on May 1, but waiting until summer is better. A Wyoming ORV permit is required.

Start: From Buffalo, head west on HWY 16 for 45.5 miles to reach the turnoff for FR 27 on the right. If traveling from Ten Sleep, drive east on HWY 16 for 17.5 miles to reach the turnoff. Follow FR 27 for 1.2 miles to a fork and bear left onto FR 24. Follow this road a little over 14 miles to reach the trailhead. The parking area is small and unsuitable for trailers. If you're towing an ATV trailer, you'll be better off going less than a mile north and unloading at Battle Park.

Description: From the trailhead, the narrow ATV path heads uphill and loosely parallels a northern tributary of Middle Paint Rock Creek. The route skirts the north edge of a large meadow before climbing steeply into more challenging terrain. Albeit short, there are two rocky sections where ATVs tend to bottleneck as drivers bobble over basketball-sized boulders. A couple of mud holes also add to the fun, though some drivers have unfortunately created additional tracks by driving around the wet spots.

At 2 miles, the track reaches beautiful Lily Lake. Be sure to kill the engine here and take in at least a few minutes along the peaceful shoreline. From the lake, the trail cuts through a meadow for a short distance before turning into FT 402. At 9,547 feet—right about treeline—the high meadows east of the lake reveal a spectacular view into the heart of the Bighorn Mountains. Of the peaks that can be seen, the closest is Elk Mountain at 11,321 feet. Look further up the drainage and you can spot the edge of Bomber Mountain, where a World War II B-17 bomber crashed in 1943.

From this vantage point, the road turns south and drops into a forested depression. You'll pass old cabin ruins here and make three easy fords of Middle Paint Rock Creek. From the crossings, the trail follows an old track for a couple miles across a high mountain plain where it tops out at over 10,200 feet. The ATV trail ends at FR 411 near the Cloud Peak Wilderness boundary. This road (route #20) continues south for 8.2 miles and connects to FR 24.

Other Nearby Drives

Buck Creek Vees/Ed Point ATV Trails—Four ATV trails (FT 360, FT 849, FT 361, and FT 359) connect to form a 15-mile trail network southwest of Battle Park. Some of these trails follow old roads, making for easy riding as you explore the western edge of the Bighorn National Forest. Other sections are found rougher, steeper, eroded, and rutted. All four routes are less than 6 miles in length, but if you park at Battle Park and then incorporate the other area roads and trails with FT 360 here, you'll create a nearly 30-mile loop. These trails are open to motorized use on May 1, but waiting until summer to visit is advised.

To reach these trails from Buffalo, head west on HWY 16 for 45.5 miles to reach the turnoff for FR 27 on the right. If traveling from Ten Sleep, drive east on HWY 16 for 17.5 miles. Follow FR 27 for 1.2 miles to a fork and bear left onto FR 24. Follow this road 11 miles to FR 360 (the southern entry point) or 15 miles to the northern entry point at Battle Park. Battle Park offers the best place to park a trailer and unload ATVs.

Tensleep Canyon—Instead of following HWY 16 through Tensleep Canyon (east of Ten Sleep), consider taking Old Highway 16 (FR 18), a gravel route that also navigates the canyon. To reach this spectacular 6.3-mile route, drive east on HWY 16 from Ten Sleep for a little over 7 miles. Turn onto HWY 435 and drive a mile to the beginning of the road. The route climbs 2,500 feet over an 8% grade and ends at HWY 16 at the upper end of the canyon. The road is open from June 16 to November 15.

22: Cold Springs/Paintrock Lakes
Rise from the desert

☒ **Backcountry Drive** Most vehicles	☒ **4WD Route** 4x4 vehicle or ORV	☐ **ATV Trail** ORV less than 50" wide

Location/Map	Northeast of Worland; Page 116
Roads	CR 268, FR 344
Distance	18 miles (last 7 miles require 4WD)
Managing Agency	USDA Forest Service—Bighorn National Forest
Starting Coordinates	N44° 16.55' W107° 31.64'

Overview: This drive follows Cold Springs Road as it climbs into the western Bighorn Mountains from the arid Bighorn Basin. Inside the national forest, you can continue on the rougher FR 344 to reach the Paintrock Lakes, as well as other remote 4WD roads and single-track motorcycle trails.

The Paintrock Lakes area is more commonly reached from the north using FR 17 (route #11), but this more adventurous approach offers a stunning overlook of the Bighorn Mountains (the best, in my opinion). If you prefer being off the beaten path, there may be no better place to spend a few days camping and four wheeling. The road is open to motorized use on April 1, but late spring and summer are better times to make the trip.

Start: From Worland, take HWY 16 north to Manderson. Turn onto HWY 31 and drive east for 21 miles to the paved Cold Springs Road north of Hyattville. Turn north onto this road, then east again after just a quarter mile. Drive nearly 4 miles to a junction marked with a Medicine Lodge Wildlife Habitat and Archaeological Site sign. Stay right on the paved road, and continue east a short distance to reach the gravel section of Cold Springs Road.

To reach the northern end of the road from the town of Shell, head east on HWY 14 for 16 miles and turn onto FR 17. Drive south for 24.5 miles on FR 17 to Medicine Lodge Campground.

Description: The initial half of Cold Springs Road (CR 268) consists of a wide, gravel surface. The driving is easy, though washboard conditions around the curves can get bothersome. After just a few miles, you'll pass the Medicine Lodge ATV Trail (which heads downhill to Medicine Lodge Archaeological Site) on the left and Paintrock Canyon Trailhead on the right.

Through a moderate climb, the road leaves behind the colorful Bighorn Basin and enters a shrubland on the lower western flanks of the Bighorn Mountains. At the end of mile 5, take the opportunity to stop and look at the countryside behind you; you'll see oddly-shaped rock outcroppings, steep escarpments, juniper woodlands, and a lush ribbon of green where Medicine Lodge Creek flows through the basin.

Scrublands along Cold Springs Road

The road continues toward the national forest boundary by weaving through a number of snake-like curves. The next stretch of the drive becomes rockier and rougher, but it is still easily driven in most vehicles.

Cold Springs Road reaches the Bighorn National Forest at 11 miles. From here, there are several secondary routes that explore the immediate area within the forest. Hunting and dispersed camping are popular activities in this area and most of the roads, though narrow, are easily traveled in pickup trucks and SUVs. Watch for FR 344 and a sign that points the way to Paintrock Lakes.

This initial stretch of FR 344 is an easy drive through a lodgepole pine and Douglas fir forest. After 2 miles, the road leaves the trees and begins climbing the southern slope of a ridge. This is where the road becomes much more rugged and narrow and the point where many people turn around. A rocky ascent ensues, and the top of the ridge is attained less than 2 miles farther.

The sagebrush-covered crest provides the most sweeping overlook of the Bighorn Mountains that I've ever seen from a road. Filling half of the entire skyline, you can see the northern portion of the range, the high country that comprises the Cloud Peak Wilderness, and a few of the peaks to the south. Cloud Peak (13,167 feet), the wilderness' namesake, is clearly visible over 11 miles of rough terrain. For the best overlook, watch for a sign marking FR 348, a short detour that isn't shown on most maps. This pullout leads to an ideal rest stop at the edge of a 700-foot drop. Continue north along the open ridgeline where you'll find easy driving when the dirt road is dry.

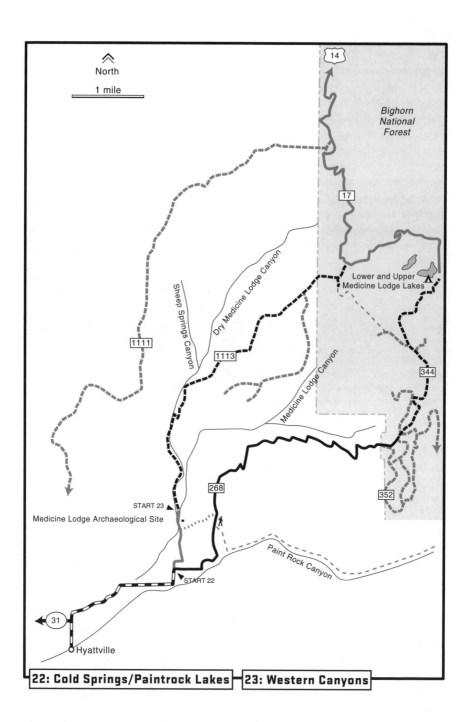

North

1 mile

U.S. 14

Bighorn
National
Forest

17

Sheep Springs Canyon

Dry Medicine Lodge Canyon

1111

1113

Medicine Lodge Canyon

Lower and Upper
Medicine Lodge Lakes

344

START 23

Medicine Lodge Archaeological Site

268

352

Paint Rock Canyon

START 22

31

Hyattville

22: Cold Springs/Paintrock Lakes — **23: Western Canyons**

A sweeping overlook along FR 344

After 15 miles, the road re-enters the timber and soon bears northeast toward the lakes. The road ends at Medicine Lodge Campground at Upper Medicine Lodge Lake. Follow the main gravel road next to the camp (FR 17) a short distance back to the south and you'll find Lower Paintrock Lake. There are two other lakes here—Upper Paintrock Lake and Lower Medicine Lodge Lake—that are reached by foot trails. The area is said to be named by American Indians who used the colorful clay in these waters to create paint for ceremonies and war.

23: Western Canyons
Rugged canyon lands on the western slope

☐ Backcountry Drive Most vehicles	☒ 4WD Route 4x4 vehicle or ORV	☐ ATV Trail ORV less than 50" wide

Location/Map	Northeast of Worland; Page 116
Roads	BLMR 1113
Distance	12 miles
Managing Agency	Wyoming State, Wyoming Game and Fish, USDA Forest Service—Bighorn National Forest
Starting Coordinates	N44° 17.99' W107° 32.41'

Overview: This spectacular 4WD road—one of the most rewarding that Wyoming has to offer in terms of natural diversity—begins at the Medicine Lodge Archaeological Site, which is located in the bottom of a canyon on the western slope of the Bighorn Mountains. After exploring one canyon, you'll climb above two others as you motor into the Bighorn National Forest. It's a very narrow road that is best suited for ATVs. It's open to motorized use from July 2 to the end of the calendar year.

The Medicine Lodge Archaeological Site itself is one of Wyoming's true treasures. Hidden within the Medicine Lodge Creek drainage, the historic site includes a brilliant red sandstone cliff of Indian petroglyphs that was discovered here in 1969. Digs since then have revealed 60 different cultural layers that date back 10,000 years. The area is complemented by a small visitor center, an interpretive nature trail, and a campground. You'll want to set aside time to enjoy the site when you visit.

The site is located within the 12,000-acre Medicine Lodge Wildlife Habitat Management Area. These lands provide winter range for elk herds that number between 500 and 1,000 animals, 300 deer, grouse, dozens of bird species, and various small game mammals.

Start: From Worland, take HWY 16 north to Manderson. Turn onto HWY 31 and drive east for 21 miles to Cold Springs Road north of Hyattville. Turn north onto this road, then east again after just a quarter mile. Drive nearly 4 miles to a junction marked with a Medicine Lodge Wildlife Habitat and Archaeological Site sign. Turn north at the sign and follow the gravel road 1.5 miles to the archaeological site. There are numerous campsites where you can park if you are staying the night, but there is also plenty of room to unload ATVs near the petroglyphs, as well as a smaller grassy area near the beginning of the road itself.

Description: Starting from the north end of the archaeological site, you'll find BLMR 113 (Dry Fork Road), which is a narrow, sandy track that runs through a canyon bottom. Tall vertical cliffs guard over the draw, which is filled with tall grasses, sagebrush, cottonwood and juniper trees. Early on, the vegetation crowds the roadway making it difficult in places to see oncoming traffic.

Aside from a couple steep and tricky hairpin turns, the going is easy through the canyon. There are a few creek crossings, but they are all insignificant. This spectacular section of trail lasts for 4 miles before the road reaches a suitable place to climb up and out of the canyon bottom. This passage travels between the two magnificent canyons—Dry Medicine Lodge Canyon and its southern neighbor, Medicine Lodge Canyon—and you'll soon get a terrific view into the northern gorge.

By 6 miles, the road steadily advances across a high slope of grass and sage that serves as winter range for a large herd of elk. At 8 miles—and now comfortably atop the western flank of the Bighorn Mountains—you get a commanding view of the region. Straight ahead is Black Butte (9,238 feet), a forested mound just inside the Bighorn National Forest. To your back is the vastness of the Bighorn Basin with all of its splendid canyons, badlands, and escarpments.

The road widens at the national forest boundary and becomes deeply rutted. The route forks after a mile of driving in the timber; a right turn leads to a single-track near a primitive camping area. Bear left and drive a short distance to reach FR 17, a dozen miles from the archaeological site.

Towering walls along Medicine Lodge Creek

Lower Bighorn Mountains

As depicted on maps, but less noticeable in person, the Bighorn Mountains extend much farther south than the Bighorn National Forest. These lower, mostly treeless mountains under 8,000 feet are known as Hole-in-the-Wall Country, a term that refers to outlaws of the Wild West who used the area's vastness and natural features to hide from lawmen. Here, you'll find expansive prairies of grass and sagebrush that are crowned with deep red escarpments—it's uniquely beautiful scenery. Hordes of pronghorn antelope and mule deer roam here, and the area serves as important winter range for these and other big game animals. Agriculturally, the lower Bighorns are used to raise cattle and sheep.

Land Ownership

Most of the land in the lower Bighorn Mountains is managed by the BLM. However, this federal land is heavily interspersed with large ranches and trespassing is a possibility if you're not careful. Some of the roads in the area are private so you can't assume that a good-looking lane is public. Watch for signs and gates and when in doubt, return to a known county road. BLM offices are located in Buffalo and Casper.

Roads and Trails

There are four highways that encompass the lower Bighorn Mountains. In the Bighorn National Forest to the north is HWY 16. To the west is HWY 20 and to the south is HWY 20/26. Running along the east side is I-25.

Within the boundaries of these highways, you'll find a wide-reaching system of interconnected gravel and dirt lanes. These are long routes that require you to be self-sufficient if you have a problem, such as running out of fuel or getting stuck in mud. Some of this land remains so isolated from development that you might drive over a hundred miles without encountering another vehicle. Conversely, there are weekends when the area is quite busy, especially during the hunting season.

A plethora of two-track paths crisscross these hills. Many of these are unsigned and unmapped. Rocks are rarely encountered on these lesser paths. Instead, you're more likely to encounter slippery ruts and mud holes.

Seasons and Conditions

Depending on seasonal precipitation, some areas in the lower Bighorns can be accessed as early as May and as late as mid-November. The challenge at these lower elevations is predicting when they will be free of snow. You can reach a stubborn snowdrift after driving miles on dry, bare ground.

A summer thunderstorm can make a route impassable even with a 4x4 vehicle. This is especially true for these roads, which have less gravel than those found in the adjacent national forest. A wait of several hours is sometimes all you'll need before the sun dries the roadbed enough to proceed.

Fuel

Before heading into this area, be sure to fill your tank. Fueling stations to the south are available in Casper and Shoshoni. On the east side, make your stops in Kaycee or Buffalo. To the north and west, you can get fuel in Thermopolis, Basin, Worland, and Ten Sleep.

Maps

This area is best navigated by using a state map such as the DeLorme Wyoming Atlas & Gazetteer or the Wyoming Road & Recreation Atlas published by Benchmark Maps. The BLM also offers topographical maps that are excellent for more precise route finding.

24: The Slip
Take the Slip (Slope) Road from the Bighorns

☒ **Backcountry Drive** Most vehicles	☐ **4WD Route** 4x4 vehicle or ORV	☐ **ATV Trail** ORV less than 50" wide

Location/Map	Southwest of Buffalo; Page 122
Roads	CR 3, CR 67
Distance	39 miles
Managing Agency	USDA Forest Service—Bighorn National Forest, BLM—Buffalo Field Office, other mixed ownership
Starting Coordinates	N44° 9.01' W106° 55.97'

Overview: This beautiful drive connects the southern Bighorn National Forest to the small community of Mayoworth where the grades on the road are almost as impressive as the scenery. With broad landscapes that show little sign of human development, it's easy to imagine the area as it was when Butch Cassidy and the Sundance Kid used it as a hideout. Today, these rugged foothills are used for sheep grazing.

Before making this drive, be mindful of the weather. Powerful summer thunderstorms can quickly flush out a parched creek bed and the Kaycee area has a history of flooding. The northern stretch of road is prone to becoming muddy and slick, but the southern half is heavily graveled and holds up better in wet weather. A truck, SUV, or similar vehicle is recommended. If you have any doubts about your vehicle, drive this road as described here, going downhill. Making this an uphill trip has the potential to overheat your rig, especially on hot summer days.

Start: From Buffalo, take HWY 16 west for 26 miles. Turn left onto Hazelton Road (CR 3). To access the road from the south, take HWY 191 north out of Kaycee for 12 miles to Mayoworth.

Description: Beginning at HWY 16, travel south on paved Hazelton Road (CR 3) toward Doyle Campground. The road changes to a good gravel surface at 3.5 miles and a string of private cabins is soon passed on the right. More noticeable, though, is the triad of mountain peaks that rise above 10,000 feet. The summits from north to south are Hesse Mountain, Hazelton Peak, and Hazelton Pyramid.

After 5 miles, the road passes Basco Creek where moose can sometimes be found foraging. The turnoff to Doyle Campground heads east at mile 6. This hidden camp rarely reaches capacity and appeals to those campers who want to escape the busier campgrounds along the highway. Beaver lodges can be found in Doyle Creek along the campground road.

At 10 miles, the backroad leaves the Bighorn National Forest and passes through privately-owned land before reaching the north edge of Dull Knife Reservoir. Much of the shoreline around the lake is also privately property, but a public parking area exists for those looking to cast a line to the trout.

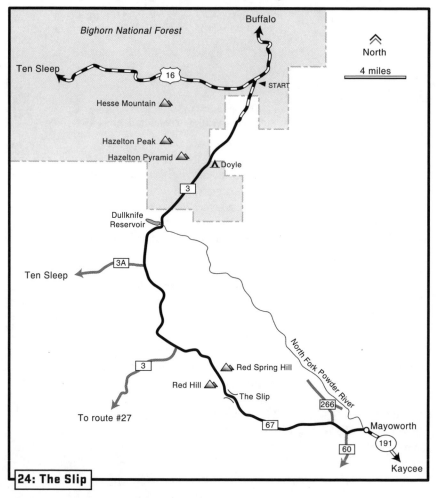

24: The Slip

A beautiful overlook over the oxbow bends of the North Fork of the Powder River is quickly reached as the road rounds the east side of the reservoir.

Continue south into an opening named Uncle Billys Flats where a junction with Rome Hill Road (CR 3A) is found. Stay south on Hazelton Road, which cuts through beautiful grassy meadows broken by bands of rock and clusters of timber.

Near mile 20, Hazelton Road breaks off to the right at Beartrap Meadows. Veer left and continue east on Slip Road (CR 67)—shown on some maps and signs as Slope Road—to climb a steep 700-foot hill. Though pulling this grade hardly warrants the use of 4WD, I watched with curiosity as a local rancher locked his hubs and used 4WD to tackle the incline. (Maybe he had a prior bad experience on this hill!) After surmounting the tree-lined crest of the hill, the road descends along Arch Creek. Colorful rock formations topped with coniferous trees create an interesting landscape.

After passing Red Spring Hill (8,189 feet) and then slightly taller Red Hill (8,221 feet), the roadway crosses Arch Creek and pulls to the bottom of The Slip, another steep incline of nearly 600 vertical feet.

From the top of the ridge, the route begins to descend and passes a tiny pond named Government Reservoir. The view from this high flank becomes progressively more impressive as red hogbacks come into view.

At 30 miles, shift into the lowest of gears and prepare for a long, steep descent across a sparsely timbered slope. In order to descend the 3,000 vertical feet to the prairie below, the roadway utilizes a 10% grade and nearly two dozen sweeping switchbacks.

Slip Road south of the Bighorn National Forest

The grade levels out over the last few miles where you pass towering red scarps. Continue east past junctions for CR 266 and Elk Mountain Road (CR 60) to reach Mayoworth and HWY 191. It's 12 miles farther on the highway to reach the town of Kaycee.

Other Nearby Drives

Rome Hill Road—This road (CR 3A/CR 56) runs 20 miles between Hazelton Road and Ten Sleep. Historically, the route began as an Indian trail and then was later used to transport logs from the high country. Today the gravel road provides little utility, other than access for area landowners and ranchers. Sightseeing is also a common use. The road reveals views of the Absaroka Range (east of Yellowstone), the high rocky caps of the Bighorns to the north, and beautiful red bluffs of the lower Bighorn Mountains to the south. Along the road itself, you'll pass Cooks Canyon, a colorful entanglement of eroded rock, pine, and aspen that cuts a groove into the landscape.

To reach the road from Buffalo, take HWY 16 west for 26 miles. Turn south onto Hazelton Road (CR 3) and drive 15.2 miles to Rome Hill Road (CR 3A). To reach the road from the west, take HWY 16 east out of Ten Sleep for 3.3 miles. Turn south onto HWY 436 and follow it 6 miles to the end of the pavement. There is some private property in this area, so you'll want to watch for signs and stay on the road where necessary. Also, watch for livestock along the way.

25: Middle Fork Canyon/Outlaw Cave
Wyoming's great hidden canyon

☐ **Backcountry Drive**
Most vehicles

☒ **4WD Route**
4x4 vehicle or ORV

☐ **ATV Trail**
ORV less than 50" wide

Location/Map	West of Kaycee; Page 126
Roads	BLMR 6214, BLMR 6217
Distance	8.5+ miles
Managing Agency	BLM—Buffalo Field Office
Starting Coordinates	N43° 39.61' W106° 54.75'

Overview: This drive leads you into remarkably beautiful country and ends at the rim of a deep and impressive canyon. The trip features photogenic scenery, hiking access to outstanding fishing, and the opportunity to further explore the area, which includes ancient Indian petroglyphs.

To prevent confusion—and people I have met here have been confused—you should know that the road ends at a campground named Outlaw Cave, not the actual cave, which is purported to be somewhere in the canyon below the camp. It also does not lead to the site of the Hole-in-the-Wall (route #26), which is only 5 miles from here but requires a 60-mile drive to reach because of private property. The mix-up over these locations is probably due to ambiguous tourism literature that suggests these hideouts are easy drives off I-25.

Start: From I-25 at Kaycee (Exit 254), travel west on HWY 191 for a mile and turn south onto HWY 190. Drive west 16 miles to the end of the pavement at Barnum. Here, turn left (south) onto the BLM road.

Description: By the time you have reached the end of the pavement, you'll realize that you are entering a special place in Wyoming. Striking red buttes and hogbacks characterize this area. The most dramatic of these formations are passed as you turn off the pavement and drive south from Barnum on the gravel road.

Before 2 miles, a two-track is seen heading west through the grassy countryside. Stay on the main course and continue paralleling the red rocks.

SIDE TRIP

The two-track is Bachus Pasture Road, a 6-mile lane that provides access to the Ed O. Taylor Wildlife Habitat Management Area. This 10,158-acre range provides year-round habitat to mule deer and serves as winter grounds for the Bighorn Mountains' elk herd.

After 3 miles, the road passes a distinct red formation named Castle Rock (5,549 feet). Along with its southern neighbor, Steamboat Rock, these rocks guard over a meadow of tall grass that is frequented by antelope. Soon after, the road passes by Bar C Ranch where the Middle Fork of the Powder River flows east.

Middle Fork Canyon from Outlaw Cave Campground

Past the ranch, the road curves to the west where BLM signs warn of worsening road conditions. Continue west a short distance to reach a fishing access point and foot trails at mile 6. The steep trails lead to the bottom of Middle Fork Canyon where you might discover Outlaw Cave, a hideout used by outlaws of the 1800s to stash their loot. If you're not driving a 4x4 vehicle, this is a good place to turn around or park and proceed on foot. From this point forward, the road surface is a crumbly, off-camber path that travels across intriguing terrain for the next couple of miles.

Just past mile 8, the road reaches a fork. Bear right to reach Outlaw Cave Campground. Here, limestone outcrops and ancient ponderosa pines line the rim above the Middle Fork Canyon, though a lightning-caused fire burned many of the trees in August 2006. Be sure to park your vehicle and walk to the edge to see into one of Wyoming's most impressive gorges. The canyon walls stand as high as a thousand feet over the Middle Fork of the Powder River.

To find the Indian petroglyphs from the campground, return to the fork near the campground entrance and turn west onto the primitive 4WD road. This sandy and rocky path travels along the evergreen-peppered brim of the canyon, though the best view into the chasm is from the campground. Continue west a short distance to reach a sign marking the location of a prehistoric rock shelter. Here, you'll be able to find the faint images on the rock.

From the rock shelter, the 4WD track continues west into the Ed O. Taylor Wildlife Habitat Management Area where there are additional 4WD trails. Some of these routes lead to fishing access points along the river, while others travel toward Hazelton Road. If you travel into these hinterlands, you'll want a land-management map to help identify state, federal, and private land. At the time of this writing, the BLM office in Buffalo offered a particularly helpful handout that showed the locations of closed roads and locked gates across this area.

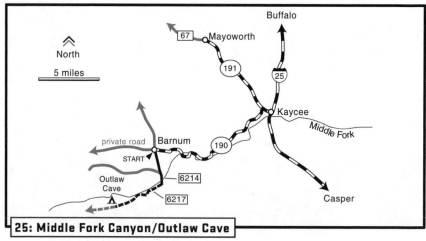

25: Middle Fork Canyon/Outlaw Cave

26: Hole-In-The-Wall
The outlaw hideout

☐ **Backcountry Drive**
  Most vehicles

☒ **4WD Route**
  4x4 vehicle or ORV

☐ **ATV Trail**
  ORV less than 50" wide

Location/Map	Northwest of Casper; Page 129
Roads	CR 51, CR 111, CR 111A, CR 105, BLMR 6214
Distance	41.8 miles (last 10.3 miles require 4WD); 4.8-mile hike
Managing Agency	BLM—Buffalo Field Office
Starting Coordinates	N43° 39.28' W106° 37.74'

Overview: This region of Wyoming, termed Hole-in-the-Wall country, is where well-known outlaws such as Butch Cassidy and the Sundance Kid hid between robberies for cash, cattle, and horses. Outlaw gangs, including the infamous Wild Bunch, enjoyed the hideout in part because it was (and still is) a secluded place where they could detect incomers from a considerable distance. Attempts to capture the bandits from this hideaway proved futile.

This route takes you across rugged country to the Hole-in-the-Wall site. In dry conditions, the first 30 miles of the drive can be done in any vehicle, though a 4WD vehicle is suggested. The last 10-mile stretch is a rutted, muddy track that requires four-wheel drive. The road ends at a primitive trailhead where a hiking trail then leads a couple of miles to the site, which is situated at the base of a gorgeous red cliff.

The remote Hole-in-the-Wall

The route described here follows the directions provided by the BLM. However, you can just as easily make your approach from the South Big Horn/Red Wall Scenic Backway (route #27), which is a better road. You could also combine both of these routes to create a fantastic tour of north-central Wyoming.

Start: From Casper, head north on I-25 to TTT Road (Exit 249).

Description: After exiting I-25, drive underneath the overpass and turn left on CR 51, known as TTT Road and often marked on maps as Lone Bear Road. The paved lane parallels I-25 a short distance and then bears southwest at a fork where it changes to a wide gravel surface. Driving off Bailey Flats, the range before you becomes quite rugged with grassy bluffs, draws, and ridges.

Follow the well-maintained course for a dozen miles until the road reaches a fork for the TTT Ranch. Turn right (the left fork is a private road) and follow the road a few more miles until it splits again at 15.5 miles. Turn right onto West Willow Creek Road (CR 111) and start driving west above Willow Creek. Although the road here is still in good shape, you might find yourself dodging mud puddles.

Near mile 21, the road comes to a curious junction with a hand-painted sign that shows CR 111 dead-ending. Turn right onto CR 111A (signed as the alternate route) and follow it up a short hill. The red surface of the road—not as heavily graveled—gets slippery when wet. After an intense overnight thunderstorm, I needed four-wheel drive to climb the squishy grade. Fortunately, underlying layers of rock give the road a good foundation making it nearly impossible to carve ruts.

The road, slightly rougher here, continues west over a series of benches, some rimmed with evergreen trees and shrubs. At mile 24, you'll top a formation called the Red Wall and then descend to a flat. While not too pronounced here, the Red Wall is a stunning geological feature that rises hundreds of feet high and is 35 miles long—the best views of it are yet to come.

The road continues west and passes a junction for the Willow Creek Guest Ranch. Some of this land belongs to the ranch and is consequently signed as private.

At 31.5 miles, you reach CR 105 just south of a striking red bluff named The Island. If you're making this trip as a backcountry drive, you can continue less than a mile west to reach CR 110 on the Big Horn/Red Wall Scenic Backway, which makes for a great return route to Casper.

To begin the 4WD portion of the drive, turn right on CR 105 and follow the primitive road around the base of The Island. You'll quickly reach the first of five livestock gates, each of which will need to be opened and closed over the next 10 miles. Though the track is deeply rutted, often muddy, and has a few tricky sections where it crosses draws, it is passable when driven carefully (an ATV would be better in wet conditions).

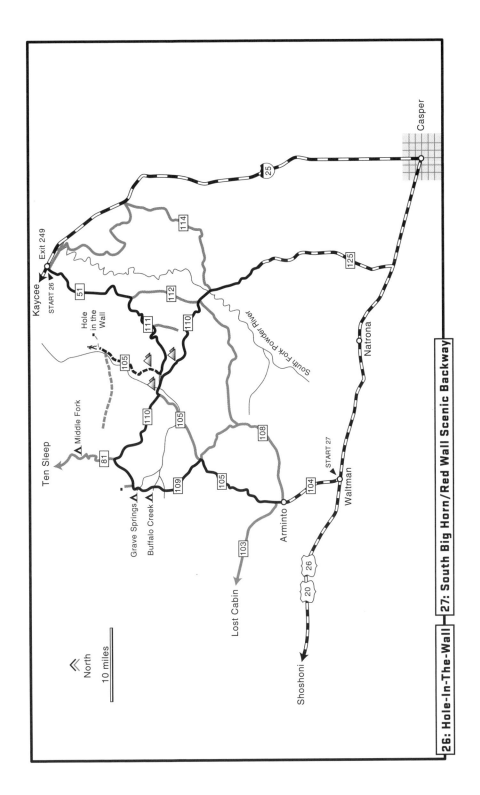

Casper

25

Exit 249

Kaycee

START 26

51

Hole
in the
Wall

114

112

111

110

105

South Fork Powder River

125

Natrona

110

Middle Fork

Ten Sleep

81

105

108

Grave Springs

Buffalo Creek

109

105

START 27

Waltman

104

Arminto

103

26

20

Lost Cabin

Shoshoni

North

10 miles

The first few miles of the 4WD road cross a lonely expanse of grass and rolling hills. Old cabins and timbers from rotting bridges speak of the rangeland's past. As the track advances north, the sheer, crimson face of the Red Wall comes into view. Three miles before the trailhead, you'll join Buffalo Creek Road (BLMR 6214), which is rockier, but usually drier, than the county track.

The trailhead is reached a short distance after a historical monument that marks the location of the Hole-in-the-Wall Fight of July 22nd, 1897, a deadly gunfight between rustlers and cowboys. From the trailhead's parking area, it's a 2.4-mile hike across rolling terrain that has occasional BLM trail markers. A shallow ford, or hop, over Spring Creek is also required. Several secondary trails and roads crisscross the indistinct hiking trail, but the destination is obvious—head for the deep indenture on the side of the Red Wall.

The trail markers cease in the meadow at the base of the cliff. This was once the location of numerous cabins used by gangs of the Wild West. Contrary to what you might imagine, or what is portrayed by Hollywood, there is no actual hole or cave at the site. Rather, it's more of a cove—a meadow encased by a cliff on three sides—with a subtle passage that leads over the top of the rock. The rock-strewn chute provides the only sensible way the outlaws could get over the wall and they'd use this steep path to drive their rustled cattle. Use caution around the escarpment; the sandstone is fragile and rocks often tumble down without warning.

27: South Big Horn/Red Wall Scenic Backway
The tail of the Bighorn Mountains

☐ **Backcountry Drive** Most vehicles	☐ **4WD Route** 4x4 vehicle or ORV	☒ **ATV Trail** ORV less than 50" wide

Location/Map	Northwest of Casper; Page 129
Roads	CR 104, CR 105, CR 109, CR 81, CR 110, CR 125
Distance	102 miles
Managing Agency	BLM—Casper Field Office
Starting Coordinates	N43° 4.27' W107° 11.76'

Overview: This designated Wyoming Scenic Backway makes a large semi-loop through the vastness of north-central Wyoming. It's a remarkable trip that crosses more than a hundred miles through the southern tail of the Bighorn Mountains.

Approximately a third of this drive is paved and the remaining unpaved portion is in relatively good condition. The rougher portion is along the "upper loop" of the drive, which follows Big Horn Mountain Road (CR 109/CR 110). This section, which can be bypassed if needed, involves steeper grades, a rocky road surface, and a few shallow fords. Snowdrifts, even into late spring, and wet summertime weather can also make travel difficult. For these reasons, consider traveling this section of the backway only if you are traveling in a 4x4. Also, while issuing notes of caution, be aware that there are no towns or services along this drive. Be sure to carry sufficient food, water, and fuel.

Start: Both ends of this backway connect to HWY 20/26 between Shoshoni and Casper. To begin the drive from the east, head out of Casper on HWY 20/26 for about 15 miles to Bucknum Road (CR 125). To start the drive from the west, as described here, take the same highway nearly 30 miles farther west to Waltman.

Description: From Waltman (at HWY 20/26), follow paved Arminto Road (CR 104) north to Arminto. Here, the road turns to a gravel surface where it becomes Buffalo Creek Road (CR 105). The only evidence of mankind here belongs to Wyoming's oil and gas companies. More often than not, there is nothing but the road to divide one horizon from the other.

Continuing north, the monotonous plain changes and gives way to more dramatic topography. The road now winds between gorgeous red scarps that contrast starkly with the sage-covered ground and bright blue Wyoming sky. One of the more notable landmarks is Deadman Butte (6,981 feet) passed at mile 17. Nearly 6 miles farther, Big Horn Mountain Road (CR 109) can be seen winding its way up into higher country. Turn left onto this road.

South Big Horn/Red Wall Scenic Backway near Grave Springs

ALTERNATE
ROUTE

If you do not want to tackle the rougher, higher portion of this drive, stay right on Buffalo Creek Road (CR 105). This will reduce the total trip by nearly 30 miles.

The backway now engages more rugged terrain as it climbs steeply along a rocky and grating roadway surrounded by sparse limber pine trees and ancient curl leaf mountain mahogany. This stretch is just a couple miles long, and easier driving is soon attained.

As you gain the south-arcing crest of the Bighorn Mountains, you'll find a beautiful and intriguing environment. Here at about 8,400 feet, the open uplands and valleys are punctuated with occasional rock outcrops and isolated stands of dense evergreens. You may encounter sheepherders and their flocks as they work over the high grassy slopes.

At 32 miles, you ford the Middle Fork of Buffalo Creek near Buffalo Creek Campground. The creek is shallow and easily crossed. Just a short distance farther is another possible ford (depending on stream flows) and a turnoff for Grave Springs Campground. These are two of the most remote campgrounds in the state and they offer plenty of solitude. If you're just driving through, consider stopping at one of them for a picnic. There are sheepherder burial sites near Grave Springs, which can be located with a little foot exploration.

Just past Grave Springs Campground, the road crosses the North Fork of Buffalo Creek—the last ford—near a sizable rock outcrop. This is the deepest ford of the three, but its waters are still easily crossed. From the creek, continue driving northeast and stay right at a fork that leads to a lodge. The road soon crosses into Washakie County where it changes to CR 81.

At 40 miles, a junction is reached in an open area named Kidd Flat. To stay on the backway, turn right (southeast) onto CR 84, which soon turns into 33-Mile Road (CR 110) where it crosses back into Natrona County.

SIDE
TRIP

The rutted road headed north at the junction, Hazelton Road (CR 81/CR 3), travels 6 miles to Middle Fork Campground where there is excellent fishing in the Middle Fork of the Powder River, a blue ribbon fishery. The road can be taken further north to Big Trails Stock Drive Road (CR 85)/HWY 434 to eventually reach the town of Ten Sleep in about 50 miles. You an also head north to reach CR 3, which will lead you to HWY 16 in the Bighorn National Forest after about 60 miles (see route #24).

Heading southeast, CR 110 descends rapidly over the next dozen miles to return to Buffalo Creek Road (CR 105). Turn left at this junction to continue the second half of the scenic backway. The county road splits a short distance later with West Willow Creek Road (CR 111). This time bear right to stay on CR 110.

Middle Fork of the Powder River at Middle Fork Campground

SIDE TRIP

A left turn onto CR 111 leads you a short distance to CR 105, a 4WD track that heads north to the Hole in the Wall (route #26). This road is dramatically different than the CR 105 you were just driving. You can also follow CR 111 farther east to reach I-25 near Kaycee.

At around 56 miles, the road reaches Roughlock Hill at the edge of an impressive natural feature named Red Wall. An interpretive sign here tells of pioneers who locked the wheels on their wagons in order to slide down the steep slope. From this vantage point, you can gaze over a beautiful grassy valley with unforgettable red escarpments. This is a very remote area of the state that must be appreciated; there are not too many places left where one can look out and not see power lines, dwellings, or other signs of the modern world.

From Roughlock Hill, the road continues an east-southeast bearing to return to the drier, lower country. Here, the rolling grassy meadows give way to sagebrush flats and draws that are peppered with ponderosa pines.

A distinctive rock feature called Broken Horn lies ahead and the road passes through the formation at mile 69. Soon after, the backway meets Lone Bear Road and bears right into Fifty-Mile Flat, an open stretch divided by the South Fork of the Powder River. In this parched region, the wide watercourse looks impressive and out of place.

From the river, the road curves further south and soon transitions to a paved surface. The remaining 21 miles to HWY 20/26 is an easy stretch that follows historical stock driveways. The view again becomes featureless as the roadway travels through working land used for livestock grazing and oil production.

28: Nowood

Country rarely seen

| ☒ Backcountry Drive | ☐ 4WD Route | ☐ ATV Trail |
| Most vehicles | 4x4 vehicle or ORV | ORV less than 50" wide |

Location/Map	Northwest of Casper; Page 135
Roads	CR 176, CR 117, CR 295, CR 82, HWY 434
Distance	80 miles
Managing Agency	BLM—Lander and Worland Field Offices
Starting Coordinates	N43° 9.73' W107° 43.61'

Overview: This backcountry drive travels across lonesome country between the community of Moneta and the town of Ten Sleep. The sprawling expanse of this open land is broken only by the fringes of the Bridger Mountains and the Bighorn Mountains. If you're starting or ending in Casper, you'll probably be driving about 160 miles between fueling stations.

Start: To begin the drive from the south as described here, drive west of Casper on HWY 20/26 for 73 miles to Moneta. Then turn north on Lysite-Moneta Road (CR 176). To start the drive from the north, turn south onto HWY 434 located on the western side of Ten Sleep.

Description: The trip begins amidst the high prairie near the exact geographical center of Wyoming. From Moneta, drive north on paved CR 176 and drive 8.5 miles to Lysite. Before you get there, you'll pass a daunting sign that warns of poisonous gas from nearby drilling sites—roadside lights flash if gas is present. Continue north, given that it's safe. The Bridger Mountains can be seen to the west, while Lysite Mountain can be found to the north.

At Lysite, follow the BLM sign eastward to Lost Cabin. The land here is ruled by the oil and gas industry—evident by the plethora of signage for pipelines, rigs, offices, stations, and gas plants. Continue through this development on Badwater Road (CR 117), which turns to gravel, to reach a fork at 16 miles. Bear left onto Nowood Road (CR 295). Drive north, passing by Bighorn Trail Road (CR 296) a few miles farther. Before the road enters more rugged land, you can look back to find the Wind River Mountains to the southwest. There are also glimpses of the taller Bighorn Mountains ahead, topping the horizon.

Continuing along a northern bearing, Nowood Road begins to slowly climb through a colorful landscape of rolling green hills peppered with red and yellowish soils and short rock outcrops. With most traces of mankind left behind, the semi-arid land here is mostly unblemished, covered with sagebrush, grasses, and occasional junipers and cottonwood trees where small creeks flow. Across the area you'll find antelope and rabbits.

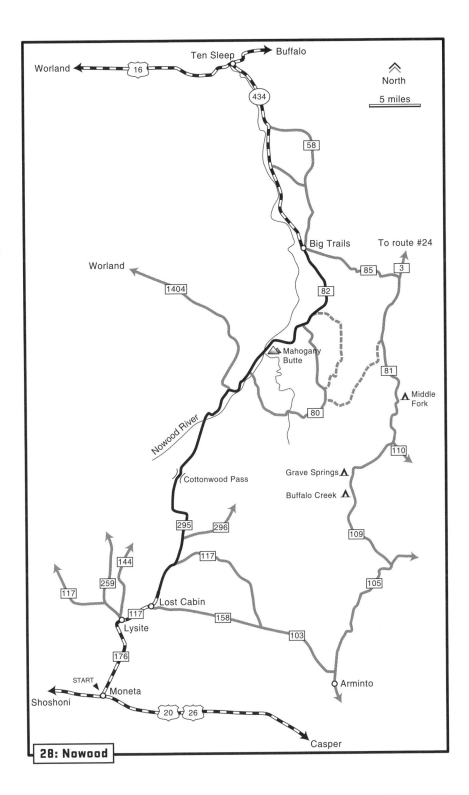

Worland

Ten Sleep → Buffalo

16

North

5 miles

434

58

Big Trails

To route #24

85

3

Worland

1404

82

81

Mahogany Butte

Middle Fork

80

110

Nowood River

Grave Springs

Buffalo Creek

Cottonwood Pass

295   296

109

117

144

105

259

117

117

Lost Cabin

117

158

Lysite

103

176

START

Moneta

Arminto

Shoshoni

20   26

Casper

28: Nowood

Headed north on Nowood Road

The drive's high point is reached at Cottonwood Pass (6,727 feet), a shallow saddle between Lysite Mountain to the west and the low scrublands that comprise the tail end of the Bighorn Mountains to the east. From here, the road descends into Washakie County where it is assigned a different number, CR 82, and is referred to as Upper Nowood Road.

A little over 3 miles from the county line, the road narrows before reaching Nowood River where the stream flows to the northeast. The backroad roughly follows the same course. This is a scenic stretch as the lane undercuts striking red beds that punctuate much of the Hole in the Wall country. The deep red coloring is a result of iron oxidation in the rock.

At 38 miles, the route reaches a fork with Nowater Trail Road (BLMR 1404), a backway that travels 47 miles to Worland. Stay right at the fork and continue past a number of ranch houses.

A sign marking Split Rock Road is reached at 41 miles. This road is actually Cherry Creek Road, a worthwhile alternative route (or side trip) that should be considered. Taking this road as an alternate route adds 13 miles to the total overall length of the drive.

SIDE TRIP

The 21-mile Cherry Creek Road travels through beautiful country that is notable for its verdant creek bottoms and generous overlooks. The route travels east to cross Deep Creek and then turns back to the northwest to return to Upper Nowood Road. The driving surface is slightly rougher than Upper Nowood Road and includes steeper grades as well as one shallow ford.

Continuing northward on the main course, you soon pass a ranch where the road crosses the Nowood River and then head toward Mahogany Butte (6,451 feet). This massive dome is bisected by a tree-lined gap where the road and river squeeze through. The butte stands hundreds of feet overhead on both sides, but it's a brief passage and the backway emerges on the northern side in less than a mile.

The road now leaves the river's banks but soon crosses over Cherry Creek and Box Elder Creek near their confluence. Soon after, Cherry Creek Road is passed where it returns to the Upper Nowood Road before mile 50.

The next dozen miles include a number of ranches where lush, irrigated pastures are nourished by Redbank Creek and Little Canyon Creek. The gravel road ends at Big Trails where paved HWY 434 begins. It then parallels the Nowood River for the remaining 21 miles to Ten Sleep.

Bighorn Basin

The Bighorn Basin separates the Bighorn Mountains of northern Wyoming from the Absaroka Range to the west—a span of nearly 100 miles. Most of this arid basin receives less than 10 inches of annual precipitation, which is evident by the parched ground that yields very little vegetation. The basin's terrain is a rugged melding of canyons, short mountains, sagebrush flats, buttes, and badlands that are colored with red and purple claystone.

When driving through the vast Bighorn Basin, it's easy to assume that it's a wasteland, and a miserable one when visited during the sweltering days of summer. But the basin is actually replete with natural resources. Underneath the powdery ground are extensive deposits of petroleum and gas. The basin's fields have already produced over a billion barrels of oil. Where the land is irrigated, farmers succeed at growing crops such as sugar beets, beans, and alfalfa.

The eastern side of the Bighorn Basin has earned global fame for its rich fossil beds, which continue to be uncovered and studied. Some of the more well-known finds include a Camarasaurus, Tyrannosaurus Rex, and a Stegosaurus that was first showcased in 2008.

Although dinosaurs no longer roam the basin, wild horses do and the BLM manages three distinct herds in the area. The Pryor Mountain Wild Horse Range, located on the north end of the basin in Montana, is perhaps the best place to spot these animals. Deer, antelope, rabbits, rattlesnakes, and a variety of birds are commonly sighted, while more elusive animals such as bobcats and mountain lions prowl the basin undetected. There is also evidence that a small number of Yellowstone's wolves have migrated across the basin to inhabit the Bighorn Mountains.

Land Ownership

The Bighorn Basin encompasses a vast expanse of federally-owned land that is managed by the BLM. The risk of running onto private property is very low if you stay on established roads. A BLM office is located in Worland.

Roads and Trails

The best roads in the Bighorn Basin include a trio of east-west highways: HWY 14 ALT, HWY 14, and HWY 16. Off these paved routes, travel can be troublesome as washouts, thick dust, rocks, and washboard are common. Even the trunk roads present difficult driving and a four-wheel drive vehicle is recommended, though a high-clearance two-wheel drive vehicle will often suffice.

If you're going to drive the area's primitive tracks, be prepared by carrying extra food and water as well as equipment to self-excavate your vehicle. Also, take note that the basin has a number of travel management areas and wilderness study areas where off-highway vehicles have restrictions. The best way to find these is to contact the BLM or to check their website.

Seasons and Conditions

The backroads of the Bighorn Basin are best driven from May through October. Although precipitation is scant, it takes but a short burst from a summer afternoon thunderstorm to turn the clay-based roads into slippery troughs that cannot be driven with any vehicle.

Fuel

You'll find fuel in nearly all of towns around and within the basin including Ten Sleep, Worland, Basin, Greybull, Lovell, Cody, Powell, Meeteetse, and Thermopolis.

Maps

The best maps for the area are those that clearly show the county roads, such as the DeLorme Wyoming Atlas & Gazetteer or the Wyoming Road & Recreation Atlas published by Benchmark Maps. For more precise route finding, especially if you're going to drive the secondary roads, check out the BLM website for the Worland Field Office. This excellent resource includes maps, regulations, and information about specific travel management areas.

29: Red Gulch/Alkali National Backcountry Byway
The edge of the Bighorn Basin

☒ **Backcountry Drive**
Most vehicles

☐ **4WD Route**
4x4 vehicle or ORV

☐ **ATV Trail**
ORV less than 50" wide

Location/Map	Southeast of Greybull; Page 140
Roads	BLMR 1109, BLMR 1111
Distance	32 miles
Managing Agency	BLM—Worland Field Office
Starting Coordinates	N44° 31.18' W107° 51.69'

Overview: This designated National Backcountry Byway travels through the Bighorn Basin, a vast arid expanse west of the Bighorn Mountains. Aside from seeing colorful bluffs along the foothills of the mountain range, the trip also offers the opportunity to see dinosaur tracks and Indian petroglyphs.

A high clearance vehicle is suggested to best handle the backway's rough and rocky stretches. Easy driving can be expected in dry weather conditions. In wet weather, the clay-based driving surface becomes a slippery hazard that can be impassable. This route can usually be driven from May through October.

Start: To begin this drive from the north, as described here, drive west of Shell on HWY 14 for 4 miles. To start the drive from the south, head east on HWY 31 from Manderson toward Hyattville. Drive 20 miles and watch for signs for the turnoff.

Description: From HWY 14, Red Gulch Road (BLMR 1109) begins by taking a southern course through the sparsely-vegetated Bighorn Basin. The first few miles of roadway are easily driven as they provide access to a heavily-visited dinosaur tracksite at mile 5—a necessary stop.

The Red Gulch Dinosaur Tracksite was discovered in 1997 after erosion is thought to have worn off the sedimentary layers that once covered the site. Here, you can clearly make out distinct, preserved footprints that were made by theropods, a meat-eating class of dinosaurs that walked on their rear legs. Interpretive signs at the tracksite provide more information about this fascinating discovery.

Heading eastward on BLMR 1109, the road narrows and becomes less friendly. It can be a jarring ride, but it's usually easily passable in dry weather, which is almost always the condition in this parched basin. The local climate is made apparent in the sagebrush-carpeted plateau that is broken by colorful bluffs, claystone badlands, and red walls that geologists know as the Chugwater Formation. These rock structures create an interesting landscape that is rarely seen, and it only gets more dramatic as you drive farther along the backway.

While your driving slows over the next 15 miles, take the opportunity to watch for some of the residents that call the Bighorn Basin home: antelope, grouse, porcupines, and cottontail rabbits. You may also find stacked rock cairns that were built as route markers by American Indians and sheepherders.

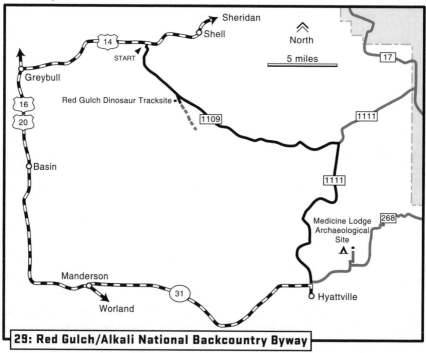

29: Red Gulch/Alkali National Backcountry Byway

At 20 miles, Red Gulch Road reaches a three-way junction along the backroad's highest point (7,070 feet). Here, Alkali Road (BLMR 1111) heads left to the Bighorn National Forest and right toward Hyattville. This historic road was built in 1897 and was used to carry mail over the Bighorn Mountains. Turn right, south, onto its slightly smoother and wider surface. Before you proceed, take advantage of the rise in elevation to catch sight of the mighty Absaroka Range to the west.

ALTERNATE
ROUTE
Turn left, northeast, onto Alkali Road and you can drive 6 miles to FR 17 (route #11) in the Bighorn National Forest. It's a rocky and rutted road that climbs nearly 2,000 vertical feet, but any high clearance vehicle can make the drive.

As Alkali Road bears south, it makes a gradual descent where it rounds the Alkali Creek Wilderness Study Area. This is one of the more interesting stretches along the drive as the land gains the color of juniper and limber pine trees while traveling through a mosaic of red cliffs, dry washes, ravines and canyons.

The scenic backway ends at Cold Springs Road near Hyattville. If this is your first time visiting the area, this drive should be just the beginning of your exploration. A left turn on Cold Springs Road will lead you to the Medicine Lodge Archaeological Site, just 5.5 miles to the east. At this state park, you can walk an interpretive trail, check out the small visitor center, and see petroglyphs on a sandstone wall.

Varied terrain in the Bighorn Basin

30: Castle Gardens/Nowater OHV Trail System
Explore the Bighorn Basin

☒ Backcountry Drive
Most vehicles

☒ 4WD Route
4x4 vehicle or ORV

☒ ATV Trail
ORV less than 50" wide

Location/Map	East of Worland; Page 143
Roads	BLMR 1435
Distance	5 miles to Castle Gardens (150+ miles of roads and ATV trails)
Managing Agency	BLM—Worland Field Office
Starting Coordinates	N44° 1.42' W107° 30.26'

Overview: The Nowater OHV Trail System consists of more than 150 miles of gravel trunk roads, secondary roads (two tracks), and ATV trails in the southeastern section of the Bighorn Basin. The trail system is located on both sides of HWY 16 between Worland and Ten Sleep. Be aware that a few routes travel through oil and gas fields where you may encounter higher volumes of traffic and infrastructure hazards, such as pipelines. In addition, some routes, including the one described here, are closed between November and April. Not all of the roads appear on published maps, but the BLM office in Worland offers a complete trail system map that is available on their website.

The short backcountry drive described here takes you to the Castle Gardens Scenic Area, likely the most popular natural attraction found in the trail system. Here, you'll find a fascinating geological area where sandstone has been shaped into unusual formations. Take note that there are no petroglyphs at this location, which is easily confused with the Castle Gardens petroglyph site located east of Riverton in Fremont County (route #12 in the Central chapter).

Start: From Ten Sleep, take HWY 16 west for 2 miles. Turn south and drive a short distance to reach the Old Tensleep Highway. Drive west for a mile and then turn south again onto BLMR 1435.

Description: From Old Tensleep Highway, drive south on the dirt lane, which is known as Two Mile Hill Road. This isn't the best of backcountry roads, but it is easily driven across the sage flat. Stay southbound when passing crossroads and follow the signs for 5 miles to reach the Castle Gardens Scenic Area. This developed recreation site consists of two campsites that are nestled within a geologically-intriguing bowl of sandstone that is peppered with juniper trees. Eroded by wind and water, the rock has been shaped into various toadstools, spires, and hoodoos.

If you want a longer backcountry drive, you can continue south on BLMR 1435 to reach Blue Bank Road (BLMR 1411). This route travels along the eastern side of the Honeycombs Wilderness Study Area and Big Cedar Ridge.

The road turns into BLMR 1410 about 22 miles south of Castle Gardens. From this point, the gravel route heads northwest to Nowater Trail Road (BLMR 1404) and ends 31 miles farther on the south side of Worland.

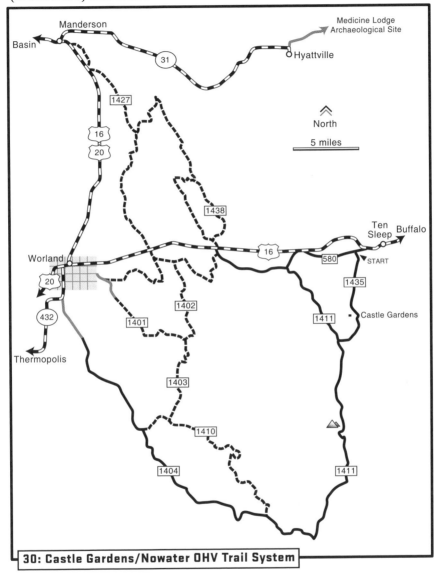

30: Castle Gardens/Nowater OHV Trail System

Unusual rock formations at Castle Gardens

Other Nearby Drives

Bighorn Canyon National Recreation Area—No trip through the Bighorn Basin is complete without a visit to this magnificent canyon on the Wyoming-Montana border. A paved road takes you to a marina, campground, hiking trails, historic ranches, and to Devils Canyon Overlook where you can stand on the rim of the canyon's 1,000-foot walls. During your visit, watch for bighorn sheep as well as wild horses, which roam the Pryor Mountain Wild Horse Range on the west side of the canyon. Visit the Bighorn Canyon Visitor Center in Lovell to learn more and also to find out about local four-wheeling routes. To reach the recreation area from Lovell, take HWY 14 ALT east for nearly 3 miles and turn north onto HWY 37.

Crystal Creek Road—This route utilizes BLMR 1129 and CR 68 to create a 32-mile gravel route that connects HWY 14 ALT near Lovell to HWY 14 near Greybull. From the north end, 14 miles east of Lovell, the road travels above the Bighorn River through a mix of sagebrush flats and irrigated pastures. Short of the halfway point, the road leaves the drainage and enters a colorful, rugged environment of bluffs and badlands. It then climbs to, and over, a monotonous bench of land before returning to rugged escarpments. A three-way junction at the south end gives you two finishing options: take Lane 33 west toward Greybull or turn left and follow the road through "Devils Kitchen" before reaching HWY 14.

Gooseberry Badlands Scenic Overlook—This roadside natural attraction offers a terrific display of the Bighorn Basin's colorful badland formations. There is also a 1.5-mile interpretive trail that can be hiked. To reach the overlook from Worland, drive south on HWY 20 for 8.5 miles. Turn west onto HWY 431 and drive 23 miles.

Boysen State Park—Located in the southwest corner of the region, this state park sits at the base of the rugged Owl Creek Mountains. The west side of the reservoir includes a couple dozen miles of backroads that follow the shoreline. These roads also access a few smaller reservoirs that are located just west of the state park. With sandy beaches and interesting rock outcrops and flora, you'll be set to take some worthwhile photographs. To reach the shoreline road from Shoshoni, drive west on HWY 26 for 5 miles and turn right.

Bighorn Canyon National Recreation Area in the Bighorn Basin

NORTHWEST

No words can adequately describe the natural splendor of northwest Wyoming. Yellowstone National Park—the nation's first—and Grand Teton National Park—possibly the most photographed—are so amazing, they draw millions of people each year from around the globe. Between the two, you'll find a land of unmatched beauty and diversity.

The grandeur of the region isn't confined to the park's boundaries. Rather, the abutting mountains bolster the national gems in both scenery and ecology. From the northern Beartooth Mountains southward to the Absaroka, Gros Ventre, and Wind River Ranges, you'll find the spirit of adventure in these very wild places.

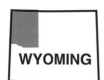

WYOMING

Northwest Areas

National Parks
Drives in and near the parks
10-18 (page 176)

Beartooth Mountains
Alpine high country
1-3 (page 149)

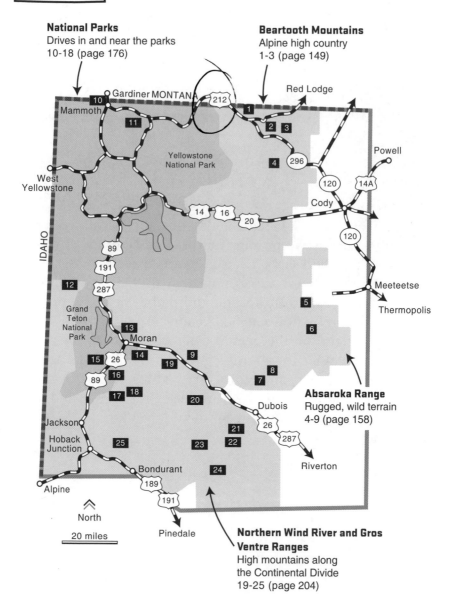

Gardiner MONTANA

Red Lodge

212

Mammoth

10

11

1

2   3

Yellowstone
National Park

4   296

Powell

West
Yellowstone

120   14A

14   16

Cody

20

120

IDAHO

89

191

12   287

Meeteetse

Grand
Teton
National
Park

13   Moran

5   Thermopolis

6

15   26   14

19   9

16   89   18

8

17   7

Absaroka Range
Rugged, wild terrain
4-9 (page 158)

20

Dubois

Jackson

26   287

Hoback
Junction

21

25   23   22

Bondurant

24

Riverton

Alpine

189

⌃⌃
North

191

20 miles

Pinedale

**Northern Wind River and Gros
Ventre Ranges**
High mountains along
the Continental Divide
19-25 (page 204)

Beartooth Mountains

The Beartooth Mountains straddle the Wyoming and Montana border just northeast of Yellowstone National Park. By Northern Rockies standards, this isn't a large range, but it is a high one. The Beartooths are home to Montana's highest point, Granite Peak (12,807 feet), as well as another 20 summits that exceed 12,000 feet. In Wyoming, just south of the high, glaciated, and snowcapped crags, you'll find expansive alpine meadows on top of the Beartooth Plateau. Geologists consider the granite that forms these mountains and plateaus to be among the most aged rock on the planet.

The Beartooth is a very diverse range that complements the balance of the greater Yellowstone ecosystem. Several hundred plant species grow here and a long list of wildlife can also be composed. Notable animals include bighorn sheep, mountain goats, wolverines, wolves, marmots, moose, elk, deer, mountain lions, and both black and grizzly bears.

Land Ownership

The Beartooth Mountains are managed by the Shoshone National Forest. Aside from a few isolated, out-of-the-way strips of private property that are clearly shown on Forest Service maps, these mountains are comprised of consolidated public land. The local Forest Service office is in Cody.

Roads and Trails

If you're thrilled by mountain views or engineering feats, you must take the drive along HWY 212, a designated national scenic byway known as the Beartooth Highway. The road steeply climbs out of southern Montana with a series of mountain-hugging switchbacks. At the top, the highway traverses the Beartooth Plateau while attaining a high point of 10,947 feet. Mountainous views at the top—replete with glaciers, valleys, lakes, and sprawling alpine meadows—are everywhere. Drive this road when it first opens in late May or early June and you'll find yourself driving between walls of snow that can be 20 feet tall.

The snow recedes by mid-summer, allowing a handful of 4WD routes to open (there are no designated ATV trails). Some of these rugged tracks cut across the tundra, others through forest. But they almost all end at a lake. Large rocks are likely to keep you at a crawling pace. There are also some very steep sections in these mountains. These are easy to handle on an ATV, but make for challenging ascents and descents in full-sized vehicles.

Seasons and Conditions

The driving season in the Beartooths is very short, around 12 weeks. Snow keeps most of the backroads closed until July 16. They then close again in October when the snow returns, though it can (and does) snow here every month of the year. You can plan on afternoon thunderstorms, which are frequent and predictable in these mountains. When the roads are open for the season, they are surprisingly dry—the sun at this altitude is quite intense.

Fuel

To the west of the Beartooths, fueling stations can be found in Yellowstone. On the other side of the range, you'll find stations in Cody and Red Lodge, Montana. There is also gas at the Top of the World Resort, located along the Beartooth Highway between Beartooth Lake and Island Lake.

Maps

Obtain the Shoshone National Forest (North Half) map or the Shoshone North Zone ORV map. Another great resource is the Forest's Motor Vehicle Use Map (MVUM).

1: Crazy Lakes
Scenic road to Lily Lake and Ivy Lake

☐ **Backcountry Drive**
Most vehicles

☒ **4WD Route**
4x4 vehicle or ORV

☐ **ATV Trail**
ORV less than 50" wide

Location/Map	Northwest of Cody; Page 151
Roads	FR 130, FR 130A, FR 130.1A
Distance	5.5 miles
Managing Agency	USDA Forest Service—Shoshone National Forest
Starting Coordinates	N44° 55.78' W109° 42.53'

Overview: This road begins with an easy drive to Lily Lake, which can be reached by most vehicles just a short distance from the highway. A 4WD route continues further to the edge of the secluded Absaroka Beartooth Wilderness where you can park and hike a short distance to Ivy Lake.

Take note that the Shoshone National Forest map shows this road as FR 128, while the MVUM shows it as FR 130. On the ground, the road sign simply reads "Crazy Lakes Jeep Road." The route is open to motorized use from May 21 to October 31, but July is a more realistic beginning for the driving season.

Start: From Cody, take HWY 120 north for 17 miles. Turn left onto HWY 296 and drive 47 miles. Turn east on HWY 212 and drive just short of 1 mile to the turnoff on the left. If you have ATVs to unload, drive north 1.5 miles on the gravel road to reach a suitable unloading area.

Description: The drive begins from the highway by climbing an open hill on a washboarded, gravel road. At 1.5 miles, the road reaches a fork at a popular parking area. To reach Lily Lake from this junction, turn right and drive a half mile on a bumpy road. The lake is popular for fishing and has a few dispersed campsites. There is a primitive boat ramp, but these waters are only open to non-motorized craft.

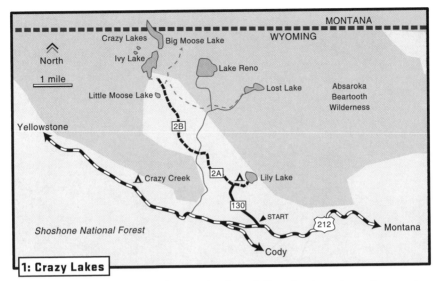

1: Crazy Lakes

To continue north toward Ivy Lake, bear left at the junction where a sign marks the Crazy Lakes Road. There is no singular characteristic of this road—it constantly changes between level and steep as it cuts through sagebrush, marshes, and pockets of timber. In the clearings, there are good views to the west of the area's most distinguishable landmarks: Pilot Peak (11,708 feet), a glacial horn, and its northern neighbor, Index Peak (11,313 feet). Where the road bores through forests of thick evergreens and berry shrubs, you'll find more challenging driving with rocks and mud.

At 3.7 miles, the road drops steeply to a crossing of Gilbert Creek (7 inches deep in August). Farther north, a side trail leads west to Little Moose Lake, a quiet little pond that is worth visiting.

Nearing the end, you pass through a burned-out forest that is now regenerating with short conifers. Then, after 5 miles, the path ends at the edge of a coniferous stand near the Absaroka Beartooth Wilderness boundary. Motorized travel is prohibited from this point, but a foot trail continues a half mile through a young forest to reach Ivy Lake, one of several high lakes collectively named Crazy Lakes.

Other Nearby Drives

Clay Butte Visitor Center—A 2.6-mile maintained gravel road, FR 142 travels uphill to reach this Forest Service facility at 9,811 feet. Once used as a fire lookout, this small tower is now staffed from July 1 through early September to offer visitors a full panorama of forests and snowcapped mountains.

To reach this road from Cody, take HWY 120 north for 17 miles. Turn left onto HWY 296 and drive 47 miles. Turn east on HWY 212 and drive nearly 8 miles to the turnoff on the left.

Marshy area near Crazy Lakes

2: Fantan Lake/Sawtooth Lake
Alpine lakes on the Beartooth Plateau

☐ **Backcountry Drive**
Most vehicles

☒ **4WD Route**
4x4 vehicle or ORV

☐ **ATV Trail**
ORV less than 50" wide

Location/Map	Northwest of Cody; Page 155
Roads	FR 149, FR 149.1A, FR 149.1B
Distance	7 miles of roads
Managing Agency	USDA Forest Service—Shoshone National Forest
Starting Coordinates	N44° 56.15' W109° 31.91'

Overview: This route includes three roads that spread out over an alpine plateau in the Beartooth Mountains. Two of the roads travel to lakes, while a third climbs a ridge where the best views of the mountain peaks await. All these roads can be driven in unmodified 4x4s, though some vacationers may not want to abuse their daily drivers. Much of this area is covered by snow through the early summer, but the road is open for the summer season on July 16.

Start: From Cody, take HWY 120 north for 17 miles. Turn left onto HWY 296 and drive 47 miles. Turn east on HWY 212 and drive 12.5 miles. If you have ATVs to unload, there are a couple of suitable unloading areas less than a mile south of the highway.

Description: From the highway, follow the narrow, but well-maintained, road south for less than a mile to a junction with FR 1B. This secondary 1.7-mile track climbs a treeless ridge to the west where you'll gain terrific views. To the north are the Beartooth Mountains' highest crags. To the west are the Absaroka, including the unmistakable Index Peak and Pilot Peak. Because of the broad vista, this road is popular for dispersed camping.

Continuing south on the main road for another tenth of a mile, you'll reach a fork. The road to the right is FR 1A, a rougher 1-mile track that ends at Fantan Lake, a sizable tarn that is frequented by anglers. The road has one tiny ford, but plenty of small rocks.

The road that bears left at the fork, FR 149, continues southward along the west side of Chain Lakes. A mile farther, the maintained roadway gives way to a rugged 4WD trail that becomes quite rocky. There is also a pair of rough crossings where small creeks drain into Chain Lakes. Pickup trucks and SUVs make this trip all the time, but it's slow going.

At 3.7 miles from the highway, the road reaches the top of a wooded ridge with Sawtooth Lake visible a short distance to the east. From this point, the road drops steeply, making for a fun climb on the return trip. Past this, the road continues a short distance and ends at Sawtooth Lake at 4.1 miles. This lake, one of the Beartooths' largest, sits in a depression just west of jagged Sawtooth Mountain (10,262 feet).

Road leading to Fantan Lake

3: Morrison Trail
Top of the Beartooths to the bottom

☐ **Backcountry Drive**
Most vehicles

☒ **4WD Route**
4x4 vehicle or ORV

☐ **ATV Trail**
ORV less than 50" wide

Location/Map	Northwest of Cody; Page 155
Roads	FR 120, FR 119
Distance	22 miles
Managing Agency	USDA Forest Service—Shoshone National Forest
Starting Coordinates	N44° 56.46' W109° 30.30'

Overview: Not many four-wheeling routes in Wyoming can rival those found in Colorado or Utah, but the Morrison Trail is one that does. This 4WD road takes you from the high alpine meadows of the Beartooth Mountains to the mouth of the Clarks Fork Canyon at the base of the mountain range. The difference in elevation between the high and low points is a whopping 5,630 feet. With steep grades, white-knuckle drop-offs, and challenging terrain, this route should only be driven by experienced drivers with a customized 4x4 or ATV. To help protect wildlife and soil, this road is only open from July 16 until October (depending on snow).

Start: To reach the northern access point from Cody, take HWY 120 north for 17 miles. Turn left onto HWY 296 and drive 47 miles. Turn east on HWY 212 and drive 14 miles to the parking area.

To reach the southern access point from Cody, take HWY 120 north for 29.3 miles. Turn west toward Clark and drive 11.5 miles to the parking lot at the end of the paved road.

Description: From HWY 212 at nearly 9,700 feet, the Morrison Trail heads south across the Beartooth Plateau with many of Montana's highest mountain peaks visible to the north. The two-track cuts through grassy alpine meadows pocketed with glacial lakes and small stands of spruce and fir. There are just enough large rocks embedded in the dirt path to warrant a slow and cautious pace.

Chain Lakes, two connected tarns, are passed within the first 2 miles. You can sometimes see vehicles on the west side of the lake, but these are traveling on a separate road (FR 149). As the road turns east away from Chain Lakes, it passes south of Dollar Lake. This is about as far as most unmodified 4x4s go.

Top Lake is reached at mile 3. The pyramid-shaped mountain seen across the water is Tibbs Butte (10,673 feet). From the lake, the road climbs a short, wooded ridge before reaching Sawtooth Meadows. Large rock slabs are encountered along the way, but they only pose problems to vehicles with poor approach or departure angles—not ATVs.

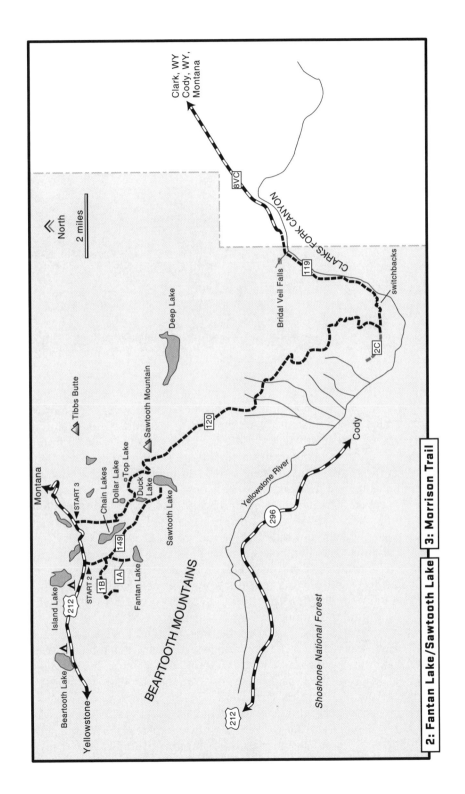

North

2 miles

Montana

Island Lake

Beartooth Lake

Yellowstone

212

START 2

1B

1A

START 3

149

Fantan Lake

Chain Lakes

Dollar Lake

Top Lake

Duck Lake

Sawtooth Lake

Sawtooth Mountain

Tibbs Butte

Deep Lake

BEARTOOTH MOUNTAINS

212

Shoshone National Forest

Yellowstone River

296

Cody

120

Bridal Veil Falls

119

2C

switchbacks

CLARKS FORK CANYON

8VC

Clark, WY
Cody, WY,
Montana

2: Fantan Lake/Sawtooth Lake—**3: Morrison Trail**

Upper section of the Morrison Trail

The Morrison Trail passes by the west side of Sawtooth Mountain (10,252 feet) in mile 4. This rocky crest is well deserving of its name, and you'll recognize it without question. Past this mountain, a slightly improved road travels across a treeless upland over the next 3 miles while attaining a high point of over 10,100 feet. On this stretch, you can peer down into the wooded drainages where the mountain falls away. Unrestricted views of the Absaroka Range are found to the west and south, including the well-known Sunlight Basin and the Dead Indian Hill areas.

At 7.5 miles, the course begins to descend and it enters a spotty forest a half mile farther. Three small streams are crossed near their headwaters within the next couple of miles. These include two forks of Dutch Charlie Creek and Barrs Creek. At the last crossing, the road cuts through the dark timber for another mile and then emerges at the Upper Dillworth Bench, an open ridge. Continue southward through this bench, along the edge of the mountain, for 2 miles. The beautiful Clarks Fork Canyon is far below, wrapping around the mountain like a horseshoe.

After passing a couple of spurs on the right, the track reaches an elevation of 8,500 feet near 13 miles. The elevation here is of particular interest because nearly half of it is going to be lost within the next 4 miles. The steep drop begins as the sometimes very rocky road tunnels through a south-facing forested slope for 1.5 miles. This is followed by another mile of downhill without trees before reaching a junction at 15.5 miles. Stay left at the fork.

The next 2 miles is what really makes the Morrison Trail unique. From the fork, drive a short distance to reach the rim of Clarks Fork Canyon. Here, you'll find nearly two dozen switchbacks, incredibly tight turns that cut into the side of the mountain. The upper switchbacks are so tight and narrow that full-sized vehicles will have to either make several-point turns to change directions or drive down some switchbacks in reverse gear. Loose rocks, an overall grade of 26%, and a severe drop-off are all reasons why this segment should only be attempted by experienced drivers in short, capable, customized vehicles. It can take over an hour to tackle this stretch.

The final switchback rolls out to the bottom of Clarks Fork Canyon. Here, the road turns to the north-northeast and follows the Clarks Fork of the Yellowstone River—a large waterway that drains much of Wyoming's Beartooth Mountains and has earned the Congressional designation as a wild and scenic river. From your new position along the river, you can now fully appreciate the incredible scale of this country. Rock spires and walls rise up to four thousand feet over the drainage. Perhaps the only thing more amazing is that there is a road that climbs out of it.

Much of the remaining road through the canyon—4.5 miles left—is narrow and very rocky. Many of the unknowing 4x4 drivers who start up through the canyon from this end get just a half mile in before they turn back, exhausted from the constant jolting. Even on an ATV, the going can be slow and your machine will take a pounding. Perhaps the most scenic part of the canyon is Cyclone Bar, a wide gravel bar that is peppered with huge boulders. This area is a real natural treasure and you can help keep it that way by staying on the defined path that cuts across the bar.

Past Cyclone Bar, the road turns rocky again. As you near the end of the trip, watch for Bridal Veil Falls where Falls Creek flows over the mountainside on the left. The trip ends a little over a mile farther at HWY 292 near Clark.

Lower section of the Morrison Trail in Clarks Fork Canyon

Absaroka Range

The Absaroka Range (commonly said as ab-sor-ka, but more properly pronounced as ab-sar-o-ka) is a large mountain range that makes a shallow arc from southern Montana, across the eastern side of Yellowstone National Park, and southward toward Dubois. The lofty volcanic range rises to a high point of 13,153 feet at Francs Peak west of Meeteetse and boasts nearly four dozen other summits that are above 12,000 feet. Flat, butte-like tops make for unique skylines and deep, narrow valleys are towered by impressive uprising slopes.

With expansive tracts of pristine wilderness, the Absaroka region is often called the wildest country in the Lower 48. While it's difficult to validate the claim—and everyone uses different criteria anyway—it's easy to recognize why the area would be considered for such a worthy title. This is a part of the Rocky Mountains that truly retains its natural character—predators like grizzlies and wolves roam at will and the skyscraping summits stand void of climbers or cars. This is awesome, raw country that demands respect.

Land Ownership

The county roads that lead up to the Absaroka Range run through and next to private property. Most of the mountains themselves are on the Shoshone National Forest, public land that is largely consolidated. When it's not, private property (such as a ranch) is usually quite obvious making the risk of trespassing quite low. The local Forest Service office is in Cody.

Roads and Trails

The Absaroka Range has three scenic highways: HWY 296 (Chief Joseph Scenic Byway) to the north, HWY 14/16/20 (Buffalo Bill Scenic Highway) through the middle, and HWY 26/287 (Centennial Scenic Byway) to the south. Most of these mountains are designated as wilderness, so backroads are few. If it weren't for the area's mining history, there would be even fewer. The routes described here begin east or south of the mountain range (the west side borders Yellowstone National Park) and have wide, gravel surfaces. But if you're going to climb far into these giant mountains, you will need an ATV or a capable 4WD rig that can handle steep, rocky terrain and stream crossings. As of this writing, there were no designated ATV trails in the area.

Seasons and Conditions

There is no single restriction or closure schedule that covers all of the roads in this area. Depending on the specific need—such as protecting grizzly bear habitat—you'll find a tailored closure for each route. The Forest Service ORV trail map is the best place to look for this information.

In general, roads at the lower elevations open by late May or June. If you're heading to elevations above 8,000 feet, you'll often be waiting until July for the snow to recede and the gates to be opened. Even when the higher roads do initially open, stream crossings may remain too swift or high for a safe ford. For these reasons, August and September are terrific months to visit the Absaroka. Roads begin to close between October and December.

Fuel
On the north end of the area, you'll find service stations in Cody and Powell. To the south, you'll want to fuel up in Dubois or at one of the stations near Togwotee Pass. If you're somewhere in between on HWY 120, your options will be Meeteetse or Thermopolis.

Maps
For general navigation in the lower elevations, use a statewide atlas such as the DeLorme Wyoming Atlas & Gazetteer or the Wyoming Road & Recreation Atlas published by Benchmark Maps. These clearly show the county roads and their junctions. For national forest roads, obtain the Shoshone National Forest (North Half) map, Shoshone North Zone ORV map, or Shoshone Motor Vehicle Use Map (MVUM).

4: Sunlight Basin
Motor into Wyoming's wildest country

☒ **Backcountry Drive** Most vehicles	☒ **4WD Route** 4x4 vehicle or ORV	☐ **ATV Trail** ORV less than 50" wide

Location/Map	Northwest of Cody; Page 161
Roads	CR 7GQ, FR 101, FR 108, FR 101.3l
Distance	35 miles of roads (last 19 miles require 4WD)
Managing Agency	USDA Forest Service—Shoshone National Forest
Starting Coordinates	N44° 45.87' W109° 25.50'

Overview: This beautiful drive burrows deep into the northern Absaroka Range to a historical mining district that is surrounded on three sides by the North Absaroka Wilderness. The first dozen miles can be driven in any vehicle and is a very worthwhile side trip off the Chief Joseph Scenic Byway (HWY 296). A 4x4 vehicle or ATV is needed to navigate further. A stock 4x4 will get you to Lee City, a good destination where you'll find cabin ruins.

The western ends of these roads (beyond mile 17) are only open to motorized use from July 16 to September 30, creating a driving season that is measured in weeks, not months. To see these roads to their ends, you'll want to be an experienced off-roader with a custom 4x4 or ATV that can handle steep grades and loose rock. The Forest Service employees with whom I spoke described the entire area as treacherous and discouraged visitor use into the far western reaches of this very remote and wild country.

Westbound in Sunlight Basin

Start: From Cody, take HWY 120 north for 17 miles. Turn left onto HWY 296 and drive 23 miles. Turn onto Sunlight Road (CR 7GQ/FR 101).

Description: From the highway, the wide gravel road heads west toward a distant blue mountain ridge often capped with snow. But it's the mountains in the foreground that are likely to catch your attention—particularly White Mountain (8,772 feet) that is seen on the right. This incredibly rugged and steep land feature is crowned with rock spires that stab the sky. Before you pass the mountain by mile 4, watch for a side road that heads north a short distance to a scenic overlook of Sunlight Falls.

The following few miles are easily driven as the backroad passes private cabins and ranches with irrigated pastures. A Wyoming Game and Fish trailhead is then passed, followed by the Sunlight Ranger Station at 7.5 miles.

From the Forest Service station, the road turns northward where a bridge spans beautiful Sunlight Creek, a popular destination for anglers fishing for brook trout. Steer your way over the bridge and around a strip of lush pasture land where stunning mountain views are revealed. From this point, you can spot the snowy crags of the North Absaroka Wilderness. Soon after, the pot-holed road reaches Little Sunlight Campground where you'll also find a wilderness trailhead.

The road narrows after the campground as it climbs out of the basin and into more timbered terrain. Some sections have a dirt surface that can get

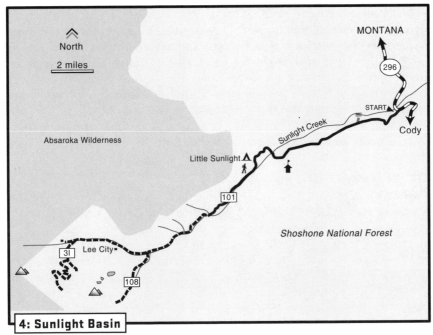

4: Sunlight Basin

muddy in wet weather. Sunlight Creek now flows along the left side, its gravel bars striking a strong Alaskan resemblance.

If you're not driving a 4x4, consider turning around by mile 16 as fords of Gas Creek and Spring Creek are a short distance ahead. The end of the maintained road, which is partially graveled, ends within the next 2 miles at Spring Creek where a gate is used to enforce a seasonal closure to protect grizzly bear habitat. The 4WD track that follows is open from July 16 through September 30.

At 18.5 miles, the route reaches a junction at the base of mountains that tower thousands of feet overhead. The lesser path, FR 108, crosses the mushy gravel bars of Sunlight Creek and then heads south through a wooded valley along Sulfur Creek. The track crosses creeks and climbs steeply for several miles, gaining elevation through some of Wyoming's most rugged mountains. It ends amidst glacier-pocketed mountains that include unforgettable peaks such as Stinkingwater Peak (11,597 feet) and Sunlight Peak (11,922 feet).

The more popular route is taken by staying straight at the junction and driving west for 1.5 miles to a swift and rocky ford of Sunlight Creek. On the other side of this crossing is Lee City, an abandoned mining area that still has a few remaining log structures. Lee City is the most common place to turn around for those who have ventured this far. From the ghost town, the 4WD road continues west for 3 more miles until it reaches the site of the Painter Cabin, which is also just 3 miles east of the Yellowstone National Park boundary. This was the home of John R. Painter, a very successful settler from Philadelphia who owned and operated several nearby mines.

Just east of the cabin site, a secondary 4WD road, 3I, cuts south into a dying evergreen forest and makes an aggressive climb over the next 6 miles to reach a gorgeous alpine world of rock, ice, and a panorama of peaks. This is where the mines operated by Mr. Painter were located. Commonly found under snow, this distant track makes an adventurous dance across steep mountain ridges full of talus—it ends in Silvertip Basin. Nobody would put roads through terrain like this unless there was money in it, which in this case came in the form of ore that held copper, gold, silver, and lead. These last segments are not routes for the casual off-roader.

Other Nearby Drives

Deer Creek—A paved highway and gravel backroad make for an easy and scenic tour to the Deer Creek area southwest of Cody. From Cody, take South Fork Road (HWY 291) south for 33 miles. This paved course travels around the south side of Buffalo Bill Reservoir and then follows the South Fork of the Shoshone River upstream into the Shoshone National Forest. From the forest boundary, FR 479, a gravel road, continues another 9.5 miles through a valley that is surrounded on three sides by the Washakie Wilderness. The best place to stop along the road is Deer Creek campground, a roadside camp that doubles as an ideal picnic site. The camp is located just 2 miles from the end of road.

5: Jack Creek/Phelps Mountain
Reach the edge of the mighty Absaroka

☒ **Backcountry Drive** Most vehicles	☒ **4WD Route** 4x4 vehicle or ORV	☐ **ATV Trail** ORV less than 50" wide

Location/Map	Southwest of Cody; Page 165
Roads	CR 4IX, CR YIX, FR 207, FR 207.2C
Distance	31 miles (13.5 miles may require 4WD)
Managing Agency	USDA Forest Service—Shoshone National Forest, other mixed ownership
Starting Coordinates	N44° 5.49' W109° 3.28'

Overview: This route travels from the genuinely western town of Meeteetse and heads west through ranch land and oil fields. Following the Greybull River upstream, it climbs to the foot of Carter Mountain on the eastern side of the Absaroka Range. From here, you can climb higher on a steep 4WD road that traverses Phelps Mountain. You'll reach exposed heights well above timberline where there are unsurpassed views of the Absaroka Range.

Some stretches pass through private property, so be sure to stay on the main road. You'll appreciate this drive much more if you first tour the most-excellent museum in Meeteetse to learn more about the area.

Start: From Thermopolis, drive 53 miles northwest on HWY 120 to Meeteetse. You can also reach this town by driving south of Cody on the same highway for 28 miles. At Meeteetse, take HWY 290 west for 11 miles to the end of the highway.

Description: The backroad begins from a fork where the highway ends and CR 4IX begins at a gate near Pappapau Butte. Stay right and continue west on Pitchfork Ranch Road. There are many junctions and forks that follow, but you can easily stay on course by following the signs to Jack Creek.

This stretch follows the lush Greybull River corridor while traveling through Wyoming's historical Pitchfork Ranch. A German emigrant named Otto Franc started this ranch in 1878 and it is said that the legendary outlaw Butch Cassidy stole his first horse from this cattle rancher. About a hundred years later, the protected black-footed ferret was discovered in this valley, and the ranch played an important role in keeping the rare mammal from becoming extinct.

Continue west, bypassing three major roads that branch off both sides of the road. Past mile 9, Pitchfork Ranch Road comes to a fork at the Four Bear Oil Field. Bear left and drive around the south side of the hilly industrial field. The side road leading to Phelps Mountain is reached to the south in mile 12.

SIDE
TRIP

The last 5 miles of the main road travel across a dusty landscape peppered with side spurs and oil tanks. The road becomes rougher as it gains on the sparsely timbered foothills. It draws parallel to the Greybull River and then ends at Jack Creek Campground and Trailhead just inside the Shoshone National Forest boundary. The overgrown camp sees little use outside of hunting season, but it's a scenic little retreat at the base of Carter Mountain and a ridge of distinctive cylinder-shaped rock caps. The trailhead offers non-motorized access into the untamed Washakie Wilderness, which is perhaps best explored by horseback. The willow-lined Greybull River, as well as Jack Creek which flows into it, provide fishing opportunities for Yellowstone cutthroat trout and mountain whitefish. The river usually flows clear by late June.

For the 4WD portion of this drive, head south on Phelps Mountain Road (near the petroleum tanks and work site). Drive past numerous drilling pads, bearing right onto FR 207. Seemingly easy at first, the road soon becomes strewn with rocks, some the size of footballs. If you're in a full size vehicle, shift into 4WD as this rock is found on a very steep incline that reaches a 23% grade. With hood to the sky, negotiate past a few tight turns to reach more level ground above a huge rock spire.

By 3 miles, the lion's share of elevation—about 2,100 feet—has been gained and the road becomes smoother as it crosses a stunning alpine landscape. The driving now becomes relatively easy as the dirt path cuts a course up

Mountainous skyline at Phelps Mountain

the northern slope of Phelps Mountain. As the last several hundred feet of elevation are gained, the views become increasingly impressive. Sunshine Reservoir comes into view to the east. To the north is Carter Mountain. In all other directions, the skyline is filled with overlapping ridgelines of mountain peaks, dozens of them, that top 11,000 and 12,000 feet. Directly below, you'll see small stands of charred evergreens that burned in the summer of 2006. Just shy of 5 miles, the road passes beneath the 10,788-foot summit of Phelps Mountain.

A junction marked by a dilapidated wooden sign is reached 5 miles from the start of this road. The road splits directions here and both routes eventually dead end. The road going right to the north, FR 2C, switchbacks downhill to Jack Creek Cow Camp, a historical cattle camp still used by ranchers. This road ends after 3 miles when it reaches a pack trail along Jack Creek.

The 5-mile track going south is the more impressive and challenging of the two routes. This road continues along the treeless crest, a full 1,000 feet above the Jack Creek drainage (not a place to be driving if you don't like heights). The road surface is initially easy to drive as it continues south along the mountain's rim, but becomes more rugged before ending at an overlook at 11,050 feet. Directly south of this rise is a towering summit of 12,490 feet. To the right of that point is what is known as the Gold Reef Tunnel—an old mining district located within a deep mountain cirque. And in the background, you'll find Francs Peak (13,153 feet), the highest peak in the Absaroka Range. If you make it to the end here—even to the first junction 5 miles prior—you'll recognize this as a very special place.

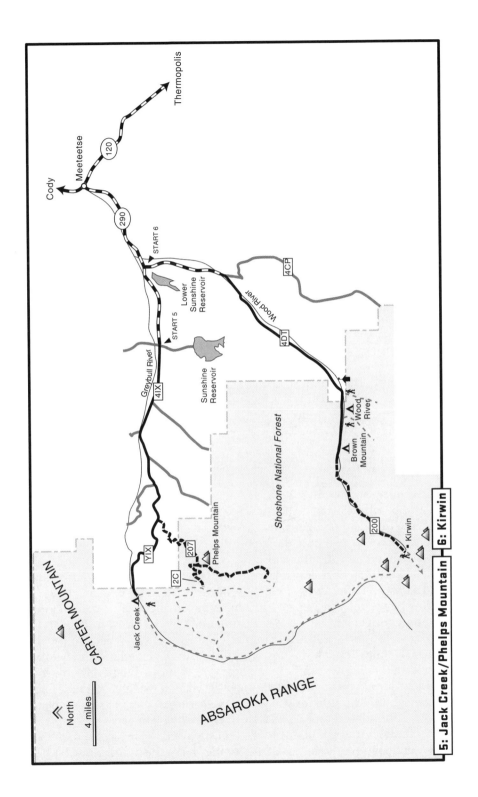

North

4 miles

CARTER MOUNTAIN

ABSAROKA RANGE

Cody

Meeteetse

290

120

Thermopolis

START 6

Lower
Sunshine
Reservoir

START 5

Greybull River

Sunshine
Reservoir

41X

Wood River

4CP

4DT

Y1X

2C

207

Phelps Mountain

Shoshone National Forest

Jack Creek

Brown
Mountain

Wood
River

200

Kirwin

5: Jack Creek/Phelps Mountain | **6: Kirwin**

6: Kirwin

Ghost town surrounded by postcard scenery

☒ Backcountry Drive
Most vehicles

☒ 4WD Route
4x4 vehicle or ORV

☐ ATV Trail
ORV less than 50" wide

Location/Map	Southwest of Cody; Page 165
Roads	CR 4DT, FR 200
Distance	27.5 miles (last 7.5 miles may require 4WD)
Managing Agency	USDA Forest Service—Shoshone National Forest
Starting Coordinates	N43° 56.14' W109° 10.75'

Overview: This exciting route runs deep into the Absaroka Range west of Meeteetse. The road is suitable for all vehicles for the first 20 miles, but a 4WD vehicle, or a skilled backcountry driver, is needed after that in order to reach Kirwin, a ghost town.

The road is closed to ATVs that only have ORV permits, but licensed ATVs are allowed. The 4WD section of the road is passable from July through September. Any earlier than this and you'll encounter snow and fords that are too deep to safely cross.

Start: From Thermopolis, drive 53 miles northwest on HWY 120 to Meeteetse. You can also reach this town by driving south of Cody on the same highway for 28 miles. From Meeteetse, drive west on HWY 290 for 7 miles and turn left onto Wood River Road (CR 4DT).

Description: From the highway, drive south on CR 4DT, which is paved for the first few miles as it passes east of Lower Sunshine Reservoir. The paved surface turns to gravel as the road follows the Wood River along pastures favored by whitetail deer. The backroad imperceptibly climbs here, drawing closer to the lightly-timbered foothills of the Absaroka Range.

Near mile 15, you pass the Wood River Guard Station, a Forest Service work center. You enter the Shoshone National Forest within another mile and it's here that the county road turns into FR 200. Wood River campground and a pair of trailheads are found just inside the forest boundary.

Brown Mountain campground, the larger of the area's two developed camps, is reached at 18.5 miles. Dwarfed by lofty summits such as Francs Peak (13,153 feet), this little camp offers plenty of visual appeal. It's also situated along the banks of the river, which come alive at dusk with wildlife. Spend an evening here and you might spot deer, moose, and a few imposing shadows as other critters move through the waning twilight. You'll be finely rewarded if this is as far as you get on the backroad, but the real dividends come to the adventurous who tackle the following 9 miles.

From the campground, the road climbs a treeless slope above the Wood River drainage. A side spur is reached at the end of the next 2 miles. It's here

Towering mounts in the Kirwin area

where road conditions noticeably worsen as the dirt track dips into a small creek. This is an easy crossing in front of the Double D Ranch site, which was opened in the 1930s and once visited by Amelia Earhart. Just past the ranch, the road reaches a ford of the Wood River, which often flows more than 12 inches deep in August. This is the deepest ford along the drive, so if you can make this one you can almost certainly make the others.

From the river, the road skirts past a mountain park on a gravel bar-like surface that weaves between the trees. The path is rocky, but easily crossed when driven carefully.

By mile 23, the road crosses back to the river's north side and advances into a very deep mountain valley. A handful of other stream crossings soon follow, but all of these are of lesser tributaries that flow into the Wood River.

The next few miles cover spectacular country. While the narrow road cuts into a hillside above the river, it passes below enormous mountain peaks and talus slopes. Soaring summits are everywhere, making this one of Wyoming's prettiest and most unique motorized routes. In this state, roads rarely penetrate such wilds.

By mile 27, ruins can be seen on the downhill side of the road—these are remains from a mining era that peaked in 1906. Although you can't see them from the road, the uphill side of the mountain along Canyon Creek is stacked with old mines.

The road ends at a parking area where you'll find interpretive signs, a trailhead, and a vault toilet. This is the site of Kirwin, a gold-mining ghost town situated at 9,200 feet. By 1906, there were more than 200 people living here among nearly 40 buildings. Then disaster struck. In the winter of 1907, over 50 feet of snow—feet, not inches—fell over the course of just nine days. The heavy accumulation triggered a massive avalanche off Brown Mountain, the towering 12,161-foot mountain that stands to the northwest. Three people died in the slide, which proved to be too much for the town. When spring came, people moved out, or evacuated rather, and never returned.

You can access the existing structures of the townsite by crossing a footbridge near the parking area. If you want to see more, consider walking up the closed road (past a locked gate) to reach the Dollar Cabin and the foundation of Amelia Earhart's home, which was never completed.

7: Burroughs Creek Loop
A loop through the southern Absaroka

☐ **Backcountry Drive**
Most vehicles

☒ **4WD Route**
4x4 vehicle or ORV

☐ **ATV Trail**
ORV less than 50" wide

Location/Map	North of Dubois; Page 170
Roads	FR 510, FR 504
Distance	12+ miles
Managing Agency	USDA Forest Service—Shoshone National Forest
Starting Coordinates	N43° 40.04' W109° 38.60'

Overview: This drive makes a rugged loop through the lower Absaroka Range outside of Dubois. Virgin Lake is passed along the main route and several other beautiful lakes are located at the end of short side spurs. You'll need a 4WD vehicle, preferably a narrow one, to complete this route. Though the roads are shown on some maps as being improved, I found them to be somewhat rocky and deeply rutted, necessitating the need for the heavy-duty drivetrain and ground clearance of a 4WD vehicle.

Start: From Dubois, turn north onto Horse Creek Road (FR 285) and drive short of 11 miles. This is the west end of the loop. The eastern end of the road is found over a mile farther past Horse Creek Campground. There are numerous places along FR 285 where ATVs can be unloaded.

Description: To begin the loop from the west, turn north off Horse Creek Road onto FR 510. The road immediately begins climbing into the mountains, beginning in mostly open terrain but soon entering a thick coniferous forest. The badly rutted route is full of kinks and tight curves on the ascent.

ALTERNATE ROUTE You can also start this drive from FR 511, which starts on Horse Creek Road just west of FR 510. This is a decent gravel road that showcases the area's beautiful mountain views. Use FR 512 or FR 1B (4WD routes) to tie into FR 510 and continue on with the main loop. This alternative route will add between 5 and 7 miles to the overall length.

At 4.8 miles, a spur signed as 1E branches off to the left. If you have a narrow 4WD vehicle or ATV, be sure to take this short half-mile track to the edge of Ramshorn Lakes. This is perhaps the most scenic lake in the area, in part because there is an excellent view over the water of Ramshorn Peak (11,635 feet).

Continuing along the main loop, the road bears east and reaches another side road that leads to tiny Rainbow Lake at 5.4 miles. This rough, short trail descends to the timbered, unimpressive shoreline of the pond. Another small pool, Virgin Lake, is passed along the main road at 6 miles. At 9,200 feet, this is also the high point of the loop.

From Virgin Lake, FR 510 continues east past an area cleared by logging, and then turns north. Watch for side roads at 7.5 and 8 miles that lead to Burnt Timber Lake and Deacon Lake Trailhead, respectively. From this northern tip of the loop, the views to the northeast are remarkable. The sprawling mountain on the horizon is Havely Rock Garden. The two impressive landmarks next to the mountain include the tower known as Cathedral Peak (11,182 feet) and the soaring spires of Lincoln Point.

Ramshorn Lakes along the Burroughs Creek Loop

After 8 miles, the route turns to the south where it begins a steady descent along a much improved surface that is easily driven. The next 4 miles pass below a steep slope of beetle-killed evergreens. The loop ends by crossing over Horse Creek and then skirting the side of private property to rejoin Horse Creek Road.

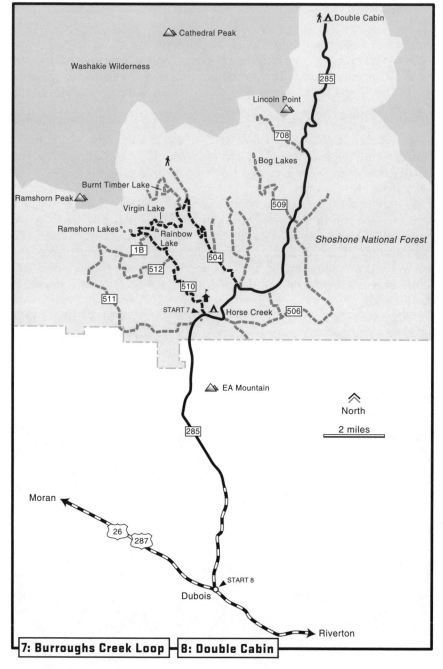

7: Burroughs Creek Loop   8: Double Cabin

8: Double Cabin
A remote mountain paradise

☒ **Backcountry Drive**
  Most vehicles

☐ **4WD Route**
  4x4 vehicle or ORV

☐ **ATV Trail**
  ORV less than 50" wide

Location/Map	North of Dubois; Page 170
Roads	FR 285
Distance	25 miles
Managing Agency	USDA Forest Service—Shoshone National Forest
Starting Coordinates	N43° 32.03' W109° 38.01'

Overview: This drive is just one of a few roads that enters the southern mountains of the Absaroka Range. Curvy and bumpy in places, the road takes you through beautiful scenery that never stops. The drive ends at a Forest Service campground and trailhead.

Start: From Dubois, turn north onto Horse Creek Road (FR 285).

Description: From Dubois, drive north on the paved road for 4 miles to a well-maintained gravel surface. The road turns to the northwest and follows Little Horse Creek upstream past a number of ranches and around EA Mountain (8,494 feet), visible to the east.

The backroad enters the Shoshone National Forest at 9 miles. Scott's Pond—a small fishing hole—is passed a mile farther, followed by Horse Creek Campground near mile 11. This scenic and popular camp is nestled up against the rugged foothills. As the road heads into a meadow east of the campground, you'll cross Horse Creek and pass through private property (stay on the road and bear right at the junction with FR 504). Tall peaks can be seen further to the north, a hint of the scenery to come.

As the road advances north and gains elevation, it travels through a light aspen and pine forest with sagebrush ground cover. At 19 miles, Cartridge Creek is crossed and the pointed rock spires of Lincoln Point, the tail of a larger mountain, are clearly seen to the northwest. The terrain is steeper here and there are several switchbacks to mitigate the grade.

Continue north through a thickening pine forest to draw parallel with a massive 11,700-foot mountain that creates a geological amphitheater. Only a mile away, the rugged cliffs rise thousands of feet above the road.

The main road ends at a trailhead near Double Cabin Campground in an incredibly scenic valley where you have a panoramic view of the Absaroka Range and Washakie Wilderness. In almost all directions, you'll find a slew of unnamed high points that stand over 11,000 feet. This valley serves as the confluence of Frontier Creek and Wiggins Fork and their broad gravel bars cover a broad path through the vale.

The name Double Cabin refers to ruins that are located on the other side of Frontier Creek. There are a few short, rough paths that branch off along the creek.

Mountain splendor at the end of Forest Road 285

Other Nearby Drives

Horse Creek Basin—Just east of Horse Creek Campground, FR 285.1A splits off and heads east. This 4WD road continues east along the fringe of the Shoshone National Forest before turning north and re-connecting to FR 285 after 6.5 miles. The road passes through an arid, badland-like landscape before wrapping around Horse Creek Basin. Be aware that there is some private land in the area.

East Fork—East Fork Road (FR 277) and Bear Creek Road offer a couple dozen miles of easy backcountry driving through the interesting country northeast of Dubois. Highlights of these roads include beautiful rivers and colorful bluffs. It also provides access to the Spence/Moriarity and Kirk Inberg/Kevin Roy Wildlife Habitat Management Areas. A number of rugged and steep 4WD tracks connect to the main routes, providing a large area to explore.

To start, drive east of Dubois on HWY 26/287 for 10 miles to the turnoff on the left. Drive north to reach a trailhead in the Shoshone National Forest or turn onto the Bear Creek Road near mile 10 to find some of the rougher tracks and primitive campgrounds.

Whiskey Mountain—Two roads explore the area southeast of Dubois, best known for its bighorn sheep winter range. From Dubois, drive east on HWY 26/287 for 3.5 miles to a turnoff on the right. Keep left at the initial fork and follow FR 411 south into Whiskey Basin. Here, a 4WD road branches off and climbs steeply to Torrey Rim on the east flank of Whiskey Mountain (11,157 feet). For the easier route, stay left on FR 411 and follow it past a series of lakes and primitive Wyoming Game & Fish campgrounds. Roadside interpretive signs describe the area and the bighorn sheep that call it home. The road ends at a trailhead on the Shoshone National Forest boundary.

9: Brooks Lake
Get up close to the Breccia cliffs

☒ **Backcountry Drive**
  Most vehicles

☒ **4WD Route**
  4x4 vehicle or ORV

☐ **ATV Trail**
  ORV less than 50" wide

Location/Map	Northwest of Dubois; Page 174
Roads	FR 515
Distance	9.2 miles (last 4.6 miles may require 4WD)
Managing Agency	USDA Forest Service—Shoshone National Forest
Starting Coordinates	N43° 42.39' W109° 57.92'

Overview: Though short, the road to Brooks Lake makes a spectacular backcountry drive. Towering pinnacles and a beautiful mountain lake are among the natural features that will keep your camera clicking. The gravel portion of the road ends at the lake. From there, the dirt driving surface is narrow, often rutted, and should never be attempted in wet conditions as it has a very steep drop-off.

Start: From Dubois, head west on HWY 26/287 for 23 miles to FR 515.

Description: Before you begin this drive, be sure to visit Falls Campground on the south side of HWY 26/287. There, you'll find a tall cascade and a terrific mountain overlook. When you're done there, drive to FR 515 and follow it north into a subalpine forest. The first 3 miles of the drive take on an uphill grade as the road climbs to 9,000 feet. Have your camera ready. There are a number of small meadows along the way that are sometimes laden with wildflowers. Towering high over the trees on the right are jagged spires known as the Pinnacle Buttes.

At 3.7 miles, the road passes a trailhead on the right side of the road. The route then bears west and reaches a junction a half mile farther. Stay left and cross Brooks Lake Creek (a right turn leads to another trailhead). Soon after, the road reaches another fork. To the right is Pinnacles Campground. To the left is Brooks Lake Campground. Unless you're looking for a campsite, turn left and go toward Brooks Lake Campground to reach a parking lot.

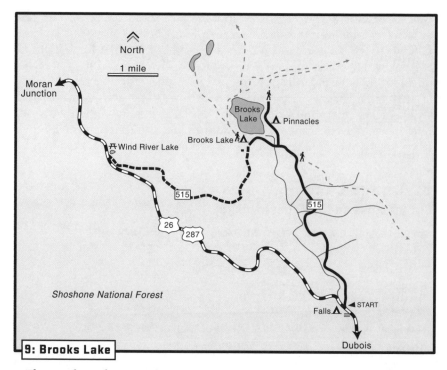

9: Brooks Lake

The road reaches Brooks Lake at 4.6 miles. The waters here reflect the eastern face of the 2.5-mile long Breccia Cliffs (pronounced bretch-yuh)—palisades that were formed by receding ice and glaciers. Words cannot describe the beauty of this setting.

Just south of the lake is the Brooks Lake Lodge, an upscale guest ranch. The road continues south past this lodge, but as a narrow lane that is terrible in wet weather (and sometimes in dry weather). In dry conditions—if you're a driver who doesn't mind heights or drop-offs—follow it southward to reach Barbers Point, a high and exposed overlook where you'll be rewarded with grand mountain views. From here, the road descends back into the forest and ends at the Wind River Lake picnic area along HWY 26/287.

Other Nearby Drives

Togwotee Pass—More terrific views of the Breccia Cliffs can be found from FR 30010, a 4-mile route in the Bridger-Teton National Forest. Found just west of Togwotee Pass (9,658-feet), this unnoticed dirt and gravel backroad cuts through the wildflower-chocked meadows of the Continental Divide and offers great views of the Absaroka Mountains. The road ends near Two Ocean Mountain (10,724) feet, which rises a thousand feet higher to the south. To reach the road from Dubois, head west on HWY 26/287 for 32.5 miles. If driving from Moran, head east for 22.8 miles.

Pinnacle Buttes near Brooks Lake

National Parks

Northwest Wyoming is famed for its two National Parks. Yellowstone National Park, the northernmost park that fills the corner of the state, sits atop North America's largest active volcano system. This isn't a place where you watch the steaming vents through binoculars, but rather, from boardwalks that weave between them. You'll see colored thermal pools and geysers that burst through the earth's crust and spray over a hundred feet in the air. You are guaranteed a show at Old Faithful, which erupts at least once every two hours.

Yellowstone is rich with other natural features aside from geysers. With 110 miles of shoreline, Yellowstone Lake is enormous, the largest high, freshwater lake in North America. Another international favorite is the Grand Canyon of the Yellowstone with its 308-foot waterfall.

Grand Teton National Park is found to the south, connected to Yellowstone by the John D. Rockefeller Jr. Memorial Parkway (a block of land also managed by the National Park Service). Perhaps no other mountains in the world find themselves on more calendars and postcards than the Tetons. With a 7,500-foot vertical rise from the valley below, these jagged peaks are dramatic and special.

Benefited by the adjacent lands of the Bridger-Teton and Shoshone National Forests, the two National Parks create one of the world's most balanced ecosystems. This wildlife sanctuary includes healthy populations of grizzly bears, black bears, gray wolves, and bison. Elk and moose are ungulates that are frequently seen, as are bighorn sheep, deer, and antelope. In the wetlands and rivers, watch for trumpeter swans and bald eagles.

Land Ownership

There are no private property concerns within the national parks, but there are well-signed service roads that are only open to park staff. The adjacent Bridger-Teton National Forest provides a huge tract of public land, though there are private properties near Moran and along the Gros Ventre River. Common sense and use of a national forest map will steer you clear of these sections. Local Forest Service offices are located near Moran and in Jackson.

Roads and Trails

It's often said that all roads in Wyoming lead to Yellowstone. This is actually true in a sense, but the main highways you'll use to access the area include HWY 89 and HWY 212 from Montana, HWY 20 from Idaho, HWY 14/16/20 from Cody, HWY 89/191 from Jackson, and HWY 26/287 from Dubois. These federal thoroughfares feed the area's other paved roads, which are numerous.

The heavily driven backroads in this section travel entirely within a National Park, begin from a park, or are proximate to a park. For this reason, they receive routine maintenance that makes them easy to drive. Aside from a few side roads in the Bridger-Teton National Forest, stock 4x4s will have no trouble negotiating the rougher roads. Though ATV use is prohibited in the national parks, there are miles of designated trails in the mountains east of Grand Teton National Park.

Seasons and Conditions

With 30 to 80 inches of annual precipitation, this region is Wyoming's wettest, which has an impact on the area's roads. Depending on snow, most of the paved roads in the parks close in late October or November and re-open in March or April. The parks' backroads have a truncated driving season that runs between June through September. Roads in the adjacent national forest vary—some routes open in May and others in June. All are closed by the end of November. The National Park Service, and the Forest Service's ORV Trail Map or MVUM, can provide specific seasonal dates.

In dry conditions, the unpaved roads in Yellowstone can be driven with any vehicle. The same is not true in nearby Grand Teton where you'll encounter more mud, ruts, and rocks (though these are minimal). The biggest obstacle for roads in the Bridger-Teton National Forest is mud. Surfaces are sloppy early and late in the driving season, as expected, but summer afternoon thunderstorms can deteriorate the roads in the middle of the summer.

Fuel

Though you'll pay a premium, fuel is available in most of Yellowstone's small villages including Mammoth Hot Springs, Roosevelt Lodge, Old Faithful, Canyon Village, Grant Village, and Fishing Bridge. West Yellowstone (the town on the western boundary) also has numerous stations. Further south around Grand Teton National Park, there are fueling stations at Flagg Ranch, Signal Mountain, Moose Village, the town of Jackson, and east of Moran.

Maps

For navigating the national parks, pick up one of the park maps available from any entrance station or visitor center. For drives located outside the park boundaries, refer to the Bridger-Teton National Forest map for the Buffalo and Jackson Ranger Districts, the Jackson-Ashton-Teton Basin ORV map, or the Bridger-Teton Motor Vehicle Use Map (MVUM).

10: Old Gardiner
The fun way to leave Yellowstone

☒ **Backcountry Drive**
Most vehicles

☐ **4WD Route**
4x4 vehicle or ORV

☐ **ATV Trail**
ORV less than 50" wide

Location/Map	Yellowstone National Park; Page 181
Roads	Old Gardiner Road
Distance	4 miles
Managing Agency	National Park Service—Yellowstone National Park
Starting Coordinates	N44° 58.64' W110° 42.08'

Overview: One of Yellowstone's first routes, Old Gardiner Road connects Mammoth Hot Springs to the park's north entrance near the town of Gardiner, MT. This historical stagecoach route offers gorgeous views of the surrounding mountains as well as wildlife viewing opportunities for the park's ungulates, including bighorn sheep.

This is a one-way road—from south to north—except for bicyclists who are granted travel in both directions. RVs and trailers are not allowed. The road is open to motorized use between May and October, but the park service can close it during wet conditions.

Start: From Mammoth Hot Springs in northern Yellowstone, drive behind the park's Engineering Building next to the Old Mammoth Hotel. A sign marks the road's entrance at the base of a hill.

Description: The narrow dirt road begins by pulling a moderate grade above Mammoth. A unique aerial perspective of the park's headquarters is soon attained, as are views into the Gardner River Canyon to the east.

From the top of the rise, the road assumes a steady descent as it advances toward Gardiner. Modern cars, especially driven downhill, make easy passage of this road, but that hasn't always been the case. When early Yellowstone visitors traversed this route in the 1880s going the other direction, it took a team of six horses to haul their yellow stagecoaches over the slope. In all, it's a difference of over 1,000 feet between ends—a respectable 7% grade.

The single lane enters Montana by cutting through hills of grass, sagebrush, and a few isolated stands of conifers. Grand mountain vistas are in abundance. To the west, you'll find the Gallatin Range, which spans the Wyoming-Montana border and features Electric Peak (10,969 feet). To the north and northeast is the Absaroka Beartooth Wilderness, which lines the horizon with numerous high summits and snow-creased crags.

After passing above Slide Lake to the east, the road rolls out across a windswept plain, then dips into a valley at the edge of Gardiner. The road ends at the park's north entrance station.

Old Gardiner Road

11: Blacktail Plateau
Leave Yellowstone's crowds in the dust

☒ **Backcountry Drive** Most vehicles	☐ **4WD Route** 4x4 vehicle or ORV	☐ **ATV Trail** ORV less than 50" wide

Location/Map	Yellowstone National Park; Page 181
Roads	Blacktail Plateau Drive
Distance	7 miles
Managing Agency	National Park Service—Yellowstone National Park
Starting Coordinates	N44° 57.48' W110° 32.49'

Overview: Nearly every public road in Yellowstone National Park is paved, offering few opportunities to get off the beaten path. One exception is the one-way lane that crosses Blacktail Deer Plateau on the north side of the park. Even though this backway doesn't draw the crowds like the world-class natural attractions found elsewhere in the park do, it is still well traveled by drivers who want to hit the dirt. You can gain more solitude yet by driving the road in the early morning or evening hours. In doing so, you'll exponentially increase your odds of encountering the plateau's wildlife, which is one of the best places to spot bears in Yellowstone. This road is open to motorized use from June through September.

Traversing the Blacktail Plateau

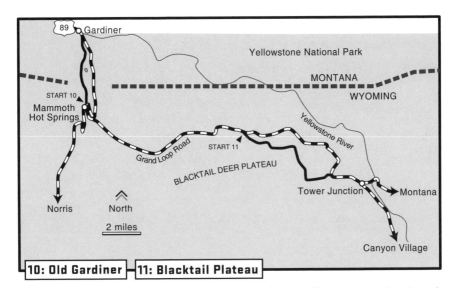

10: Old Gardiner — 11: Blacktail Plateau

Start: From Mammoth Hot Springs in northern Yellowstone, take Grand Loop Road east 9.4 miles toward Tower Junction. The turnoff is on the right side of the road.

Description: The dusty, gravel backroad begins by passing through a thin evergreen forest that quickly gives way to gentle slopes covered by sagebrush and thick grass. The road parallels a small stream for a short distance and then crosses over Oxbow Creek before 3 miles.

Broad views of northeastern Yellowstone are revealed as the road climbs above 7,500 feet. At 4 miles, the high point of the drive is attained at what is named The Cut. Here, distant mountain peaks can be seen poking over the horizon directly ahead.

From the high point, the road descends sharply into heavier timber as it kinks tightly into the Elk Creek drainage. This stretch provides good midday cover for wildlife and is worth spying. Black bear sightings are common along this road and I've spotted both black bear and grizzly within these trees—once at the same time.

The road now heads east and rolls through a burned-out valley. These charred trees were among those burned in the great Yellowstone fire of 1988 that ultimately had a third of the park ablaze.

The road reconnects to Grand Loop Road near a small wooden footbridge that spans a tiny brook. Turn right to reach Tower Junction in 1.5 miles or turn left to return to Mammoth Hot Springs.

12: Grassy Lake Road/Cave Falls
Land between the parks

☒ Backcountry Drive	☐ 4WD Route	☐ ATV Trail
Most vehicles	4x4 vehicle or ORV	ORV less than 50" wide

Location/Map	Between Yellowstone and Grand Teton National Parks; Page 184
Roads	FR 261, FR 582
Distance	34 miles (53 miles to Cave Falls)
Managing Agency	USDA Forest Service—Bridger-Teton National Forest, Caribou-Targhee National Forest, National Park Service—Yellowstone National Park
Starting Coordinates	N44° 6.51' W110° 40.08'

Overview: This long backcountry drive—an old American Indian route—travels west from Flagg Ranch, near Yellowstone's south entrance, to the farmlands surrounding Ashton, Idaho. Much of the road burrows through a dense forest, but there are lakes and bogs along the way. To just drive into Idaho and turn around, you probably won't find this drive worth its time. But if you are willing to drive another 19 miles (one way), you can reach Cascade Corner, the virtually unknown southwestern area of Yellowstone. There, you'll find a photogenic cascade known as Cave Falls, along with a campground, foot trails, good fishing, and plenty of good picnic sites.

While most of this route can be driven with a 2WD vehicle, high clearance is recommended. You can expect ruts, mud, and potholes on the road near Grassy Lake Reservoir. Plan on spending an entire day to make this drive if you go the full distance to Cave Falls, which makes a roundtrip of more than 100 miles. The route is best driven from mid-June to mid-September, depending on conditions.

Start: From Moran, head north for 25 miles on HWY 89/191/287 to Flagg Ranch. The ranch is 2.4 miles from Yellowstone's south entrance. Drive to the north end of the large parking lot near the fuel pumps to find Grassy Lake Road, also called Ashton-Flagg Ranch Road or Reclamation Road.

Description: Grassy Lake Road begins by bearing west to a crossing where Polecat Creek flows into the Snake River. The next 2 miles parallel this waterway and are among the most scenic along the entire trip. Across the gravel bars and tree breaks, you can catch sight of the northern Teton Range. There are numerous free campsites that can be found on both sides of the road over the next several miles.

After 5 miles, the road joins Glade Creek and follows this meandering stream through its marshes for the next few miles. With most of the popular areas now behind you, you'll find that the road surface deteriorates the

Cave Falls in southwestern Yellowstone

farther you drive. While manageable by most vehicles during the summer, expect some potholes, rough patches, and occasional mire.

At 9.4 miles, the backroad reaches the eastern tip of Grassy Lake Reservoir. The road rounds the timbered northern shore of the lake and then crosses the dam at mile 11. On the far side, you'll find FR 26, a 4WD road that leads to Tillery Lake and Lake of the Woods. Drivers wanting a smoother side route will find a turnoff for FR 27 a little over a mile farther. This 2.3-mile route leads to a Boy Scout camp and the west side of Lake of the Woods—one of the area's larger bodies of water.

Grassy Lake Road continues west through an evergreen forest, briefly running along the southern boundary of Yellowstone National Park. It may not look too wild, but the next several miles of road pass through some of the most pristine wilderness in the Lower 48. To the north is the tiny Winegar Hole Wilderness, which abuts Yellowstone. The larger Jedediah Smith Wilderness flanks the south side of the road. This elongated wilderness runs along the western slope of the Teton Range.

At 19 miles, the road enters an old glacial plain that is covered with streams, marshes, and lakes. Not many of these riparian features can be seen from the road due to the timber, but a few side spurs do lead to some nearby lakes. The first of these is the short track that leads to Loon Lake. A similar side road leading to Moose Lake is found a short distance farther at 20.6 miles. Be sure to watch for moose while visiting these wetlands. Bending further south, the road passes through numerous large meadows, such as Gibson Meadows at mile 21 and the larger Squirrel Meadows at mile 23.

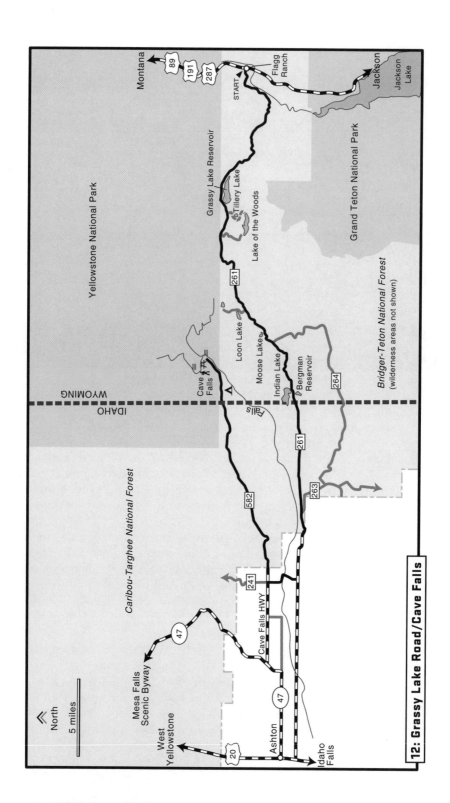

12: Grassy Lake Road/Cave Falls

SIDE
TRIP
Between the two large meadows is FR 264, which heads south into the Caribou-Targhee National Forest. The road can be used as an alternative route west or to access other backroads. If used as an alternative route, follow it west until it intersects FR 263. Then bear right and drive a few more miles to the northwest to rejoin Grassy Lake Road.

After Squirrel Meadows, the road reaches Indian Lake, a sizable body though most of its waters are covered with lily pads. On the other side of the road, a turnoff leads to Bergman Reservoir. The road continues west from the lake to enter Idaho where it is often shown on maps as Reclamation Road. The worst of the roadway is now over and the driving surface soon becomes smoother and wider.

The next 8.5 miles present little change as you drive west through the coniferous woods before reaching the national forest boundary where the road becomes paved.

For the shortest route to Yellowstone's southwest corner, continue west on the paved road for 2.8 miles and turn north onto a secondary road (if you stayed westbound, you'd reach the town of Ashton in about a dozen miles.) Drive north for 2.3 miles, through farmland and over a canal, to reach an intersection with Cave Falls Highway. Turn right, back to the east, and you'll re-enter the Caribou-Targhee National Forest within a mile on FR 582. Continue east on this well-maintained gravel road for another 14 miles to reach a parking lot at the Cave Falls recreation area, which collectively includes a campground, picnic area, and trailhead.

The road ends here on the banks of the wide-flowing Falls River where a stunning cascade flows over a broad shelf. Rainbow and cutthroat trout swim these waters, but a Yellowstone fishing permit is required to fish here. The greater Bechler Area, the region around Cave Falls, has many trails that can be explored on foot. A brochure at the picnic area includes a map and trail descriptions. Among the best is a 3-mile trail to Bechler Falls.

ALTERNATE
ROUTE
An easier but slightly longer route to Cave Falls can be made from West Yellowstone. Simply follow HWY 20 southwards to Ashton and then head east on Cave Falls Highway. This is an 80-mile route that is mostly paved. Incorporate Idaho's Mesa Falls Scenic Byway into the route—which takes you through the Caribou-Targhee National Forest instead of through Ashton—and you'll save a few miles while you discover two spectacular waterfalls.

13: Pacific Creek/Two Ocean Lake
Take a Wyoming wildlife safari

☒ **Backcountry Drive**
  Most vehicles

☐ **4WD Route**
  4x4 vehicle or ORV

☐ **ATV Trail**
  ORV less than 50" wide

Location/Map	Grand Teton National Park; Page 187
Roads	Pacific Creek Road, Two Ocean Lake Road, FR 30090
Distance	10.5 miles
Managing Agency	National Park Service—Grand Teton National Park, USDA Forest Service—Bridger-Teton National Forest
Starting Coordinates	N43° 51.25' W110° 31.22'

Overview: The two roads that comprise this backcountry drive explore the northeast corner of Grand Teton National Park; one ends at a beautiful lake, the other at a Forest Service campground. Driven at first light or in the fading evening glow, the duo often serve as one of the most rewarding wildlife tours in Wyoming. Elk forage among the aspen stands and moose are usually nearby. Black bears are scattered across the area, but it's the larger grizzly that roams here that has repeatedly made headlines over the years. During a single evening in late spring, I spotted moose, elk, a coyote, a fox, and signs of bear. Another outing revealed a young grizzly.

  Both of these roads are rough with ruts and potholes and the National Park Service considers Two Ocean Lake Road to be a 4WD route. This can

Two Ocean Lake in Grand Teton National Park

certainly be true in wet conditions, but both of these routes are navigable with a 2WD vehicle if you have decent ground clearance and drive them when they are dry. The road that passes through the national forest is open to motorized use on May 1, though it may still be sloppy in spots.

Start: From Moran (30 miles north of Jackson), go north on HWY 89/191/287 for 1 mile and turn right onto Pacific Creek Road.

Description: From the highway, follow the paved Pacific Creek Road for 2 miles to a fork. A left turn here puts you on Two Ocean Lake Road, a 2.3-mile route that passes above a lush mountain meadow where moose and elk are commonly sighted. A picnic area is located at the end, as is a scenic, mountain-capped lake. Foot trails continue around the lake.

To continue on to Pacific Creek, stay right at the first fork and drive a short distance to reach a second one. Here, turn left onto the dirt road and follow it north through sagebrush parks that are flanked by aspen and conifers. The first few miles are easily driven where the road continues through Grand Teton National Park, but this changes when you enter the Bridger-Teton National Forest near mile 6. Routine maintenance ends at the forest boundary and the ensuing road is rough and rutted. The boundary is also

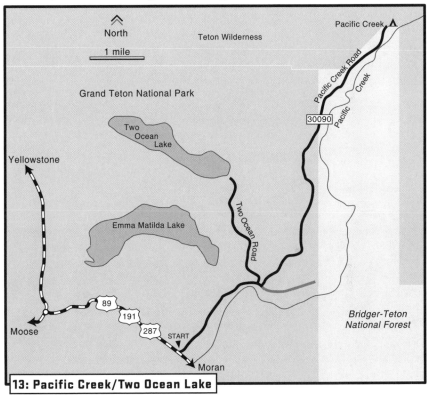

13: Pacific Creek/Two Ocean Lake

where the road draws close to Pacific Creek. Watch for bald eagles and other large birds along the stream.

The bumpy lane ends at Pacific Creek Campground 2 miles inside the national forest. The trailhead camp is situated against the Teton Wilderness, one of the wildest backcountry areas in the nation.

14: Flagstaff/Lily Lake
Discover the Mount Leidy Highlands

☒ **Backcountry Drive**
Most vehicles

☐ **4WD Route**
4x4 vehicle or ORV

☐ **ATV Trail**
ORV less than 50" wide

Location/Map	Northeast of Jackson; Page 190
Roads	FR 30160, FR 30100
Distance	16 miles
Managing Agency	USDA Forest Service—Bridger-Teton National Forest
Starting Coordinates	N43° 49.47' W110° 21.28'

Overview: This beautiful backcountry drive explores the mountains east of Grand Teton National Park that are known as the Mount Leidy Highlands. The trip takes you uphill to an overlook of the Tetons, and then passes Lily Lake before it descends back to HWY 26/287 on Flagstaff Road. There are numerous secondary roads off the main route that can be taken to further explore the Highlands. The road is open to motorized use from May 1 to December 15. Many of the side roads open in July.

Afternoon thunderstorms build over Flagstaff Road

Start: From Moran (30 miles north of Jackson), drive east on HWY 26/287 for almost 9 miles to the turnoff for Hatchet Campground (just west of the Blackrock Ranger Station). If traveling from Dubois, you can reach the eastern end of the road by driving west on HWY 26/287 for 47 miles. If driving an ATV, you can park and unload at the Ranger Station and follow a roadside ATV trail to reach the starting point.

Description: From the highway, FR 30160 begins by cutting through Hatchet Campground, an under-utilized Forest Service site that offers campers quick access into Grand Teton National Park. From the camp, the gravel road climbs a moderate grade and enters a forest comprised of evergreens, aspens, and a thick understory. In the clearings, you'll be able to look out over the mountainous countryside.

A side road, FR 30200, is passed at 3.5 miles and offers a more primitive route through these mountains. From here, the lane works further south toward Sagebrush Flat. As you enter this large aspen-dotted park by mile 5, watch for the junction with the 4-mile side road, FR 30180. Just past this junction, there is a tremendous view of the Teton Range and Jackson Hole Valley. Yet another side trip—an old road (FR 30165) now designated as an ATV trail—heads south from Sagebrush Flat for 3 miles to Skull Creek Meadows.

SIDE TRIP

For the best views of the area, including the majestic Tetons to the west, steer your 4x4 up to Baldy Mountain on FR 30161. This track can be found before mile 8, just before you reach Lily Lake. The 1.5-mile road gains 400 feet and ends in a clearing at 8,542 feet—well above the surrounding terrain.

Lily Lake is reached at the drive's halfway point. This is not your typical mountain fishing lake. With a marshy shoreline and an interior filled with lily pads and beaver dams, these waters are better suited for a camera than a fishing line. Above the lake, Grouse Mountain (10,337 feet) rises over a forest that is being transformed by the recent dying of mature trees and the regeneration of past clearcuts.

Continuing east, FR 30160 ends at an intersection less than a mile east of the lake. Here, FR 30100 is found going both directions. To continue along the backcountry drive, bear left on Flagstaff Road.

SIDE TRIP

A right turn takes you deeper into the forest while paralleling the South Fork of Spread Creek—a popular choice for locals who make the 7-mile drive to Leidy Lake. To reach the lake, drive south on FR 30100 and then turn right on FR 30250. This is a rockier road, but still passable by most vehicles. The road ends at a saddle about a mile past the lake where you'll find a faint 1-mile foot trail that leads to the summit of Mount Leidy (10,326 feet).

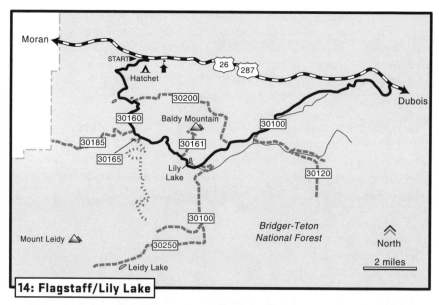

14: Flagstaff/Lily Lake

The backroad now turns to the northeast as it returns to the highway. The first mile of this stretch cuts through Preacher Park. The road then tops a short rise only to drop to an intersection with North Fork Road (FR 30120). From the junction, the road follows Flagstaff Creek as it drains downhill. This makes for a picturesque drive as the mountain stream is lined with thick vegetation and wildflowers such as Indian Paintbrush. The pinnacles near Togwotee Pass are also visible at times.

At 12.5 miles, Flagstaff Road climbs out of the shallow drainage and runs the length of a lightly-timbered ridge. In the last mile of the drive, the road crosses over Blackrock Creek before ending at HWY 26/287.

Other Nearby Drives

Pilgrim Creek Road—This bumpy 2.7-mile route is located just east of Colter Bay Village and provides access to the Bridger-Teton Wilderness. The road travels across sagebrush covered meadows and ends at a trailhead next to the gravel bars of Pilgrim Creek. Grizzlies and wolves frequent this area.

Sheffield Creek—This short access road is located just a few miles south of the Yellowstone boundary. A shallow ford over rough concrete blocks will get you to a trailhead and primitive campground.

Buffalo Valley Road—A 12-mile route, FR 30050 connects to HWY 26/287 at both ends. The western end is found near the east entrance of Grand Teton National Park, 3.5 miles east of Moran. From there, the paved road follows Buffalo Fork, a broad stream, through Buffalo Valley to reach Turpin Meadows trailhead and campground. The gravel portion of the road then returns to the highway by tunneling through a thick forest for nearly 5 miles.

15: Snake River
Follow the river below the mighty Tetons

☐ **Backcountry Drive**
Most vehicles

☒ **4WD Route**
4x4 vehicle or ORV

☐ **ATV Trail**
ORV less than 50" wide

Location/Map	Grand Teton National Park; Page 192
Roads	River Road
Distance	15.5 miles
Managing Agency	National Park Service—Grand Teton National Park
Starting Coordinates	N43° 49.37' W110° 36.87'

Overview: This road presents the rare opportunity to go four wheeling in a national park. It also offers the chance to escape the crowds and experience a part of Grand Teton National Park that is rarely visited. Known as River Road, this easy 4WD track travels between the Snake River and the Teton Range, making it one of the most worthwhile drives in Wyoming. As with other roads in the area, June through September is the best time to drive this route.

Start: From Moran (30 miles north of Jackson), drive north on HWY 89/191/287 for 4 miles to Jackson Lake Junction. Turn south onto Teton Park Road and drive 4.3 miles to an unsigned dirt road on the left. You can also access the road from the south by driving north from Jackson on HWY 26/89/191 for 12 miles. Turn left onto Teton Park Road and drive north for 4 miles to the road on the right.

Description: From the northern access point, River Road heads east across the flat sage-filled valley floor. Early morning drivers may spot elk in the open here or along the treeline. Bison and antelope are also frequently seen.

At 2 miles, the road comes to a fork. The east-bearing route (that goes straight ahead) descends 1.5 miles to the banks of the Snake River. The main route turns south where you'll find a number of large dips. Hereafter, the road settles into a distinct two-track flanked on both sides by sagebrush. While usually passable with ease, there are some sections that get large puddles, though these are usually dry during the height of summer when the sun scorches the 6,800-foot high valley.

Much of this stretch parallels the Snake River along a high bench where the watercourse isn't always in sight. Numerous tracks sprout from the main road to reach overlooks of the river. Most of these unsigned junctions are clearly discernible, but if there is any question, bear westward toward the Tetons to stay on the main route. If you choose not to explore any of the side roads, you'll still find plenty of scenic overlooks of the beautiful river.

After 8 miles, the trickiest part of the road is reached at the bottom of a steep incline with loose gravel and a series of dips. It's a brief climb that may require four-wheel drive in slick or wet conditions. The road cuts away from the river here, but returns within 2 miles on an increasingly rocky surface. You now skirt directly along a rim above the river. Combined with the surrounding mountain views, you'll surely agree that it doesn't get any better than this. A particularly worthwhile overlook is reached near 11 miles.

After 13 miles, the road passes a gated road that leads to the Bar BC Dude Ranch, an old cluster of buildings listed on the National Register of Historic Places. Constructed in 1912, the dude ranch was a significant contributor to the area's economy until it stopped accommodating guests after World War II. You can walk down the road to visit the site, but pets are prohibited.

From the ranch, the road travels west 1.5 miles directly toward the mighty crags of the Teton Range to return to Teton Park Road. Large puddles are common early in the driving season along the last straight and level mile.

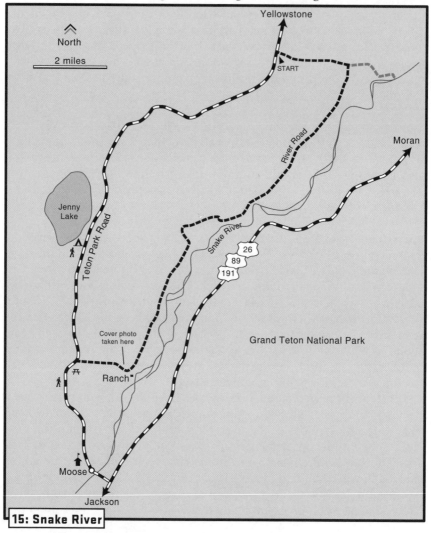

15: Snake River

Overlooking the Snake River from the River Road

Other Nearby Drives

Signal Mountain Summit Road—If you're spending time in Grand Teton National Park, a drive to the top of Signal Mountain is well worth your time. The paved road climbs 800 feet in 5 miles to a terrific pair of overlooks near 7,600 feet. I spent an evening at the top listening and watching the valley's elk. A black bear sighting on the way back down made it all the more worthwhile. To reach the road from Moran, head north for 4 miles to Jackson Lake Junction. Turn left onto Teton Park Road and drive 4 miles to the turnoff, just 1 mile south of Signal Mountain Campground.

Wilson-Falls Creek Road—This route, FR 31000, travels 18.3 miles between Wilson and HWY 26/89 (between Hoback Junction and Alpine). Almost five miles of the northern end are paved to accommodate access to subdivisions. The remaining distance consists of a wide gravel road that passes through the forested terrain of the Snake River Range.

Moose-Wilson Road—This 15-mile connector travels between the small settlements of Moose and Wilson. Though most of this length is paved, several miles have a gravel surface. This segment is a tight, curvy lane that winds through a forest ripe for wildlife viewing. Lucky observers can find moose, deer, bears, and a variety of birds. The gravel section is closed to trailers, motorhomes, and large trucks.

16: Shadow Mountain
Hit the dirt in Jackson Hole

Backcountry Drive
Most vehicles

4WD Route
4x4 vehicle or ORV

ATV Trail
ORV less than 50" wide

Location/Map	Northeast of Jackson; Page 195
Roads/Trails	Antelope Flats Road, FR 30340, FT 4209, FT 4210, FT 4211, FT 4212, and FT 4213
Distance	15 miles (backcountry drive); 11+ miles of ATV trails
Managing Agency	National Park Service—Grand Teton National Park, USDA Forest Service—Bridger-Teton National Forest
Starting Coordinates	N43° 39.89' W110° 41.68'

Overview: Shadow Mountain is a foothill at the edge of the Gros Ventre Range that is popular for camping, mountain biking, and ATV riding. From this forested mountain, you get views of the Teton Range and Jackson Hole Valley. The main road (FR 30340) can be driven by most vehicles, but a 4x4 is recommended since it's prone to becoming muddy with large puddles and ruts. (ATVs on this road must be street legal.) This road is open to motorized use on May 1, but many of the side routes and ATV trails open on June 1. These routes close on November 30. A Wyoming ORV permit is required for the ATV trails.

Start: To reach the southern end of the backcountry drive from Jackson, head north on HWY 26/89/191 for 13 miles. Turn right at the Antelope Flats sign.

The northern end of the mountain (including the ATV network) can be reached by driving south from Moran on HWY 26/89/191 for 10 miles to the turnoff. If you have ATVs to unload, drive east on a bumpy road to reach a large parking area and trailhead just inside the Bridger-Teton National Forest boundary.

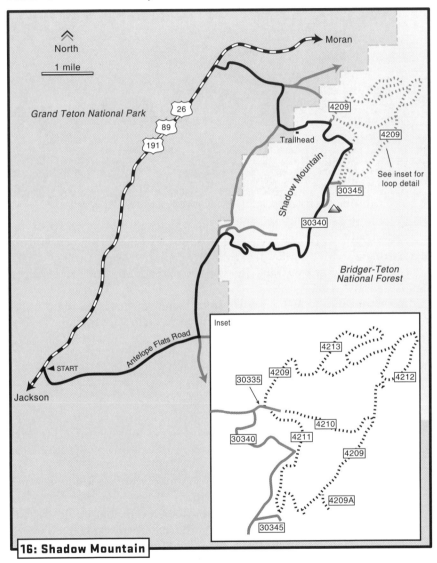

16: Shadow Mountain

The Teton Range from FR 30340 on Shadow Mountain

Description (Backcountry drive): From the highway, drive east across the sage-covered valley on Antelope Flats Road for 3.3 miles to a junction. Turn left, north, and drive 2 miles to a primitive camping area at the edge of the timber where you leave Grand Teton National Park and enter the Bridger-Teton National Forest.

Turn right onto FR 30340, which immediately begins climbing through an aspen stand. It doesn't take long before you can look over your shoulder to find the Teton Range spread out across the horizon. Blacktail Butte, rising starkly from the valley floor, is also easily spotted to the southwest.

The views improve as the road climbs atop the grass-covered upper slopes of Shadow Mountain. There are numerous dead-end 4WD spurs that branch from the main road that are used for camping.

At 8 miles, the road makes a tight turn to the north and climbs along the open crest of the mountain to undercut its 8,252-foot summit. This ridge is usually passable with ease, but after wet weather, the driving surface gets mottled with mud.

From the high point, the road begins a rapid descent on the mountain's northern flank. As is common of northern slopes, this side is covered with a thick evergreen forest. You'll soon pass a sign that marks the site of a lodgepole pine provenance test. As the signboard explains, the area was logged in July 1983 and reseeded a couple months later. The seed for these trees was collected from 60 sites in Wyoming and Idaho. Researchers now analyze the trees to determine which seeds provide the most favorable growth characteristics.

A two-track ATV trail on Shadow Mountain

Along the wooded descent, you'll pass access points for the ATV trail network. Gates at these points enforce the 50-inch vehicle restriction.

At 13 miles, the road reaches the bottom of the mountain, leaves the forest, and re-enters Grand Teton National Park. Follow the road to the north for another mile to a junction. A right (east) turn leads you to Lost Creek Guest Ranch. Turn left toward the Tetons to return to the paved highway near the Snake River Overlook.

Description (ATV trails): The upper slopes of Shadow Mountain have around a dozen miles of intersecting ATV trails. The longest of these is FT 4209 with a length of nearly 6 miles. This trail follows an old road for most of its length, making it one of the easier routes. Watch for a pair of short spurs on the south end of this trail, such as FT 4209A, for an outstanding overlook of the Gros Ventre Range to the east and southeast.

For a more challenging trail, take FR 4210. In just 1.3 miles, this trail climbs a whopping 700 feet. Where it passes through a shadowy forest, you'll be grinding over roots and rocks while branches crowd the trail. The other three trails—FT 4211, FT 4212, and FT4213—are also timbered routes that can be used to form a number of loops.

Remember that travel on FR 30340 requires a street-legal ATV. Also know that these trails are frequently used for commercial guided ATV rides; watch for large groups of riders.

17: Gros Ventre Slide/Red Hills

A look into the Gros Ventre Range

☒ **Backcountry Drive**
Most vehicles

☒ **4WD Route**
4x4 vehicle or ORV

☐ **ATV Trail**
ORV less than 50" wide

Location/Map	Northeast of Jackson; Page 200
Roads	FR 30400
Distance	29 miles (last 11 miles may require 4WD)
Managing Agency	National Park Service—Grand Teton National Park, USDA Forest Service—Bridger-Teton National Forest
Starting Coordinates	N43° 38.49' W110° 37.39'

Overview: This drive begins on the east side of Jackson Hole and follows the Gros Ventre River into a mountain range with the same name. The first part of the backroad is paved to Lower Slide Lake, but it then turns to washboarded gravel followed by soft dirt that gets sloppy when wet. There are no seasonal restrictions for the road leading to Lower Slide Lake, but the remaining distance past the lake is open to motorized use on May 1, though it still may not be passable at that time.

There are numerous 4WD tracks and ATV trails that branch off the main backroad. A Wyoming ORV permit is required for the ATV trails.

Start: From Jackson, head north on HWY 26/89/191 for 6.5 miles to Gros Ventre Junction. Turn east and take Gros Ventre Road 8 miles to a junction north of Kelly. Turn and follow the paved road east here to begin the drive. If you have ATVs to unload, continue east 6 miles to one of the parking areas near Atherton Creek Campground.

Description: The drive starts by passing Kelly Warm Spring, an 81-degree pool of water that is open to the public but remains largely unknown. The paved road continues east, gradually climbing to the Bridger-Teton National Forest boundary at mile 2. Over the next couple of miles, take notice of the landslide scar on Sheep Mountain to the right. After days of heavy rain in 1923, the northern slope of this mountain broke loose and dammed the Gros Ventre River to form a lake. Two years later the water broke through the dam and flooded the area downstream, killing six people. As you approach Lower Slide Lake at 5 miles, watch for an interpretive overlook that describes this natural disaster.

The road travels above Lower Slide Lake and passes Atherton Creek Campground at mile 6. After the campground, the paved surface gives way to a washboarded, gravel one that can be very jarring. This lane soon wraps around the lake to reach mile 8.

The next few miles travel through a unique part of Wyoming. While irrigated ranchland is found on the right side, there are stunning deep-red

Rugged hills in the Gros Ventre Range

hills above the road on the left. Standing against a blue sky and a pretty river, you'll find some good photo opportunities, especially around Red Hills and Crystal Creek Campgrounds, reached near mile 12. With the most popular areas now behind you, you'll find that the road gradually takes on more of a natural surface that doesn't hold up well in wet weather. Just over 13 miles, the dirt road on the left leads to the Slate Creek/Dry Dallas ATV trails (route #18).

After passing through a broad valley along the river, the backroad reaches a little pond called Goose Lake after 17 miles, and then Upper Slide Lake a mile farther. Plan on stopping at Upper Slide Lake to look for trumpeter swans. The lake is an established refuge for these majestic birds.

SIDE
TRIP

A more adventurous excursion can be made on FR 30410 and FR 30415, starting from the east side of Upper Slide Lake. This 9-mile 4WD route travels through a sagebrush flat and then skims the edge of an escarpment before ending near burned-out Gunsight Pass. The road gains 2,000 feet of elevation and provides awesome views of the surrounding area. Additional four-wheeling can be found by taking FR 30410 further east—this ties into FT 4202, an ATV trail that runs up Cottonwood Creek, or FT 4204, which travels along Bacon Creek.

From Upper Slide Lake, the backroad continues to the southeast by spanning Yellowjacket Flat and then rolling into a large basin. A pair of side

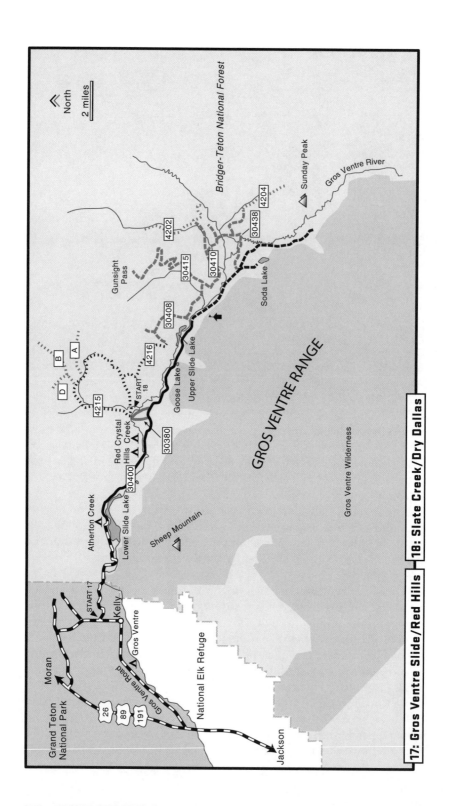

17: Gros Ventre Slide/Red Hills — **18: Slate Creek/Dry Dallas**

roads is reached at 23.5 miles. The route to the left leads to three ATV trails that dead end (FT 4202, FT 4203, and FT 4204). The rutted 1.3-mile track on the right (FR 30437) goes to Soda Lake, a small body of water that sits on the Gros Ventre Wilderness boundary.

From the two cutoffs, the road advances through the valley and then bears south, turning rougher. The Gros Ventre River meanders wildly here, creating miles of oxbow bends. The drive ends at a turnaround at mile 29 across the valley from Sunday Peak (8,976 feet).

18: Slate Creek/Dry Dallas
ATV trails in the Gros Ventre Range

☐ **Backcountry Drive**
  Most vehicles

☐ **4WD Route**
  4x4 vehicle or ORV

☒ **ATV Trail**
  ORV less than 50" wide

Location/Map	Northeast of Jackson; Page 200
Trails	FT 4215, FT 4216
Distance	12-18 miles
Managing Agency	USDA Forest Service—Bridger-Teton National Forest
Starting Coordinates	Slate Creek Trailhead: N43° 37.22' W110° 24.74' Dry Dallas access point: N43° 35.64' W110° 20.40'

Overview: The Slate Creek/Dry Dallas OHV Trail System is considered one of Wyoming's best ATV riding areas. Interesting terrain, gorgeous mountain valleys, flourishing creek bottoms, the Gros Ventre River, and views of truly wild mountains all contribute to the area's allure.

Much of the route is smooth and easy to drive, offering outstanding riding that allows you to soak up the scenery. However, this is an area that demands a healthy dose of respect for several reasons. First, there are some tricky spots where the trail floods. Secondly, this is known grizzly bear country. Third, when accessed from the west end, a deep ford of the Gros Ventre River is required (consider mid-July to be the earliest this should be attempted). Due to these factors, I'd encourage you to be appropriately prepared and, if possible, do not travel alone. The trails get high use on weekends, but visitation is lighter during the week. Commercially-guided ATV riders use these trails, though I didn't see another ATV on the summer day that I spent here.

The main loop (FT 4215) is 12 miles long. Accessing this loop from the east on FT 4216 adds an additional 3.5 miles. There are also several peripheral trails that dead end after branching off the loop. In all, there are nearly 20 miles of trails within the system.

The loop itself can only be ridden in its entirety from July 1 to September 9 (the northeastern segment closes at that time), but the other trail segments are open through November. A Wyoming ORV permit is required.

Start: From Jackson, head north on HWY 26/89/191 for 6.5 miles to Gros Ventre Junction. Turn east and take Gros Ventre Road 8 miles to a junction north of Kelly. Turn east and follow this road for over 13 miles to FR 30380. Follow this secondary road north 1 mile to reach the Slate Creek Trailhead where you will find plenty of space for ATV unloading.

If the Gros Ventre River is too high to cross (common in July), continue another 6.5 miles east to FR 30410 and turn left. Drive over the bridge and then bear left onto FR 30408. Follow this lesser road for 3.5 miles to tiny Dallas Lake where FT 4216 begins.

Description: From the Slate Creek Trailhead, the trail immediately begins with a steep descent to the Gros Ventre River where a deep ford is required (15 inches in late August). The crossing is 120 feet across and deeper in the middle than it appears. On the other side, the trail ascends a short distance to a fork—this is the other end of the loop. Bear left and proceed through the flanks of the Lavender Hills. This is easy driving here along a narrow two-track that cuts through broad expanses of grass, sagebrush, and pockets of mixed timber. Continue northward to enter the more vegetated Slate Creek drainage at 1.3 miles.

A small ford of Slate Creek is reached at 1.5 miles. The trail now parallels the creek along its east side. A fantastic view northward across a brushy valley awaits at 2 miles—this is someplace special. Gain a little distance in this valley and then take a moment to look back to the south to see the 11,000-foot peaks of the Gros Ventre Range.

At nearly 3.5 miles, the trail tops McKinney Pass (7,530 feet) before descending into the heart of the valley. Here, Slate Creek collects waters from the Carmichael Fork from the northwest and the Bear Paw and Dallas forks from the northeast. Cut eastward through this photogenic valley, trending uphill, to reach the junction with 4215B at 4.5 miles. This side-trail runs northward, splits with FT 4215D, and ends after 2 miles.

To continue the loop, stay right at the junction and drive southeast. A potentially nasty mud hole is encountered by mile 5. Innocent at first glance, this knee-deep bog swallowed my right two tires and nearly put my machine on its side before I was able to seize firmer ground on the other side.

From the creek bottom, the trail climbs through small stands of evergreens. At 5.3 miles, FT 4215A splits off the left and heads further up the valley for less than a mile. Again, stay right here to continue the loop.

A few shallower mud holes can be expected as the halfway point is attained on the northern end of the loop. Watch for flooded ruts that are lined with logs and boards from those who tried to bridge their way across the mire. While there are a few bridges, and some trail hardening has been done, more work is needed to prevent further resource damage.

At roughly 7 miles, on the southbound leg of the loop, the trail tops Bear Paw Pass (8,161 feet) where there are good views of Gros Ventre Range to the south. From this high point, it's now a long descent back to reach the Gros Ventre River.

Northbound on FT 4215 near McKinney Pass

As the trail heads southward, it passes through the wet meadows of the Haystack Fork drainage. The track cuts along the edges of these lowlands, making passage easier and drier.

The junction with FT 4216 is reached at 9.3 miles. This 3.5-mile side trail tops Lightning Pass (8,060 feet) and connects to the eastern trailhead at Dallas Lake and FR 30408. From the junction, stay right and navigate around the eroded, barren south faces of the hills. The westbound trail becomes slightly more rocky, dipping into some dry draws and crossing several narrow ATV bridges. Slate Creek is forded a second time at 11 miles. From here, the trail runs southwest along a bench above the Gros Ventre River.

The last fork is reached by mile 12. Turn left to complete the loop and return back to the river to make another deep ford near the trailhead.

Other Nearby Drives

Curtis Canyon Overlook—A bumpy 7.3-mile drive from Jackson takes you to a terrific overlook of Jackson Hole and the Teton Range. This is often a windy perch and it's popular with paragliders who sail from its heights. Curtis Canyon Campground is found in the timber on the other side of the road. To reach the overlook from Jackson, drive east on East Broadway Street and follow this road through the National Elk Refuge. It then turns north, then east again where it changes to FR 30440 and climbs a steep hill. If you want to explore this area further, drive east for 1.7 miles and take the rougher Sheep Creek Road (FR 30445) for 5 more miles to its end.

Northern Wind River
and Gros Ventre Ranges

Where a mountain range starts or ends is sometimes obvious, but that's not the case for the northern end of the Wind River Range. These highlands roll into the Gros Ventre Range, a separate cluster of limestone mountains that stands between the Winds and the Tetons. The union between these two ranges creates a small valley occupied by the Green River. North of this valley you'll find Union Pass where broad subalpine meadows are dimpled with glacial ponds. This relatively gentle upland lends itself to motorized travel and you'll find many roads here to explore.

The two ranges create a continuous landmass that is a rich wildlife habitat. Many of the species you find in the Yellowstone area are also found here. Bighorn sheep live among the rocky summits and bears—both black and grizzly—roam the parks and forests. Keep watch for moose, elk, deer, and even pronghorn antelope. The high divide between the mountain ranges is part of the antelope's migration route, which extends from the Tetons to wintering grounds south of Pinedale. A mountain goat sighting was also confirmed here in 2009—the first for this mountain range.

Land Ownership

This area is divided between the Bridger-Teton National Forest to the west and the Shoshone National Forest to the east. There are numerous private ranches within these national forests, so refer to your map and watch for signs when in doubt. These ranch lands are concentrated along the Green River, the Gros Ventre River, and the Wind River. Above these large drainages, you'll find continuous expanses of public land. Forest Service offices are located in Dubois and Pinedale.

Roads and Trails

Two federal highways flank these mountains ranges: HWY 26/287 (Centennial Scenic Byway) to the north and HWY 189/191 to the south. The ranges themselves are protected by four designated wilderness areas: the Gros Ventre, Bridger, Fitzpatrick, and Popo Agie. As a result, the high, mostly rock-and-ice core of the mountains have no roads, which are unsuitable for mechanized travel anyway. There is, however, an extensive network of roads between the two ranges at Union Pass. A maintained trunk road traverses this pass and offers access to miles of rougher 4WD routes and ATV trails. Many roads here are simply dirt two tracks that are easily driven in any 4WD vehicle. However, the tracks that travel closer to the high peaks get progressively rockier and more challenging. High clearance and skid plates are recommended.

Seasons and Conditions

Driving conditions vary greatly across the area and are dependent on factors such as slope aspect and the amount of shade on the road surface. I found some roads to be heavily rutted, though they held up well when I drove them during multiple days of rain. I can only deduce that the ruts are a result of driving the roads too early in the season. Most of the roads and trails in the area have no specific seasonal closure. Of those that do, it's from the middle of November to the middle of May. However, these mountains receive a lot of precipitation and many areas are closed with snow into June. For easy planning, don't count on finding any of the higher roads to be accessible before July.

Fuel

On the north side of the ranges, service stations can be found near Moran and in Dubois. A couple of stations are also located between these two towns on HWY 26/287. On the southern side, you can fuel up at Hoback Junction (south of Jackson), in Pinedale, and at Daniel Junction (west of Pinedale).

Maps

No additional maps are needed for the well-signed trunk roads, but to reliably navigate the confusing maze of spurs around Union Pass, you'll need a Bridger-Teton National Forest map for the Pinedale Ranger District, the Pinedale ORV map, or the Bridger-Teton or Shoshone Motor Vehicle Use Map (MVUM).

The northern slope of the Wind River Range, near Togwotee Pass, is split between two Forest maps: the south half of the Shoshone National Forest map and the Bridger-Teton National Forest map for the Buffalo and Jackson Ranger Districts. There is some overlap on both maps, so you might be able to get by with just one of these two.

19: Pelham Lake
The local fishing hole

■ Backcountry Drive
Most vehicles

■ 4WD Route
4x4 vehicle or ORV

☐ ATV Trail
ORV less than 50" wide

Location/Map	Northwest of Dubois; Page 206
Roads	FR 532, FR 540
Distance	6.3 miles (last quarter mile requires 4WD or short hike)
Managing Agency	USDA Forest Service—Shoshone National Forest
Starting Coordinates	N43° 38.58' W109° 55.16'

Overview: This drive leads to Pelham Lake, a trophy trout fishing hole on the west side of the Shoshone National Forest. Most of the road can be driven in any vehicle, but the last quarter mile requires a 4WD vehicle or short hike. You can expect to find ice on the lake into June.

Start: From Dubois, head west on HWY 26/287 for 17.5 miles to the turnoff on the left. The best place to unload ATVs is south of the highway near some dispersed campsites on FR 532. As an alternate starting point, some riders park at the beginning of FR 537 (along the highway to the north) and then follow an ATV trail eastward to reach this route.

Description: Beginning from the highway, drive south over the Wind River to reach a junction. Bear right onto FR 540 and head west. The maintained gravel road travels through a pine forest across fairly level terrain.

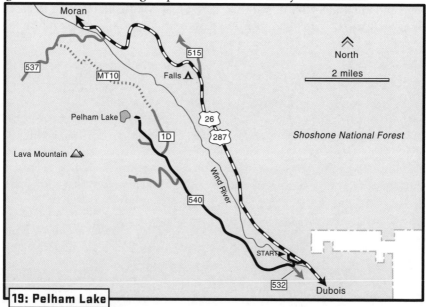

19: Pelham Lake

Pelham Lake

At mile 3, the road begins climbing higher into the forest. At 5 miles, a side road, FR 540.1D, branches off to the north. (This road ties into FT MT10, an ATV trail that connects to FR 537 a few miles to the northwest near Pilot Knob.) A fork is reached a short distance farther. Stay right and follow the main road northward.

A small parking area is reached at 6 miles where the road turns rougher. The remaining distance—a little more than a quarter mile—has rocks, roots, and some small mud holes. This track ends at Pelham Lake, a small body of water that is ringed by timber and shale. Lava Mountain (10,452) stands high over the lake.

Other Nearby Drives

Moccasin Basin Road—Although on a map it looks like one of the longest roads in the area, FR 537 (located west of Falls Campground), is only open to motorized use between HWY 26/287 and the Bridger-Teton National Forest boundary—a distance of just 3 miles. However, the road does offer access to a 3.75-mile ATV trail that connects to FR 540 near Pelham Lake.

Long Creek—An assortment of various roads and spurs can be found off FR 513, located 17 miles west of Dubois on HWY 26/287 near the Tie Hack Historical Monument. Among the two dozen miles of routes, you'll find everything from the maintained trunk road, which ends at a trailhead, to short dead-ending 4WD tracks.

20: Fish Lake
A lake on the Continental Divide

☒ **Backcountry Drive**	☒ **4WD Route**	☐ **ATV Trail**
Most vehicles	4x4 vehicle or ORV	ORV less than 50" wide

Location/Map	Northwest of Dubois; Page 209
Roads	FR 532, FR 544, FR 534
Distance	21.2 miles (12.5 miles to Fish Lake; 4WD required past the lake)
Managing Agency	USDA Forest Service—Shoshone National Forest
Starting Coordinates	N43° 38.58' W109° 55.16'

Overview: This drive climbs to Fish Lake on the Continental Divide. The lake can serve as either a destination or just a waypoint for a longer trip through the beautiful high country of the Wind River Range. In good conditions, you can reach the lake in a 2WD vehicle, but you'll need a 4x4 if you continue past the lake to follow the Continental Divide to Union Pass.

Start: From Dubois, head west on HWY 26/287 for 17.5 miles to the turnoff on the left. The best place to unload ATVs is south of the highway near some dispersed campsites. If carrying an ATV in the back of your pickup, you could also unload at the lake and use the ATV to explore the more rugged road south of the lake.

Description: Beginning from the highway, drive south over the Wind River to reach a junction. Stay left at the fork to pass some dispersed campsites and an outhouse, then proceed south on FR 532, a maintained gravel road.

The road now makes some sweeping curves as it moderately climbs a wooded slope for the next several miles. After topping a rise, the route drops into a beautiful valley at mile 6. This broad mountain park holds the confluence of numerous streams including Trout Creek, Warm Spring Creek, and Green Creek.

Drive into the heart of the meadow to reach a fork. If you stay on FR 532, you'll find a slew of secondary roads and short ATV trails. To continue to Fish Lake, bear right at the fork onto FR 544. Follow this good road west along Warm Spring Creek, a beautiful drainage that runs through a narrow finger of the valley. After crossing over the creek, the road bears south into the evergreen forest and begins climbing. Ignore a couple of side spurs to find FR 534. Much of the next 2 miles travel through the blackened remains of the once thick forest. The lightning-ignited Purdy Fire burned thousands of acres here in August of 2006.

After 12 miles, the road reaches the northern tip of Fish Lake at an elevation of 9,238 feet. This is far as the easy driving will take you. If you have an ATV or 4WD vehicle, you can continue for nearly 10 more miles to reach Union Pass Road. From the lake, follow the 4WD trail around the open shoreline, crossing a number of tiny streams along the way.

On the far side of Fish Lake, the road enters the forest and begins gaining on the steep western flank of Fish Lake Mountain (10,073 feet). After a challenging climb, you'll reach the Continental Divide, which is also the boundary line between the Shoshone National Forest and the Bridger-Teton National Forest.

Two miles from Fish Lake, the road reaches a clearing on the south side of Fish Lake Mountain. Watch for an ATV trail that soon branches off to the north—ATV riders can use this 4-mile connector to make a loop back to FR 532.

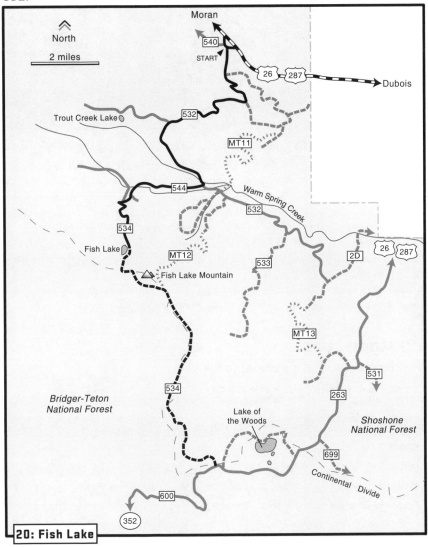

20: Fish Lake

Fish Lake near the Continental Divide

From Fish Lake Mountain, the road enters the treeless hinterlands of the Wind River Range. This is still the Continental Divide, and the views soon make it apparent that the road is on the spine of the mountain range, especially after attaining a high ridge of more than 9,600 feet a couple miles farther.

From the high point, the road descends from the high meadows to the edge of a sparse forest. The last couple of miles continue along the treeline until you reach Union Pass Road (FR 263). From here, you can turn east and follow Union Pass Road 17 miles to HWY 26/287 or turn west and drive roughly 30 miles to reach HWY 352 north of Pinedale.

21: Moon Lake

Journey to a distant subalpine lake

☐ **Backcountry Drive**
Most vehicles

☒ **4WD Route**
4x4 vehicle or ORV

☐ **ATV Trail**
ORV less than 50" wide

Location/Map	North of Pinedale; Page 211
Roads	FR 531
Distance	8.1 miles
Managing Agency	USDA Forest Service—Shoshone National Forest
Starting Coordinates	N43° 31.29' W109 50.52'

Overview: This 4WD road travels from Union Pass to a remote lake on the northern side of the Wind River Range. The driving gets progressively more challenging the closer you get to the lake. Virtually all stock 4WD vehicles are found parked on the side of the road within the first 6 miles before the terrain turns rocky. The road necessitates a raised suspension; I had rocks scraping my skid plates even with a generous 12 inches of ground clearance. There are no seasonal restrictions for this route but July is a good starting time. Be prepared to encounter equestrian traffic along the way.

Start: To access the road from the north, drive west of Dubois on HWY 26/287 for 9.3 miles to the signed turnoff for Union Pass on the left. Drive south on Union Pass Road (FR 263) for 10.5 miles to FR 531 on the east side of the road. There is plenty of space to unload ATVs at the beginning of the road.

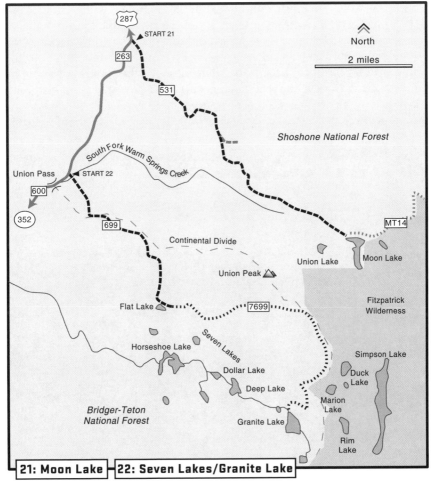

To access the road from the south, drive west of Pinedale on HWY 191 for 6 miles. Turn north onto HWY 352, drive 28.5 miles (the first 25 miles are paved), and bear left onto Union Pass Road (FR 600). Then drive a little over 34 miles to FR 531 on the right.

Description: The trip begins by crossing the high meadows of the Continental Divide. The first 2 miles of this open terrain present easy driving, and some people opt to tow their ATV and horse trailers to the end of this initial stretch.

After 3 miles, the road reaches a large meadow thick with shrubs at the foot of an unnamed 10,147-foot mountain. The road used to cut through the middle of this park, but it has since been rerouted through the whitebark pine trees that run along the western side. After a half mile, the road turns east and crosses the meadow as well as a small tributary to Warm Springs Creek. The water level isn't a problem, but the channel is rocky. Union Peak (11,491 feet) and its receding glaciers is now clearly visible to the south.

After passing through a short stretch of timber at mile 4, the track returns to the Warm Springs Creek drainage where a huge mountain massif to the south offers a beautiful backdrop. After following the waterway for over a mile to its headwaters, the road re-enters the trees after mile 6. At this point, all vehicles with average ground clearance will go no farther. The path now becomes riddled with large rocks that impede progress, especially during the last mile.

Moon Lake at the end of Forest Road 531

After 8 miles, you'll find yourself above the northern shore of Moon Lake, a hammer-shaped body of water. Because of the unique shape, not all of the lake is visible from this vantage point. A downhill hike is required to reach the shore.

Those traveling by ATV can continue east on FT MT14. This 4-mile track runs along the timbered Fitzpatrick Wilderness boundary. Near its end, it steeply climbs a treeless ridge of Windy Mountain (10,194 feet) where you'll earn a wide-reaching view across the Wind River Range and beyond. From this high point named Salt Barrels Park, a 4WD road leads a little over a mile to the Shoshone National Forest boundary.

22: Seven Lakes/Granite Lake
An alpine traverse

☐ **Backcountry Drive** Most vehicles	☒ **4WD Route** 4x4 vehicle or ORV	☒ **ATV Trail** ORV less than 50" wide

Location/Map	North of Pinedale; Page 211
Roads/Trails	FR 699, FT 7699
Distance	10.1 miles
Managing Agency	USDA Forest Service—Bridger-Teton National Forest, Shoshone National Forest
Starting Coordinates	N43° 29.07' W109 51.89'

Overview: This 4WD road and ATV trail combo, often called Seven Lakes Road, begins at Union Pass and follows the Continental Divide to Granite Lake. An alpine ascent that reaches elevations of 11,400 feet, the trail is among the most scenic in Wyoming. Expect a rough ride; this is a landscape carved out by glaciers (some of which still exist) and the rocky debris left behind is very much part of the driving surface. The first 4 miles are open to licensed vehicles and ATVs. The remaining distance to Granite Lake is open to ATVs that have a Wyoming ORV permit.

This is a summertime route and July is the earliest that you'll want to visit. When you go, keep weather in mind as this is treeless, exposed high country—not a good place to be during afternoon thunderstorms.

Start: To access this road from the north, drive west of Dubois on HWY 26/287 for 9.3 miles to the signed turnoff for Union Pass on the left. Drive south on Union Pass Road (FR 263) for 13.6 miles to FR 699 on the east side of the road. There is plenty of space to unload ATVs at the beginning of the road.

To access the road from the south, drive west of Pinedale on HWY 191 for 6 miles. Turn north onto HWY 352, drive 28.5 miles (the first 25 miles are paved), and bear left onto Union Pass Road (FR 600). Drive 31 miles to FR 699 on the right.

High country above Granite Lake —Wesley Gooch photo

Description: The trail begins from Union Pass Road, near the pass itself, with an immediate ford of the South Fork of Warm Creek Springs. From the crossing, the trail passes through a spotty evergreen forest while climbing to the Continental Divide, reached at 1 mile.

Nearing the third mile, the road approaches a marshy trough where a number of tracks have been created. Slosh your way to the other side and follow the road into a saddle between two 10,500-foot high points. On the other side of the saddle, the route bears south and soon reaches Flat Lake, a tiny alpine tarn. Another small ford is found here where the trail once again turns eastward. Ignore the side spurs on the right and stay on course by keeping to the left.

At 5 miles, an intermittent stream is reached at the base of Union Peak (11,491 feet). From this point the trail climbs steeply—1,200 in less than 2 miles—to pass over a high ridge of this large mountain. The route to the top has a number of paralleling tracks—try to stay on the main course to help prevent further damage and future restrictions.

At the top, 11,400 feet, you'll find an incredible skyline of snowy peaks and sprawling alpine terrain. Look to the southeast for Granite Lake, tucked into a shadowy cirque off Three Waters Mountain. From this vantage point—even greater if you scramble up one of the nearby rock outcrops—you'll see what western Wyoming is all about: mountain lakes, lofty peaks, and vast expanses of evergreen forests.

From Union Peak, the trail descends the southern flank of the mountain, staying just below the Continental Divide rim that obscures views of several lakes to the east. As tempting as it may be to veer off onto one of the sidetracks, don't. The area to the east is within the Fitzpatrick Wilderness area and some of trails that go in that direction have been illegally created. A view does open up as you pass above Marion Lake at 9 miles.

From a trail-side pond near Marion Lake, the trail cuts back to the southwest and enters some trees. Follow this track downhill for another mile to its end at Granite Lake—this is a very photogenic setting in the Winds high country.

23: Union Pass
Cross the Wind River Range

☒ **Backcountry Drive**
Most vehicles

☐ **4WD Route**
4x4 vehicle or ORV

☐ **ATV Trail**
ORV less than 50" wide

Location/Map	North of Pinedale, Southwest of Dubois; Page 218
Roads	FR 600, FR 263
Distance	45 miles
Managing Agency	USDA Forest Service—Shoshone National Forest, Bridger-Teton National Forest
Starting Coordinates	N43° 15.61' W110° 1.0'

Overview: The only motorized crossing over the Wind River Range is a historical passage called Union Pass that is located between Pinedale and Dubois. This corridor is made possible not over the jagged crags for which the Winds are known, but rather on the range's western fringe, where more gentle, rolling terrain is found. This drive takes you over this pass where you'll cross the Continental Divide and discover its beautiful vistas. An interpretive site at the top of the pass makes a good destination.

A word of caution regarding maps—of the five maps I referenced in researching this drive, not one accurately reflected the road as it was marked on the ground. On most maps, the route is shown as a patchwork of meandering roads that have varying numbers and driving surfaces. At least one map plotted the roadway 2 miles from its actual course. The most accurate reference is the Bridger-Teton National Forest map for the Pinedale Ranger District. Fortunately, you'll find the mostly gravel road to be very well-signed and easy to navigate. Most side roads and junctions are marked or obvious. The Bridger-Teton portion of the road is open to motorized use on April 15, but it'll be mid-June before you want to drive into this high country.

Start: To access the road from the south, drive west of Pinedale on HWY 191 for 6 miles. Turn north onto HWY 352, drive 28.5 miles (the first 25 miles are paved), and bear left onto Union Pass Road (FR 600). There is ample parking here at the beginning of the road for ATV unloading. To access the road from the north, drive west of Dubois on HWY 26/287 for 9.3 miles to the signed turnoff on the left.

Description: The backroad begins next to the Green River in the bottom of a verdant valley. At 3.5 miles, the road bears left at a fork and then curves away from the river by rounding the northeastern slope of Klondike Hill (9,280 feet). The base of Bacon Ridge is then soon reached and the road switchbacks over the southern tip of this steep crest to reach its eastern side. The bumpy driving surface is at its worst along these few miles.

The backroad passes through timber stands of pine and aspen as it travels further into the backcountry. As elevation is gained, views of the Wind Rivers' glaciated crags become visible to the southeast. After a dozen miles, the road reaches Mosquito Lake, a large but shallow pond that fills a depression in the sagebrush-covered upland.

From the lake, the route continues for another 15 miles across a broad mountain plateau, occasionally through the evergreens, but more often across a landscape of grass, sagebrush, and wildflowers. There are numerous well-signed side roads that depart from the main route, including those for Kinky Creek, Park Creek Meadow, and the Fish Creek Guard Station. These are popular spurs for ATV riders and those looking to get further off the beaten path.

SIDE TRIP Near mile 27, watch for a secondary road that heads north. This is the Lake of the Woods Road, a route that you'll have to take if you want to see the large lake of the same name. The loop road is only a few miles in length and rejoins the main route before you reach Union Pass.

Broad meadows at Union Pass

After 30 miles (the Forest Service signs show 32 miles), the road reaches the Continental Divide and Union Pass at 9,210 feet. A short foot trail leads to a historical site, a ring of interpretive signs that explain how Union Pass was utilized by aboriginal natives, Shoshone Indians, fur trappers, explorers, surveyors, and loggers. The signs also describe how the Continental Divide splits waterways two ways, or three, as this geographically unique area is able to do.

Across the pass, the same high peaks of the Wind River Range are still visible, but new summits to the southeast are now in view. The closest of these are a string of high points over 10,000 feet on Three Waters Mountain—a treeless mount pocketed with lakes and glaciers. There are also views on the other side of the compass, including the Breccia Cliffs and Pinnacles, which are visible 20 miles to the northwest.

From Union Pass, the backroad leaves the Bridger-Teton National Forest and enters the Shoshone National Forest. The road, now numbered as FR 263, is better maintained on the Shoshone side. Expect less washboard and more gravel—sometimes too much gravel.

The road advances north and continues to climb to a high point of 9,655 feet near the junction of FR 531, a 4WD road that leads to Moon Lake. Union Pass Road enters the timber a short distance farther. Now on the northern slope of the massive mountain range, the forest is thicker and the generous vistas become hidden by flora.

The 10 miles that follow are steep as the road drops 2,300 feet of elevation. Overall, it's a grade of just 6%, but much of the elevation loss comes on two distinct downhill sections.

At 39 miles, the road exits the national forest on the west side of Warm Spring Mountain (9,514 feet) and continues its rapid elevation loss. The remaining distance of 6 miles continues, in zigzag fashion, through lightly timbered terrain that is spotted with private homes, lodges, and ranches. The road ends at HWY 26/287.

Other Nearby Drives

Upper Green River/Union Pass Routes—Between the upper Green River and Union Pass areas, there are more than 175 miles of 4WD roads and ATV trails. Much of this is a patchwork of dead ends, but there are also some loops. For exact routes and seasonal restrictions, be sure to obtain the Bridger-Teton and Shoshone National Forest Motor Vehicle Use Maps (MVUM).

To access the area from the north, drive west of Dubois on HWY 26/287 for 9.3 miles to the signed turnoff on the left. The best place to unload ATVs is in the high meadows near Union Pass, 12 miles to the south.

To access the area from the south, drive west of Pinedale on HWY 191 for 6 miles. Turn north onto HWY 352, drive 28.5 miles. Unload ATVs near the bridge where Union Pass Road (FR 600) crosses the Green River.

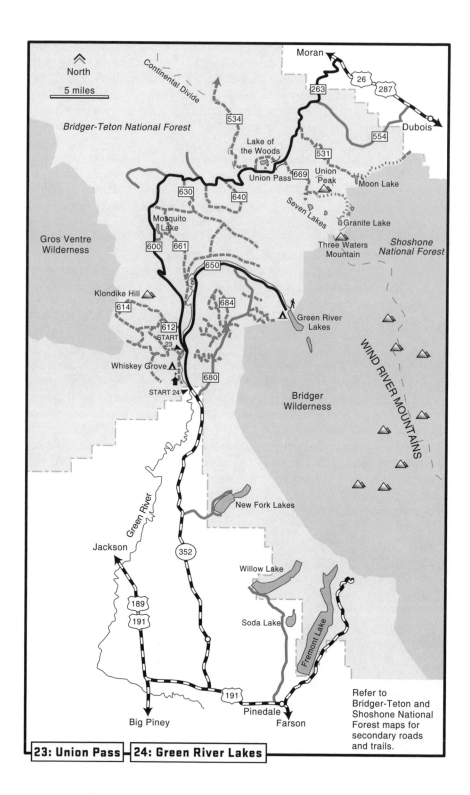

North

5 miles

Continental Divide

Moran

26

287

263

554

Dubois

Bridger-Teton National Forest

534

Lake of
the Woods

531

Union Peak

Moon Lake

Union Pass

669

630

640

Seven Lakes

Granite Lake

Mosquito
Lake

Three Waters
Mountain

Shoshone
National Forest

Gros Ventre
Wilderness

600

661

650

Klondike Hill

684

614

Green River
Lakes

612
START
23

WIND RIVER MOUNTAINS

Whiskey Grove

680

START 24

Bridger
Wilderness

Green River

New Fork Lakes

Jackson

352

Willow Lake

189

191

Soda Lake

Fremont Lake

191

Refer to
Bridger-Teton and
Shoshone National
Forest maps for
secondary roads
and trails.

Big Piney

Pinedale

Farson

23: Union Pass ⊢ **24: Green River Lakes**

24: Green River Lakes
Find the headwaters of a 700-mile river

☒ Backcountry Drive
Most vehicles

☐ 4WD Route
4x4 vehicle or ORV

☐ ATV Trail
ORV less than 50" wide

Location/Map	North of Pinedale; Page 218
Roads	FR 650
Distance	19 miles
Managing Agency	USDA Forest Service—Bridger-Teton National Forest
Starting Coordinates	N43° 13.28' W110° 0.48'

Overview: This backcountry drive takes you into the Wind River Range through the Upper Green River Valley. The road follows the Green River to its headwaters where it ends at a campground, trailhead, and mountain lake of stunning beauty. The road is open to motorized use on April 15, but it'll be mid-June before you want to come here (and that's when the campground opens, too).

Start: Drive west of Pinedale on HWY 191 for 6 miles. Turn north onto HWY 352 and drive 25 miles to the end of the pavement.

Description: The drive begins where paved HWY 352 leaves off, which is the Bridger-Teton National Forest boundary. From here, a gravel, but heavily washboarded road continues north and soon passes the Kendall Forest Service Work Center and a side road that leads to Whiskey Grove Campground.

The junction with Union Pass Road (FR 600) is passed near mile 3. Stay right and continue north on FR 650. The road now follows the Green River upstream toward its headwaters. The waterway—an important one to the West—flows more than 700 miles before draining into the Colorado River. Continue along the oxbows of the river and watch for Dollar Lake at 9 miles.

At 10 miles, the route makes a sweeping curve to the east, keeping the mountains to the right and the river on the left. The area here is known as the Big Bend—a marshy meadow where the Green River bends its way out of the mountains to establish its southern downstream course.

The following several miles present similar terrain and views, but this changes as you steer to the southeast. As you near the end, beautiful mountain peaks fill the skyline. The most distinct of these is Squaretop Mountain (11,823 feet), a soaring tower with a blunt summit. Along with the Tetons, this mountain is one of the most popular landmarks in Wyoming to photograph. You are sure to be struck by its dominance.

Green River Lakes and Squaretop Mountain

The road ends at Green River Lake Campground. Stay on the road to the left of the camp to reach a parking lot and small boat ramp at the edge of the water. There is also a trailhead here where you can explore the surrounding Bridger Wilderness on foot.

Other Nearby Drives

Gypsum-Moose Road—An alternative route between HWY 352 and Green River Lakes is FR 680. This 14.5-mile course parallels Gypsum Creek though sagebrush, pines, and aspen trees to reach Gypsum Park. The road gets rough as it wraps around Little Sheep Mountain (10,182 feet), but improves again as it descends the last couple of miles to FR 650.

North Fork of Fisherman Creek—FR 30650 runs along the North Fork of Fisherman Creek. The first 4 miles offer a maintained gravel surface that rolls through evergreen stands and sage-covered parks. The road then roughens and splits into a pair of 4WD tracks. The longer road, on the left, fords the creek and heads north several miles toward the Shoal Creek Wilderness Study Area. Here, ATV trail (FT 2149) continues for 3 more miles. This scenic route is located 7 miles east of Bondurant on HWY 189/191.

Raspberry Ridge ATV Loop—FR 30652 and FT 2146 create a fantastic 11-mile route across the meadows and southern flanks of the Gros Ventre Range. There are a few boggy spots where the trail crosses Jenny Creek. The trail is located 6 miles east of Bondurant on HWY 189/191.

25: Granite Creek
Follow a raging stream to its hot springs

☒ **Backcountry Drive**
Most vehicles

☐ **4WD Route**
4x4 vehicle or ORV

☐ **ATV Trail**
ORV less than 50" wide

Location/Map	Southeast of Jackson; Page 221
Roads	FR 30500
Distance	9 miles
Managing Agency	USDA Forest Service—Bridger-Teton National Forest
Starting Coordinates	N43° 16.99' W110° 32.03'

Overview: The bumpy road that follows Granite Creek has more than its share of highlights. Beautiful scenery, abundant wildlife, a waterfall, and hot springs are among them. There is also a large campground near the end of the road where you can spend the night and a trailhead if you want to hike this impressive area. The road is open from May 1 to November 30.

Start: From Jackson, drive south 11 miles to Hoback Junction. Turn left onto HWY 189/191 and drive east 11.5 miles. Turn north onto the well-signed road on the left side.

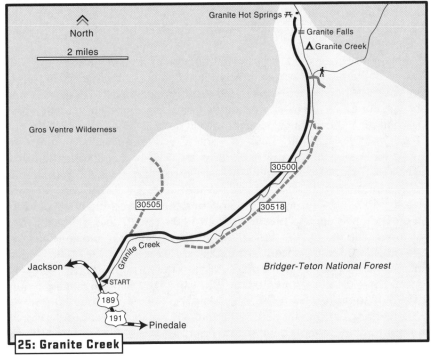

Gros Ventre Range from Forest Road 30500

Description: From the highway, FR 30500 gets underway by tightly following Granite Creek upstream for the first several miles. The road is washboarded and potholed, but the scenery is worth every bump.

After 6 miles, the road turns north into a valley and the peaks of the Gros Ventre Wilderness are revealed. A wildfire has burned some of the forest, but the post-fire regrowth has created a lush understory. Watch for deer and moose along this drive—both can often be seen around sunset when they descend from the timbered slopes to reach the water.

As you approach mile 8, near Granite Creek Campground, look to the rocky mountainside on the right to locate a well-named structure called "The Open Door." Continue north past the campground to find Granite Falls, a thunderous roadside cascade. A short distance farther, the road ends at a developed hot spring that consists of a changing cabin and 45x75-foot pool. The site is open to the public from 10:00 a.m. to dusk unless the road is impassable due to too little snow in the winter (for snowmobiles) or too much mud in the spring. During the spring months, the melting snow mixes with the pool's water supply and cools the spring to approximately 80 degrees. It gradually warms after the spring thaw to reach a high temperature of about 110 degrees by midwinter.

In addition to the main pool at the end of the road, there are undeveloped hot springs just 50 yards downstream on the eastern side of the creek. These springs offer free wading and soaking without restrictions. You can reach them by following a foot trail down from the developed pool.

CENTRAL

Central Wyoming presents a transition between the Great Plains and the Rocky Mountain West. On the east side of the region, Wyoming's prairies and farmland fold up into sparsely-timbered hills and breaks. Further west, vast sagebrush flats are divided by numerous mountain chains, including the stately Laramie Mountains. Flowing three different directions around and through these mountains is the North Platte River. This impressive watercourse fills central Wyoming's enormous reservoirs and drastically impacts the region with its many uses.

Central Areas

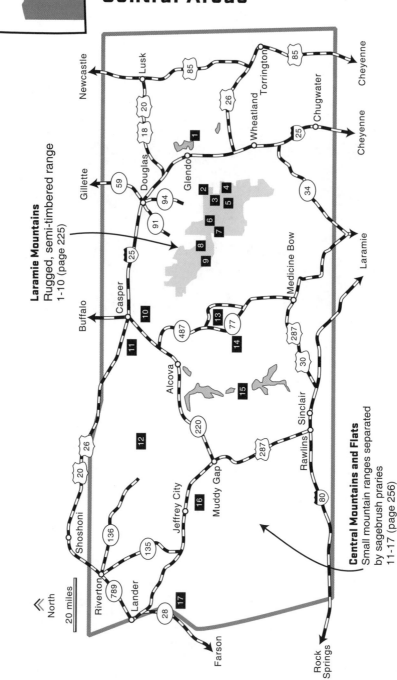

Laramie Mountains
Rugged, semi-timbered range
1-10 (page 225)

Central Mountains and Flats
Small mountain ranges separated
by sagebrush praries
11-17 (page 256)

North
20 miles

Sand Creek, Black Hills

Bear Lodge Mountains, Black Hills National Forest

East Tensleep Lake, Bighorn National Forest

Southern Bighorn National Forest

Lily Lake, Bighorn National Forest

Brooks Lake, Bridger-Teton National Forest

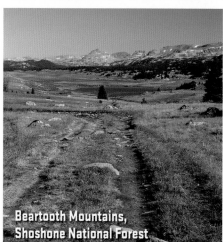
Beartooth Mountains, Shoshone National Forest

Red Hills, Bridger-Teton National Forest

Laramie Mountains, Medicine Bow National Forest

Fremont Canyon

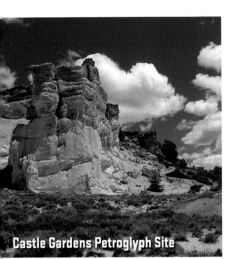
Castle Gardens Petroglyph Site

Seminoe Reservoir

Snowy Range, Medicine Bow National Forest

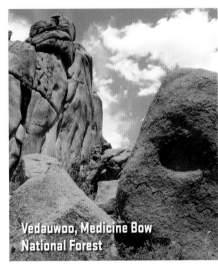
Vedauwoo, Medicine Bow National Forest

Sierra Madre, Medicine Bow National Forest

Big Spring Scenic Backway,
Bridger-Teton National Forest

Warren Bridge Recreation Area

Smiths Fork, Bridger-Teton National Forest

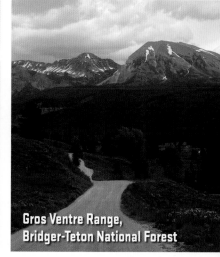

Gros Ventre Range,
Bridger-Teton National Forest

Louis Lake Road, Shoshone National Forest

Laramie Mountains

An extension of Colorado's Front Range, the Laramie Mountains stretch nearly 150 miles from Colorado to Casper. The range is characterized by towering granite outcroppings, widespread slopes of sagebrush and grass, and forests that are dominated by ponderosa and lodgepole pine. Spruce and fir trees can be found on the highest mountains including Twin Peaks, Laramie Peak, and Casper Mountain. Creeks are small and often intermittent, and lakes are relegated to beaver ponds.

By Rocky Mountain standards, the southern half of this chain is unimpressive and goes mostly unnoticed. Conversely, it's impossible to ignore the rugged northern half of the range where timbered ridges culminate to Laramie Peak at 10,274 feet. For emigrants migrating west, this peak proved to be a sentimental landmark as it was the very first mountain that many of them had ever seen. From slow-moving wagons on Wyoming's eastern plains, the distinct summit was seen at a distance that would take several days to travel.

The Laramie Mountains provide habitat for a diverse range of animals. At the southern end of the range near Colorado, small numbers of moose can be found among the creeks. Further north in the area described here, it's antelope, deer, and elk that you are likely to spot. You may also encounter wild turkeys, dusky grouse, and sage grouse. Also present in these mountains, but rarely seen, are bighorn sheep, black bears, and mountain lions.

Land Ownership

A large section of the northern mountains is covered by the Medicine Bow National Forest, managed by an office in Douglas, but it is heavily fragmented by private land. Many of the landowners do not grant public access across their property, which limits nearly all of the 4WD routes in the range to just a few miles in length. The western mountains of the range, Casper Mountain and its southern neighbor, Muddy Mountain, have a mixed land ownership that is mostly private.

When driving roads in this area—particularly if you like to explore the unbeaten paths—be mindful of posted private property signs. Local stories abound about conflicts with armed landowners in a snit. I personally have never had any such encounters, but I did meet one owner who drove out to his fence and made it clear that I was not allowed to pass through his gate.

Roads and Trails

Interstate 25 travels along the entire length of the Laramie Mountains, making for convenient access and offering a multitude of entry points. Cutting across the southern half of the range is HWY 34, which travels through beautiful Sybille Canyon between Wheatland and Laramie. On the far north end, a paved road traverses Casper Mountain. Other major routes in these mountains are long, remote county and forest roads.

Secondary roads are often short and vary from easy tracks to rocky, challenging paths. Nearly all of these can be traversed in stock 4x4 vehicles as long as you travel slowly and cautiously. There are also a number of designated ATV trails. Though these are also short, they make for fun trips in scenic areas.

Seasons and Conditions

Seasonal restrictions and closures are uncommon for the roads in the Laramie Mountains, leaving travel to your discretion. In general, the main roads are navigable in May, though sloppy conditions can leave some stretches closed until June. This is especially true at higher elevations such as those around Laramie Peak and Muddy Mountain. Summer days can be scorching hot, which helps fuel the buildup of violent afternoon thunderstorms. Access in the fall months is good in September and October, but snow—and the wind that drives it horizontally—forces the roads closed after November. The road to the top of Casper Mountain is open all year.

Fuel

The roads that traverse the Laramie Mountains are very long; always start a trip with a full tank. On the north and east side of the mountains, you'll find fueling stations in the towns along I-25. To the south, you'll find fuel in Laramie.

Maps

A statewide atlas works well for navigating the main backroads in this area. Two good ones include the DeLorme Wyoming Atlas & Gazetteer and the Wyoming Road and Recreation Atlas published by Benchmark Maps. For more detailed route-finding, refer to the Medicine Bow National Forest map for the Laramie Peak Unit, the Medicine Bow ORV map, or the Medicine Bow National Forest Motor Vehicle Use Map (MVUM).

1: Glendo State Park
Follow the Glendo Reservoir shoreline

☒ **Backcountry Drive**
Most vehicles

☐ **4WD Route**
4x4 vehicle or ORV

☐ **ATV Trail**
ORV less than 50" wide

Location/Map	Southeast of Douglas; Page 228
Roads	Lake Shore Drive, Glendo Park Road (CR 17, CR 160, CR 146)
Distance	32+ miles of roads
Managing Agency	Wyoming State Parks, other mixed ownership
Starting Coordinates	N42° 29.14' W105° 0.72'

Overview: Glendo State Park covers a rugged area east of the Laramie Mountains that is of historical significance. The North Platte River that now fills a large reservoir here was a critical resource sought by natives and pioneers alike. Archaeologically rich, many ancient artifacts have been discovered here and are now being displayed in museums. While you may still chance upon a remnant of this history—such as a tepee ring or evidence of the Oregon-Utah-California Trail—some of the opportune land is now submerged under 12,000 acres of water.

Today, Glendo is one of Wyoming's most popular recreation areas, especially in mid-summer when boaters from several states converge on the park. The Fourth of July weekend is the rowdiest time. If crowds aren't for you, visit the park in the spring or fall. Entering the park requires a reasonable day-use fee for both residents and non-residents. Be aware that you may be charged a fee for ATVs, as these can qualify as second vehicles.

There are two backroads in Glendo State Park: the shorter Lake Shore Drive that travels through the short hills on the west side of the reservoir and the longer Glendo Park Road (CR 17) that wraps around the reservoir's southern and eastern shorelines.

Start: From Douglas, take I-25 south to Glendo (Exit 111). Turn east from the Interstate and drive into the small town. Follow the Glendo State Park signs for 1.3 miles to the south to reach the park's main entrance booth.

Description (Lake Shore Drive): This 6.7-mile drive follows the west shoreline of Glendo Reservoir. From the main entrance, drive south a short distance and turn left onto a gravel road. Within a couple of miles, the curvy road passes Custer Cove Campground and then reaches a thinly wooded area filled in with private residences. Continue through the development and watch for a side road leading to Reno Cove—this is one of several places where you can access the shoreline.

The main roadway continues through varied terrain to reach the Red Hills area. The pale red and tan brim here contrasts sharply with the sky, water, and sprinkling of trees.

From the colorful halfway point, the road bends to the west to traverse flatter terrain. It's a relatively featureless few miles to reach the Airport Fee Booth—a park entrance point located just north of the town of Glendo. When you reach the paved road, turn left to return to town.

Description (Glendo Park Road): For a longer drive of 35 miles (round trip), begin by following the paved road from the main entrance as it wraps around the reservoir's southern end. The park's marina and headquarters are soon passed before Two Moon Campground on the left and a scenic pullout on the right. From this viewing area, you can see the North Platte River and a small power plant some 300 feet below. Along the horizon are miles of rugged and timbered hills that largely comprise Camp Guernsey, training grounds for Wyoming's Army and Air National Guards.

Past the overlook, a short side road descends to an excellent 1.6-mile foot trail near the river. A stroll along this wildlife-rich path takes you to the reservoir's dam.

Staying on the main paved route, the road bends around and crosses the dam, a 167-foot structure that was completed in 1957. Climb up the ensuing switchback to find another scenic pullout. At 4,800 feet, this high perch

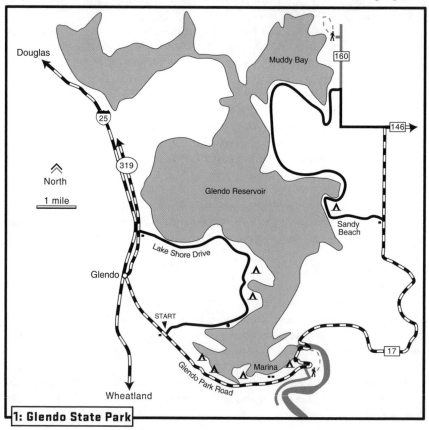

1: Glendo State Park

offers views of the reservoir and the Laramie Mountains to the west. Laramie Peak (10,272-feet) is the dominant summit that is easily recognized.

By 6 miles, the road exits the state park and crosses beautifully semi-timbered prairie where deer and pronghorn antelope are common. Continue along the paved route until you reach a signed junction near mile 12 for Sandy Beach. Turn left onto the gravel road and drive a short distance to reach a state park entrance sign where fees are collected.

At Sandy Beach, you'll find a very popular campground and day-use area. The beach is lined with thick cottonwood trees that shade campsites. The sand here is part of a belt of shallow dunes that stretch from the Great Divide Basin near Rock Springs to Nebraska.

Continue north along the sandy road as it curves around Cottonwood Creek Bay on the reservoir's east side. The road is narrow and has some shallow ruts, but is easily negotiated with any car. The exception to this is if you venture onto any of the sandy side spurs. Even 4WD vehicles get stuck in this innocuous-looking dune field.

The single lane continues on for several miles to reach Muddy Bay, a marshy cottonwood-lined bulb on the northeast side of reservoir. The route parallels the trees until reaching a good gravel county road at 21 miles. From here, you can turn left on CR 160 to reach the Muddy Bay Wetland Nature Trail—a short 1.5-mile foot trail. Otherwise, turn right and head south to a junction. Turn left here (a right turn leads to private property) and drive east on Meadowdale Road (CR 146) for a mile. Then turn right to return to the paved Glendo Park road. It's a little over 14 miles back to the main park entrance from this point.

Sandy beach at Glendo State Park

Other Nearby Drives

Glendo-Guernsey—The hilled country between Guernsey and Glendo State Parks is dotted with pine trees and rugged breaks. County roads such as Patton Creek Road (CR 208) and Emigrant Hill Road (CR 214) between these parks are worth a drive. However, be attentive to signs that mark private property and especially restricted areas as some of this land belongs to the military.

2: Sunset Ridge

A loop across the top

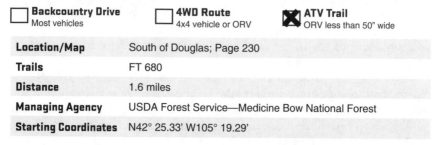

☐ **Backcountry Drive** Most vehicles	☐ **4WD Route** 4x4 vehicle or ORV	☒ **ATV Trail** ORV less than 50" wide

Location/Map	South of Douglas; Page 230
Trails	FT 680
Distance	1.6 miles
Managing Agency	USDA Forest Service—Medicine Bow National Forest
Starting Coordinates	N42° 25.33' W105° 19.29'

Overview: This short ATV loop surmounts the top of Sunset Ridge (shown as Sunset Hill on USGS maps). From the crest, you'll discover a full panorama of the northern Laramie Mountains and eastern plains. A Wyoming ORV permit is required.

Start: From Douglas, head south for 28 miles on HWY 94/CR 5 to Esterbrook. The first 17 miles of this road are paved. Drive east 2.3 miles

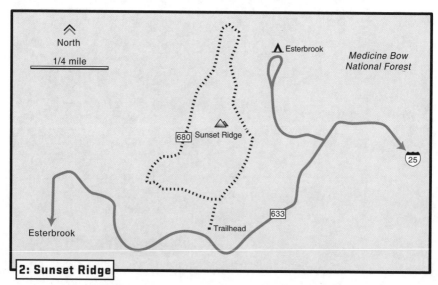

Sunset Ridge Trail

to the Sunset Ridge Trailhead. If traveling from Glendo, take I-25 south to Horseshoe Creek Road (Exit 115) and proceed west on the well-maintained gravel road for 16.5 miles. Turn north onto FR 633 and drive 2.6 miles to the trailhead.

Description: The ATV trail begins by heading north through a pine forest dotted with rock outcrops. The other end of the loop is passed within a tenth of a mile. Bear right at this fork and continue northward where the trail runs below the ridge. Rocks on the trail provide a little bounce, but are easily driven over.

On the far side of the hill, the trail passes a short ATV that heads north into more open terrain. The loop trail, though, climbs higher along a couple of grass-lined switchbacks to gain the top of the ridge. From the east side of this crest, there are far reaching views of Wyoming's eastern plains, including Glendo Reservoir.

Follow the trail southward to reach the top of the rocky ridgeline where you'll attain a sweeping view across the mountain range to the southwest. Some of the highest summits in these mountains that can be seen include Rock Mountain (7,200 feet), Black Mountain (8,000 feet), and the range's dominant point, Laramie Peak (10,272 feet), just 12 miles away as the crow flies.

From this point, the trail begins descending as it heads east to reach the end of the loop. Turn right at the junction to return to the trailhead.

3: Eastern Laramie Mountains
Tour the eastern front

⬛ Backcountry Drive
Most vehicles

☐ **4WD Route**
4x4 vehicle or ORV

☐ **ATV Trail**
ORV less than 50" wide

Location/Map	South of Douglas; Page 233
Roads	CR 135, CR 6, FR 633, FR 71, FR 721, CR 204
Distance	85 miles
Managing Agency	USDA Forest Service—Medicine Bow National Forest, other mixed ownership
Starting Coordinates	N42° 30.20' W105° 1.94'

Overview: This extended drive tours the eastern side of the Laramie Mountains by utilizing a number of different roads—some are smooth, others a bit rougher. There are sections that are tight and steep so towing a long trailer is not recommended.

Start: From Douglas, take I-25 south to Glendo (Exit 111) and turn west.

Description: From I-25 at Glendo, drive west on Ridge Road (CR 135), also named Esterbrook Road or Glendo Road (depending on the map), which later turns into CR 6 where it enters Converse County. This heavily graveled lane climbs gently over the grassy prairie to the higher forested hills of the Laramie Mountains, some 20 miles away. It's beautiful—especially in late spring—and for many, it's this kind of open space that makes the heart sing. The shift from the Great Plains to the Rocky Mountains becomes evident as gentle flats gain rounded knolls, occasional rocks, and a light measure of trees.

After 20 miles, a fork is reached with a road headed north to Douglas. Stay left to continue south and enter the Medicine Bow National Forest. It's a mile farther to Esterbrook, a tiny settlement of summer cabins hidden among the ponderosa pines.

In Esterbrook, continue straight past a junction for CR 5 (headed west) and then turn left, back to the east, on FR 633. The forest's road surface is noticeably rougher than the county roads, but still easily driven with any vehicle.

Near 25 miles, the road passes an ATV trail at Sunset Ridge Trailhead (route #2). A short distance further is Esterbrook Campground, a sleepy camp that sees light use except on holiday weekends.

From the campground, the road turns south and passes a junction with Horseshoe Creek Road (FR 614), which travels 16.5 miles east to I-25. Continue south on what is now Harris Park Road. This course climbs and descends, sometimes steeply, over the rugged eastern mountain front, which consists of a light ponderosa pine forest and granite outcrops. A number of secondary roads leave the main route, but private land interwoven throughout the area leaves these short spurs better suited for parking and picnicking than driving.

As the road works southward, massive spires of granite tower over the forest to the west. The road bends around shorter outcroppings to get through the rugged terrain. You'll find the trip to be smooth at times, bumpy at others. At 32 miles, FR 633 passes by a number of cabins and then settles down into Harris Park near a Boy Scout camp.

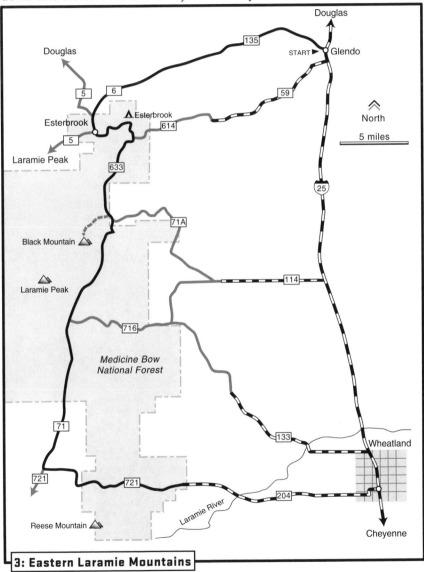

3: Eastern Laramie Mountains

SIDE TRIP A 4WD road, FR 667 passes through the scout camp and climbs nearly 2,000 feet to reach the top of Black Mountain (route #4). This 3.4-mile drive requires a high clearance vehicle to clear some rock slabs.

At mile 35, Harris Park Road briefly leaves the national forest and reaches a junction. Here, it turns left and eventually joins Fish Creek Road en route to I-25. To continue with the backcountry drive, turn right onto Cottonwood Park Road (FR 633), re-enter the national forest, and continue south. The road now travels below the rocky folds of Black Mountain (8,000 feet) where 16,000 acres of pine forest burned in 2002.

You'll soon parallel Cottonwood Creek over the next few miles through a park of the same name. The clearing of this little valley affords perfect views of Laramie Peak (10,272 feet) with its summit looming just three miles to the west. The blackened flanks of this mountain burned in a massive 100,000-acre fire in 2012.

Continue southward until the park narrows and reaches Fletcher Park Road at 44 miles. This is another east-bearing route that leads back to Wheatland. For the last time, stay south at this junction.

The road now leaves Cottonwood Park and cuts through a groove between lightly timbered slopes. The North Laramie River is soon crossed and then the road exits the national forest near a ranch. The following few miles take you across mountainous ranch land before the road breaks out into the flats by mile 52. This is beautiful open country adorned with unexpected rock outcrops and the now distant timbered summits of the mountain range.

Laramie Peak seen from the east

A few miles to the southwest, the road reaches Palmer Canyon Road (CR 721). Turn left here, east, and drive over gentle terrain to reach the national forest boundary again within a few miles. The terrain gets suddenly rugged here, with steep, rocky ridges. The road's grade becomes much steeper, too, and you soon begin a 2,400-foot descent through Palmer Canyon.

The sinuous backroad becomes rougher in the so-called canyon, but these are scenic miles worth the bumps. Two summits of which to take note are Collins Peak (7,915 feet) and the higher Reese Mountain (8,152 feet), both to the south. Interpretive roadside signs are soon passed that highlight these craggy massifs. One mentions the Collins Peak fire of 1986 that burned 4,520 acres. The other tells of the Reese Fire that scorched nearly 20,000 acres in 2002—that was an especially ravaging year for wildfires in these mountains.

By mile 70, the road leaves the Medicine Bow National Forest for the last time and rolls out of the mountains and onto the plains. Luman Creek soon parallels the roadway for a short distance before draining into the larger Laramie River, which is crossed. It's now a straight shot east through farmland to reach Wheatland by mile 84. The road ends at the residential edge of town. Here, make a short jog to the north and then turn back to the east on the next street to return to I-25.

4: Black Mountain
Climb to a staffed fire lookout tower

☐ **Backcountry Drive**	☒ **4WD Route**	☐ **ATV Trail**
Most vehicles	4x4 vehicle or ORV	ORV less than 50" wide

Location/Map	South of Douglas; Page 237
Roads	FR 667
Distance	3.4 miles
Managing Agency	USDA Forest Service—Medicine Bow National Forest
Starting Coordinates	N42° 19.91' W105° 20.485'

Overview: This rugged 4WD road climbs over 1,700 feet to reach a staffed fire lookout tower on the summit of Black Mountain. You'll encounter steep grades and rock slabs as well as intermittent easy stretches.

Start: From Douglas, head south on I-25 to the El Rancho Road exit (Exit 94) between Wheatland and Glendo. Drive west on Fish Creek Road for 8 miles, bearing right at the Harris Park fork. Follow Harris Park Road (CR 71A) for 12 miles to a Boy Scout camp. The 4WD road, FR 667, begins from this camp.

Description: The drive begins from Harris Park, a grassy meadow found at the base of the Laramie Mountains. A smattering of private cabins is found

Fire lookout on top of Black Mountain

here, as is a Colorado-based Boy Scout camp. Locate the main road traveling through the camp, FR 667, and follow it west into the timber. The first half mile passes through private property and gets progressively more rocky as you go.

Once the road enters public land, it gets significantly more challenging as you motor up rock slabs on the steep roadway. You'll need a vehicle with high clearance, possibly four-wheel drive, and good approach angles (things like trailer hitch balls or low hanging exhaust pipes might scrape).

A tiny trailhead for the Harris Park Trail is reached near 1 mile. If you make it to this point, you can certainly make it the rest of the way. From the trailhead, the road enters a broad clearing that offers the first glimpse of the fire lookout tower on top of Black Mountain, some 1,000 feet higher in elevation. The opening also reveals a rugged landscape of towering rock pinnacles and outcrops. The surrounding pine forest—filled with elk, deer, mountain lion, and bear—has seen its share of disasters. Damaging bark beetles initially killed many trees in this area. This infestation only helped fuel the Hensel Fire in 2002 as it roared across 16,000 acres of the Laramie Mountains. The evidence of this fire is still very fresh today, though the landscape is slowly showing signs of recovery.

The driving is relatively easy through the clearing as the grade levels and the road surface becomes smoother. This is only a half mile stretch, though, and by the end you'll have reached the base of Black Mountain. From this point, the road begins to switchback up the northeastern flank of the mountain while maintaining a relatively steep incline—an average grade

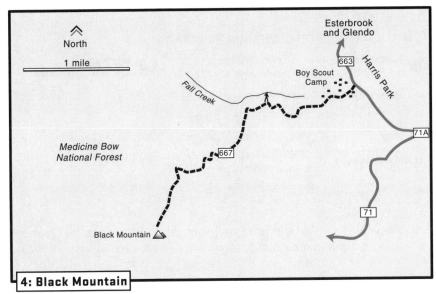

4: Black Mountain

of 14%. The road also gets rockier, but many of the rocks are of the looser, smaller variety that poses minor traction problems if any at all.

Much of the final last mile traverses the long ridgeline of the mountain. From this narrow, high strip, you can begin to scan the vast area to the west. The road ends at a parking area where a short spur leads to the base of an impressive rock formation. On top is a metal fire lookout that was built in 1958. This is one of the nation's last remaining lookouts to be staffed, as aerial surveillance and satellite imaging have now become the tools of wildfire detection. When visiting, remember that this tower also serves as a residence so only proceed to the tower if you are invited to do so.

The view from the top of Black Mountain is excellent. Laramie Peak commands the western skyline, but there are many lesser peaks that also paint the backdrop. You also get a better look of how much of the area was consumed by wildfire. Looking east, you'll scan miles of prairie land as well as the timbered hills near Glendo State Park.

Other Nearby Drives

Cow Camp Road—FR 641 is a 4WD route that runs 4 miles across a burned-out ridge high above the North Laramie River. There is no view of the river, but a nearby foot trail can get you there. Deer, elk, and bighorn sheep live here. The road is open to motorized use from May 1 to November 14. To reach the road from Douglas, head south on I-25 to the El Rancho Road exit (Exit 94). Drive west on Fish Creek Road, staying left at the Harris Park fork. After 13.7 miles, turn right at the junction onto Fletcher Park Road (FR 716) and continue 5.5 miles west. Turn south at the trailhead sign on FR 641/FR 642. If traveling from Wheatland, you can take Fletcher Park Road for 22 miles to reach this turnoff.

5: Laramie Peak

Drive to the top of the Laramie Mountains

☒ **Backcountry Drive** Most vehicles	☐ **4WD Route** 4x4 vehicle or ORV	☒ **ATV Trail** ORV less than 50" wide

Location/Map	South of Douglas; Page 239
Roads/Trails	CR 5, FR 671, FR 661, FT 602
Distance	28.5 miles (backcountry drive), 5.25 miles (ATV/foot trail)
Managing Agency	USDA Forest Service—Medicine Bow National Forest, other mixed ownership
Starting Coordinates	Backcountry drive: N42° 45.29' W105° 24.52' ATV trail : N42° 15.41' W105° 29.07'

Overview: This beautiful trip takes you from the prairies of central Wyoming into the very heart of the Laramie Mountains. The backcountry drive ends at a trailhead located at the base of the range's highest summit, Laramie Peak. From there, you can continue to the top of the mountain on foot, horse, or ATV. The roads that comprise the backcountry drive are well maintained, but the last couple of miles can be sloppy, especially before mid-June.

The rugged ATV trail that leads to the summit climbs nearly 3,000 vertical feet and should only be driven by experienced ATV riders as it is steep, narrow, and rocky—traits that don't appeal to most recreational riders. Many a rider here has expressed regret, surprise, and misery while trying to throttle an ATV up the rugged path.

If such a trail is just the challenge for which you've been looking, there are a few more things to know. First, be ready to share the trail—hikers and horsemen are common. Yielding to a party riding 1,000-pound animals that can be skittish, on a trail barely wide enough for your ATV, is a good reason to tackle this trail on a weekday when visitation is lighter. Another concern is snow. The last mile of this trail often has knee-deep drifts through June; it's very deceptive when it feels like summer at the trailhead. Last, remember that a Wyoming ORV permit is required.

Start: From I-25 at Douglas, take Exit 140 and drive south to HWY 94. Follow the highway south for 17 miles until you reach the end of the pavement where the backcountry drive portion begins. To continue on to the trailhead, drive south for 28 miles on HWY 94, which turns into Esterbrook Road (CR 5) after 17 miles. At Esterbrook, turn west on CR 5, following the signs to Friend Park Campground. Drive 15 miles to FR 671, turn left and drive just short of 3 miles. Turn onto FR 661, drive 1 mile, and then bear left at the split to reach the trailhead.

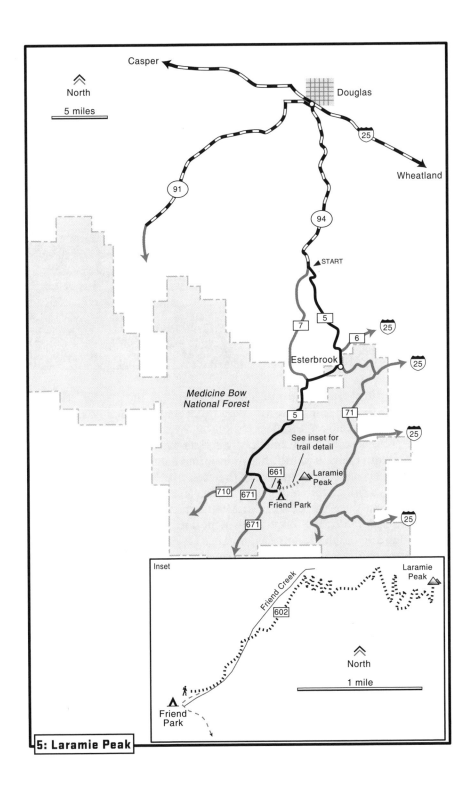

North

5 miles

Casper

Douglas

25

Wheatland

91

94

START

7

5

25

6

25

Esterbrook

Medicine Bow
National Forest

5

71

25

See inset for
trail detail

Laramie
Peak

661

710

671

Friend Park

671

25

Inset

Friend Creek

602

Laramie
Peak

North

1 mile

Friend
Park

5: Laramie Peak

A distant look at Laramie Peak

Description (Backcountry drive): The drive begins at the end of HWY 94 where two gravel roads, Esterbrook Road (CR 5) and Braae Road (CR 7), split into separate directions. Bear left onto CR 5 to continue a southward advance. Esterbrook Road immediately crosses LaBonte Creek and begins tackling rougher terrain, which becomes immediately obvious as the road surface also becomes more uneven with occasional rough patches.

A few miles farther, the county road mimics Mill Creek for a short distance before passing the west side of Elk Mountain. The road now enters the fringes of a sporadic pine forest—mostly ponderosa and lodgepole pine—that is found across the Laramie Mountains.

At nearly 9 miles from the end of the pavement, you pass a fork with CR 6, which heads east to Glendo. Stay right, or south, to enter the Medicine Bow National Forest—this briefly changes the road number from CR 5 to FS 653. Just a mile farther, the road splits into two directions at Esterbrook, a small mountain community. Bear right at this fork and drive west through Ullman Park. Here, a small photogenic chapel sits dwarfed by Laramie Peak's large presence on the horizon.

Continuing west, the now smooth gravel lane passes by an assortment of homes, cabins, and trailers that are nestled into the light pine woods. Past this development, you enter a grassy prairie and briefly leave national forest land. There are many side roads that are passed, but the main course is obvious and there are numerous signs that show the destination: Friend Park Campground.

After passing Braae Road (CR 7) a second time, Esterbrook Road bends to the south. Here, the path divides into two separate routes, but they both unite after just a quarter of a mile so it makes no difference which leg you choose. The road then re-enters the national forest soon after this point.

The next 11 miles proceed through open country that runs through the heart of the Laramie Mountains. Here, you get unobstructed views of the landscape features that typify these central Wyoming mountains: meadows of grass and sage, fractured stands of pine, unique granite boulder piles, and short but jagged peaks.

At mile 25, turn left onto the rougher FR 671. Drive east on this lane to round the northern base of Eagle Peak (9,167 feet), one of the area's highest summits. A trailhead for Roaring Fork Creek is passed at 2 miles, followed shortly thereafter by FR 661. Turn left and drive along this narrow road for a mile as it dips into Friend Park before ending at a popular Forest Service recreation area. This site is split between a large trailhead on the left and Friend Park Campground on the right. Parking fees are required at both sites.

Laramie Peak (10,272 feet) is the highest summit in this range and it towers thousands of feet above its surrounding terrain. The mountain's crown can be seen over a hundred miles away on clear days. Impressive, but from the end of this drive, at a higher elevation of 7,500 feet, the peak has lost a little of its towering dominance. As you explore this area, you can see areas that burned during the massive 2012 Arapaho Fire. The nearly 100,000-acre blaze spared the west side of Laramie Peak (including the trail), but consumed the south and eastern faces.

Visitation to Friend Park is high during the summer as people come to picnic, sightsee, camp, or climb the large mountain. The trail to the top is just over 5 miles in length—one easy mile to start followed by four more that tackle the mountain's relentless uphill switchbacks that gain nearly 3,000 feet of elevation. The view at the top is terrific, a true aerial view of eastern and central Wyoming.

When driving back to Douglas, consider taking CR 7 (near Esterbrook) as an alternative to CR 5. It provides a different view for 14 miles of the return trip. Of course, it is also possible to take one ALTERNATE ROUTE of the major trunk roads south to Laramie or east to Wheatland. These are long roads so consider your fuel level.

Description (ATV trail): The trail begins with an easy one-mile ride above Friend Creek. At the end of this stretch, the trail intersects the miniature creek at a bridged crossing. This is your last good chance to do any adjustments as the trail immediately turns onto a steep, uphill grade. There will be but one level, wide spot on the trail between this point and the summit.

The switchbacks that ascend the mountainside travel through a gorgeous blend of lodgepole pines and massive boulders. The trail surface itself varies as you go. A few lengths consist of an easily driven dirt surface, but there are many rock-strewn stretches that demand your attention. Some rocks on the trail are large enough to high-center your machine.

The trail reaches Friend Creek Falls by the end of mile 2. This is a tiny cascade shadowed by aspen trees, a refreshing stopping point before taking on the next dusty switchback.

The next several miles consist of much of the same thing—elevation gain. Watch for mile markers high on the trees. As the trail pushes through 9,000 feet, the forest begins to transition to subalpine trees such as spruce and fir. Dusky grouse are commonly seen at these higher elevations. As the forest changes, so do the views. The Medicine Bow Mountains, including the Snowy Range and Elk Mountain, can be seen from the southern ends of the switchbacks.

In mile 4, you'll get a glimpse of the summit, its rocky point crowded with a small shed and antennas. A mile farther, you'll be on the final approach to the pinnacle. There are not good places near the summit to pull off the trail and park an ATV, and turning around can also be challenging. With this in mind, keep a lookout for suitable (wider) spots in the trail as you near the top of the mountain. The last few yards to the summit will need to be walked on foot.

At 10,272 feet, the view of eastern Wyoming from the top of Laramie Peak is unsurpassed. To the east, the Laramie Mountains fall away to the Great Plains, but they stretch toward Casper to the west.

Narrow and rocky trail on Laramie Peak

6: LaBonte Canyon
Laramie Mountains' wildlife-rich habitat

☐ **Backcountry Drive**
  Most vehicles

☐ **4WD Route**
  4x4 vehicle or ORV

☒ **ATV Trail**
  ORV less than 50" wide

Location/Map	Southwest of Douglas; Page 245
Trails	FT 624
Distance	2.9 miles
Managing Agency	USDA Forest Service—Medicine Bow National Forest
Starting Coordinates	N42° 24.45' W105° 37.35'

Overview: The short trail through LaBonte Canyon is likely the most stunning route in the Laramie Mountains. This trip takes you into a beautiful valley bound by hills of granite. The passage is rich with opportunities for wildlife watching and scenic photography. The trail is open to motorized use from May 1 to November 14, but waiting until later in May is suggested. A Wyoming ORV permit is required.

Start: From I-25 at Douglas, take Exit 140 and drive south to HWY 91. Continue along HWY 91 for 23 miles, then Cold Springs Road (CR 24) for 3 miles to a fork. Bear left onto Fort Fetterman Road (CR 16) and drive 13 miles. Turn east onto FR 658 and proceed 4.5 miles to Curtis Gulch Campground. The road begins at the camp.

Description: The trail begins from a pole fence that runs along LaBonte Creek at the east side of Curtis Gulch Campground. From here, the trail immediately dips to a rock-strewn crossing of LaBonte Creek—a shallow east-flowing stream that rarely has much depth to it. This is the first of six times that the path crosses the meandering creek.

Follow the stream to the east through a riparian corridor lined with aspens, shrubs, and coniferous trees. Aside from some occasional large rocks at the beginning, and at each creek crossing, the trail is smooth and easily driven, especially on an ATV.

At 1 mile, the trail enters the LaBonte Canyon Wildlife Range. This superb habitat supports bighorn sheep, deer, elk, grouse, wild turkeys, and bears. Here, the road passes through grassy mountain meadows that are flanked by towering granite pinnacles.

Just shy of 3 miles, the track ends at LaBonte Canyon Trailhead. This is as far as motorized travelers can go, but you can continue another mile on foot before reaching private property.

Track leading through LaBonte Canyon

7: Big Bear Canyon/Devils Pass
Climb through a timbered gorge

☐ **Backcountry Drive**
Most vehicles

☐ **4WD Route**
4x4 vehicle or ORV

☒ **ATV Trail**
ORV less than 50" wide

Location/Map	Southwest of Douglas; Page 245
Trails	FT 657, FT 615, FT 610, FT 604, FT 655
Distance	10+ miles
Managing Agency	USDA Forest Service—Medicine Bow National Forest
Starting Coordinates	N42° 24.28' W105° 37.9'

Overview: Big Bear Canyon and Devils Pass are among the best four-wheeling areas in the Laramie Mountains. Here, you'll find a small network of old roads that have been converted to designated ATV trails. These paths offer more family-friendly riding than some of the other challenging trails in the Laramie Mountains.

This area is fragmented with parcels of private property, which kills the potential for some excellent extended routes. However, as of this writing, the Forest Service is working on connecting some of the trails here to provide a longer, connected trail system. The trails are open to motorized use from May 1 to November 14. A Wyoming ORV permit is required.

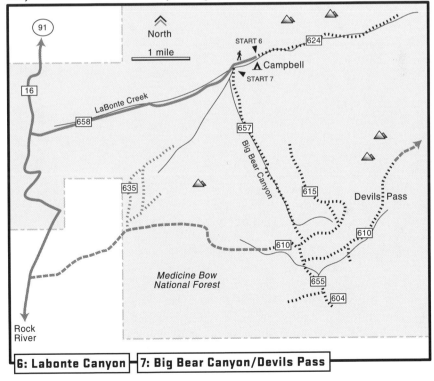

Approaching Big Bear Canyon

Start: From I-25 at Douglas, take Exit 140 and drive south to HWY 91. Continue along HWY 91 for 23 miles, then Cold Springs Road (CR 24) for 3 miles to a fork. Bear left onto Fort Fetterman Road (CR 16) and drive 13 miles. Turn east onto FR 658 and proceed 4 miles to Big Bear Canyon Road on the right. There are numerous pullouts along the incoming road where you can unload ATVs.

Description: The trail, long known as Big Bear Canyon Road (FT 657), begins from the south side of FR 658. Once you turn onto the trail, you immediately ford LaBonte Creek, which is usually not too deep. The track then travels westward a short distance before curving to the south and entering a heavily timbered canyon.

The next several miles ascend through a beautiful area consisting of ponderosa pines, quaking aspen, and massive boulders. It's a mostly dirt path with few rocks, but it is often found wet. You're likely to encounter at least seven shallow water crossings as well as a couple sizable mud holes. Another challenge can be downed timber. While many of the smaller logs can be driven over, at least one that I came upon required some vigorous axe work before I could continue the drive.

At 3.7 miles (4 miles according to the Forest Service), the trail reaches a junction at the top of the canyon. A left turn here puts you on the Sawtooth Trail (FT 615). This is a slightly rockier path that ends 3 miles farther at private property. While this trail is worthy of exploring, the more interesting Devils Pass route makes a more scenic drive.

To reach the pass, turn right to reach FR 610, and then turn left to head south. (Following FR 610 to the west here leads to a road that is not enrolled in the state ORV program.) After a quarter mile, FR 610 turns east to cross an exposed sagebrush-covered slope that affords excellent views to the south. From this vantage point, you can peer over the Medicine Bow National Forest and pick out tall, unsung summits like Windy Peak.

As the trail continues east, you'll pass several spurs that branch off both sides, but none of these go far. At 5.5 miles, the main track enters a scrubby pine stand where it becomes rocky on its final ascent to reach Devil's Pass (8,140 feet). Reaching the pass is a bit anti-climatic, as most views are obscured by rock outcrops and pines. It does, however, make a terrific place to picnic and watch for wildlife that wander over this high passage. From here, the trail continues past a gate and descends through a denser forest to end at the national forest boundary.

8: Twin Peaks
Short ride to a small high point

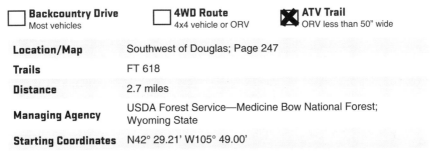

| ☐ **Backcountry Drive** Most vehicles | ☐ **4WD Route** 4x4 vehicle or ORV | ☒ **ATV Trail** ORV less than 50" wide |

Location/Map	Southwest of Douglas; Page 247
Trails	FT 618
Distance	2.7 miles
Managing Agency	USDA Forest Service—Medicine Bow National Forest; Wyoming State
Starting Coordinates	N42° 29.21' W105° 49.00'

Overview: This moderate ATV trail climbs to the top of a landing between two rocky summits. Views at the end of the trail reveal an expanse of low timbered mountains that see little visitation. A Wyoming ORV permit is required.

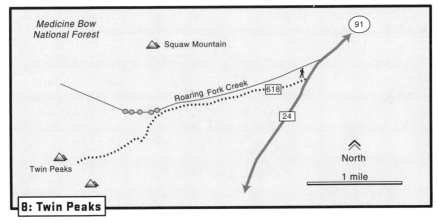

Twin Peaks Trail

Start: From I-25 at Douglas, take Exit 140 and drive south to HWY 91. Continue along HWY 91 for 23 miles, then Cold Springs Road (CR 24) for 3 miles to a fork. Bear right to stay on CR 24 and drive another 8.5 scenic miles to the trailhead on the right side of the road. The trailhead can accommodate small ATV trailers.

Description: A dirt path departs the trailhead and travels across gentle terrain dotted with trees. Part of this initial stretch crosses a section of private property (as well as state-owned land) so be sure to stay on the trail.

Approaching the end of the first mile, the vegetation thickens as the trail reaches the Roaring Fork drainage. Despite its name, this is a tiny brook that is mostly concealed by brush along the banks. There are only a couple of places where you can spot the stream and some tiny ponds.

At 1.5 miles, the trail bears southwest away from the creek and soon takes on a steeper grade through a coniferous forest. While the lower woodland consisted mostly of pine and aspen, the forest transitions to subalpine fir and spruce as the route gains elevation. Watch for grouse along the way.

After ascending for just a half mile, the trail reaches more moderate terrain. At 8,800 feet, the forest begins to thin and trees become displaced by large rock outcrops.

The trail ends at a level area between the rocky summits of Twin Peaks. The view from your ATV seat isn't too impressive, but if you scramble up one of the smaller rock outcrops, you'll get a sweeping look around the rugged countryside, including a burned area to the north.

9: Western Laramie Mountains
Tour the west side of the range

☒ **Backcountry Drive**
Most vehicles

☐ **4WD Route**
4x4 vehicle or ORV

☐ **ATV Trail**
ORV less than 50" wide

Location/Map	Southeast of Casper; Page 251
Roads	CR 24, CR 62, FR 660, CR 97, CR 402
Distance	62 miles
Managing Agency	USDA Forest Service—Medicine Bow National Forest, other mixed ownership
Starting Coordinates	N42° 45.33' W105° 24.53'

Overview: This long backcountry drive travels through a remote portion of the Laramie Mountains in the all-but-forgotten sections of the Medicine Bow National Forest—its lonely country. Be sure to have a full tank of gas before starting out as this drive travels over 100 miles between towns.

Start: From I-25 at Douglas, take Exit 140 and drive south to HWY 91. Continue along HWY 91 for 23 miles to reach Cold Springs Road (CR 24).

Description: The trip begins on Cold Springs Road (CR 24), a well-maintained gravel road that cuts into the edge of a steep hill above Blue Nose Creek. The road reaches a fork at 3 miles; stay on CR 24 by bearing right. The road now climbs as it bends to the west to cross a broad grassy valley. While this stretch is easily driven in any vehicle, occasional bumps in the roadway will give you a good knock if you hit them at full speed.

By 6 miles, the landscape is overtaken by awesome and unusual rock outcrops. The rolling hills that have been covered in grass and sagebrush since Douglas now begin to support small clusters of trees, while large boulders are strewn about the prairie like litter. After crossing aspen-lined Rabbit Creek, the road passes Bear Rock, one of the more pronounced outcrops. LePrele Creek, a larger stream, is then soon crossed near the Medicine Bow National Forest boundary.

The next several miles become increasingly more wooded as the road nears a number of Forest Service sites. The first of these is the Twin Peaks Trailhead (route #8) at 11.5 miles followed by the LaPrele Guard Station at 13.8 miles. Among the cabins found here is a two-bedroom cabin that the Forest Service rents out for overnight stays (check www.recreation.gov). For a more primitive and affordable night in the forest, you'll find Campbell Creek Campground just a quarter of a mile farther south. Much of the forest along this stretch is privately owned, so resist the temptation of turning off onto one of the numerous sidetracks that are found near the recreation sites.

Past the campground, CR 24 surmounts the high point along this drive at 8,400 feet. A section of this high country was hit by a tornado in the summer of 1997 and you'll find tree stumps and a large wood sign on the right side of the road that marks the site. Shortly thereafter, the pine forest concedes to the sprawling, empty Shirley Basin. Look to the southern horizon to find Elk Mountain and other high peaks of the Medicine Bow Mountains.

When CR 24 exits the southern boundary of the Medicine Bow National Forest at 18 miles, it also crosses into Carbon County and becomes Little Medicine Road (CR 62). A half mile past this line, turn west onto Balsh Road (FR 660), a lesser road found near the Little Medicine Bow River.

ALTERNATE ROUTE
If FR 660 is found too rough or muddy for your liking—it is often heavily rutted—you can detour around this stretch by continuing south on CR 62 for a little over 15 miles to Utah Mining Road (CR 97). Turn north on CR 97 and drive north for a little over 10 miles to reach Bates Creek Road (CR 97/CR 402).

Driving west on FR 660, the route skims the national forest boundary while paralleling the base of the Laramie Mountains. The timbered ridge seen here is among the western remnants of this long, arcing range. At 25 miles, FR 629 is passed on the right, a scenic route that leads to Glenrock.

ALTERNATE ROUTE
A terrific alternate route for this drive is to return to I-25 on Box Elder Road, shown on maps as FR 629/CR 17. This 31-mile road heads north to parallel Box Elder Creek for a good distance, and then passes beautiful columns and mounts of rock. Be aware that there is a considerable amount of private land on both sides of the road. The road is a good dirt surface with only a few bumpy spots. The southern end of the road sometimes resembles a two-track path, but it becomes more distinct and gets more use further north. Nearly halfway, the road splits with CR 18. Stay right on CR 17 and drive another 8 miles to hit pavement. From this point, the road continues another 8 miles to pass underneath I-25 and reach HWY 20/26/87. Turn left toward Glenrock or right to reach I-25 at Exit 160.

One of the best places to access the mountains from this stretch is from FR 659 reached at mile 28. This rough track goes northward 5 miles to the Deer Creek Trail, a footpath closed to motorized traffic. From the junction with FR 659, the main road continues 7 miles to reach Bates Creek/Bates Hole Road (CR 97/CR 402). The last few miles of FR 660 are often found rutted and rough.

At mile 35, turn west on CR 97/CR 402, which offers a much improved gravel surface. This puts you along a high bench of BLM and state-managed land. Out the left window, you'll find that the countryside drops away into the basin while it rises into timbered knolls on the opposite side.

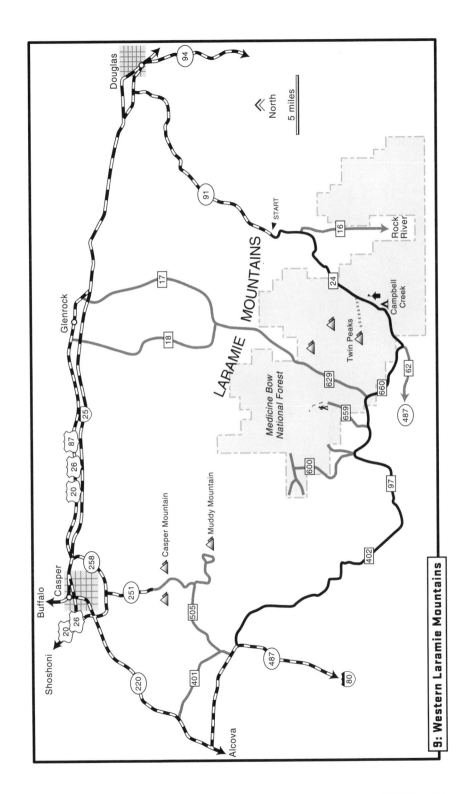

9: Western Laramie Mountains

Weaving road in the western Laramie Mountains

Bates Creek Road covers gentle terrain for the next dozen miles. But soon after it turns northward toward Casper, the landscape becomes more dramatic with colorful ridges of claystone and sandstone. Small junipers are also found on these hills—the only trees that will grow on this parched fringe of the Laramie Mountains.

The county road crosses over Corral Creek near mile 58, and then follows the stream a short distance through a lightly timbered trough. At mile 62, the backcountry drive ends at HWY 487. To reach Casper from this junction, turn right and drive 9 miles to HWY 220. Turn right again and drive 16 miles to town.

10: Casper Mountain Loop
Tour a trio of central Wyoming mountains

☒ **Backcountry Drive**
Most vehicles

☐ **4WD Route**
4x4 vehicle or ORV

☐ **ATV Trail**
ORV less than 50" wide

Location/Map	South of Casper; Page 254
Roads	HWY 251, CR 505, BLMR 6409, CR 401
Distance	37 miles
Managing Agency	BLM—Casper Field Office, Natrona County, other mixed ownership
Starting Coordinates	N42° 48.312' W106° 19.8'

Overview: This drive climbs to the top of Casper Mountain and then to an overlook on Muddy Mountain. After topping these two mountains, the route bears west and wraps around Coal Mountain. The road over Casper Mountain is open all year, but the road leading to Muddy Mountain is only open from mid-June to late November (it's also open to snowmobiling in the winter).

Start: From the west or east side of Casper, take Wyoming Boulevard (HWY 258) south to Casper Mountain Road (HWY 251).

Description: Begin the trip by driving south on paved Casper Mountain Road. As the road approaches the base of the mountain, watch for Garden Creek Road (HWY 252) on the right. In the spring and early summer, a small waterfall at the base of the mountain can be seen from here. Stay left at the junction and continue uphill.

SIDE TRIP
To access the waterfall, bear right onto Garden Creek Road, and then take an immediate left onto the access road. A Rotary Park sign marks the turn. The recreation area features the waterfall, excellent hiking trails, and picnic sites.

The incline immediately intensifies as you climb the northern face of Casper Mountain. Using tight switchbacks to manage a 13% grade, this is one of the steepest paved roads that you'll find in the state. A large pullout is reached at 4 miles where the sprawling city of Casper can be seen in its entirety as well as the snowcapped Bighorn Mountains to the far north.

Further south, and higher still, the road levels off and reaches a fork at 5.5 miles. Keep left and continue to Beartrap Meadows, a county-operated recreation area that includes five separate campgrounds. It's a great place to have a picnic or enjoy the cool mountain air during the height of summer.

In mile 7, the road tops Casper Mountain at 7,985 feet and begins to descend along a much more open southern slope. The pavement ends here

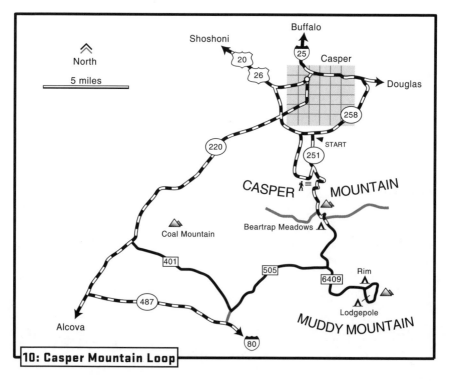

10: Casper Mountain Loop

and a wide gravel road—signed as Circle Drive—resumes the course. From this point, its downhill to the bottom of a valley where CR 505 heads west at 10.5 miles.

From the junction, stay left (south) and follow the road uphill where it cuts into the steep north flank of Muddy Mountain. When the road reaches a clearing in mile 13, look south to find the Medicine Bow Mountains on the distant horizon. Two miles farther, the gravel path reaches a large kiosk on the mountain's broad summit. Turn right at the junction and drive south on Loop Road. This segment of the drive makes a 2.3-mile circuit across the top of Muddy Mountain. Though it's a short distance, the loop offers a good sampling of the area's pine forest and wildflower-covered meadows. You'll also find a pair of campgrounds and a number of trails where you can walk about on foot.

SIDE
TRIP

A short distance south of the Lodgepole Campground, a rough spur branches off the main route and travels 1.5 miles into the pine forest to Corral Creek. Signs and maps show this road looping back to the main route, but it reaches private property soon after the creek.

Loop Road ends back at the kiosk near Rim Campground. Watch for a viewing platform on the right and check out the view across the valley toward Casper Mountain. From here, return to the base of Muddy Mountain

Loop Road on Muddy Mountain

to the CR 505 junction. Instead of driving back over Casper Mountain, turn left onto CR 505 and follow it west through the colorful Big Red Creek drainage. A mix of rock, junipers, and sagebrush, as well as the Seminoe Mountains to the south, make this a scenic and worthwhile stretch.

About a mile before HWY 487, turn right onto Coal Mountain Road (CR 401). Follow this 8-mile gravel road to the northwest as it cuts into the edge of Coal Mountain. This mountain has a history of wildfire, but its biggest blaze blackened 6,000 acres here in 2000 and the effects can still be seen.

The drive ends at HWY 220. To reach Casper from this junction, turn right onto the highway and drive a dozen miles to town.

Central Mountains And Flats

Central Wyoming is home to nearly a dozen mountain ranges that are virtually unknown—the Granite Mountains, Green Mountains, Ferris Mountains, Crooks Mountain, Pedro Mountains, Freezeout Mountains, Shirley Mountains, Seminoe Mountains, Haystack Mountains, Bridger Mountains, and Owl Creek Mountains. In addition to these masses, you'll find scores of other named summits, hills, and breaks that spread out across the interior of the state. These mostly roadless uplands range between 7,000 and 9,000 feet—dwarfs compared to Wyoming's larger mountain chains.

Surprisingly, it's not the mountainous country that you're likely to notice in central Wyoming, but the extensive shortgrass prairies and sagebrush steppes. For as uninhabitable as these flats may appear, they support a long list of animals. Biologists have identified 87 mammals, nearly 300 species of birds, and more than 60 types of reptiles that live in this environment. The most commonly sighted mammal is the pronghorn antelope. A fun statistic that you often hear in Wyoming is that three-quarters of the world's pronghorn population is found within a 125-mile radius of Casper. Other notable animals include deer, elk, moose, bighorn sheep, mountain lion, black bear, coyote, bobcat, fox, ferret, rabbit, bald eagle, grouse, hawk, and waterfowl.

Another natural feature of central Wyoming is the North Platte River. Nearly half of the river's 680-mile length is in this area where it fills numerous large reservoirs such as Seminoe, Pathfinder, Alcova, Glendo, and Guernsey. Aside from the most vital uses that this river provides—city water supplies, irrigation, wildlife habitat, and energy production—it also provides tremendous recreational opportunities. These waters, and the reservoirs they fill, draw people from even neighboring states.

Historically, the North Platte River was a lifeline for those traveling west on the Oregon Trail. Some of that history is still visible today from both developed sites and backroads. To learn more about this area's interesting past, be sure to visit the outstanding National Historic Trails Center located on the west side of Casper.

Land Ownership

Most of this area consists of BLM-managed land with isolated State sections. Ranch lands and mining areas are also common, but these are either obvious or well-signed. BLM offices are located in Casper, Rawlins, and Lander.

Roads and Trails

Two major expressways provide easy access to central Wyoming. The eastern and northern part of the area is served by Interstate 25. To the south, there is I-80. Only two-lane highways connect the towns of Rawlins, Casper, Riverton, and Lander. Backroads are maintained by the counties and are found in good condition, though washboard is common. Secondary roads are often two-tracks where you'll tackle mud and ruts on the flats and rockier terrain nearer to the mountains. Though the area has no designated ATV trails, it does offer an ORV park where you'll find a cobweb of trails.

Seasons and Conditions

Central Wyoming receives less than 15 inches of annual precipitation allowing some of the main backroads to remain accessible throughout the year with a 4WD vehicle. However, snowdrifts and muddy conditions can pose problems. For the best conditions, plan your trips between May and October. Higher elevations, or those prone to severe drifting, often remain closed until early June. This is highly variable on seasonal weather.

Fuel

On the east side, fueling stations can be found in the towns along I-25, including Chugwater, Wheatland, Glendo, Douglas, and Casper. Further west, you'll find fuel in Shoshoni, Riverton, and Lander. Aside from a little station at Alcova, the vast stretch between the eastern towns and the western towns offers little in terms of reliable gas stations. Sometimes you'll find an operating pump, other times you'll find a vacated building. Fueling stations are few to the south and are only found in towns and interchanges along I-80 and in the town of Medicine Bow.

Maps

The best maps for this area are statewide atlases such as the DeLorme Wyoming Atlas & Gazetteer or the Wyoming Road & Recreation Atlas published by Benchmark Maps. Both show the many trunk roads and a few of the secondary routes. For more detailed route finding, you'll need a BLM surface management map.

11: Poison Spider Off-Road Vehicle Park
Romp, rumble, and roll

☐ **Backcountry Drive** Most vehicles	☒ **4WD Route** 4x4 vehicle or ORV	☒ **ATV Trail** ORV less than 50" wide

Location/Map	West of Casper; Page 258
Roads	Not applicable
Distance	8 miles of trails
Managing Agency	BLM—Casper Field Office
Starting Coordinates	N42° 50.65' W106° 33.16'

Overview: The Poison Spider ORV Park is an easily accessible place to romp. It's a terrific place to try out a new ATV or 4x4, or just hone your off-road skills. More established places like this are needed; show your support to the BLM by keeping the park clean and following the posted rules.

Start: From Casper, take I-25 to Exit 189. Drive west on HWY 20/26 Bypass for 3 miles and merge onto HWY 20/26 toward the airport. Less than a quarter mile after turning on the highway, turn left onto Zero Road (CR 202). Follow Zero Road for 8.1 miles to the large parking area on the right.

Description: Poison Spider ORV Park spans 200 acres in an area known as Emigrant Gap. Pioneers traveled through this passage between the 1840s and 1880s. Today it's ATVs and dirt bikes that kick up dust, not stock animals and covered wagons.

There are about 8 miles of widely strewn trails that cover the park's rugged moonscape terrain. The middle of the park, where you start, sports a couple of wet troughs where you can mud bog without reprimand. The steep banks

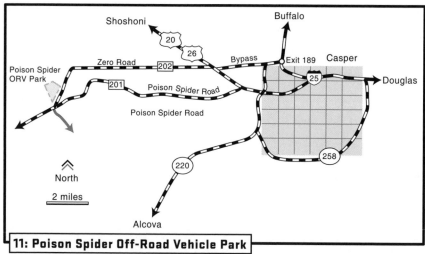

11: Poison Spider Off-Road Vehicle Park

Poison Spider Off-Road Vehicle Park

on the north side of the park are a favorite for the hardcore 4x4 enthusiasts who push their vehicles to the limits. To the south, a hill sprinkled with evergreens provides more varied topography with plenty of dips and rises. Most of the dirt-encrusted paths throughout the park offer easy riding, but there are places where it's possible to dump your machine or get high centered.

12: Central Hills/Castle Gardens
Discover Wyoming's solitude and history

☒ **Backcountry Drive** Most vehicles	☐ **4WD Route** 4x4 vehicle or ORV	☐ **ATV Trail** ORV less than 50" wide

Location/Map	West of Casper; Page 261
Roads	CR 201, CR 202, CR 212, HWY 136, CR 507, BLMR 2107
Distance	111 miles
Managing Agency	BLM—Casper and Lander Field Offices
Starting Coordinates	N42° 50.56' W106° 24.89'

Overview: This route travels through central Wyoming's rolling sage prairie along the base of the rugged Rattlesnake Hills. You'll pass through an old uranium mining district in the Gas Hills that once fueled the nation's appetite for atomic weapons. Further, you'll visit the Castle Gardens archeological site, which boasts some of the best petroglyphs found in the western United States. In good conditions, these roads can be traveled in any vehicle, but a 4WD vehicle is needed if the roads are not dry—particularly on the access road leading to the petroglyphs. Development is nearly non-existent in this country and even ranch houses are few and far between. Be sure to have a full tank of gas before heading out.

Start: From Wyoming Boulevard on the west side of Casper, take HWY 220 west for 2.5 miles and turn north on Robertson Road. Drive 2.4 miles and then turn west on Poison Spider Road (CR 201). If traveling from Riverton, head east on HWY 136 for 43 miles to the Gas Hills Road.

Description: From Casper, head west on paved Poison Spider Road (CR 201). The pavement is replaced by a good gravel road at 5.3 miles. Just 1.5 miles farther, you pass the Emigrant Gap Interpretive Site on the north side of the road. This break in Emigrant Ridge provided passage to many emigrants on the Oregon Trail as they left the North Platte River and advanced west into more rugged country.

At 8 miles, make a right turn at a fork, followed immediately by a left turn onto paved Zero Road (CR 202)—this will soon become CR 201 again. Continuing west, you'll soon pass rural Poison Spider School. Several ridges can be seen to the south from this point including Casper Mountain, Coal Mountain, and the beautiful bluffs of Bessemer Bend. The pavement transitions back into a gravel surface after several miles of driving.

Rock outcrops near Emigrant Gap

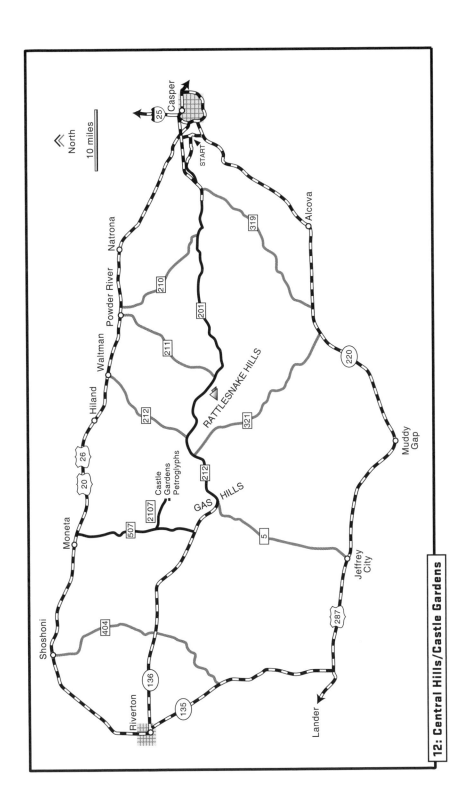

North

10 miles

Casper

25

START

Alcova

319

Natrona

Powder River

210

201

Waltman

211

RATTLESNAKE HILLS

Hiland

212

321

26

220

20

Castle
Gardens
Petroglyphs

212

Muddy
Gap

Moneta

2107

GAS   HILLS

507

5

Jeffrey
City

Shoshoni

404

287

136

Riverton

135

Lander

12: Central Hills/Castle Gardens

The following 10 miles present interesting geology. The first of these are flat-topped outcroppings that are scattered across the range. Stay left at the junction for CR 210 and an intriguing progression of rocks is soon found. The small, rocky mounds on the south side of the road seemingly grow in size as they continue to the north. Then as you travel west through rolling sage and grassy terrain, the Rattlesnake Hills begin taking shape. The road approaches the base of these rugged mountains by 40 miles and soon passes by Garfield Peak (8,244 feet). Though it can be tempting to do some cross-country exploration here, there is little access to public lands along this stretch.

Just past 57 miles, make a left turn onto Gas Hills Road (CR 212), which is shown on some maps as Dry Creek Road. A large strip mine to the south is soon passed and the white caps of the Wind River Range can be seen due west.

The mining that occurred in the sandstone Gas Hills is impressive. Benefiting from the nation's largest uranium reserves, Wyoming has led the country in ore production for more than a decade. All current production is now in the Powder River Basin, but historically, it was here at the Lucky Mc site where much of the extraction occurred. Over the thirty years between 1958 and 1988, 12 million tons of ore was processed in this region. Today the land is being reclaimed, though renewed interest has resulted in some recent exploratory drilling.

The road descends gently over the next 8 miles while passing old mining sites now signed as the Gas Hills Reclamation Project. At 72 miles, the gravel

Petroglyphs at Castle Gardens

course reaches a paved road that leads to HWY 136. There are numerous side roads along this stretch, but the main course is easily discernible.

A fork is reached at the beginning of the highway. The left-bearing Ore Road (CR 5) goes 26 miles to Jeffrey City, a once thriving mining town that is now a virtual ghost town. The right fork, which is the highway itself, leads 43 miles into Riverton. Stay right and follow the highway for 6 miles to Castle Gardens Road (CR 507). Turn north on this gravel road and drive 6.4 miles to a junction. To reach Castle Gardens, turn east onto narrow BLMR 2107, which has the reputation of being a nasty road in wet weather. This is semi-arid country, though, and you'll likely find the road dry and easily passable—if not badly rutted—during the summer months. Follow the lane past colorful sandstone formations for 6 miles to a parking area with a pit toilet, picnic tables, and an interpretive sign.

Off-road travel is prohibited in and around the petroglyph site, but several primitive foot trails wind around the tall orange spires and cliffs to several petroglyph walls. Protected by chain-link fences, the carved pictures depict people, animals, and warrior shields—common art forms for the culture of that time. Unfortunately, more modern carvers have marred the sandstone by scratching names, years, and other pointless clutter into the walls for all of us to regret. Please do your part to keep this historical site preserved.

To finish the backcountry drive, return to Castle Gardens Road and turn right. Follow the road north for a little over 15 miles to its end at HWY 20/26. From this point, it's 20.5 miles west to Shoshoni or 75 miles east to Casper.

13: Shirley Basin
Wide open spaces

☐ **Backcountry Drive**
Most vehicles

☒ **4WD Route**
4x4 vehicle or ORV

☐ **ATV Trail**
ORV less than 50" wide

Location/Map	Southwest of Casper; Page 266
Roads	BLMR 3129, CR 2, BLMR 3127, BLMR 3137, BLMR 3123
Distance	100+ miles of roads
Managing Agency	BLM—Rawlins and Casper Field Offices
Starting Coordinates	N42° 19.63' W106° 24.95'

Overview: Dozens of miles of roads are found in central Wyoming's Shirley Basin. Less than an hour out of Casper, the basin is a great place to explore the state's empty open spaces without the hassles of gates, private property, and traffic. During the fall, hunting is common here for antelope and sage grouse. The endangered black-footed ferret also resides in the basin.

All of the roads in the basin vary in condition, ranging from gravel surfaces to dirt two-tracks that create ribbons across the plain. Some minor washouts, ruts, and rocks can be expected on the routes near Chalk Mountain.

Start: From Casper, head southwest on HWY 220 (toward Alcova) and drive 16 miles. Turn east onto HWY 487 and follow the highway for 27 miles to a fork. Here, you can take HWY 77 into the western side of the Shirley Basin or continue south on HWY 487 to drop directly through it. If driving south on HWY 487, focus more on roads that head west. The area east of the highway has a mix of land ownership and uranium mines. The two highways converge to the south after about 23 miles.

Deciding where to start is simply a matter of preference, but a good starting point is along HWY 77 between BLMR 3129 and BLMR 3144. This spot gives you good access to most of the area's roads.

Description: The most exciting area of the Shirley Basin is found on its west side where Chalk Mountain (7,984 feet) rises abruptly from the basin. The rim of this mesa is peppered with evergreens, adding variety to the sandstone and claystone formation. You can reach this high point by driving 6 miles south on HWY 77 from where the highways split. Here, Chalk Mountain Road (BLMR 3129) heads west for a few miles and then ascends the mountain's southwest flank. Any truck or SUV can handle this road. The view from the top is wide-reaching.

Along the way to Chalk Mountain, you'll find short spurs that branch off to the north. These lead to the rim of Bates Hole, a beautiful valley filled with grass, sagebrush, and greasewood. There are some excellent overlooks that can be attained with little effort.

For more gentle terrain, you'll find primitive county and BLM roads that crisscross the 10 miles between HWY 77 and HWY 487. To the north is Shirley Ridge Road (CR 2). Crossing the midsection is Antelope Road (BLMR 3144). The southern portions are accessible by BLMR 3127, BLMR 3137, and BLMR 3123. There are also many miles of unnumbered, lesser trails that intersect these main courses.

Not all of these routes are signed from the highway. In addition, some of the signs that do exist refer to the roads by name, which are not shown on many maps. And while carrying a map is always a good idea, it's relatively easy to keep your bearings here since the area is bound by the two highways. You can also use Chalk Mountain as a major landmark.

East of HWY 487, Shirley Ridge Road (CR 2) can be taken a short distance to reach Walker-Jenkins Lake where there is fishing access. This county road also connects to CR 97 and CR 62, which lead north toward the Laramie Mountains. This area of the basin (east of HWY 487) has many intersecting roads and a detailed Wyoming atlas is very useful.

An overlook near Chalk Mountain

14: Shirley Mountains
A loop around a remote mountain range

☒ **Backcountry Drive**
Most vehicles

☐ **4WD Route**
4x4 vehicle or ORV

☐ **ATV Trail**
ORV less than 50" wide

Location/Map	Southwest of Casper; Page 266
Roads	CR 102, BLMR 3115
Distance	35 miles
Managing Agency	BLM—Rawlins Field Office
Starting Coordinates	N42° 15.27' W106° 25.79'

Overview: This drive encircles a remote mountain range on the edge of the treeless Shirley Basin. In sharp contrast to the basin, the Shirley Mountains are carpeted with a forest of aspen, pine, spruce, and fir. Most lengths of the road are easily traveled, but there are rough spots with rocks, washouts, ruts, and one ford. While you're unlikely to need 4WD, you'll want a vehicle with high clearance (any pickup or SUV) to handle these short sections.

Start: From Casper, head southwest on HWY 220 (toward Alcova) and drive 16 miles. Turn east onto HWY 487 and follow the highway for 27 miles to a fork. Bear right onto HWY 77 and drive south for 12 miles to a signed turnoff for CR 102.

Description: Drive west on the county road, which is known as the Leo-Shirley Basin Road. Continue through the dry basin and keep watch for antelope, which are found in large numbers to the east of the Shirley Mountains. At 9.2 miles, turn south onto BLMR 3115 toward Prior Flat Campground. After passing through the camp, the road immediately begins climbing through an aspen and evergreen forest. The course soon reaches a clearing and begins crossing open mountain country.

A secondary track, BLMR 3117, splits off at 14 miles. Stay left and pass an old ruins site. Here the road turns west and you'll ford Cave Creek over a concrete lining that makes it an easy crossing. The ensuing hill can be easy— or tricky. On one visit during hunting season, I encountered knee-high ruts and washouts, though it was possible to steer around them. On my most recent visit in late spring, the road was smooth and maintained. Seasonal weather, maintenance, and prior use are all factors that will determine the condition of the road during your drive.

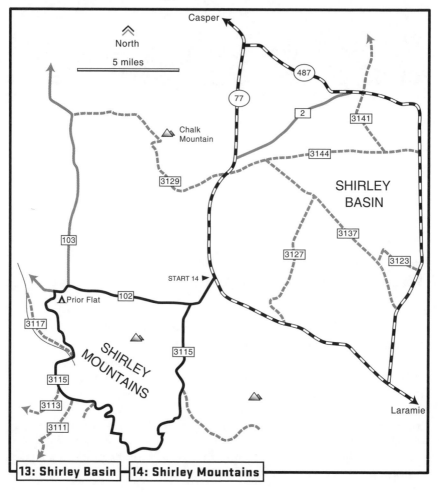

13: Shirley Basin — 14: Shirley Mountains

SIDE
TRIP

The road (BLMR 3117) that splits off before Cave Creek is a rough track that descends into the Cave Creek drainage before dividing into several separate spurs. There are several square miles of BLM land here that can be explored, but the Shirley Mountains also include private land. You should obtain a land ownership map (such as a BLM surface management map) if you plan on exploring these secondary routes.

The next few miles involve a series of ascents and descents as the backroad travels over rocky, rougher terrain. There are many side tracks that are passed, and many of these dead-end at dispersed campsites. Three of the more established roads that you'll find lead to Bear Park, "The Sinks" along Austin Creek, and to Troublesome Creek. At least two of these are signed along the main course.

The drive's high point of 9,100 feet is attained at 17.5 miles. Coincidentally, this is also the drive's half-way point. By 20 miles, the road begins revealing views over the Shirley Basin to the east as well as Elk Mountain and the Snowy Range to the south. These views precede a gradual descent along a surface that is often much smoother.

As you lose elevation, the drive takes you through mountain parks and stands of aspen. If you can plan your trip in September, you'll be rewarded with brilliant colors as the leaves turn gold.

At 27 miles, the road returns to the Shirley Basin and turns northward. It's an easy 8-mile drive back to HWY 77 from this point.

The east side of the Shirley Mountains

15: Seminoe-Alcova Backcountry Byway
Weave between mountains and reservoirs

☒ **Backcountry Drive**
Most vehicles

☐ **4WD Route**
4x4 vehicle or ORV

☐ **ATV Trail**
ORV less than 50" wide

Location/Map	Northeast of Rawlins; Page 271
Roads	CR 351, CR 291, CR 407
Distance	71 miles
Managing Agency	BLM—Rawlins and Casper Field Offices
Starting Coordinates	N41° 48.14' W107° 6.67'

Overview: This drive, one of Wyoming's designated scenic backways, utilizes both paved and gravel roads to travel over the rugged Seminoe Mountains and past three reservoirs fed by the North Platte River. You'll also discover the unsung mountain ranges of central Wyoming as well as one of the best fishing spots in the state. There are some steep, rough grades north of Seminoe Reservoir that are unsuitable for large trailers or motorhomes. The best time to drive the backway is May through November.

Start: From Rawlins, head east on I-80 to Sinclair (Exit 219). Drive through the refinery town and head north on well-signed Seminoe Road (CR 351) to a kiosk where the designated scenic byway officially begins. If traveling from Casper, take HWY 220 for 27 miles to CR 407 at Alcova.

Description: From the byway's information board near Sinclair, the route heads north on a paved roadway in which only the most disciplined drivers will be able to maintain the posted 50 mph speed limit. Rocky escarpments are seen on the left and Elk Mountain and the Medicine Bow National Forest occupy the far horizon to the right. Deer, antelope, and rabbits are common animals spotted in this high prairie.

By 8 miles, the North Platte River comes into view as it flows a north-bearing course. Dugway, a primitive BLM campground, is situated along Fort Steele Breaks, a stretch of photogenic rock above the river. It's a good place for a picnic or to use as a launch point. Watch for waterfowl and pelicans while you visit this section of the river corridor.

At 24 miles, the first view of Seminoe Reservoir comes into sight as the road begins to pass through the fragmented rock structures that comprise the Haystack Mountains. You soon wrap around the Ferris Dune Field and then work north along Seminoe State Park where several campgrounds are passed. The dune field and nearby shoreline used to be a hot spot for ATV riding, but higher water levels and tighter restrictions have since significantly reduced the areas that are open to ORV use.

By 32 miles, the pavement ends and a gravel road begins to climb the rugged southern side of the Seminoe Mountains. There are several excellent

Sand dunes south of the Seminoe Mountains

overlooks of the state park along the switchbacks here. With 180 miles of shoreline, Seminoe is Wyoming's largest reservoir. The 295-foot high dam—passed just a couple miles from the end of the pavement—was built in 1939 and sits 85 feet wide at the base.

From the overlook pullouts on the southern flank of the Seminoe Mountains, the road weaves between ridges and enters a fertile canyon, which is unexpectedly lush for this parched region of Wyoming. The Morgan Creek Wildlife Habitat Management Area occupies much of this area and is home to a feeble bighorn sheep population. For decades, wildlife biologists have tried unsuccessfully to bolster the herd by mostly bringing in sheep from Whiskey Basin near Dubois. But those animals were acclimated to a far different environment than the low-lying, semi-arid Seminoe Mountains, and the herd of more than 200 eventually declined to just 20. In the winter of 2009/2010, another couple dozen sheep were transplanted here from similar habitats found in the Bighorn Mountains and Oregon. This new approach may give the sheep new hope, as they should have less adaptation stress to their new habitat.

Leaving the green canyon foliage behind, the road becomes washboarded and climbs to 7,500 feet to expose a glorious view of rocky peaks and a vast, grassy basin to the north. The view is brief as the road literally drops out of the Seminoe Mountains by descending nearly 1,500 feet in just 3 miles. This grade, coupled with the tight curves and steep hills near Seminoe Dam, is why large trailers are not recommended for this drive.

With the Seminoes now to your south, the countryside opens up where the backway crosses the North Platte River at the renowned Miracle Mile. World-class fishing for walleye, brown, and rainbow trout—thousands of them per mile—draw people to this remote stretch of the river. Anglers are found on the banks during all seasons of the year. Near the bridge, you'll find a side road that leads to covered picnic tables and primitive campsites. A paved road on the right leads to another fishing access point as well as Kortes Dam.

From the North Platte River, the byway follows Kortes Road, which is paved for the next several miles until it reaches a fork. Here, bear left to stay on Kortes Road and follow it northward along a wide gravel lane.

After mile 50, the backroad travels east along the Pedro Mountains. This small granite range is known for a deformed infant mummy that was discovered by gold prospectors in 1932. The mummy was probably born from a prehistoric tribe, but there is little factual information and its whereabouts have been unknown for the last several decades. A web search for "Pedro Mountain Mummy" will get you a picture of the creepy-looking corpse. At the northern end of these mountains, the road becomes paved again and continues toward Pathfinder Reservoir.

SIDE TRIP Watch for paved CR 408 that leads to Fremont Canyon and Pathfinder Reservoir near mile 64. It is 2.5 miles to the deep gorge where rock climbers have established hundreds of routes on the steep rock walls. Pathfinder Reservoir and a number of campgrounds are located 4 miles farther.

Past the turnoff for Pathfinder Reservoir, it's just a few miles to scenic Alcova Reservoir on CR 407. The striking red bluffs that surround this popular lake create a beautiful setting. A pair of 1-mile side roads lead to campgrounds and the shoreline. The one leading to Cottonwood Campground takes you pass Cottonwood Creek Dinosaur Trail, a footpath with interpretive signs that describe the huge animals that once lived here and the fossils that have been found.

The byway ends shortly after passing Alcova Dam in the town of Alcova. A sign near the junction of HWY 220 alludes to the area's popularity during the summer months. It figures Alcova to have 100 residents, except in the summer when it runs around 35,000. The sign concludes with "It's a dam site."

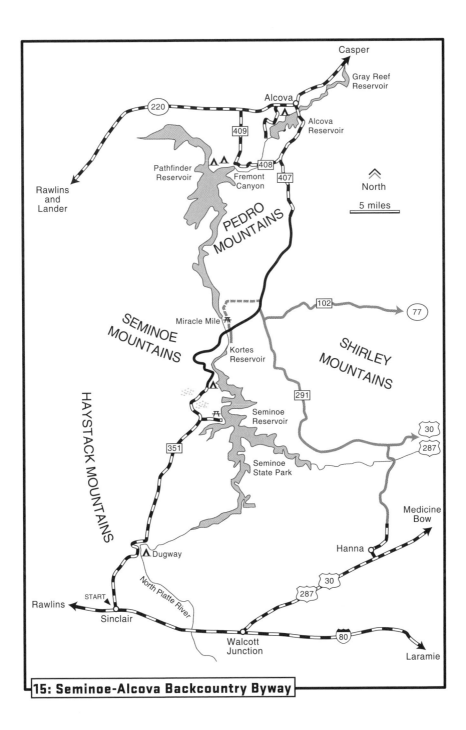

15: Seminoe-Alcova Backcountry Byway

Other Nearby Drives

Miracle Mile—In addition to route #15, there are other gravel roads that can be used to access the Miracle Mile fishing area north of Seminoe Reservoir. These include the Hanna Leo Draw Road (CR 291) and Medicine Bow Road (CR 121), which come from the towns of Hanna and Medicine Bow along HWY 30/287. Further north, you can use the Leo-Shirley Basin Road (CR 102), which comes off HWY 77 in the Shirley Basin.

Ferris Mountains—This small mountain range is located in central Wyoming between Casper and Rawlins. With dark, wooded slopes and a sharp crest that rises above 10,000 feet, this isolated mass would easily qualify as a state park in many other states. But this is Wyoming, and the mountain is reduced to just another hump on the horizon. No developed trails or roads traverse the Ferris, which is currently protected as a wilderness study area, but there are many roads that probe the mountain's lower flanks. One rugged approach is BLMR 3147 (Cherry Creek Road), which ascends to a gorge at the foot of the mountains before turning back.

To reach the road from Casper, travel southwest on HWY 220 for 61 miles and turn left onto Bar-V-Ranch Road. This turnoff is about 32 miles past Alcova Reservoir. From here, drive south on the maintained road for 2 miles and stay straight at the first junction. Turn right onto BLMR 3147, a rutted two-track. Follow this road (and it's not really a road) for several miles, then stay right when the track forks to reach a small ford of Cherry Creek after 6 miles. From here, the course turns directly southward and becomes increasingly rocky as it gains elevation. These conditions improve as the road nears the mountain.

Another tiny ford is reached in a wooded draw near 10 miles. From this high point of 7,680 feet, the dirt track turns east through another two drainages, but neither of these have much water.

By 11 miles, the road reaches the mouth of a canyon. A sign here clearly indicates that the trail headed south is now closed to motorized use and that motion-activated video cameras may be used to catch violators. Since this is the wilderness study area boundary, park here and hoof it up the short hill. With a little effort, you can peer into a rocky gorge and into the heart of the Ferris Mountains.

From the perch above the creek, the road now turns back to the north and then drops down a steep bank to another ford. To finish this 20-mile drive, follow the rough track to the north as it travels along a bench above the stream. As you reach junctions for secondary roads, stay left to rejoin Cherry Creek Road after mile 15. It's 5 miles back to the highway from this point.

To further explore the area, you can follow some of the tracks that branch off the last stretch or several other BLM roads near the eastern half of the range. Much of this land in managed by the State or BLM.

16: Green Mountain
A mountain island in a sea of sagebrush

☒ Backcountry Drive
Most vehicles

☐ 4WD Route
4x4 vehicle or ORV

☐ ATV Trail
ORV less than 50" wide

Location/Map	Southeast of Lander; Page 274
Roads	BLMR 2411
Distance	28 miles
Managing Agency	BLM—Lander Field Office
Starting Coordinates	N42° 29.18' W107° 42.39'

Overview: For years, Green Mountain was a hidden Wyoming secret, just another distant mount in the vast sagebrush flats that separate the southern and northern Rockies. But Green Mountain really is a mountain, complete with clear brooks, shadowy pines, wildflower-laden parks, and enough elevation to bring a crisp chill to a summer night. When I first wandered upon this remarkable timbered island at the north end of the Great Divide Basin, I saw but one other person, a local rancher. The last time I visited, the BLM campground and picnic areas were nearly full and the mountain was abuzz with activity. Apparently, the large Green Mountain signs that were erected along the highway finally revealed one of the best hideaways in central Wyoming.

A view to the east from the top of Green Mountain

This drive travels from the semi-arid high plains to the top of the mountain where you'll discover a charming campground, a wild horse overlook, and a picnic area. Stretches of this road are rough, so a high clearance vehicle is suggested. The road is open to motorized travel from mid-June through November.

Start: From Jeffrey City (between Lander and Muddy Gap), take HWY 287 east for 6 miles to Green Mountain Road (BLMR 2411).

Description: From the highway, travel south on BLMR 2411. This road is heavily washboarded making for a jarring ride. When the road splits after 6 miles, bear left and pilot your way to the base of the mountain. Here, the road meets East Cottonwood Creek and follows the stream uphill into a pine and aspen forest. Cottonwood Campground, a BLM-maintained recreation site, is reached just 2 miles farther.

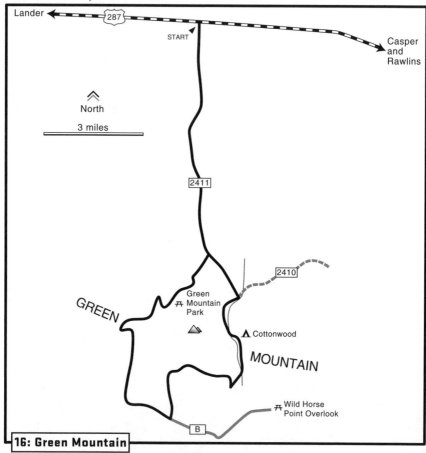

A short distance past the camp, the road bends to the west where a sign warns of steep, rough conditions ahead. Unless the road has been improved since this writing, you'll find that the sign doesn't exaggerate. The next 2 miles involve ruts, rocks, and grades that exceed 14%. This is not a road you want to negotiate if the weather is or has been especially wet.

By mile 12, the road reaches level ground near Green Mountain's highest point (8,951 feet) and the driving becomes easier. There is a junction within 2 miles where BLMR 2411B splits off to the Wild Horse Point Overlook and Picnic Area.

SIDE
TRIP

The 3-mile drive to the overlook is a must-do if you're already here. The road ends at a high point in the center of the mountain where you can look north and east across Wyoming's varied topography and south over the Great Divide Basin (the Continental Divide runs along the south side of the mountain). If you're fortunate, you'll spot wild horses from the overlook, and I've also spotted elk here.

The loop continues from the junction by entering Sagebrush Park, which feels a bit like the rooftop of Wyoming. From here you gain a vantage point over the west side of the mountain toward the mighty Wind River Range. One of the most unnerving moments experienced during the research of this book came when a powerful lightning storm caught us in this park—it was quite a show!

From the meadow, the loop road returns to the mountain's north side where the course descends through the heavily-logged forest. This was once another rough stretch of roadway, but it has been improved in recent years.

A small county-operated picnic area is found at the base of the mountain on a grassy site along the West Fork of Middle Cottonwood Creek. From this point, drive 2.5 miles back to the original fork and then turn left and drive 6.2 miles to return to HWY 287.

17: South Pass
Return to the old wild west

☒ **Backcountry Drive** Most vehicles	☐ **4WD Route** 4x4 vehicle or ORV	☐ **ATV Trail** ORV less than 50" wide

Location/Map	South of Lander; Page 276
Roads	BLMR 2324, BLMR 4108
Distance	20 miles
Managing Agency	BLM—Lander Field Office
Starting Coordinates	N42° 31.63' W108° 43.33'

Overview: This drive tours South Pass—a natural passageway across the Continental Divide—where emigrants traveled along the Oregon Trail and miners converged to discover their fortunes. The route visits three historic mining towns including Atlantic City, South Pass City (a Wyoming historical site), and an abandoned ghost town. Plan to spend some time in South Pass City to experience what an authentic mining town was like in the 1800s.

Start: From Lander, head south on HWY 287/28 for 27 miles to Atlantic City Road.

Description: To start this tour from the highway, drive southward for a half mile and then turn left on Fort Stambaugh Road (BLMR 2324). Follow this gravel lane for a half mile to Big Atlantic Gulch Campground, situated across from a shallow channel of the same name. Here, the tiny waterway nourishes willows and aspen trees to give life to what is an otherwise empty upland.

From the camp, follow the road uphill through evergreen stands that fill the bottoms of gullies. When the roadway tops out at 8,400 feet, a grand view is revealed of central Wyoming and the soaring peaks of the Wind River Range.

Keep watch for an old cabin on the left and then, at 3.5 miles, turn left onto a spur next to a cemetery. This is the old Miners Delight Townsite where you'll find the remains of a gold mining community gone bust. From the parking area, there is a quarter-mile footpath that leads down into a remarkable ghost town where half a dozen structures still stand with cans, tables, and

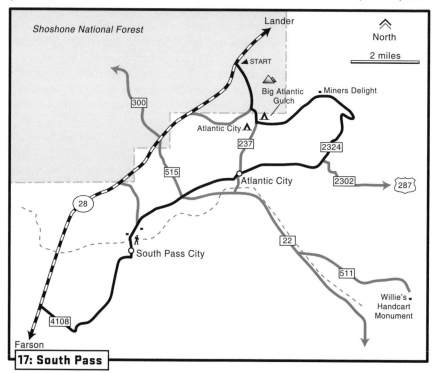

other items from the 1800s. It's an absolutely intriguing place to visit. Return to the main roadway and follow it east below a horizon of rimrocks followed by pockets of sparse forest. This eastern side of the backcountry drive travels through BLM land so there are numerous side tracks that are used for ATV riding and dispersed camping.

At mile 7, the road reaches a junction with Hudson-Atlantic City Road (BLMR 2302), which travels 24 miles to HWY 287. A nearby monument marks the spot of Fort Stambaugh, a former military post that was established here to protect miners from Indians. Stay straight at the junction to roll into Atlantic City 3 miles farther.

Atlantic City is a historic mining town that sits on the windswept cusp of the Wind Rivers. The town, along with the Miners Delight townsite, was erected in 1968 as gold prospectors rushed in with hopes of getting rich. Seven years later the boom ended leaving the once bustling towns to dwindle, though successive, lesser booms kept the community active over the next few decades. Atlantic City is now home to a smattering of buildings consisting of private residences, a restaurant, and a general store.

SIDE
TRIP
Willie's Handcart Monument—a mass grave for dozens of Mormons who died on the Oregon-Mormon trail in a 1856 blizzard—can be reached by driving 3.7 miles on Three Forks Road (CR 22) and then another 3.5 miles on Lewiston Road (CR 511). Ruts from the Oregon-Mormon Trail can still be seen near the site.

An old cabin at the Miners Delight Townsite

To continue with the tour, follow South Pass Road to the southwest for 4.5 miles to reach South Pass City. As the first town to be built in the mining district, it was once home to almost 2,000 people before the gold bust sent the miners packing. Today, it's a fascinating Wyoming Historic Site. A couple dozen buildings still remain, including a saloon, blacksmith shop, general store, and hotel. After paying a small visitor's fee, you can wander down the main street, imagining life as it was over a century ago.

To finish the drive, continue following the main road for 5.5 miles to reach HWY 28. Lander is 38 miles to the north from this point.

Other Nearby Drives

Hudson-Atlantic City Road—BLMR 2302 makes a nearly 70-mile arc from the tiny town of Hudson to historic Atlantic City. The southern half of the road (a 31-mile stretch from HWY 287 to Atlantic City) is the portion that receives the most interest because it loosely parallels the Oregon Trail. While the trail itself remains a couple miles to the south, it can be accessed by a few primitive 4WD tracks.

Several significant historical locations are found along this stretch of the Oregon Trail including Rocky Ridge, the Lewiston Lakes, and the Willie's Handcart Company Monument where dozens of Mormon travelers died when they were caught in a severe storm in 1856.

If you drive the southern portion, there are two things of which to be mindful. First, the road is usually impassable between November and June due to snow. Even in warmer months, muddy conditions can impede access, as was the case when I attempted the route in July (August was better). Getting a vehicle stuck is somewhat common and deep ruts along some stretches indicate that drivers have pushed further than they should have. As a general rule, the west end of the road, near Atlantic City, is the wetter and most troublesome. Secondly, Mormons still use the road for handcart trips during the summer. As a result, you may encounter heavy pedestrian use of the road near Sage Camp, which is a group staging area.

To reach the road's northern terminus, take HWY 789 from Lander to Hudson. To reach the road's midpoint, take HWY 287 east of Lander and drive roughly 32 miles to Hudson-Atlantic City Road, which is found on both sides of the highway. For the southern and most popular starting point, drive south of Lander to Atlantic City on HWY 287/28. Then follow BLMR 2324 to the east until you reach BLMR 2302.

SOUTHEAST

Southeastern Wyoming is a microcosm of the entire state. You'll find many of the state's natural communities here—plains, mountains, high deserts, forests, and alpine tundra. In the corner, gentle windswept prairies are covered with grasslands. These end at a timbered upland where jumbled boulders of granite provide intriguing scenery. Further west, a pair of mountain chains—the Medicine Bow and the Sierra Madre—give rise to striking landscapes. On the opposing side of the Continental Divide, the highlands relent to Wyoming's high deserts.

Southeast Areas

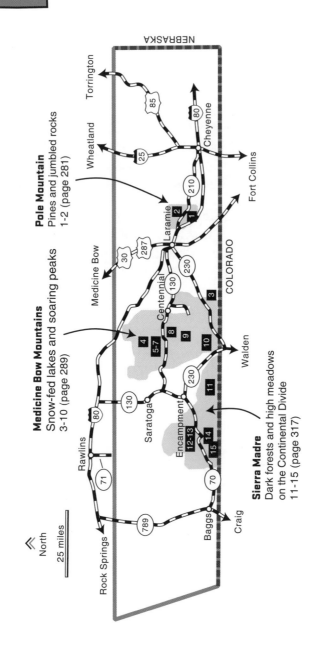

Pole Mountain
Pines and jumbled rocks
1-2 (page 281)

Medicine Bow Mountains
Snow-fed lakes and soaring peaks
3-10 (page 289)

Sierra Madre
Dark forests and high meadows
on the Continental Divide
11-15 (page 317)

North

25 miles

Pole Mountain

Pole Mountain is a small, isolated unit of the Medicine Bow National Forest that encompasses 87 square miles of lightly timbered, rocky terrain. The southern part of this area is best known for what is called Vedauwoo, a band of fascinating rock formations. The northern half consists of rolling, windswept uplands that are intermixed with sparse pine and aspen forests. Small creeks flow eastward off the mountain and many, if not all, are chocked with beaver dams.

The Pole Mountain area is southeastern Wyoming's recreational playground. It takes just 30 minutes to reach this 8,000-foot hill from the capitol city of Cheyenne, and only half that from the college burg of Laramie. This proximity to the state's first and third largest towns, respectively, and easy access from Interstate 80, make Pole Mountain a terrific place to get outdoors if you only have a few hours. But if you can, stay longer.

Land Ownership

Pole Mountain is a continuous chunk of federal land managed by the Medicine Bow National Forest. You'll encounter no private roads and the forest boundary tends to be well-signed, gated, or fenced. The local Forest Service office is located in Laramie.

Roads and Trails

Pole Mountain is hardly a remote place and you'll find a motorized route virtually anywhere you want to go. The most significant thoroughfare that passes through the national forest here is Interstate 80, a transcontinental highway connecting California to New Jersey. Wyoming Highway 210 (Happy Jack Road) is another paved road that cuts through the hills. Connecting to this highway are three wide gravel roads that access picnic areas and trailheads. The lesser routes, the dozens of 4WD roads and primitive two-tracks, are everywhere. With a few exceptions, these are easy to moderate paths that can be handled by stock 4x4s—they are perfect for beginners or those who want to venture off the main roads without completely punishing their vehicle. As of this writing, there were no designated ATV trails in this area.

Irresponsible ORV use such as driving off designated routes and damaging wetlands has become far too common here and some roads have been closed permanently has a result. Currently, more roads are being petitioned for closure. If you're interested in keeping these roads open, stay on the designated route and encourage others to do the same.

Seasons and Conditions

Pole Mountain is at its best during the late spring and fall. Though summer days can be perfect here, hot afternoons often breed frequent and severe thunderstorms. Many roads are open to motorized use during the winter, but strong perpetual winds create impenetrable snowdrifts that keep them closed until the spring thaw. Even then, some roads remain closed from March 1 to May 25 to protect wildlife and prevent road damage.

Fuel

Since Interstate 80 runs across Pole Mountain, service stations are both abundant and in close proximity. Look no further than Cheyenne to the east or Laramie to the west.

Maps

Statewide maps and atlases don't show enough detail to be useful for the Pole Mountain area. The Medicine Bow National Forest map is good for most navigation if you're going to stay on the main roads, but doesn't include many of the secondary spurs. For the best detail, get the Forest's ORV map or Motor Vehicle Use Map (MVUM).

1: Vedauwoo
Wyoming's rock jungle

☒ **Backcountry Drive** Most vehicles	☐ **4WD Route** 4x4 vehicle or ORV	☐ **ATV Trail** ORV less than 50" wide

Location/Map	East of Laramie; Page 284
Roads	FR 700
Distance	7.5 miles
Managing Agency	USDA Forest Service—Medicine Bow National Forest
Starting Coordinates	N41° 9.51' W105° 24.11'

Overview: The word Vedauwoo (pronounced vee-da-voo) is an Arapahoe Indian word that means "Earthborn." It's a term they used to describe the ancient Sherman Granite rocks that characterize the area in the most unusual ways. Here, you'll find boulders balanced precariously on top of boulders. There are rock piles, spires, towers, slabs and all sorts of intriguing shapes that get informal names like "mushroom" and "potato chip."

This backcountry drive makes a short and easy tour through Vedauwoo along a gravel road that is easily driven from late spring into fall. Driving the road from one end to the other can be done quickly, but this is an area that deserves to be taken in more slowly and there are many places to pull off where you can do just that.

Start: From Laramie, head east on I-80 for 13 miles and take Exit 329. Turn left (northward) to cross under the overpass. The backroad begins on the north side of this interchange.

A jumbled pile of granite at Vedauwoo

Description: From the Interstate, follow Vedauwoo Road (FR 700) for about a mile as it crosses the windswept plain. The pavement ends at the turnoff for the Vedauwoo Recreation Area.

SIDE
TRIP

This Forest Service recreation area is itself a destination. Here at the base of Turtle Rock—a huge, fascinating mound of granite—you'll find a campground, large picnic area, trailheads, boulders to be scrambled, and technical routes that draw rock climbers from around the region. Many visitors just mill around and take great photos, but you can get a good sampling of this area by hiking the easy 3-mile Turtle Rock loop. A day-use fee is required to park inside the recreation area.

Continuing along Vedauwoo Road, the roadway transitions to a pebbly gravel surface that is soft on the edges. Use caution when getting over to the side. I pulled one SUV back onto the road after the loose shoulder sucked the vehicle off the road and the driver sank it to its axles.

The road descends into a patchy pine forest punctuated with large rock "complexes" and smaller, odd-shaped boulders. Along the way, you'll pass about a dozen spurs. These are places where you can park to camp, picnic, hike, or climb and they are incredibly popular with the locals on summer weekends. Due to the area's high use, shooting of all types is banned from the end of March through mid-September.

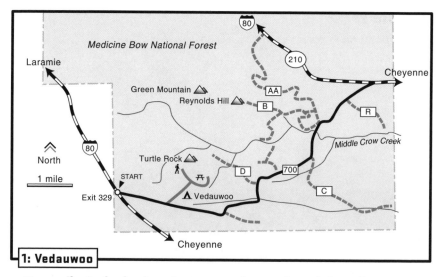

Near mile 3, the backroad curves to the north and then dips to cross the South Fork of Middle Crow Creek. A parking lot near the next curve is a popular starting point for hikes to Devils Playground and Reynolds Hill, which are the rock towers seen a mile to the northwest. Beaver ponds and aspen stands with vertical slabs of granite as a backdrop make this a particularly beautiful place.

Follow Vedauwoo Road as it cuts northeast along an open stretch. With few trees and an elevation of 8,000 feet, you can look across the unique country to the north and northwest. This broken land is the southern tip of the Laramie Mountains, much lower than the range's high points near Wheatland, but every bit as interesting.

At mile 5.5, the road drops to its lowest point to cross Middle Crow Creek. It's a tiny creek, though the lushness of the drainage would indicate otherwise. The backroad now climbs out of the draw through the most wooded section of the drive. The side road soon reached on the left, FR 700B, offers some of the better four-wheeling opportunities in this area (route #2).

The final 2 miles of the drive roll along a treeless flat. The tour ends when you reach HWY 210. You can turn left here to return to I-80 (a little over 10 miles to the west) or turn east and drive 26 miles to Cheyenne.

2: Pole Mountain
Fun routes near I-80

☐ **Backcountry Drive**
Most vehicles

☒ **4WD Route**
4x4 vehicle or ORV

☐ **ATV Trail**
ORV less than 50" wide

Location/Map	West of Cheyenne; Page 287
Roads	Eagle Rock Loop: FR 703, FR 715, FR 713D, FR 713, FR 714 Crow Creek Loop: FR 701G, FR 701GA, FR 701DC, FR 701D Sherman Mountains: FR 707A, FR 707AA, FR 700B South Branch of Crow Creek: FR 708
Distance	50+ miles
Managing Agency	USDA Forest Service—Medicine Bow National Forest
Starting Coordinates	Eagle Rock Loop: N41° 15.19' W105° 26.28' Crow Creek Loop: N41° 12.93' W105° 20.35' Sherman Mountains: N41° 12.43' W105° 20.05' South Branch of Crow Creek: N41° 12.48' W105° 20.0'

Overview: Pole Mountain is crisscrossed with four-wheeling tracks that are short, rarely loop, and often dead end. Yet even with these shortcomings, they are surprisingly satisfying. Interesting scenery, wildlife sightings, and an infinite number of attractive places to take a break all contribute to a good day behind the wheel.

There are many tracks at Pole Mountain that beg to be explored. The four routes described here will get you started. All of these roads, except FR 708, are closed to motorized use from March 1 to May 25 to protect wildlife and prevent road damage.

Start: From Laramie, drive east on I-80 for 7 miles and take Exit 323 for the Summit Rest Area. Turn left (eastward) to cross over the interstate to a fork. Bear left onto HWY 210 (the road to the right goes to the rest area). Follow the highway to reach the route of your choice.

Description (Eagle Rock Loop): This first route is a nearly 20-mile loop that travels across the northern portion of Pole Mountain. It is reached off HWY 210 just 1 mile from Interstate 80. Turn left onto Pilot Hill Road (FR 703) and follow it 2.5 miles to FR 715. Turn left onto the 4WD road here and drive steeply down a hill to cross the North Branch of Middle Lodgepole Creek. This is the steepest, sandiest part of the drive and four wheel drive may be needed to climb it if going the other way. The road then climbs out of the drainage and turns east—stay right at the next junction to follow FR 713D. The next 6 miles of road travel across mild terrain covered in pine and aspen. Aside from a few rocky and narrow sections, this is an easy 4WD stretch that offers many side spurs to stop or camp. Cattle grazing is common here and you may need to open a gate or two. Turn south when you reach FR 713, and then west onto FR 714 about a mile farther. Continue west on this easy lane to pass Eagle Rock and complete the loop.

Lightly timbered and rocky terrain on Pole Mountain

Description (Crow Creek Loop): This 9-mile loop explores the intriguing scenery found on the east side of the Pole Mountain area. This is one of the most challenging routes in the area, and pieces from vehicles—like license plate holders and hitch covers—can sometimes be found around the larger rocks and ruts.

To begin, follow HWY 210 east for 7.5 miles and turn northward onto FR 701. Drive 1 mile north to 701 G, a 4WD road that begins at a corral. Take this track east past a large bunker-like structure and through a popular dispersed camping area. When you reach a junction near the meadow, bear left onto FR 701 GA. The road now deteriorates into a true off-camber 4WD track as it descends steeply through gorgeous country to the national forest boundary near Upper North Crow Reservoir. Turn north onto an unmarked path to ford Crow Creek and connect to FR 701 DC. This connector isn't shown on official Forest maps, but a Forest Service employee who happened to be on the road confirmed that it was opened to motorized travel. Continue north about a mile and then turn left onto FR 701 D. Follow this easy track west to return to FR 701, and then drive south to reach the starting point. There are numerous side roads that beg to be explored along this loop; be prepared to spend more time than it would normally take you to drive an 8-mile loop.

Description (Sherman Mountains): There are more than 20 miles of 4WD roads that cut across the broken terrain between Turtle Rock and HWY 210, an area obscurely known as the Sherman Mountains. You'll find a little bit of everything on these paths—easy and smooth straights to awkward, rock-strewn paths. This isn't a place to drive if you're looking for a destination; this is where you go to explore each track to its end and then start again. Some days you'll find this maze of roads busy with ATVs and dispersed campers. On others, you'll have the mountains to yourself.

For a convenient starting point, drive east on HWY 210 for 8 miles and turn right onto FR 707A. Follow this road a short distance to a fork. Stay right, and you'll head directly west toward Headquarters Road (FR 707) on a path that sometimes has huge mud puddles. There are several secondary tracks that branch off this route to reach the base of Twin Mountain.

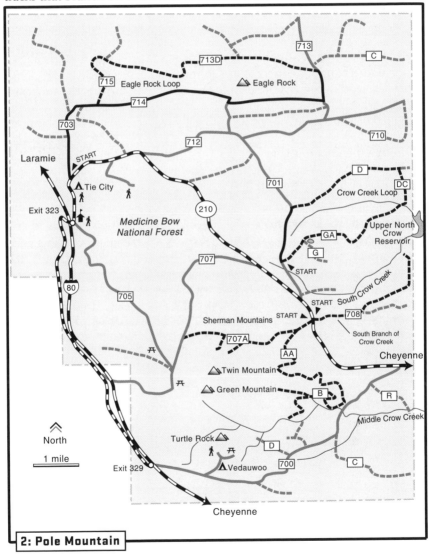

2: Pole Mountain

Bear left at the junction and you'll be on FR 707AA, a 4-mile course that weaves through a pine forest and ends at Vedauwoo Road (FR 700). To extend your trip, turn onto FR 700B and choose one of the numerous spurs. Though short, these tracks make worthwhile trips.

Description (South Branch of Crow Creek): This short 3.2-mile two-track leads to the edge of the national forest where you can see Upper North Crow Reservoir. It's an easy drive that can be done in a 2WD vehicle if driven carefully in dry conditions.

To start, take HWY 210 for 8 miles and turn left onto FR 708. Now drive east along the pebbly road, which has a few small, insignificant dips. Large granite rocks are stacked across the prairie and there are many smaller ones that stick up like headstones in a cemetery. Stay left at the junction with FR 708A, and continue a northeast bearing. When the road reaches the fenced national forest boundary, it turns and follows it northward and Upper North Crow Reservoir becomes visible. At the end, the road turns back to the west and approaches the South Branch of Crow Creek where a primitive campsite is located near a sizable rock outcropping. I have seen moose foraging along this creek.

Though the reservoir is within just a half mile of the end point, there is no motorized access to it. To get there, return to HWY 210 and drive about a mile east of the national forest to a gravel access road that heads north.

Other Nearby Drives

Curt Gowdy State Park—This state park features a 5-mile backroad that takes you around Granite Reservoir and Crystal Reservoir. The rugged hills that surround the lakes make for interesting scenery. To reach Curt Gowdy State Park from Cheyenne, take I-25 to Exit 10D. Drive west on HWY 210 (Happy Jack Road) for 24 miles. If traveling from Laramie, take I-80 east to the Summit Rest Area at Exit 323. Then drive east on HWY 210 for 15 miles. The road begins from the park's main entrance.

Medicine Bow Mountains

From their northern point along Interstate 80 in Wyoming, the Medicine Bow Mountains extend southward to Rocky Mountain National Park in Colorado. Wyoming's share of these lofty mountains is called the Snowy Range, or just "the Snowies," in reference to a dramatic quartzite crest that rises sharply to 12,013 feet.

The mountains' lower elevations are covered in forests of aspen and lodgepole pine. Spruce and fir trees dominate the higher elevations, though they get relegated to shrubby groundcover at treeline (about 10,500 feet). On the roof of the mountain range, tiny plants and wildflowers comprise an alpine tundra that is filled with dozens of alpine lakes and kettle ponds.

The Medicine Bow is a recreational playground and an extensive road network provides easy access throughout the range. Wildlife viewing is common and elk and moose are easily found during the summer. Campgrounds are abundant along the Snowy Range and fill even on weekday nights during the summer. Anglers have many choices, as streams, reservoirs, and lakes are plentiful. The area is also a mecca for day hiking and four-wheeling, and these two pursuits are often combined.

Land Ownership

Most of the Medicine Bow Mountains are within the Medicine Bow National Forest, while the surrounding foothills are managed by the BLM. Within the national forest, there are numerous private landholdings, but these are well-signed or gated. Public access is almost always granted along arterial roads, which are also signed well. Ranches are interspersed with BLM and State lands, so watch for signs indicating private property. Forest Service offices are located in Laramie and Saratoga. The local BLM office is in Rawlins.

Roads and Trails

No other national forest in Wyoming is as laden with roads as the Medicine Bow—this is very accessible "backcountry." To start, there are two highways that traverse the range. Cutting through the southern half is HWY 230, which offers year-round access to the lower mountains. Going over the top of the range is HWY 130—the Snowy Range Scenic Byway—which accesses the high country, but only when it is open from late May to October (it's open to snowmobiles in the winter). Interstate 80 runs along the forest's northern boundary, making for a fast and convenient thoroughfare.

Off the pavement, there is an excess of gravel trunk roads that crisscross the mountains. These are excellent, well-maintained paths that only suffer from occasional patches of washboard. Secondary dirt roads are also usually found in good condition. Four-wheel drive roads up high are the exception. Expect a lot of mud and a lot of rock—where there is one, you will find less of the other. In the southern reaches, you'll find the primitive roads to be much easier to drive. They present fewer challenges and are perfect for casual cruises through the woods.

The Medicine Bow has numerous designated ATV trails. None of these are very long in length, and some are just connectors. Yet combined with the broader network of backroads, you can create extended routes that will provide a full day of riding.

Seasons and Conditions

The Medicine Bow Mountains receive a lot of precipitation. Summer comes late and leaves early here. In the highest terrain around the Snowy Range (10,000 feet), you'll find that the roads are snowed in until mid-July. Even the mid-range routes between 8,000 and 9,000 feet often hold snowdrifts until the middle of June. Many a driver gets buried in these banks. I've liberated more stuck cars from the Medicine Bow than I've even seen stuck in the rest of the state. In researching this book, this is the only place I got stuck (and yes, in a snowdrift).

When the Medicine Bow dries out at the end of July, it's absolutely spectacular country to explore. But some routes never really do, so be prepared for that. Fall and the first snows come in September, but that month is still an excellent time to visit these mountains. Deeper, closing snows come in the middle of October though many roads remain officially open until the middle of November.

Fuel

On the east side of the range, you'll find many fueling stations along I-80 in Laramie. To the north, also along I-80, there are gas stations at Walcott Junction (Exit 235) and Elk Mountain (Exit 255). On the west side, you can fill up in Saratoga and Encampment. On the south side, you might be able to get gas at stations in Woods Landing (southwest of Laramie on HWY 230) and at Tie Siding (south of Laramie on HWY 287), though these locations are not always reliable. Fuel is also readily available further south in Walden, Colorado.

Maps

Obtain the Medicine Bow National Forest map and supplement it with either the Forest's ORV map or Motor Vehicle Use Map (MVUM).

3: Jelm Mountain/Laramie River Overlook
Romp to the top of these high overlooks

☒ **Backcountry Drive**
Most vehicles

☐ **4WD Route**
4x4 vehicle or ORV

☐ **ATV Trail**
ORV less than 50" wide

Location/Map	Southwest of Laramie; Page 292
Roads	Jelm Mountain: BLMR 3429 Laramie River Overlook: BLMR 3431
Distance	Jelm Mountain: 5.3 miles Laramie River Overlook: 2.6 miles
Managing Agency	BLM—Rawlins Field Office
Starting Coordinates	Jelm Mountain: N41° 3.96' W106° 0.41' Laramie River Overlook: N41° 1.83' W105° 59.73'

Overview: These two short roads climb to high overlooks near the Wyoming/Colorado border. The first is Jelm Mountain Road, which climbs steeply to a lone mountaintop east of the Medicine Bow National Forest. Jelm Mountain is named after a tie hack—a laborer who hews logs into railroad ties—who worked on the mountain. Today, the summit is home to the Wyoming Infrared Observatory.

The second and shorter route, Laramie River Overlook Road, climbs to a high point overlooking the Laramie River. This is an easy drive, but if you're driving a low clearance vehicle, you'll likely need to park below the overlook and walk the final tenth of a mile to the top.

Approaching the summit on Jelm Mountain

Start: From Laramie, drive west on HWY 230 for 25 miles to Woods Landing. Then drive south on HWY 10 for 3.4 miles to Jelm Mountain Road on the left or 6.6 miles to the Laramie River Overlook Road on the right.

Description (Jelm Mountain): The drive begins by heading east on BLMR 3429 above Sunrise Spring Creek. Follow the gravel road as it wraps around the southern flank of Jelm Mountain and then turns north onto a steeper grade. As you climb the long ridge of mountain shrubland, views of the Laramie River Valley are revealed to the east. The higher you climb, the better the views—the snowcapped mountains of Colorado to the south and the Medicine Bows to the northwest. Further north, the Snowy Range comes into view behind the closer Sheep Mountain.

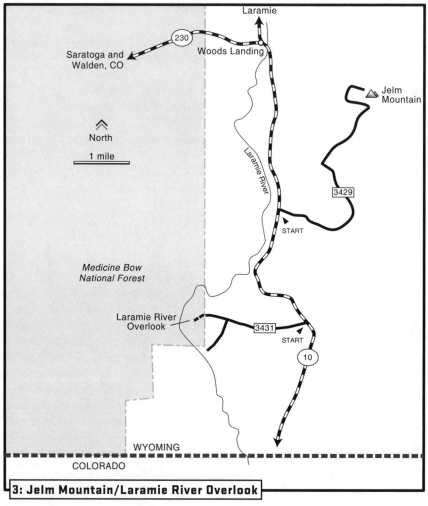

3: Jelm Mountain/Laramie River Overlook

By 3 miles, the road begins climbing through a spotty pine and aspen forest. There are lots of small, loose rocks on the road, but it's still an easy ascent. Nearing the top, the road leaves the forest and makes a final cut to the east to attain the mountain's 9,656-foot summit.

Description (Laramie River Overlook): From the highway, follow the road west across open terrain to a split at 1.6 miles. The left-bearing track descends 500 feet in a little over a mile to reach the Laramie River—a good route for the return trip. To attain the overlook, stay right and continue along the edge of a treeless ridge.

At 2.1 miles, the road splits again with a spur leading off to the north. Stay left here and drive another .4 mile to a pullout, which is a good place to park if you're driving a 2WD vehicle. The road continues another tenth of a mile to the southwest, but it's rocky and has no good turnaround at the end.

The road ends at a lightly-timbered high point of 8,203 feet just inside the Medicine Bow National Forest boundary. From this vantage point, you can look southward into the Laramie River drainage, which creates a lush corridor in an otherwise empty and parched valley. On the distant horizon are the snowcapped peaks of the Medicine Bow Mountains in Colorado, better known as the Rawah Wilderness. To the immediate west are the treeless foothills of Wyoming's share of the same mountain range.

4: Northern Medicine Bow
Tour the northern mountains

☒ **Backcountry Drive**   ☐ **4WD Route**   ☐ **ATV Trail**
Most vehicles   4x4 vehicle or ORV   ORV less than 50" wide

Location/Map	West of Laramie; Page 294
Roads	FR 101, FR 100
Distance	47 miles
Managing Agency	USDA Forest Service—Medicine Bow National Forest
Starting Coordinates	N41° 20.39' W106° 10.09'

Overview: This drive makes an easy arc through the northern Medicine Bow Mountains. Highlights include Sand Lake, Turpin Reservoir, historical ruins, and a side trip to the top of Kennaday Peak. The gravel road has a relatively smooth surface but there are blind curves that you'll want to handle carefully. Since the road travels over 10,000 feet, snowdrifts keep the road closed until mid-June. The drive begins and ends near two Forest Service Visitor Centers where you can learn more about the area.

Start: To start from the eastern end of the road, take HWY 130 west of Laramie for 28 miles to Centennial. Continue west from Centennial for 4 miles and turn right onto Sand Lake Road (FR 101). To reach the western end from Saratoga, take HWY 130 for 20 miles and turn north onto FR 100.

Description: Sand Lake Road (FR 101) begins from HWY 130 at 8,900 feet. This first stretch is paved as the road passes trail markers for the Little Laramie cross-country ski trails on both sides of the road.

A number of side roads are soon reached. At 1.3 miles you pass FR 330, a rough 3.3-mile track that travels to the North Fork River. On the other side of the road, you'll find Fallen Pines Road (FR 329), which cuts 13 miles across the eastern side of the national forest. Then, before mile 2, the entrance to North Fork Campground is passed on the left. With 60 long sites, this campground is one of the largest in the Medicine Bow. Mountain pine beetles have ravaged the forest here in recent years, and the campground's trees have been cleared.

From the campground, Sand Lake Road turns to gravel and begins ascending the west slope of a heavily-wooded hill. You can gauge this climb at the North Fork Overlook, located 3 miles north of the campground on a curve that tops 10,000 feet in elevation. With altitude comes a transition in the forest. Aspen and pine trees are replaced with spruce and fir, species of the subalpine communities. From this point northward, there are many side roads that are now closed to motorized traffic but are still open to other

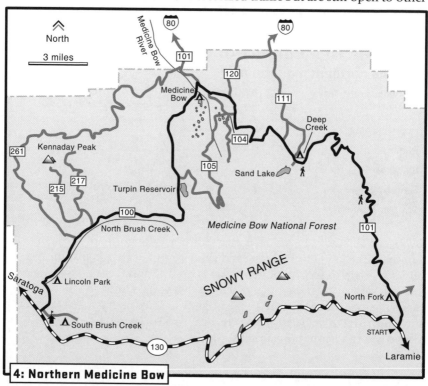

4: Northern Medicine Bow

Boggy meadows near Sand Lake

pursuits such as mountain biking and hiking. If it's a hiking trail that you're seeking, check out the little-acclaimed Trail Creek Trail, reached at 8.7 miles. The trek will lead you 3.3 miles to a pair of high country lakes.

The following 7 miles bring an increasingly curvy route that climbs to a high point of 10,200 feet. Then, at nearly 18 miles from the highway, you'll roll into a mountain park that is rich with recreational opportunities. On the right is Deep Creek Campground, an out-of-the-way camp that receives light use. There are also two trailheads, one on each side of the road. The large one on the left provides access to the backcountry lakes south of the Snowy Range. The trail on the right descends through the Deep Creek/Rock Creek drainage toward Arlington. A bit further, a spur on the left leads to Sand Lake, a large subalpine fishery.

The road now begins a gradual descent as it tracks to the northwest. A side road, FR 111, splits off to the north and leads to Arlington. Less than a mile farther, the Bow River Overlook at mile 20 offers a good view of Elk Mountain (10,981 feet). The lone mountaintop stands 16 miles from this vantage point.

Four miles further downhill, the road reaches FR 104, a worthwhile alternate route. Look in the trees at the junction and you'll find a pair of old cabins.

A dirt road, FR 104 heads west toward the marshy interior of Stillwater Park where scores of ponds are adorned with lily pads. Within a mile, the road intersects Stillwater Park Road (FR 105), which can be taken north 1.6 miles, or south for 11 miles. Both directions return to the main route, but the south bearing road is the more exciting of the two. After cutting through Stillwater Park, the road follows the Medicine Bow River upstream, a drainage frequented by moose. At 5.5 miles, it crosses the river over a bridge to reach a slope of younger conifers. This is the site of a tornado that flattened 250 acres of the forest in the summer of 1976. From this point, the road switchbacks up the steep wooded mountain gaining 600 feet in 2 miles. The view from the top, at 10,080 feet, is far reaching—you can see clear out of the mountains to the northern prairie. The last 3 miles of the road descend along a rocky, bumpy lane before joining FR 100 just north of Turpin Reservoir.

ALTERNATE ROUTE

Continuing north on FR 101 from the junction, the backroad intersects FR 120, another good route that leads north to Arlington. Stay on FR 101 for another 2 miles and then turn left onto FR 100 (FR 101 continues northward to Cedar Pass Road and Elk Mountain). The route now travels southwest and soon crosses the beautiful Medicine Bow River near Bow River Campground. Soon after, a short spur is passed on the left—this offers access to non-motorized trails around Long Lake.

The following 6 miles present easy driving. In mile 33, you'll pass the southern end of FR 105 (the alternate route) and then roll past Turpin Reservoir where you can toss a line for trout. Follow the road south around Cecil Park, and then west along Brush Creek to mile 41 where a secondary route, FR 215, climbs to the top of Kennaday Peak.

The exhilarating 6.5-mile drive on FR 215 takes you above timberline to an abandoned fire lookout tower on the windswept summit of Kennaday Peak (10,810 feet). The current tower was built in 1964 and is used intermittently to spot flare-ups. The dirt road climbs over 2,000 feet but is easily driven, unless you're afraid of heights and steep drops. The reward at the top is a sweeping view of the entire region.

SIDE TRIP

Near 42 miles, you pass Cedar Pass Road (FR 261), a 23-mile route that loops around the west side of Kennaday Peak and ends near Bow River Campground. Also keep watch for splash dams and decrepit cabins that are remnants of the area's logging history.

Further south, you'll find several 4WD roads and ATV trails around Lincoln Park Campground. Past the camp, the backroad passes briefly through private property and the junction with FR 200, which leads to South Brush Creek Campground. The road then pulls into a sage flat and ends at HWY 130 at the foot of Barrett Ridge. Pine beetles have decimated the surrounding forest here, and you'll find the hillsides covered with dead pines. Turn left to go over the Snowy Range or turn right to exit the national forest and reach Saratoga.

Other Nearby Drives

Cedar Pass Road—This gravel lane (FR 261) can be used to loop around Kennaday Peak on the northwestern slope of the Medicine Bow Mountains. This is a heavily timbered drive that has no destination. However, there are interpretive signs along the way that describe the various trees and animals that comprise this forest. To reach the southern end of the road from HWY 130, drive north for 5 miles on FR 100. The northern end of the road ends at the Medicine Bow National Forest boundary, which is 12 miles south of the town of Elk Mountain.

Pass Creek Road—This easily driven road (CR 404) runs between the town of Elk Mountain and HWY 130 north of Saratoga. In 29 miles, it wraps around Elk Mountain (11,156 feet) and parallels beautiful Pass Creek for several miles. The road is best driven in September when the area's flora displays brilliant autumn colors. To reach the western end of the road from Saratoga, drive north on HWY 130 for 12 miles. To reach the eastern end from I-80, take Exit 255 and drive a few miles to Elk Mountain (the town) on HWY 72.

5: Snowy Range
Tour of the high lakes

☐ **Backcountry Drive**
  Most vehicles

☒ **4WD Route**
  4x4 vehicle or ORV

☐ **ATV Trail**
  ORV less than 50" wide

Location/Map	West of Laramie; Page 300
Roads	FR 103
Distance	9.5 miles
Managing Agency	USDA Forest Service—Medicine Bow National Forest
Starting Coordinates	N41° 19.69' W106° 21.81'

Overview: This rugged road tours the western side of the Snowy Range where half a dozen lakes can be seen. Take off on foot and you can hike to a dozen more. Both ends of the road travel through subalpine forest, but the middle stretch spans exposed high meadows that will have you reaching for your camera.

Most full-sized vehicles on this road have been modified with higher ground clearance. Stock 4x4s can make it, but it takes a skilled backcountry driver. The road is open to motorized travel from July 2 to October 31.

Start: To reach the southern end of the road, drive west from Laramie on HWY 130 for 28 miles to Centennial. Then continue west on the highway for 18.2 miles and turn right onto FR 103 where there is a parking lot for unloading ATVs.

A northern access point can be reached by continuing west on the highway for another 10 miles and turning right onto FR 100. Follow this road for 11.5 miles to FR 103 on the right.

Description: Starting from the south end, follow the maintained road northward for a mile and then bear right at a fork. You'll soon wrap around the west side of the trip's first lake, South Twin Lake. The good road continues only about another half mile where a small parking area usually holds a car or two. North Twin Lake is up ahead in the trees to the right, but is not as visible as its predecessor.

From this point forward, the road becomes a true 4WD route. The initial stretch here is cluttered with deep potholes, mud, and large rocks. Getting through it is more a result of your comfort level than your vehicle's capability. I've seen stock pickup trucks finish this route and a lifted, modified 4WD rig turn back.

Continuing north, the ground becomes boggier as small streams flow along and over the road. Two shallow fords are required before reaching mile 3. The trees thin considerably from this point and Dipper Lake soon comes into view. A trailhead at the lake offers foot access to the east where you'll find trails that lead to Heart Lake and the top of Medicine Bow Peak.

Next to Dipper Lake, the road runs next to an unnamed loch with a tiny timbered island. With the Snowy Range now spread out over the horizon behind the lake, the setting is quite photogenic. This is also the trip's high point at 10,700 feet.

The road now becomes an oft-muddy track as it cuts through meadows and over two small rises in a light forest. At mile 5, it reaches a pair of old cabins at Quealy Lake, which sits in a small depression on the other side of the road. Here, another foot trail heads east to a chain of alpine lakes. You now pass through high, wildflower-loaded meadows. Watch for elk herds here in the summer as they forage in the parks and take refuge along the treeline.

The rutted road now descends gradually where you'll have to contend with an occasional boulder. Since the path is so narrow, usually the only option is to go up and over these impediments. Even with 12 inches of ground clearance, a few of these mashed my skid plates.

Nearing mile 7, the road dips through the headwaters of the Medicine Bow River as it returns to the edge of a spruce and fir forest. These are shallow fords, but wet tires and muddy banks can make them trickier.

Westbound, the road skirts north of Cascade Lake, which is surrounded by timber. What follows is perhaps the most challenging stretch of the route. Large rocks, a steeper grade, and tight sections with lots of overhanging limbs will have you driving with care. Near the end, you reach an improved

Forest Road 103 crosses high meadows near the Snowy Range

road that forks just a tenth of a mile before reaching FR 100. Stay left to finish FR 103. A right turn takes you onto a short road that leads to Banner Lakes and also connects to FR 105 further to the north.

6: Campbell Lake
Motor in to a remote mountain lake

☐ **Backcountry Drive**
 Most vehicles

☐ **4WD Route**
 4x4 vehicle or ORV

☒ **ATV Trail**
 ORV less than 50" wide

Location/Map	West of Laramie; Page 300
Trails	FT 211, FT 211.1C
Distance	1.9+ miles
Managing Agency	USDA Forest Service—Medicine Bow National Forest
Starting Coordinates	N41° 24.17' W106° 23.26'

Overview: This mostly-timbered ATV trail travels to Campbell Lake on the west side of the Snowy Range. The shortest and most common way to reach the lake is from the north, where the lake can be reached in less than 2 miles. A longer trip can be made by continuing southward toward HWY 130, tying into a 4WD road near a trio of high lakes. The trail is open for motorized use from July 1 to November 15. A Wyoming ORV permit is required.

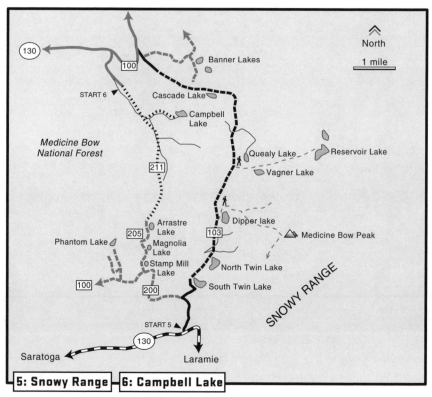

5: Snowy Range — **6: Campbell Lake**

Start: To reach the southern access point for this trail, drive west from Laramie on HWY 130 for 28 miles to Centennial. Then continue west on the highway for 18.2 miles and turn right onto FR 103 where there is a parking lot for unloading ATVs. For the shortest distance to the lake, continue west on the highway for another 10 miles and turn right onto FR 100. Follow this road for 10.5 miles to FR 205 on the right. Drive southward about a mile to reach the trailhead. There are numerous places to park and unload ATVs along this road and at the trailhead.

Description: Beginning from the northern trailhead near FR 100, the wide trail climbs through the North Brush Creek drainage. A narrow meadow sometimes filled with cattle is passed on the right. The trail here gains quite a bit of elevation on short, rocky steeps as it advances through spruce and fir. There are several shallow fords before reaching the end of the first mile.

At 1 mile, the trail enters a meadow of wildflowers. Here, you'll find an intersection with FT 211.1C. Turn left onto this trail and ford North Brush Creek. Continue through the meadow where the trail is lined with plastic tread to prevent erosion.

The remainder of this stretch—a little less than a mile in length— becomes rougher and narrower. The trail passes around a rocky abutment and tackles challenging terrain with plenty of mud, rock, deep ruts, and tree

A ford of North Brush Creek near Campbell Lake

roots. Various detours have been made, but stick to the main trail and you'll reach the end at an embankment just below the lake.

The quiet waters sit in a small basin surrounded by higher ground—views are limited and the Snowy Range remains hidden. Moose are commonly seen in this area and pikas can sometimes be heard within the rocks.

The lake is a popular final destination, but a longer route can be made by returning to FT 211. From this junction, the trail makes another ford (the ATV bridge was out at the time of this writing) and continues southward another half mile to ford the upper waters of North Brush Creek. The trail gets rougher yet, and steeply climbs 500 feet over the next mile.

As this is the western slope of the Medicine Bow Mountains, streams are flowing westward and downhill along the trail, so you'll find bogs and channels along the way. A high point of 10,500 feet is reached in a small boggy park. From here, the trail descends to Arrastre Lake, some 3.5 miles from the northern trailhead. The trail now turns into FR 205, a narrow and rocky 4WD road that is open to full-sized vehicles.

From this point, it's another 5 miles to HWY 130 to the south. To reach it, continue along FR 205 to reach Magnolia Lake, followed later by Stamp Mill Lake. A No Trespassing sign here reminds you to stay on the road as there are small parcels of private property. Just south of this third lake, the road reaches FR 200. This road (route #7) heads to Phantom Lake and South Brush Campground. Turn east here and follow a smoother road as it passes dispersed campsites and reaches FR 103. Turn south onto this improved road and follow it less than a mile to reach HWY 130.

7: South Brush Creek/Phantom Lake
Head upstream to Phantom Lake

☐ **Backcountry Drive** Most vehicles	☒ **4WD Route** 4x4 vehicle or ORV	☐ **ATV Trail** ORV less than 50" wide

Location/Map	West of Laramie; Page 304
Roads	FR 200, FR 234, FR 200.2A
Distance	7 miles
Managing Agency	USDA Forest Service—Medicine Bow National Forest
Starting Coordinates	N41° 20.66' W106° 29.85'

Overview: This fun route starts at a Forest Service campground on the west side of the Medicine Bow National Forest and follows a creek upstream to Phantom Lake. The rocky route makes for a jarring ride on an ATV, and an even worse one in a full-size vehicle. While stock 4x4s can make the drive, it takes a patient and careful driver.

Start: From Laramie, take HWY 130 west for 28 miles to Centennial. Then continue west on the highway for 28.2 miles and turn right onto FR 100. If you're driving from Saratoga, follow HWY 130 for 20 miles to reach FR 100. Upon reaching Brush Creek Road (FR 100), drive north for a third of a mile and then turn right onto narrow FR 200. Head east for 1.6 miles to the end of the maintained road.

Description: The 4WD road begins where the maintained portion of FR 200 ends, near South Brush Creek Campground. The path heads east through the mixed evergreen forest and is completely pocked with rocks. In some places, the road resembles a dry creek bed. Though not overly large, the sheer volume of rocks will keep your pace slow and steady.

A junction with FR 281B (marked as FR 200.1B on the MVUM) is soon passed and the road continues a gradual uphill climb as it parallels South Brush Creek. While dodging rocks, keep watch for a pair of cabin ruins as well as moose, which are commonly found along the willow-lined creek.

SIDE TRIP
A left turn onto FR 200.1B will lead you to several additional 4WD roads such as FR 222 and FR 220. There are no notable destinations along these routes, but they do offer decent off-roading opportunities in the forested terrain above Lincoln Park Campground.

Near 2.5 miles, the road reaches a fork where a lesser road runs northeast along Little Brush Creek. Keep right at the fork to connect to FR 234, and then turn left (a right turn takes you back to the highway). Use this smoother road to quickly advance eastward for another 2 miles at which point the road will deteriorate back to a 4WD surface.

At 6.2 miles, turn north onto FR 200.2A. The rocks are larger along this rough side track, some nearly knee-high. It's just short of a mile on this steeper road to reach a dispersed camping area at the edge of shallow Phantom Lake. At 10,040 feet, the subalpine loch is timbered on all sides in a forest of spruce and fir.

If you want to see more of this country, there are additional options for your way out. When you return to FR 200, turn east and follow it over half a mile to FR 205. This 4WD road heads north to several lakes on Gold Hill,

Rocky road to Phantom Lake

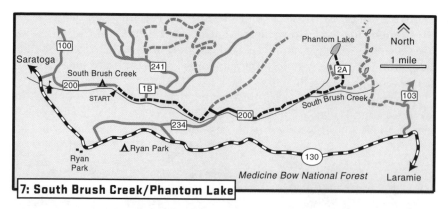

7: South Brush Creek/Phantom Lake

which is an old mining district. This is also where you can catch an ATV trail to Campbell Lake. Continuing east on FR 200, you'll reach FR 103 in 2 miles and HWY 130 in 3 miles.

Other Nearby Drives

Lincoln Park Trails—The northwest area of the Medicine Bow National Forest has several designated ATV trails. These serve as short connecting routes between 4WD roads in a quiet, heavily timbered part of the mountain range. To reach these from HWY 130 (on the west side of the Snowy Range), drive northward on FR 100 for 2.7 miles to Lincoln Park Campground. From here, you can take Stump Hollow Trail to the northwest where it ties into other secondary roads and trails. Another option is to follow FR 241, which runs southeast beside the campground. This road connects to several other roads, including FR 200 along South Brush Creek. For exact routes, refer to a Medicine Bow National Forest map.

8: Bear Lake/Silver Run Lake/Libby Flats
Atop Snowy Range Pass

☐ **Backcountry Drive**
  Most vehicles

☒ **4WD Route**
  4x4 vehicle or ORV

☐ **ATV Trail**
  ORV less than 50" wide

Location/Map	West of Laramie; Page 306
Roads	FR 275, FR 336, FR 396, FR 396A, FR 343
Distance	3.6 miles to Bear Lake (12+ miles of roads)
Managing Agency	USDA Forest Service—Medicine Bow National Forest
Starting Coordinates	N41° 20.75' W106° 17.47'

Overview: This drive is likely the most popular four-wheeling route in the Medicine Bow National Forest. A local favorite that can be handled by most 4x4s, the road tops 10,700 feet at Libby Flats on Snowy Range Pass. It's the third highest 4WD route in the state, or at least in this book.

Most drivers start at the top on HWY 130 and only go to Bear Lake or Silver Run Lake, a distance of 3.6 and 4.5 miles, respectively. A longer route can be made by following roads off of Libby Flats and into the dark timber to the south. The entire route is open to motorized use from July 16 to October 31. You can expect sloppy conditions throughout the driving season.

The Snowy Range from Libby Flats

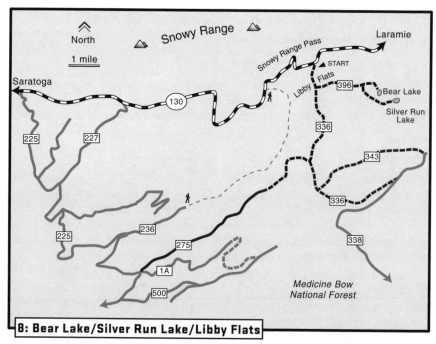

8: Bear Lake/Silver Run Lake/Libby Flats

Start: To reach the northern end of the road from Laramie, drive west on HWY 130 for 28 miles to Centennial. Then continue west for 11.3 miles to the turnoff on the left. To reach the southern end of the road from Centennial, drive west on HWY 130 for 21.5 miles and turn left onto FR 227. Follow this road south for 4 miles to join FR 225, and then continue south on curvy FR 225 for 10.6 miles to the intersection with FR 275. For access from the east, use Elhin Road (FR 338), 1.3 miles west of Centennial.

Description: From the northern starting point, FR 336 begins by heading south across Libby Flats, a high alpine plain with magnificent views of the Snowy Range. The road here has some occasional rocks and puddles, but is easy when driven slowly. Follow this road southward to a junction with FR 396. Turn left and follow the path down an often-wet slope that leads to the timber. Numerous side tracks parallel the main route, but stick to the main path to prevent further resource damage.

The next junction is reached at the edge of the trees at 3 miles. A left turn here leads a half mile to Bear Lake, a photogenic gem that fills a rocky and wooded bowl. This last stretch is sometimes found with massive mud holes that are unsuitable for stock trucks. If you need an easier and drier route, turn right and follow the narrow lane 1.5 miles to Silver Run Lake, a slightly larger lake.

The two lakes are the most popular destinations in the Libby Flats area, but more four-wheeling can be found to the south. To continue, return to FR 336 and turn southward. A jumbled pile of shin-high rocks is found

1.5 miles further. Some stock vehicles may scrape something on the undercarriage here, but it's a short stretch that is quickly passed. Soon after, the road leaves the alpine landscape and enters a mature subalpine forest. The rocky lane has some potholes, but 4WD vehicles will have no trouble negotiating the obstacles.

At nearly 4 miles from the northern starting point, the road forks. The left fork, FR 336, heads more than a mile downhill into Nelson Park where there are some historical cabins as well as a junction with FR 343. From there, you can take either 4WD road about 4 miles to Ehlin Road (FR 338), a popular route that runs from HWY 130 to Rob Roy Reservoir. Driving both of these roads, and using FR 338 to connect the two, creates an additional 12-mile loop. You'll encounter multiple fords and some mud holes along these roads, especially on the western end of FR 343.

The easier route in this area is FR 275. This cobble track has some large mud puddles and a heavy dose of tree roots over the next few miles, but is easy to drive as it traverses a ridge high above the French Creek drainage. The road connects to main trunk roads on the west side of the Medicine Bow Mountains.

Other Nearby Drives

Brooklyn Lake Road/Towner Lake Road/Sugarloaf Recreation Area—For such short lengths, these three roads are very scenic as they lead to the edge of the highest crest in the Snowy Range. Within 2 miles, Brooklyn Lake Road (FR 317) takes you past two lakes and three trailheads. About halfway along the road, Towner Lake Road splits off to the left and travels 3 miles past several unnamed lakes to return to HWY 130. It's a bumpy path poked with potholes, but the Forest Service may be improving it in the future. The third road in the area leads to the Sugarloaf Recreation Area, which includes a picnic area, trailhead, and campground. This might very well be one of the most scenic roads in the state as it ends at the foot of Medicine Bow Peak. Snowdrifts typically keep all three of these routes closed until late July. To reach the roads from Centennial, drive west on HWY 130 for 8 miles to Brooklyn Lake Road, 10.5 miles for Towner Lake Road, or a little over 11 miles to the Sugarloaf turnoff.

Elhin Road—FR 338 is a 14-mile road that runs between the Forest Service Centennial Visitor Center at HWY 130 to Rob Roy Reservoir. It's commonly used for dispersed camping and ATV riding, especially at the southern end in Cinnabar Park. The narrow and sometimes steep road is bumpy—expect a rough ride. To reach the northern end of the road, drive west from Laramie on HWY 130 for 28 miles to Centennial. Then continue west on the highway for 1.3 miles to the turnoff on the left. To reach the southern end from Laramie, drive west on HWY 130 for 21 miles to HWY 11. Then head south on HWY 11 for 11 miles to Albany. Drive west on FR 500 for 7.7 miles and turn right onto FR 338.

Barber Lake Road—Paved FR 351 departs from HWY 130 just 2 miles west of Centennial and makes an alternative route to the Snowy Range high country. The road maintains a steady ascent through the Libby Creek drainage while passing several Forest Service campgrounds and a picnic area at man-made Barber Lake. It ends after 5 miles where it reconnects to the highway. This is not a fast-driven road as there are numerous tight curves and switchbacks.

9: Southern Medicine Bow
A traverse of the southern mountains

☒ **Backcountry Drive** Most vehicles	☐ **4WD Route** 4x4 vehicle or ORV	☐ **ATV Trail** ORV less than 50" wide

Location/Map	West of Laramie; Page 310
Roads	FR 500, FR 542, FR 543, FR 206, FR 225, FR 227
Distance	45 miles
Managing Agency	USDA Forest Service—Medicine Bow National Forest
Starting Coordinates	N41° 10.96' W106° 7.99'

Overview: This tour of the southern Medicine Bow Mountains includes several of the area's features including Rob Roy Reservoir, the old mining town of Keystone, and a scenic overlook. Due to deep snowdrifts on the west side of the range, this drive may not be passable in its entirety until the beginning of July.

Start: To reach the eastern end of the drive from Laramie, drive west on HWY 130 for 21 miles to HWY 11. Then head south on HWY 11 for 11 miles to Albany. Drive through the small town to reach the gravel road. To reach the western end from Saratoga, head south and then east on HWY 130 for 23 miles to FR 225.

Description: From Albany, follow the wide road—known as French Creek Road—around a tight curve and then along a steady climb through a pine forest. The first of many junctions is reached at mile 2. Here, FR 513 turns south toward Lake Owen and Fox Park. Stay straight at the junction and continue west for a half mile to Keystone Road (FR 542) and then turn left.

ALTERNATE ROUTE
Staying straight on FR 500 will take you past Spruce Mountain where a fire lookout tower can be rented for overnight stays (check www.recreation.gov). It then passes along the north side of Rob Roy Reservoir before rejoining this backcountry drive in 7 miles. This detour cuts about 12 miles off the total distance.

Travel along Keystone Road as it climbs and dips over the next 5.5 miles to the Keystone Work Center on the right side of the road. This Forest Service facility includes a 1930s two-bedroom cabin that can be rented out for the night (again, check www.recreation.gov). From the work center, roll another quarter mile to reach FR 543. Stay right to reach Keystone where you'll find a curious assortment of structures, including some touristy, false storefronts.

Keystone was part of the widespread Douglas Creek gold-mining district that started producing in 1878. Though fair amounts of gold were extracted from the ore here, miners came and went over the next couple of decades. By 1939, parcels of the land were being sold off and they now comprise a small mountainous retreat of summer cabins. Even though the land has been repurposed, remnants of the area's heavy mining is still very much visible, especially along Douglas Creek.

From the small townsite, FR 543 (now called Douglas Creek Road) curves to the north and follows the stream of the same name to Rob Roy Reservoir. Stay straight at the junction with FR 511.

SIDE
TRIP

Head west on FR 511 and you'll reach FR 512 in just 2.5 miles. You can then take FR 512 further west between two designated wilderness areas—the Savage Run to the north and the Platte River to the south. The road ends a little over 10 miles further at the cottonwood-lined banks of the North Platte River. There, you'll find a pair of Forest Service campgrounds, a trailhead, and plenty of river-loving people.

Rob Roy Reservoir as seen from Forest Road 543

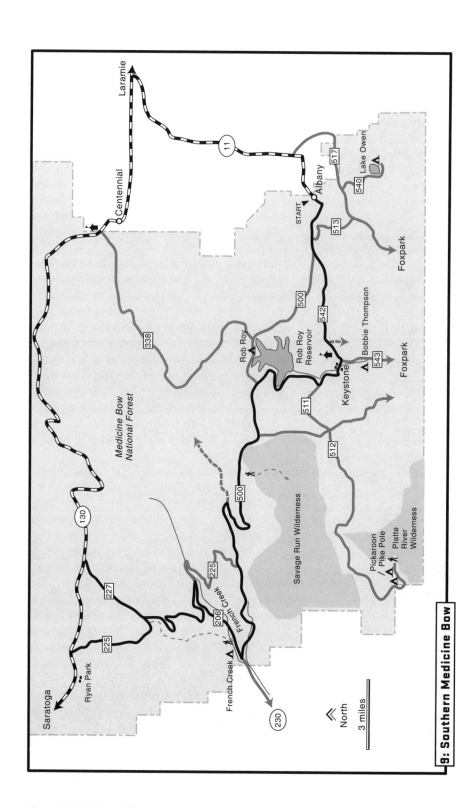

9: Southern Medicine Bow

The Rob Roy Reservoir dam is reached in mile 11, but the road continues to wrap around the western shoreline of the large lake for the next few miles. Construction on the reservoir was completed in 1965 to help collect water for Cheyenne.

The road rejoins FR 500 (French Creek Road) in mile 14 near the historical Holmes mining district. This was another active mining area that even had a post office that operated until 1950. More recently, the Forest Service operated a campground at the junction, but it's now closed. A right turn at this junction will take you to a campground and boat ramp on the north side of Rob Roy Reservoir. To continue with this backcountry drive, turn left on FR 500 and drive west. One note of caution: if it's before July and you've already encountered snow along or on the road, there's a good chance that the second half of this drive will be impassable.

Just a half-mile west from Holmes is the site of the Rambler Mine, a gold mine that was rebirthed for copper extraction in 1900. The Rambler's copper ore was of reportedly good quality, but the mine couldn't compete with the larger open pit mines found elsewhere in the country and it was eventually shut down.

While attaining an unnoticeable high point of 9,930 feet, the backroad reaches FR 511 in mile 16. Bear right and continue to follow FR 500 as it skirts along the Savage Run Wilderness boundary on the left side of the road. This stretch has been devastated from the mountain pine beetle epidemic, and many pine trees have been cut and harvested. Further west, watch for an interpretive sign that describes the Laramie and Encampment Wagon Road, which served the area's mining districts. As the sign reads, it took up to 8 hours to travel from Laramie to Keystone with a stagecoach.

After passing through a heavily logged area with occasional overlooks to the south, the backroad begins a steady descent off the western slope of the Medicine Bow Mountains. The well-maintained gravel roads up to this point are replaced with a rockier, bumpy surface as you rapidly change elevation. Upon curving into the North Mullen Creek drainage, the road straightens out and heads toward French Creek Campground. Along the way, you'll find that the dark evergreen forest transitions to lighter woodlands of aspen and shrubs. The roadway also improves.

You reach FR 206 at 30 miles. At 7,800 feet, this junction marks the drive's lowest point. Turn right onto the lesser road and you'll immediately pass French Creek Campground. The road now begins to climb back uphill as it follows French Creek to the northeast. A large footbridge that accesses the Tie Hack Trail is soon passed on the left.

 SIDE TRIP If you continue west on FR 500 from the campground, you'll exit the national forest and reach BLMR 3404 a couple of miles farther. This 7-mile route accesses two BLM campgrounds and a trailhead along the North Platte River.

Continue upstream along French Creek until you reach FR 225 near mile 34. Here, make a tight left turn to get onto FR 225 and then follow it west across a steep slope of aspen. This road cuts into the side of the mountain and offers a terrific view into the drainage in which you just traveled. A short pullout for a scenic overlook is found right before the road cuts back into the timber. From this vantage point, you can see Wyoming's Sierra Madre as well as the snowy crags of Colorado's Mount Zirkel Wilderness.

The backroad now winds northward through the pine forest by following an elevation contour that doesn't allow for a straight shot. At mile 40, the road intersects FR 227. Here, you can take either road—both are around 4 miles—to reach HWY 130 and end the drive. If you're ultimately going to drive back east to Laramie, take FR 227. If you're headed west to Saratoga, stay on FR 225, which ends in just 4.5 miles.

10: Pelton Creek
Explore rich wildlife habitat

☒ **Backcountry Drive** Most vehicles	☐ **4WD Route** 4x4 vehicle or ORV	☐ **ATV Trail** ORV less than 50" wide

Location/Map	Southwest of Laramie; Page 314
Roads	FR 898
Distance	8.6 miles
Managing Agency	USDA Forest Service—Medicine Bow National Forest
Starting Coordinates	N40° 59.76' W106° 12.45'

Overview: This road follows a meandering creek from the Colorado border to a Forest Service recreation site on the eastern tip of the Platte River Wilderness. Wildlife is abundant in this part of the national forest and sightings are common. The road also serves as an access point for many secondary roads that branch off to the west and east.

Start: From Laramie, drive southwest on HWY 230 for 40 miles. Turn right onto FR 898, located just inside the Colorado state line.

Description: From the highway, the gravel road heads into the forest for a short distance and enters Wyoming. Just over a mile, the road reaches a trailhead for the Medicine Bow Rail Trail, a 23-mile stretch of railroad bed that has been converted to non-motorized use. The old line was named the Laramie, Hahn's Peak, and Pacific Railroad, known as the L, HP & P. Constructed between 1902 and 1911, it was used to carry livestock, lumber, passengers, mail, and coal along its 111-mile length between North Park, Colorado and Centennial, Wyoming. With the tracks now removed, the recreational path is open to hiking, biking, and pack animals.

Shrubby banks of Pelton Creek

Continuing to the northwest, the backroad reaches Pelton Creek by mile 2. In earlier times, the meandering stream was called Beaver Creek and West Beaver Creek, appropriate names given its numerous beaver ponds, but was later named after Clark Pelton, "The Kid." Clark was an outlaw who was imprisoned in the Midwest for robbing stagecoaches and then later served time in Laramie for murder. Upon his last release in 1882, he turned his life around and became a highly-regarded citizen.

The road now travels downstream through the open drainage. The creek is flanked on both sides by low-rising ridges of conifers where willows and aspens fill the tributaries. At mile 5, you pass FR 516, a decent west-bearing road that accesses a handful of 4WD roads that reach the wilderness boundary. A little further north is FR 530, which leads eastward to Fox Park. It also has numerous tracks that make fun and easy four-wheeling trips.

As you drive deeper into the backcountry, watch for moose and deer which are sometimes seen along Pelton Creek. Elk can also be found, especially near the beginning of autumn when they begin migrating from higher elevations. Other notable inhabitants of the area include bear, mountain lion, and bighorn sheep.

A few dispersed campsites are passed before you reach the end of the road at Pelton Creek Campground. The shrubby confluence of Pelton Creek and Douglas Creek is found here and the resulting riparian corridor draws all sorts of wildlife during the day's early and waning hours. A trailhead is located on the far end of the campground. From there, you can hike or ride a horse into the Platte River Wilderness.

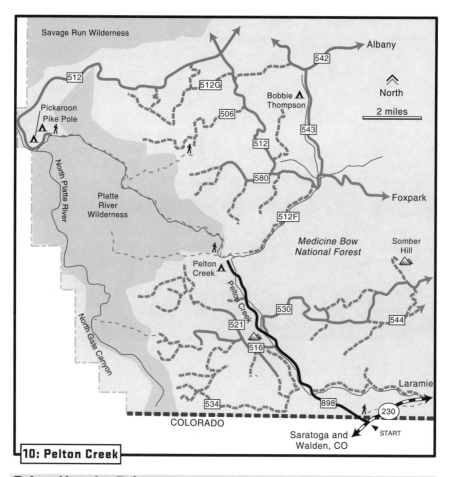

10: Pelton Creek

Other Nearby Drives

Somber Hill—Fun, family-oriented ATV rides can be made on FR 530, which connects Fox Park to Pelton Creek Road (FR 898). This easy road sees little traffic, has mild inclines, and almost no terrain challenges. Be sure to drive to the top of Somber Hill (9,422 feet) where you'll get an overlook of the surrounding forest. For slightly rougher driving (but still quite easy on an ATV), incorporate FR 530Q and FR 544 into your trip.

Platte River Wilderness Routes—The Platte River Wilderness on the southwest side of Medicine Bow National Forest has many 4WD roads that reach its eastern boundary. These routes are narrow and often muddy. Because of snowdrifts, the roads can remain closed as late as July. September is a particularly good time to drive here as the aspens are colorful and the conditions are usually drier.

A narrow road that follows Douglas Creek through a valley, FR 512F is a muddy, rutted route that has plenty of challenges. These include downed timber, shin-high rocks, inclines, and washouts. It ends before mile 4 at the base of Castle Rock. There, a footpath continues into the wilderness.

Another route in the area is FR 506/FR 506D, which leads to the Devils Canyon Trailhead on the northeastern side of the Platte River Wilderness. The drive is nothing spectacular, but the hike into the canyon is. The remainder of FR 506 becomes much rougher and a 4WD vehicle is necessary to handle it. The road ends in 5.7 miles at the wilderness boundary. Another nearby 4WD road, FR 512G, can be found to the north. This route travels through a heavily logged area of the forest.

There is a widespread maze of secondary roads that is accessible to the west of Pelton Creek Road (FR 898). These routes run westward through dark timber to reach slopes of aspen and sagebrush at the edge of the Platte River Wilderness. Many of these 4WD spurs are easy, save for endless dips and some monster mud holes. A modified 4x4 or ATV is required to get through some of the trickier sections. With the exception of FR 534 and 516A near the Colorado border, these are dead-end routes that don't connect to form any loops. One note of caution: these roads travel through beetle-killed timber and trees are often found over the roads.

To reach these roads from Laramie, head southwest on HWY 230 for 34 miles to the turnoff for FR 512 (Fox Park). Take this road to the northwest for 8.8 miles to 512F or 13.6 miles to FR 506. Additional 4WD routes can be accessed by staying on the highway for another 6 miles and turning right onto Pelton Creek Road (FR 898), located just inside the Colorado state line. Drive north on this gravel road for 5 miles, and then turn left on FR 516 to locate several secondary roads.

State Line Routes—Between the small communities of Mountain Home and Woods Landing, look for FR 532 and FR 528 on the north side of HWY 230. With few rocks and little mud, these secondary roads can be driven in stock 4WD vehicles. Watch for both elk and moose on these routes. If you like these roads, similar ones can be found on the south side of HWY 230 near Chimney Park as well as around Gramm, an old railroad town built in 1915.

Prospect Creek—Prospect Creek Road (BLMR 3423), labeled on many maps as the Prospect Peak Road, is a 6.1-mile route that leads from HWY 230 to the North Platte River. The road begins by crossing several miles of open terrain where views are generous. This portion can be driven in any vehicle, but the last 1.3 miles require four-wheel drive and some skill. At this point, the road descends steeply, 750 feet over an 11% grade, with deep ruts. Drop a tire into one of these grooves and you'll likely catch the undercarriage of your vehicle. The road ends at the banks of the North Platte River.

To reach the road from Saratoga, drive south 18 miles to Riverside-Encampment. Then take HWY 230 toward Colorado for 19.5 miles to the well-signed turnoff on the left.

Laramie, Hahn's Peak, and Pacific Railroad—On the southeast side of the Medicine Bow Mountains, you'll find FR 552, which parallels an old railroad course for 5 miles from Lake Owen to FR 517 near Fox Park. The first couple of miles south of the lake are rocky and there is a muddy ford, but the 4WD course smoothes out considerably after that. No motorized use is allowed on the railroad bed except to cross over it, which the road does a few times.

North Platte River from the end of Prospect Creek Road

Sierra Madre

The northern end of Colorado's Park Range spills over the Wyoming state line where it is known as the Sierra Madre. These beautiful and serene mountains still retain much of their wild character, even though they have been heavily mined, logged, and bisected by a paved highway. Two designated wilderness areas—the Huston Park and the Encampment River—ensure that the best of these mountains remain primitive and unspoiled.

The Sierra Madre are not especially rugged and only a few summits approach timberline. The two highest peaks are Bridger Peak (11,004 feet) and Blackhall Mountain (10,979 feet), both of which can be reached by a road. Sagebrush slopes are mixed with a diverse forest that includes aspen, lodgepole, and limber pine. At higher elevations, verdant meadows are ringed by dense stands of spruce and fir. The western slope of the range is covered extensively with some of the largest aspen communities in the state.

Recreation throughout the Sierra Madre includes several pursuits; chief among them is hunting for antelope, deer, elk, and grouse. Even though the mountains are carved by drainages with rapid-flowing waters, natural lakes are few. There are, however, a number of reservoirs that offer fishing and boating opportunities, mostly at Hog Park Reservoir near the Colorado border. Another draw is the Continental Divide Trail, which brings long distance hikers across the backbone of the range.

Land Ownership

The Sierra Madre are managed by the Medicine Bow National Forest; the local office is located in Saratoga. This land has numerous private landholdings that are signed or gated. Many of these are carryovers from old mining districts. Even considering these, the national forest lands are well consolidated.

Roads and Trails

A single paved road known as Battle Highway (HWY 70) traverses the Sierra Madre from east to west. Before this road was paved and upgraded in the late 1990s, it was a gravel backroad that helped contribute to the area's wild and remote character. Today it offers easy access to the range's high crest where it crosses Battle Pass (9,955 feet) along the Continental Divide.

Although there are only a few good, well-maintained trunk roads that cut through these mountains, they are sufficient to get you where you want to go. There are many secondary roads that branch off these main routes, making this a very accessible range.

The Sierra Madre's 4WD routes are generally easy to drive. Ruts, tree limbs, snowdrifts, and occasional large rocks create the most challenges. There are few roads that a skilled backcountry driver couldn't tackle with a decent, stock 4x4 vehicle. With that said, the roads shouldn't be underestimated.

Although the going seemed easy, these mountains caused the most physical damage to my ride, including a busted side panel and a rock that punched a hole through the floorboard. It's too easy to build up speed on the easy stretches and then suddenly find yourself grappling for control when you least expect to need it.

Seasons and Conditions

Battle Highway is usually opened by Memorial Day Weekend, or shortly thereafter. However, many of the backroads aren't accessible until the middle of June. Secondary roads at higher levels are often snowed-in until the middle of July. Imagine my surprise when I went four-wheeling near Battle Pass on the Fourth of July and drove up to a 4-foot snowdrift! Winter snows begin in October, but usually don't make roads impassable until November.

Fuel

You're well advised to fuel up before heading to the Sierra Madre. To the north, you can make your stops is Rawlins or Saratoga. To the south in Colorado, your choices include Steamboat Springs and Walden. Closer to the range, you'll find fuel on the east side in Encampment and on the west side in Baggs.

Maps

The Medicine Bow National Forest map and Medicine Bow ORV map are the best maps for the Sierra Madre.

11: Southern Sierra Madre
Tour the southern mountains

☒ **Backcountry Drive**
Most vehicles

☐ **4WD Route**
4x4 vehicle or ORV

☐ **ATV Trail**
ORV less than 50" wide

Location/Map	South of Rawlins; Page 319
Roads	FR 550, FR 496, FR 409, CR 211
Distance	46 miles
Managing Agency	USDA Forest Service—Medicine Bow National Forest
Starting Coordinates	N41° 10.58' W106° 53.61'

Overview: This backcountry tour makes a loop around the Encampment River Wilderness in the southeastern portion of the Sierra Madre. It offers a look back into the mountains' history as well as a chance to spot animals such as bighorn sheep, deer, and elk. Plan on a full day to complete this trip if you're interested in incorporating some of the numerous stops, side trips, or hikes that are found along the way.

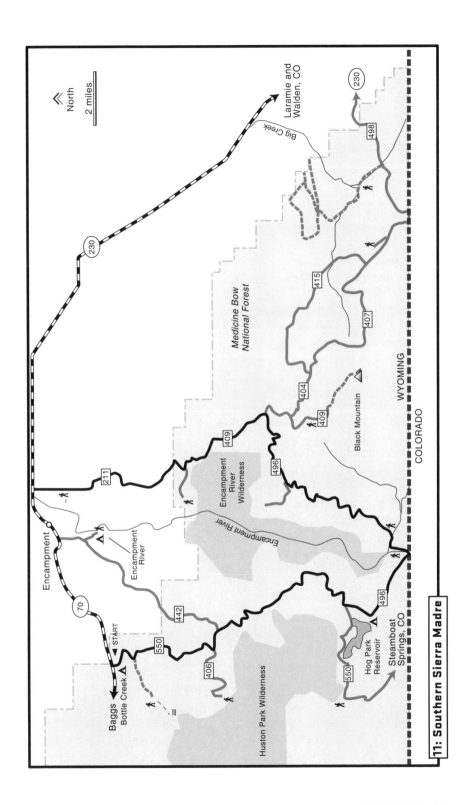

11: Southern Sierra Madre

The Forest Service has designated this route as the "Sierra Madre Auto Tour," which has 21 marked points of interest. However, the signs at each stop have no information other than a number, so you have to rely on the Forest Service's tour brochure to learn the significance of each point. Unfortunately, the brochure box located at the beginning of FR 550 is almost always found empty, so a summarized version of its information is included in this description.

Start: To access the west end of the loop from Encampment, drive west on HWY 70 for 6 miles and turn left onto FR 550. To access the eastern end, drive east from Encampment on HWY 230 for less than a mile to reach Blackhall Mountain Road (CR 211).

Description: The tour begins from HWY 70 by driving south on FR 550, a washboarded, gravel road. A turnoff for Bottle Creek Campground is soon reached on the right. From this point, you get a good overlook of the surrounding mountains before the road drops into the dark timber. At 2 miles, you cross the North Fork of the Encampment River where there is a trailhead and 4WD road.

SIDE TRIP

If you have a 4WD vehicle, you can follow FR 550.2H along the creek to another trailhead located 2 miles upstream. Here, a 1.2 mile-foot trail continues to Green Mountain Falls, a spectacular cascade at the edge of the Huston Park Wilderness.

Continuing southward, the backroad weaves through the pine forest and passes a sign marking the Halfway House. Built in 1902, this structure stood at the halfway point between Encampment and the camps that were once in Hog Park. A short distance farther, the road crosses the lower flank of Green Mountain (10,303 feet). A bumpy side road (FR 406) is soon passed on the right, which leads to a trailhead near the top of the heavily-wooded mountain.

The next several miles take you through a dark forest that transitions to spruce and subalpine fir. Closing in on Hog Park, you'll catch distant glimpses of Blackhall Mountain, where there is an old lookout tower on the top, and the Mount Zirkel Wilderness area in Colorado. Then, at mile 16, the road reaches the junction with FR 496 at the north end of Hog Park. Bear left on FR 496 and continue through the photogenic park and over a creek of the same name.

The odd naming of Hog Park by tie hacks—loggers who crafted railroad ties for the Union Pacific Railroad—is not entirely known. Several explanations exist, ranging from a description of the prostitution and gambling that went on during the mining and logging days to the "ground hogs" (marmots) that live here. Today, the park is known for its recreation rather than its resources. A short spur leads to Hog Park Reservoir where there is a picnic area, boat launch, and campground.

From the park, drive southeast to reach Commissary Park, another meadow that was once occupied by throngs of loggers. Here, you'll find a trailhead that serves the Encampment River Wilderness. Just past the trailhead, you'll cross over the Colorado state line near a bridge spanning the Encampment River. On the other side of the drainage, turn left to stay on FR 496 where it turns northward back into Wyoming.

Physical remnants of the Sierra Madre's logging and mining history are common in this area of the national forest. One accessible place to explore the past is on the East Fork Trail, reached at 22 miles. Numerous decaying cabins can be found along this 7-mile footpath including the first pair that is reached only about a mile from the road. The creek next to the cabins served as a way to transport the logs—they were floated downstream, usually during late spring when flows were high.

The backroad roughens as it curves to the northeast. This is a mostly timbered stretch, but there are occasional overlooks and old logging clearcuts that afford glimpses of the Sierra Madre's rolling mountains. You'll soon attain the tour's high point of 9,550 feet and then reach a junction with FR 404 at mile 33. Turn left here to follow CR 409 to the northwest.

SIDE
TRIP

A right turn onto FR 409 puts you on a lesser road that heads 6.3 miles to the top of Blackhall Mountain (10,979 feet). After passing a trailhead for the East Fork Trail, continue about another half mile until the road begins to degrade into a rough track containing more rocks, ruts, and mud—you will want a 4WD vehicle to continue driving from this point.

The last 3.1 miles tackle a steady 8% incline while passing through a spruce and fir forest. Near the end, the road breaks above treeline, wraps around the east face of the mountain, and then makes a final turn to reach the summit where there is an old fire lookout tower. This upper section is often snowbound until the middle of July, so you may not be able to drive to the very top.

The summit of Blackhall Mountain is comprised of a rocky crest that stands upwards of 2,000 feet above the surrounding mountains—it provides one of the best views in southern Wyoming. In the immediate foreground, you'll find rolling mountains that have been heavily logged. The southern horizon is filled with a glorious view of the Mount Zirkel Wilderness in northern Colorado.

Now driving back toward Encampment, the road traverses steeper, drier slopes that reveal the best views yet. With a steep drop off the left side of the road, you can look west across a rugged landscape comprised of ridges, canyons, and high mountainous points. The intermittent forest is comprised of light aspen and limber pine.

Hog Park Reservoir along Forest Road 496

SIDE
TRIP
At mile 38, the road passes FR 409.2A. This steep and narrow 4WD road goes to a small trailhead at the northern end of the Encampment River Wilderness.

In mile 39, the road leaves the Medicine Bow National Forest and descends quickly from the mountains. From this point forward, you drive across sage-covered terrain managed by the BLM. Nearing mile 45, watch for a sign marking the Indian Bathtubs Trail on the left side of the road. This short foot path (less than a mile) leads to a rock outcropping with small pools of water on the top that were used by Native Americans for bathing during the summer months. From the trail, the backroad ends a mile to the north at HWY 230. Turn left and drive a mile west to reach Encampment.

Other Nearby Drives
Continental Divide—Just west of Hog Park Reservoir, there is a 4-mile 4WD road that climbs to the top of the Continental Divide to gain awesome views of the area. The road is suitable for most 4x4 vehicles. To get there from Encampment, drive west on HWY 70 for 6 miles and turn left. Drive south on FR 550 for a little over 16 miles and bear right at the fork to stay on FR 550. Head west around the north side of Hog Park Reservoir for 6 miles to the turnoff for FR 550.2E on the right.

Big Creek—This is a 30-mile route that offers access to hiking trails and 4WD routes in the eastern Sierra Madre. To reach the beginning of the road, take HWY 230 south from Encampment for 25 miles or drive north from Walden, Colorado for 24 miles. Turn onto Holroyd Road (CR 498).

Drive west toward the national forest on Holroyd Road, a gravel lane. Within the forest, the road significantly narrows and climbs steeply in places. You'll roll into Holroyd Park near mile 7. Here, FR 498.2A branches off to the northwest and accesses the Big Creek Trail (a foot trail) and a small network of worthwhile 4WD roads. From this point, the road dips southward to the Colorado state line and then cuts back to the northwest as FR 407. Travel through beautiful Big Creek Park, which is private land, and you'll pass FR 407.1B, a spur that leads to another trailhead for the Big Creek Trail. From this halfway point, the road weaves wildly as it works to the northwest and ends roughly a dozen miles farther at FR 409. A left turn here takes you to Blackhall Mountain. A right turn gives you the option to head north to Encampment or southward on FR 496 to Hog Park Reservoir.

12: Northern Sierra Madre
Tour the northern mountains

☒ **Backcountry Drive**	☐ **4WD Route**	☐ **ATV Trail**
Most vehicles	4x4 vehicle or ORV	ORV less than 50" wide

Location/Map	South of Rawlins; Page 328
Roads	FR 443, FR 452, FR 830, FR 801
Distance	46.5 miles
Managing Agency	USDA Forest Service—Medicine Bow National Forest
Starting Coordinates	N41° 10.56' W106° 54.12'

Overview: This drive makes a large arc across the northern Sierra Madre, crossing the Continental Divide along the way. You'll navigate through several drainage systems, cut into the steep sides of heavily wooded mountains, and finish by passing through a remarkable aspen stand. Watch for elk and dusky grouse as you traverse this range. This route is open in its entirety for the summer season on June 16.

Start: From Encampment, drive west for 6.5 miles on HWY 70 to FR 443 on the right. To reach the western end of the route, continue west for nearly 18 more miles to FR 801.

Description: The trip begins on FR 443 by cutting northward across the eastern flank of the Sierra Madre. You'll almost immediately spot trail markers for the Bottle Creek cross-country ski trails that interlace the hills near the highway. Past this, the road begins weaving through a heavily logged forest of old clearcuts that are now thick with young lodgepole pines. Outside of the logging units, you'll find sagebrush-covered slopes and shallow gullies filled with aspen.

By mile 5, a pair of tight turns briefly take you across the national forest boundary. Two miles farther, the road turns westward and passes through more logging units before reaching a junction at mile 12. Here, FR 440 bears northeast toward HWY 130 just south of Saratoga. Stay left at the junction and continue following FR 443 as it slices into the side of a steep mountainside above the South Spring Creek drainage.

Towering aspen stands in the Sierra Madre

The road becomes rougher as it descends to cross South Spring Creek. You can now see the road climbing out of the drainage on the opposing hillside. When you get there, you'll find a revealing view across the forest. This is fun driving. The next several miles take you further north where the forest is thinner and includes more aspen. Approaching the northern-most point of the trip, you pass below Sharp Hill (9,439 feet) before reaching the junction with FR 452. Turn left here and follow the road back to the southwest where it soon improves with a wider gravel surface.

SIDE TRIP

Among the numerous side roads that are passed, one of the notable ones is FR 450 that is passed near mile 24. This maintained road heads south for several miles before it degrades into a 4WD track that connects to FR 412 on the Continental Divide. The route provides a couple of different loop options if you're interested in motoring across the crest of the Sierra Madre.

Nearing mile 26, the road reaches FR 830. You'll need to turn left onto this road to complete the drive, but before doing that, consider staying right to first visit the Jack Creek area.

SIDE TRIP

Staying right on FR 452, you'll soon pass the Jack Creek Guard Station, which includes a single-room cabin that can be rented for overnight stays (check www.recreation.gov). The cabin was completed in 1934 by early forest ranger Evie Williams, who is now buried near the cabin. A short distance farther, you'll roll into scenic Jack Creek Park where there is a campground. The road continues northward out of the national forest and ends at Saratoga.

Turn south on FR 830 and drive to the Continental Divide at mile 29. This is a heavily wooded area and the divide is only discernible because of a roadside trailhead for the Continental Divide Trail. A few miles farther west, you'll pass FR 412, a 4WD track that follows the Continental Divide along the backbone of the Sierra Madre (route #13).

At 32 miles, the road turns to the south and briefly skirts the western boundary of the Medicine Bow National Forest. You'll soon discover that the western slope of the Sierra Madre is covered extensively with aspen stands. The trees here are comprised of what is often said to be the largest continuous aspen grove in the state of Wyoming.

Follow the road southward while it descends to lower elevations. A junction with Deep Creek Road (FR 801)—a road that connects HWY 70 to Rawlins—is reached at mile 39. Turn left here and continue southward.

At mile 40, the road drops steeply to cross Sandstone Creek. It then snakes to the southeast to reach an area known as Aspen Alley. This half-mile stretch of road is one of the most photographed in Wyoming as straight, towering aspen trees grow upwards of 50 feet tall. The road passes under the overlapping canopy, creating a timbered tunnel. The beauty of this backroad is no secret—it becomes a parking lot here when the leaves change colors in September. Take note that a part of the road passes through private property.

The drive ends less than a mile south of Aspen Alley at HWY 70. Turn left here to return to Encampment or turn right to drive to Baggs.

13: Bridger Peak
Traverse the spine of the Rockies

☐ **Backcountry Drive**
Most vehicles

☒ **4WD Route**
4x4 vehicle or ORV

☐ **ATV Trail**
ORV less than 50" wide

Location/Map	South of Rawlins; Page 328
Roads	FR 412
Distance	12.5 miles
Managing Agency	USDA Forest Service—Medicine Bow National Forest
Starting Coordinates	N41° 9.69' W106° 58.92'

Overview: This spectacular 4WD road climbs to the top of the Sierra Madre where it then follows the Continental Divide to the western reaches of the Medicine Bow National Forest. Along the way, you pass Bridger Peak, the Sierra Madre's highest summit. With elevations near 11,000 feet, this is the second highest road described in this book. As a result, it's often impassable due to deep snowdrifts until middle or late July.

This road parallels the Continental Divide Trail, and you may see signage and cairns that mark this Canada-to-Mexico footpath. Expect to encounter hikers and possibly horses and other pack animals.

Start: From Encampment, drive west for 12.5 miles on HWY 70 to the turnoff on the right (this is just a half mile past Battle Pass). A large parking area provides plenty of room to unload ATVs. Here, you'll find two separate 4WD roads—you want the one on the left, closest to the highway.

Description: The dirt road begins by climbing through a shadowy evergreen forest. By mile 2, you reach the high meadows of the Continental Divide and broad views of the region become far and wide.

By 3.5 miles, the road skirts below the rocky, windswept summit of Bridger Peak (11,004 feet). If you want to "bag" the mountain range's highest summit, this is your chance to do so with little extra effort. A short foot scramble will gain you the top. From this high point, you get the best possible view of the Sierra Madre, including landmarks such as Battle Lake, seen less than 3 miles to the south. Further in the distance are the rugged mountains of north-central Colorado. Look to the north toward Rawlins and you'll find drastically different terrain—a semi-arid and empty high desert.

High country near Bridger Peak

Past the high point, the dirt track briefly splits into separate routes (the lower route is less rocky) and then converges before reaching FR 450 on the right, which heads downhill to the north. A short distance further, you pass North Spring Creek Lake, which sits nearly a thousand feet lower than the roadway.

To this point, the high crest has only had isolated pockets of stunted spruce and fir. But by mile 8, the road has dropped back to an elevation of 10,200 feet and the forest soon becomes more substantial. Watch for dusky grouse as you drive through this transition zone.

Most 4x4 vehicles can be driven to this point. However, the road's remaining distance becomes narrow and much more difficult to negotiate. With a path littered with large rocks and downfall, you'll need a capable vehicle that you won't mind getting knocked by branches. There are some steep sections, and overall you're tackling a 10% downhill grade.

By mile 10, the Continental Divide cuts to the north taking the famous Continental Divide Trail (a footpath) with it. The road continues to the northwest, burrowing through a dense, dark forest. It ends before mile 13 at FR 830, an arterial road that provides access to the west side of this mountain range. A right turn here puts you on course to go to Saratoga and Rawlins. A left turn returns you to HWY 70.

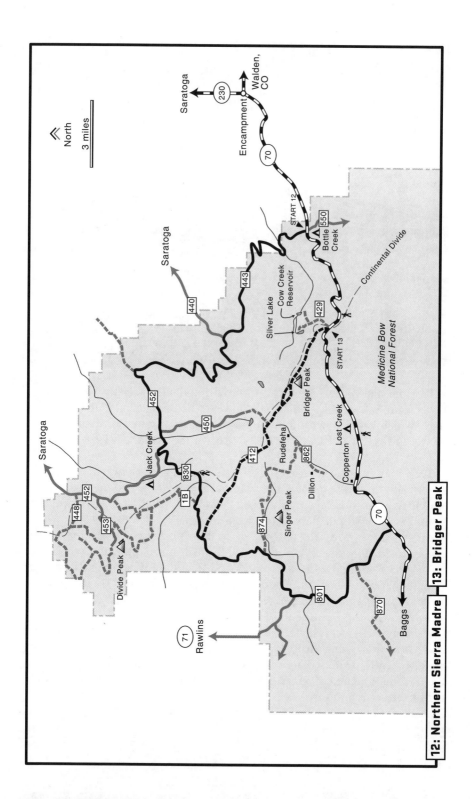

12: Northern Sierra Madre — 13: Bridger Peak

Other Nearby Drives

Silver Lake/Cow Creek Reservoir—Forest Road 429 is a narrow and fairly rocky 2.1-mile 4WD route that leads to a pair of hidden mountain lakes. The steep road descends 800 vertical feet from the Continental Divide to a bowl that is filled by Silver Lake. A 1.9-mile side road along the way can be taken to reach Cow Creek Reservoir. Geographically, the lakes are similar as they both sit surrounded by sharp slopes covered with spruce, fir, and scree. Silver Lake, being the higher and more shadowed of the two, is often found amidst snowdrifts until the later part of July.

To reach the road from Encampment, drive west for 12.5 miles on HWY 70 to the turnoff on the right (this is just a half mile past Battle Pass). A large parking area provides plenty of room to unload ATVs. Here, you'll find two separate 4WD roads—you want the one on the right.

Copper Mines/Dillon—Forest Road 874 and a portion of 862 are 4WD tracks that can be used to reach an area where copper was mined at the turn of the 20th century. From FR 830, take FR 874 eastward through the Sandstone Creek drainage where the muddy track makes numerous fords. Overhanging limbs also make this a challenging route.

After 6 miles, you reach a fork that leads to the largest copper mine in the Encampment Mining District, the Rudefeha, which received its name from the first two letters of the owners names: Rumsey, Deal, Ferris, and Haggarty. The mine started operating in 1898 and continued for 10 years. During that time, a 16-mile tramway—the longest in the world at the time—transported ore from the mine to a smelter in Encampment. Today, the site remains on private property and public access is not allowed. However, from the road on Forest Service land, you can still see significant ruins. Further south, cabin ruins from the Dillon townsite can be found. The town was reportedly built, in part, to accommodate the area's hard-drinking rowdies. When the decision was made to close the saloons at the nearby Rudefeha mine, the bar owners simply moved down the road a short distance and set up business here, where they operated until 1917.

To reach this road from Encampment, drive west for 18 miles on HWY 70 to FR 801. Drive north on FR 801/830 for 10 miles.

14: Huston Park

Overlook primitive wilderness

☐ **Backcountry Drive**
Most vehicles

☒ **4WD Route**
4x4 vehicle or ORV

☐ **ATV Trail**
ORV less than 50" wide

Location/Map	South of Rawlins; Page 333
Roads	FR 811
Distance	9 miles
Managing Agency	USDA Forest Service—Medicine Bow National Forest
Starting Coordinates	N41° 8.43' W107° 4.74'

Overview: This track skirts the boundary of the beautiful Huston Park Wilderness area, which straddles the crest of the Sierra Madre. You'll revel in the beauty of this country as you descend the western slope of the mountain range. Narrow and short 4x4 vehicles are preferred to negotiate tight curves in thick timber.

Start: From Encampment, drive west on HWY 70 for 19 miles to the turnoff on the left (across the road from Lost Creek Campground). To reach the southern end of the road, continue west along HWY 70 for another 5.6 miles or east from Baggs for 32.5 miles. Turn south onto FR 807 and drive 3.5 miles to reach FR 811 on the left.

Description: Upon turning off the highway, bear left at the first fork and follow the road uphill for less than a half mile to reach a trailhead and dispersed camping area. Find the 4WD track on the far side of the parking area and follow it as it climbs through a mixed forest of conifers and aspen. Aside from a few dips, mud holes, and loose rocks, this initial stretch is relatively easy to navigate.

The track now follows the boundary of the Huston Park Wilderness, which is heavily signed on the left side of the road. As a primitive area designated by Congress, there are restrictions that govern this land's use—the most notable is the prohibition of motorized and mechanical equipment. Simply put, if you're planning on using a chain saw or hunting game cart, make sure you do it to the north and west of this road, which is outside of the wilderness.

A saddle is reached less than a mile from the highway. This is the route's highest point at 9,050 feet. Just west of this, you'll enter a wildflower-sprinkled meadow where you can see out over the wilderness. Here, you'll find parks and an alarming number of conifers that have been killed by a widespread mountain beetle epidemic. On the far horizon, you'll find the uniquely rugged country of north-central Colorado. Aside from the dead trees, this is elk country at its finest.

At 1.5 miles, the road bends to the south and retains its fair condition. While four-wheel drive may be needed to handle the steeper sections where there is loose rock, the route lacks the skid-plate scarring boulders and deep potholes that characterize some of the other routes in the Medicine Bow National Forest.

Continue south along a narrowing path that is often shadowed by the overhanging canopy of the forest. There are a few tight spots as the road descends along the spine of a long, wooded ridge above the Battle Creek

Forest Road 811 along the Huston Park Wilderness boundary

drainage. At points, you'll pass through openings that reveal stunning vistas.

At 3 miles, the road tunnels through the dark timber to reach the west flank of the ridge. You'll now descend several hundred feet over the next few miles to more level terrain and into a very different place. The spruce and firs found in the higher elevations are replaced with sprawling stands of aspen. A verdant understory of tall grass and shrubs contrast sharply from the environment where you started.

Follow the road as it bears west for a little over a mile. Approaching mile 8, you'll reach the end of the hill above a broad valley. Here, the road drops over 600 feet to the valley floor in just over a mile—it's a steep 12% grade. Battle Creek is reached near the end of the road and must be forded. This stream typically flows between 12 and 18 inches.

The drive ends on the other side of the creek at FR 807. To continue exploring this awesome country, turn left. To return to the highway, turn right and follow the road uphill for 3.5 miles.

15: Battle Creek
Skirt the Colorado-Wyoming border

☒ **Backcountry Drive** Most vehicles	☒ **4WD Route** 4x4 vehicle or ORV	☐ **ATV Trail** ORV less than 50" wide

Location/Map	South of Rawlins; Page 333
Roads	FR 807, FR 851
Distance	19 miles (last 14 miles may require 4WD)
Managing Agency	USDA Forest Service—Medicine Bow National Forest
Starting Coordinates	N41° 6.84' W107° 9.56'

Overview: This backcountry drive takes you 3 miles to the scenic Battle Creek drainage, which is a popular day-use area near the Colorado state line. Those with a 4x4 can then continue eastward and explore the unique southern Sierra Madre that is used for sheep herding. There are many side roads along the way if you want to get even further off the beaten path.

Start: From Encampment, drive west on HWY 70 for 24.6 miles to FR 807 on the left. If driving east from Baggs, go 32.5 miles to reach the turnoff.

Description: Starting from the highway, follow the road downhill and through an aspen forest. At 1 mile, you'll reach four tight switchbacks that drop into a valley filled with tall grass. At the bottom, 1,000 feet below the highway, you'll find Battle Creek Campground, a primitive site that mostly sees day use. Continue along the rutted road to a bridged crossing of Battle Creek, which receives heavy visitation on weekends. Most visitors never make it past this point.

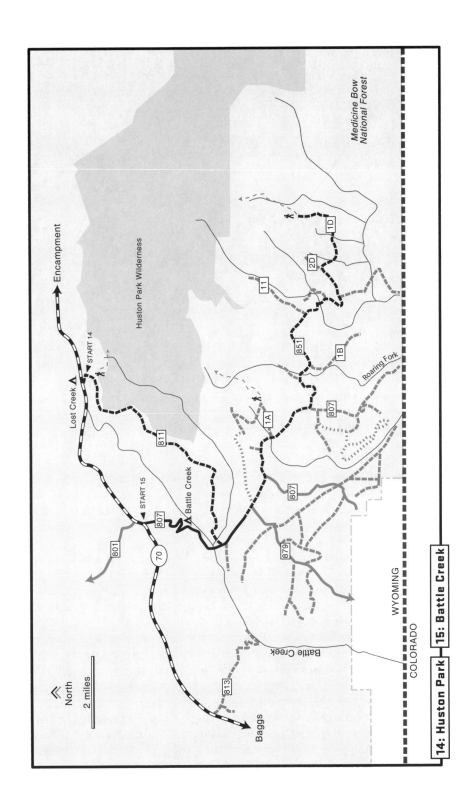

North

2 miles

Encampment

Lost Creek

START 14

811

Huston Park Wilderness

START 15

807

801

70

Battle Creek

807

879

813

Battle Creek

Baggs

11

1D

2D

851

1B

1A

807

807

Roaring Fork

Medicine Bow
National Forest

WYOMING

COLORADO

Narrow track between Battle Park and Cottonwood Park

A narrower road now curves to the east and passes FR 811, a rugged track that heads uphill for 9 miles to HWY 70 (route #14). From this junction, stay straight and drive uphill and through the trees to reach Cottonwood Park by mile 5.

SIDE TRIP You'll find FR 879 branching off to the south through Cottonwood Park. This decent road leads to several of the area's 4WD tracks that split out across shrubby terrain. These are fun routes to spend an afternoon exploring.

A small creek is forded on the east side of the park just before FR 807 turns to the south. To continue eastward, stay straight and follow FR 851 as it ascends out of the park. You'll soon pass a spur that leads to private property followed by FR 851.1A, which leads to the remote Fletcher Park Trailhead for the Huston Park Wilderness.

The next few miles pass through a mosaic of coniferous stands, aspen groves, and tall grass. The grass here in the southern Sierra Madre is especially unique because it grows to chest-high levels, a very rare occurrence in Wyoming, the country's fifth driest state. Keep an eye out for grouse, antelope, deer, and elk, all of which favor this habitat.

At 10.5 miles, the track reaches the Roaring Fork of the Little Snake River. There is a sheep bridge to the north, but the road runs through the creek (14 inches in July). On the other side of the stream, you'll find that the road degrades into a true 4WD track with steep sections and a rougher driving surface.

Before mile 14, another ford is made next to a sheep bridge. This time the crossing is of the West Branch of the North Fork of the Little Snake River (16 inches in July). The road splits a little over a mile from the drainage. The spur on the right leads to the Colorado state line. The left-bearing track continues to the east as FR 851.1D.

Stay left and take the narrower path through a thicker evergreen forest. Unless they've been cleared, there are many downed trees along the road that will keep full-sized vehicles from getting through and only ATVs will be able to proceed. There are two more fords and another section of steep terrain to tackle before reaching the end of the road at mile 19. This is as far as you can drive, but you can continue northward on foot using the Verde Mine Trail. It's about a mile to reach the old Verde Mine and about 2 miles to reach the Huston Park Wilderness.

Other Nearby Drives

Western Sierra Madre—There are several secondary roads that cross the lower western slopes of the Sierra Madre. These include roads on both sides of HWY 70 including the Savery Stock Driveway (FR 852) as well as FR 870, FR 850, and FR 813. These routes travel through a blend of grassy parks, sagebrush flats, and aspen groves. They are often found rutted and muddy with few rocks. Side spurs are found overgrown by the lush grasses that grow on this side of the mountain range.

Big views along HWY 70 in the Sierra Madre

SOUTHWEST

Though most of southwest Wyoming is not known for its allure, it's certainly not absent. The region holds a tremendous unsung beauty that is discovered by those who follow their curiosity and go where few others do. Much of this area is a high desert where vast sagebrush steppes and alkali flats stretch to every corner of the horizon. And on those horizons, beyond the desert's lone mounts and buttes, are the snowcapped summits of unspoiled mountain ranges—the Wyoming, Salt River, Wind River, and Uinta.

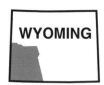

WYOMING **Southwest Areas**

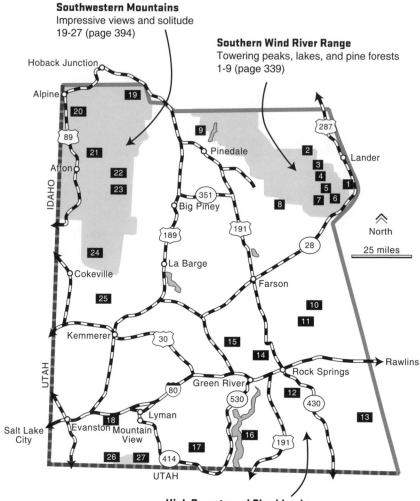

Southwestern Mountains
Impressive views and solitude
19-27 (page 394)

Southern Wind River Range
Towering peaks, lakes, and pine forests
1-9 (page 339)

Hoback Junction

Alpine

19

20

89

9

Pinedale

287

Lander

21

Afton

2

IDAHO

22

3

23

4

5

351

Big Piney

6

7

8

189

191

North

28

25 miles

24

Cokeville

La Barge

Farson

25

10

11

Kemmerer

30

15

14

Rawlins

Green River

Rock Springs

UTAH

80

12

Lyman

530

430

13

Salt Lake City

18

Evanston Mountain View

16

191

26

27

17

414

UTAH

High Deserts and Shrublands
Sprawling open spaces and lone mounts
10-18 (page 365)

Southern Wind River Range

The Wind River Range (affectionately referred to as just the "Winds") spans a 100-mile distance from Lander to Togwotee Pass northwest of Dubois. These granite mountains are topped by glaciated peaks and jagged spires, including Wyoming's highest, Gannett Peak (13,804 feet). In all, there are 53 summits that rise above 13,000 feet.

Much of this rock-and-ice high country is preserved as designated wilderness, making these mountains a favorite of backpackers, anglers, and horsepackers. The lower elevations that are open to motorized use vary from the drier foothills to the thick pine forests near timberline. In most cases, the roads that traverse these mountains end at mountain lakes, which make for scenic and worthwhile destinations.

The Wind River Range supports a long list of common mountain wildlife species, but this habitat is anything but ordinary. The seemingly empty foothills near Pinedale are known to be among the continent's most prolific waterfowl breeding areas. Grizzly bears have returned to these mountains by slowly expanding their range from the greater Yellowstone area, but you're more likely to spot deer, moose, elk, and black bear.

Land Ownership

The Wind River Range near Pinedale is within the Bridger-Teton National Forest while the southern section near Lander falls within the Shoshone National Forest. There is very little private land within these Forests and the risk of trespassing is low. Local Forest Service offices are located in Lander and Pinedale.

Where you should be more vigilant is on the mountain range's fringe areas, which have substantial amounts of private property that are interspersed with BLM land. This includes the Wind River Reservation, which should be treated as private property since it requires a permit for public access (for those not living on the reservation). These permits can be purchased from sporting good stores in the area as well as a few businesses in the town of Fort Washakie, where the tribal headquarters are located.

Roads and Trails

The Wind River Range near Pinedale is accessed by numerous county and national forest roads that start from HWY 191, HWY 352, or HWY 353. Most of these gravel routes end at a destination, such as a lake, and secondary roads are few. For the area southeast of Pinedale, access is made from a number of remote county roads that are easily driven.

The far southern end of the range near Lander offers excellent four-wheeling routes. These mountains are bound to the east by HWY 287/28. The most popular entry point here is on HWY 131, which leads from Lander to Sinks Canyon State Park. From the park, Louis Lake Road arcs across the range and provides access to numerous secondary roads.

The secondary roads in these mountains are quite possibly Wyoming's most challenging. Not only is 4WD necessary, but a customized vehicle is often in order. In the higher elevations, the roads are covered with rock and a lot of it. To conquer these routes, you'll need tough tires, higher than average ground clearance, and four-wheeling experience. Don't hesitate to turn back if the terrain gets too difficult. Most of the area's ATV trails are also difficult and should only be considered by experienced riders.

Seasons and Conditions

The driving season in the southern Wind River Range begins by the middle of June when Louis Lake Road opens for normal vehicle traffic (it's open in the winter to snowmobiles). However, many of the campgrounds in the area don't open until late in June or July, so factor that into your travel plans.

Seasonal closures and restrictions in this area are uncommon—it's mostly on you to decide when you want to try them. For many of these routes, it would be foolish to attempt them before the middle of the summer due to snowdrifts and dangerously high runoffs in the creeks. August and September are good months to explore this high country. One thing of which to be to be mindful during the summer months is that the weather in the Wind Rivers changes quickly and severely. Be prepared for intense thunderstorms and even snowstorms.

The first decent snows, sometimes with season-ending accumulations, can be expected in October. In warmer, drier years, the lower areas can be accessed through November.

Fuel

The closest fueling stations are found in towns to the east and south of the mountains, including Lander, Farson, and Pinedale.

Maps

Obtain the Shoshone National Forest (South Half) map. Referring to the Forest's ORV map or Motor Vehicle Use Map (MVUM) is also useful, especially for differentiating between ATV trails and 4WD roads.

1: Red Canyon
Drive along a crimson ridge

☒ **Backcountry Drive**
Most vehicles

☐ **4WD Route**
4x4 vehicle or ORV

☐ **ATV Trail**
ORV less than 50" wide

Location/Map	South of Lander; Page 341
Roads	CR 235
Distance	10.3 miles
Managing Agency	BLM—Lander Field Office, The Nature Conservancy, Wyoming Game & Fish, other mixed ownership
Starting Coordinates	N42° 35.69' W108° 38.0'

Overview: The Red Canyon at the foot of the Wind River Range is among Wyoming's most stunning landscapes. This drive takes you across a dusty lane that snakes through a valley below striking crimson cliffs. The road is open from mid-June through November.

Start: From Lander, head south on HWY 287/28 for 20 miles to the turnoff on the right. If traveling north from Farson, drive 57 miles on HWY 28 to the turnoff.

Description: The drive begins from the top of the sandstone canyon where you can peer down along its length. Flanked on one side by a broad hillside

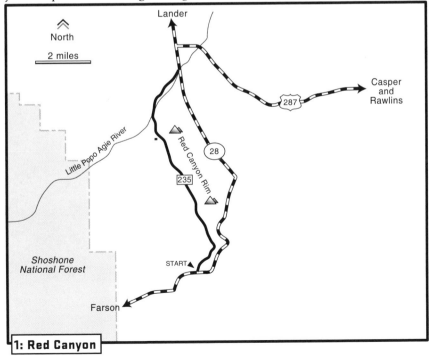

1: Red Canyon

of grass and sagebrush, the other side of the canyon is rimmed by a 500-foot cliff of magnificent brick-red rock.

For the first 2 miles, the bumpy, fairly rocky road assumes a 9% grade as it descends sharply from 7,075 feet to reach the bottom a thousand feet lower. This initial stretch crosses the Red Canyon Wildlife Management Area, a 1,785-acre tract that serves as winter range for deer, elk, and moose. From the canyon floor, the course parallels Red Canyon Creek where you may spot a variety of wildlife such as gray partridges and yellow-bellied marmots.

The now powdery road—dusty when dry, terrible when wet—continues its course below the towering rim for the next 4 miles until it reaches Red Canyon Ranch at 6.5 miles. The Nature Conservancy owns this ranch and operates it by raising livestock and growing hay in the surrounding pastures.

From the ranch, the canyon becomes shallower allowing the skyline to expand. The roadway also improves here and gains an all-weather surface. A mile farther, at 7.5 miles, the route reaches and crosses the Little Popo Agie River where there is a public access point. A second access point to this rushing waterway is then passed just a mile later.

The remaining distance of this drive crosses much gentler terrain as the wall recedes entirely. The drive terminates 9 miles south of Lander at HWY 28. A car wash will almost certainly be in order.

Red Canyon near Lander

2: Dickinson Park
Steep climb into the Winds

☒ **Backcountry Drive**
Most vehicles

☐ **4WD Route**
4x4 vehicle or ORV

☐ **ATV Trail**
ORV less than 50" wide

Location/Map	Northwest of Lander; Page 344
Roads	Trout Creek-Moccasin Lake Road, FR 329
Distance	17 miles
Managing Agency	USDA Forest Service—Shoshone National Forest, Wind River Indian Reservation
Starting Coordinates	N42° 57.45' W108° 56.6'

Overview: This route climbs the steep eastern face of the Wind River Range to reach Dickinson Park. This isn't a gentle ascent, but rather an uphill ramble that will have you shifting into low gear and hoping nobody is coming the other way.

Most of this drive passes through the Wind River Indian Reservation and their rules are not always clear or disseminated. For years, tribal litigation denied non-Indian access through the reservation, and thus to federal public land on the other side. Even after the dispute was settled, tribal and Forest Service staff evaded questions on the status of the road. As of this writing, the current understanding is that you (and everyone in your vehicle) must purchase a tribal fishing permit as well as a recreation stamp to drive through the reservation to reach Forest Service land. The permit serves as a sort of trespass fee and is required by any non-Indian, not just anglers. Permits can be purchased at most sporting good stores and gas stations in the greater area (Lander, Riverton, Dubois, Thermopolis, and Fort Washakie). Prices vary depending on the license purchased and resident status, but expect to pay at least $25 for just a one-day permit.

Start: From Lander, head north on HWY 287 for 14 miles toward Fort Washakie. Turn left onto Trout Creek-Moccasin Lake Road. Take this paved road west for 5.2 miles to reach a gate where the road turns to dirt.

Description: From the end of the paved road, continue west on the gravel road and stay right at the first fork. The road climbs slowly at first while crossing the grassy foothills of the mountain range.

At 2 miles, the grade intensifies, the road surface becomes rocky, and the first switchback is soon reached. This is just one of several direction-reversing turns that the single lane makes over the next few miles. While passing oncoming vehicles is distressing (especially if you're on the outside edge), it's usually possible except for a few places along the switchbacks themselves.

At 5.5 miles, the road reaches more level terrain after having gained nearly 2,000 vertical feet. This gives you an opportunity to look back to the east and survey the Wind River Basin before the road enters its first stand of trees. Also, keep watch to the south where a small ravine dilates into an impressive canyon. Trout Creek flows through the bottom of the thousand-foot gorge. From the rim, the next 4 miles consist of fairly level driving through a dying forest of limber pine.

At 9 miles, the road exits the forest to cross the upper waters of Trout Creek. The route before you is now easily seen as it cuts seven switchbacks—each layered above the other—into the open northern face of Bald Mountain (9,937 feet). This second set of switchbacks is much smoother than the first, though occasional ruts can make for some tricky uphill turns.

At the top of the mountain, some 3,600 feet higher than at the start of the drive, the road re-enters the timber and reaches a fork before mile 14. A right turn here takes you 4 miles to Moccasin Lake. Instead, bear left at the fork and drive into the Shoshone National Forest, which is marked by a very cool log sign and improved road surface. It's just a half mile farther to a crossing of Dickinson Creek. From this point you get the first glimpses of what characterizes the Wind River high country—jagged snow-creased crags.

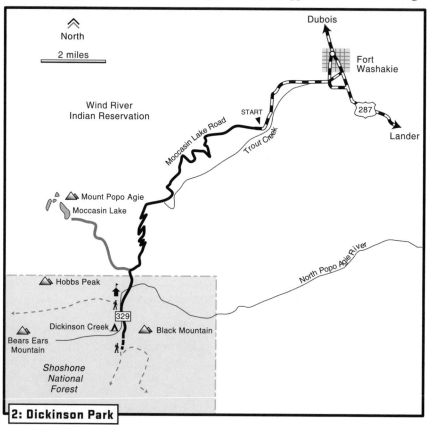

2: Dickinson Park

Jagged skyline above Dickinson Park

The last mile of this trip is made by entering a small subalpine meadow where there is a Forest Service guard station and a side road that leads to Bears Ears Trailhead. Continue straight and follow Dickinson Creek into beautiful Dickinson Park, a sprawling mountain meadow ringed by a skyline of lofty mountain peaks. A campground is found at the north end of the meadow and makes a scenic setting for a picnic or chilly overnight stay. From the camp, a rougher track skirts the edge of the park and leads to the Smith Lake-North Fork Trailhead where you can park and further explore the area on foot.

3: Shoshone Lake via Cyclone Pass
The 4WD road to the reservoir

☐ **Backcountry Drive**
   Most vehicles

☒ **4WD Route**
   4x4 vehicle or ORV

☐ **ATV Trail**
   ORV less than 50" wide

Location/Map	West of Lander; Page 348
Roads	Shoshone Lake Road, FR 350
Distance	8.5 miles
Managing Agency	USDA Forest Service—Shoshone National Forest, other mixed ownership
Starting Coordinates	N42° 49.9' W108° 53.49'

Overview: Of the two motorized routes that lead to the large mountain reservoir known as Shoshone Lake, this is the most popular. But this isn't a route that can be approached casually. Steep grades, loose rock, and plenty of boulders make this a difficult drive that should only be tackled by experienced backcountry drivers with ATVs or capable, modified 4x4s. If driving an ATV, this route can be combined with route #4 to create a partial loop, though the machine will need to be street-legal (to return to Lander on paved roads) or you will need to arrange a shuttle at both ends of the route.

Start: From the west side of Lander, follow either Baldwin Creek Road (CR 193) or Squaw Creek Road (CR 14) about 5.5 miles west of town to reach CR 212, an unsigned gravel road near Red Butte. Take the well-maintained road less than a mile to a fork near Baldwin Creek and bear right onto Shoshone Lake Road. Follow this red, dusty lane for 3.5 miles to a large parking area where ATVs can be unloaded. With six steep, narrow switchbacks, it's not an easy access road and I had to use 4WD just to get enough traction to pull a trailer to the top of the 1,400-foot incline.

Description: The adventure begins in Mormon Basin on the eastern front of the Wind River Range. It's a shallow depression that is covered in grass, sagebrush, and a peppering of short evergreens. Although terrain like this is usually traversed quickly, the road here has just enough yellowish-limestone rock patches that it hinders a steady pace.

Shoshone Lake from Cyclone Pass—Michelle Buzalsky photo

After slowly climbing for 3 miles, the road reaches a bald hillside on Suicide Point (9,409 feet) where you'll find a gate. While you'd expect unparalleled mountain views from this elevation, all you get is the top of Mount Arter (11,078 feet) and its blanketing, wooded slopes. Follow the dirt path across the exposed mount and into the timber. From this point, the rule of the road is simply this: the farther you go, the rougher it gets.

For most of the next 2 miles, the trail takes on the appearance of a riverbed that is referred to as "The Chute." It's an all rock and boulder surface made wet by an uphill spring. Most rocks are football-sized or smaller, though there are plenty of basketball-sized ones as well. The only way through this stretch is to slog through, and you'll feel the jolt each time one of the wheels comes off a large rock or a stone kicks out from under the tire and smacks your undercarriage. It can be tiring work on an ATV, but it's no better in a full-sized 4x4. The occupants of an old Scout I saw clambering up this stretch looked like they were taking a beating.

At 6.2 miles, the road surmounts gorgeous Cyclone Pass at 10,600 feet. Here, unsurpassed views of the southern Winds come into full view. The jagged granite crags and peaks of this expansive range make this among Wyoming's most scenic overlooks that can be attained by a motorized vehicle. Below the skyline lies Shoshone Lake, clearly visible in a timbered basin. Wind River Peak (13,192 feet), the triangular summit to the left of the lake is the highest peak in the southern half of the range.

To reach the lake from Cyclone Pass, the route descends a treacherous 15% grade littered with rocks and knee-high boulders, some of which are loose and sometimes wet. Choose your lines carefully. After 1.5 miles of downhill work, you roll into Cyclone Basin. From this marsh, follow the track to the southwest to reach Shoshone Lake's dam at its northern end at mile 8.

With nearly five miles of shoreline, the size of Shoshone Lake cannot be overstated. The lake is surrounded by timbered slopes on all sides with a skyline of higher mountain peaks visible to the west. Follow the road around the east side of the reservoir to join a rugged ATV trail that leads to Sinks Canyon State Park (route #4).

4: Shoshone Lake via Petes Lake
The ATV route to the reservoir

☐ **Backcountry Drive**
Most vehicles

☐ **4WD Route**
4x4 vehicle or ORV

☒ **ATV Trail**
ORV less than 50" wide

Location/Map	Southwest of Lander; Page 348
Roads/Trails	FR 351, FR 369, FT MT01
Distance	12 miles
Managing Agency	USDA Forest Service—Shoshone National Forest
Starting Coordinates	N42° 44.21' W108° 50.38'

Overview: This ATV trail is one of two motorized routes that lead to Shoshone Lake, a high reservoir at the edge of the Popo Agie Wilderness. Due to segments that are very wet, tight, and choked with large rocks, this trail is challenging enough that only experienced riders should give it a go. A Wyoming ORV permit is required.

Start: From Lander, drive 9 miles on HWY 131 through Sinks Canyon State Park to a turnoff on the right. The highway pullout is long enough for a couple vehicles with trailers. Another parking area is found about a quarter mile farther in on the gravel road.

Description: The trip begins in Sinks Canyon at an elevation of 6,900 feet. When you look up and see FR 351, the dirt path that cuts into the side of the canyon, you'll know this is one steep ascent. The average grade is

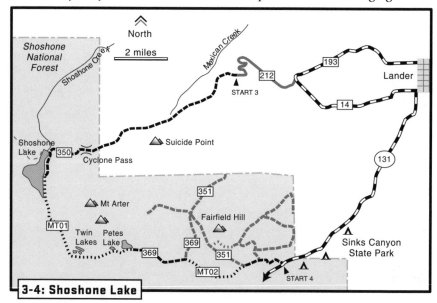

13% and more than 1,000 feet of elevation is gained by the first 1.5 miles. Fortunately, the track consists of dirt and mostly embedded rocks, nothing here to worry about for ATVs.

At 2 miles, the road divides on the southeast side of Fairfield Hill. Bear left and continue west to find the ATV trail marked by a small green arrow.

SIDE TRIP A right turn at the fork takes you across the open slopes of Fairfield Hill where you'll find a number of roads that can be explored, including a loop further east near the Shoshone National Forest boundary. You can also follow this road to the northwest and then return to the ATV trail on FR 369, a very rocky path.

The trail continues to climb as it makes a 2.5-mile arc across a sparsely treed slope of pine and aspen. This is where the wide, easy trail turns nasty. Large rocks, or boulders rather, litter a very narrow path that leaves no room for maneuvering. Stretches like these make this route suitable only for skilled riders—even hikers complain about the trail's condition.

Less than a mile after entering the dark timber, the trail smoothes temporarily as it reaches McMahone Park. You'll find FR 369 on the far side of the meadow. Continue west on this road to reach Wild Horse Meadow at 6 miles. The track skirts the south side of this boggy park and then reaches Petes Lake less than a mile farther. A suitable fishing destination in of itself, the lake is ringed by timbered slopes of pine.

The shoreline at Shoshone Lake —Ryan Twomney photo

The trail advances to the west, passing a marsh before mile 8 and bypassing Twin Lakes at mile 9. The path is rougher again here, but soon smoothes out considerably. The highest point of the route, 9,800 feet, is achieved as the trail follows the Popo Agie Wilderness boundary on the left.

At 9.5 miles, the trail bears north and passes through the timbered edge of Shoshone Basin, a beautiful sprawling meadow bisected by Shoshone Creek. Known locally for its black bear habitat, this mile-long grassy park reveals a stunning skyline of mountain crags, domes, and cliffs. The tough-again trail, which used to run through the basin, has plenty of rocks and trees that will force you to drive carefully.

The final stretch utilizes an improved trail surface that follows Shoshone Creek to the grassy inlet of Shoshone Lake. At an elevation of 9,500 feet, this massive lake is surrounded by trees, but numerous rocky summits on the horizon exceed 11,000 feet. The ATV trail continues along the eastern shoreline to join FR 350, which can be taken back toward Lander (route #3).

5: Louis Lake
Easy drive through the southern Winds

☒ **Backcountry Drive**
Most vehicles

☐ **4WD Route**
4x4 vehicle or ORV

☐ **ATV Trail**
ORV less than 50" wide

Location/Map	Southwest of Lander; Page 351
Roads	FR 300
Distance	26 miles
Managing Agency	USDA Forest Service—Shoshone National Forest
Starting Coordinates	N42° 43.75' W108° 51.48'

Overview: Louis Lake Road cuts through the southeastern tip of the Wind River Range, providing access to four lakes as well as numerous campgrounds, trailheads, and picnic areas. Though narrow in places and steep at the beginning, the road is easy to drive. It has no designated opening season—it's dependent on conditions—but it can usually be driven by the middle of June. Many of the side roads will be impassable until July.

Start: To reach the north end of the road from Lander, drive 10 miles on HWY 131 through Sinks Canyon State Park. To access the area from the south, take HWY 287/28 south of Lander for 30 miles and turn right onto FR 300.

Description: This tour of the Wind Rivers begins with an impressive climb out of Sinks Canyon. From the Bruce Picnic Area and Trailhead, the road ascends Fossil Hill (9,089 feet) by utilizing nearly a dozen steep switchbacks, which are paved. Before this stretch was improved, the tight and bumpy

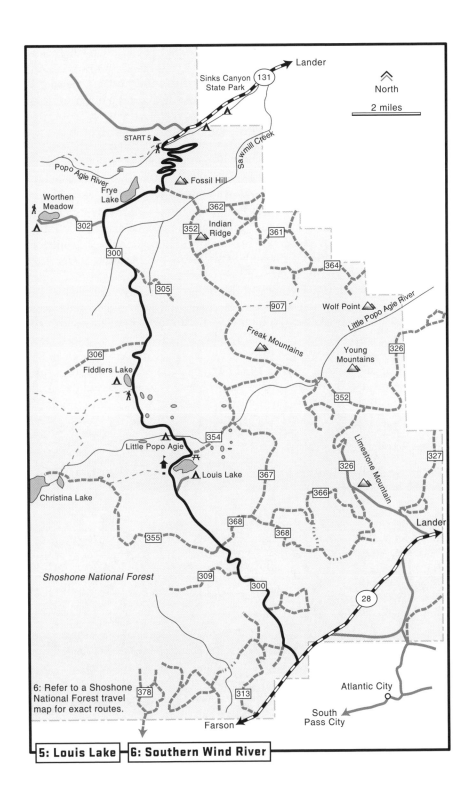

Lander

Sinks Canyon
State Park

131

North

2 miles

START 5

Popo Agie River

Frye
Lake

Worthen
Meadow

Fossil Hill

Sawmill Creek

302

362

352

Indian
Ridge

361

300

305

364

306

Fiddlers Lake

907

Wolf Point

Freak Mountains

Little Popo Agie River

Young
Mountains

326

352

Little Popo Agie

354

326

327

Christina Lake

Louis Lake

367

366

Limestone Mountain

Lander

355

368

368

28

Shoshone National Forest

309

300

6: Refer to a Shoshone
National Forest travel
map for exact routes.

378

313

Atlantic City

South
Pass City

Farson

5: Louis Lake ─ **6: Southern Wind River**

turns were the center of many conversations. The road is much easier now, on both the driver and the vehicle.

At 4 miles, before the road levels off and slips into the trees, be sure to take a look around the surrounding area. Below the road is a bird's-eye view of the canyon and tall mountain peaks can be seen to the west. From here, continue on toward the treeline where some of the trees were cut to create a migration corridor for bighorn sheep.

At 5.5 miles, the road reaches the shoreline of Frye Lake. Water levels are highest in the late spring and early summer before irrigation demands dwindle the supply during the later summer months. The massive mountain visible over the lake is Wind River Peak (13,192 feet), the highest summit in the southern part of the range. A mile past the lake, at mile 7, you'll find a turnoff for Worthen Meadow. This narrow side road leads 2.4 miles to Meadow Reservoir, which is ringed by a trailhead, campground, picnic area, and boat ramp for small watercraft.

From the turnoff, the pavement ends and is replaced by a gravel lane. The next several miles along Louis Lake Road slowly climb and twist through the pines of the Shoshone National Forest. The high point of the drive is reached at 11.5 miles when the road reaches Blue Ridge at 9,576 feet. Here, a separate 4WD track leads west to a clearing on the ridge where there is a historical stone lookout built in 1938 by the Civilian Conservation Corps.

A little more than a mile from Blue Ridge is a turnoff to Fiddlers Lake where you may find loons on the water's surface. A nice campground is

Louis Lake along Forest Road 300

located on the west side, but it's the east side near the boat ramp where you'll find stunning views of the mountains located within the Popo Agie Wilderness. These peaks are often speckled with snow, even as late in the year as August.

Watch for moose as you continue south through the curves—the road here travels past numerous ponds and marshes that make excellent habitat for these large ungulates. One particularly photogenic stream is the Little Popo Agie River, reached at 15.5 miles near a campground of the same name. A mile after crossing the river, the road reaches a picnic area on the north side of Louis Lake. This mountain lake lies below tall rock outcrops and slopes of scree. Steer your way around the lake to find a Forest Service guard station and Louis Lake Resort on the west side. A short distance farther, FR 308 can be used to access the lakes southern shore as well as a small campground.

Twenty miles into the drive, Louis Lake Road enters Grannier Meadows, a popular park for camping. Rugged 4WD roads can be found on both sides here and are favored by ATV riders. As the main route leaves the meadow, it climbs a treeless ridge. Before dropping over the other side, look behind you to the west. A long line of impressive mountain peaks ranging between 11,000 and 12,000 feet fill the horizon.

The terrain over the remaining five miles of the drive changes quickly. The road leaves the forest behind and breaks into large clearings as it descends. These openings offer views over the lower foothills that comprise the South Pass and Continental Divide area. The trip ends at mile 26 at HWY 28. Turn left and you'll find Lander 30 miles to the north. A right turn takes you to Farson, some 46 miles to the southwest.

6: Southern Wind River
An assortment of four-wheeling routes

☐ **Backcountry Drive**
Most vehicles

☒ **4WD Route**
4x4 vehicle or ORV

☒ **ATV Trail**
ORV less than 50" wide

Location/Map	Southwest of Lander; Page 351
Roads	North routes: FR 352, FR 361, FR 362, FR 364 Central routes: FR 354, FR 367 South routes: FR 368, FR 366, FR 326
Distance	50+ miles
Managing Agency	USDA Forest Service—Shoshone National Forest
Starting Coordinates	North routes: N42° 42.69' W108° 51.43' Central routes: N42° 36.01' W108° 50.52' South routes: N42° 33.7' W108° 49.59'

Overview: This collection of 4WD roads and ATV trails covers an area of the Wind River Range where each ridge and mount seems to have a name of its own: Indian Ridge, Meyer Lookout, Wolf Point, Freak Mountains, Bayer Mountain, Young Mountain, Limestone Mountain, and Iron Mountain.

These individual landmarks comprise the southeastern tip of the Shoshone National Forest. It's also one of the largest areas in the range that you'll find open to motorized use since much of these mountains are designated as non-motorized wilderness.

With more than 50 miles of roads and trails, there are many trip options. Road conditions across the area vary greatly. Many of them are two-tracks that travel across open sagebrush terrain with a mostly dirt and rutted surface. Others travel into the forest or across rough ridges where roots and rocks make for more challenging driving. Nearly all of these routes include some steep grades and there are also major water crossings that present hazards. The fords involve Sawmill Creek in the north and the tributaries to the Little Popo Agie River in the central part of the network (a bridge spans the river itself). These fords are clearly marked on the Forest Service ORV Trail map. A Wyoming ORV permit is required if you take any of the short ATV trail segments.

Start: The best access from the north is found at Fossil Hill near Sinks Canyon. To get there from Lander, drive 10 miles on HWY 131 through Sinks Canyon State Park, and then follow FR 300 for several more miles up steep switchbacks. Turn left onto FR 352, which is found at the top of the hill. There is ample parking for ATV unloading.

To access the area from the south, take HWY 287/28 south of Lander for 24 miles to FR 326, which feeds directly into the road network. You can also take the highway 6 miles farther and turn right onto FR 300. Take this gravel road north for 5.5 miles to FR 368, which begins from a large meadow. Parking can be found in the nearby dispersed campsites.

A more centralized access point is located on the north side of Louis Lake and is signed as FR 354 to Maxon Basin. Parking is limited in this area.

Description (North routes): The northern sections are accessed from the area's main route, FR 352, known as Indian Trail. This is a scenic road to explore as the views are seldom limited by trees. From Fossil Hill, the road quickly descends to ford Sawmill Creek. I found this crossing to be a foot deep in August of a drought year.

From here, the road climbs out of the shrubby drainage and cuts into a steep, open hillside before reaching a fork. While the east-bearing route (FR 362) explores the rugged terrain along the Shoshone National Forest boundary, Indian Trail continues to carve a line across rock-crowned Indian Ridge (9,232 feet). The track retains this characteristic until it reaches a heavily wooded canyon. Here, the road splits again. The main course continues south into the dark timber while a narrower, single-track motorcycle trail (FT 907 – Wolf Trail) heads east.

From the canyon, FR 352 continues through the forest for only a mile before resuming its course across open terrain. This eventually terminates on the east side of Young Mountain several more miles to the east. You can use FR 326 to exit the area.

Primitive road in the southern Wind River Range

Description (Central routes): The central part of this network is accessed by FR 354, a rocky path that traverses a forested landscape that is pocketed with kettle ponds. This road accesses Maxon Basin, where lesser creeks drain into the Little Popo Agie River. Be prepared for potentially sloppy conditions here.

Description (Southern routes): The southern area is accessed by FR 368 at Grannier Meadow. This dirt track travels across open, rolling terrain and splits into separate roads that are more suitable for family riding than many of the other roads in these mountains. While dusty and hot during the summer, these roads have no major fords and fewer rocks. There are some steep sections, however. Junctions are well signed and there are plenty of overlooks where you can get a panorama of the surrounding mountains to the west and high prairie to the east.

7: Christina Lake
Reach a pair of distant high country lakes

☐ **Backcountry Drive**
Most vehicles

☒ **4WD Route**
4x4 vehicle or ORV

☐ **ATV Trail**
ORV less than 50" wide

Location/Map	Southwest of Lander; Page 356
Roads	FR 355
Distance	8.6 miles
Managing Agency	USDA Forest Service—Shoshone National Forest
Starting Coordinates	N42° 33.55' W108° 49.34'

Overview: This challenging drive takes you to Gustave Lake and Christina Lake near the boundary of the Popo Agie Wilderness. The first few miles of this road can be handled by most 4WD vehicles, but usually only modified rigs and ATVs make it all the way to the end of the road. Due to snow in the higher elevations, this is a route that you'll want to save for mid-summer.

Start: From Lander, drive 10 miles on HWY 131 through Sinks Canyon State Park to FR 300. Follow this road for nearly 21 miles to a large meadow where you'll find FR 355 on the right.

The road can also be accessed from the south by taking HWY 287/28 south of Lander for 30 miles. Turn north on FR 300 and drive for 5.5 miles to the turnoff for FR 355 on the left. If you have ATVs to unload, drive west on FR 355 for a half mile to reach a large parking lot.

Description: From the beginning of FR 355, head west along the edge of Grannier Meadow where dispersed camping and ATV riding are popular. A large parking area with Forest Service signs is found at a half mile.

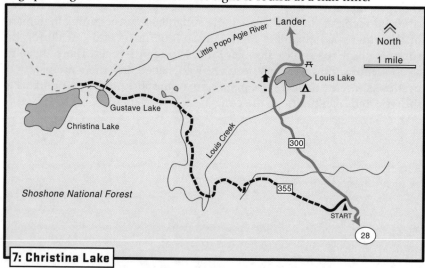

7: Christina Lake

Rock-strewn road near Christina Lake

The next several miles are easily driven as the dirt path travels uphill through a light pine forest that is broken by small grassy parks. The clearings offer glimpses of some of the Wind River's higher summits.

The road deteriorates considerably at 5 miles where it heads north toward Deer Park. The driving surface now holds sizable rocks that require a slower pace to negotiate. This condition only worsens as you advance deeper and higher into the backcountry.

Deer Park is reached at 6 miles and it takes another mile for the road to reach the wet meadow's western side. Here at mile 7, the track is strewn with rocks, some of which are a foot or taller. This is as far as most stock 4x4s dare to go, and you're likely to see a few trucks parked off to the side.

The road continues to climb as it heads west, reaching an elevation of nearly 10,000 feet. Some of this elevation is gained (lost and regained) in short but very steep chunks. Add tree roots, mud, and big rocks to the grade and you've got tricky sections that demand careful driving.

At 8 miles, the road passes to the north of Gustave Lake, but you can take a secondary track through the trees to get closer to the water. To continue to Christina Lake, cross the boulder-chocked Little Popo Agie River where the roadway all but disappears. Some people decide to spare their machines the beating by parking at the smaller lake and hiking to Christina Lake, which is reached at 8.6 miles—just a little over a half mile. Since these lakes are the headwaters for the river, depth is usually not an issue, at least not by late summer when this road sees its highest visitation.

At 9,942 feet, Christina Lake is situated about 600 feet below timberline and is surrounded by towering peaks on three sides. Large snowdrifts at least several feet deep linger here into August, feeding the lake and outbound creek throughout the summer. Wind commonly blows across the water, bringing a chill to even the warmest of days.

8: Lander Cutoff
Parallel the mighty Wind Rivers

☒ **Backcountry Drive** Most vehicles	☐ **4WD Route** 4x4 vehicle or ORV	☐ **ATV Trail** ORV less than 50" wide

Location/Map	Southeast of Pinedale; Page 359
Roads	CR 446, CR 132, CR 118
Distance	41 miles
Managing Agency	BLM—Lander Field Office
Starting Coordinates	N42° 22.33' W108° 54.54'

Overview: This route follows the Continental Divide along the foot of the Wind River Range. It's a beautiful and easy backroad that runs between South Pass and Pinedale. Along the way, you can take several side roads north to reach picturesque campgrounds and trailheads, such as Big Sandy. Historically, the Lander Cutoff was a 256-mile shortcut between South Pass and Fort Hall, Idaho that was used by emigrants traveling by wagon. Today it's primarily used to access recreation sites.

Big Sandy River along the Lander Cutoff

Start: To start the drive from the east end on HWY 287/28, drive 33 miles northeast of Farson or 43 miles southwest of Lander to the turnoff on the west side of the road. To reach the west end from Pinedale, head south on HWY 191 for 12 miles to HWY 353 and then east on this highway for 19 miles to Big Sandy-Elkhorn Road.

Description: The east end of the road begins at South Pass, across the highway from Oregon Buttes Road. Heading northwest along the Continental Divide, the wide gravel lane begins with a lot of washboard but becomes smoother as you travel west. The divide is what separates waterways to the eastern or western oceans. The streams to the right, including the Sweetwater River just north of the road, drain to the Atlantic Ocean. Creeks to the left of the road flow into the Green River en route to the Pacific.

The driving is easy over the next several miles and the views of the Wind River Range are unobstructed to the north. By 7 miles, the gentle sage flats begin to break as the road runs into more broken terrain. The rugged hills to the left are the Prospect Mountains. The road skirts this dwarfed range and passes Sweetwater Gap Road (BLMR 4105) at 15 miles, which leads to a pair of BLM campgrounds 8 miles to the north.

Another junction is reached 4.5 miles farther at Elkhorn Cutoff Road (BLMR 4108). A left turn here would take you 30 miles south to reach HWY 28 near Farson. Instead, turn right (north) and follow the road toward Jensen Meadows and Little Sandy Creek.

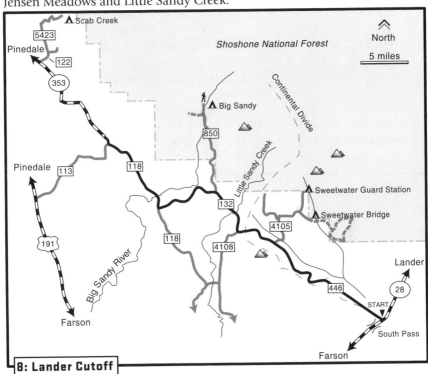

8: Lander Cutoff

With its conifer-lined banks, Little Sandy Creek is a popular place for primitive camping. It is also where the Continental Divide breaks from the Lander Cutoff and turns upstream along the east side of the creek. From this drainage, the road swings to the northern timbered front of Little Prospect Mountain (8,866 feet) where a junction is reached. The road headed north here is BLMR 4113, which later turns into FR 850 where it enters the Bridger-Teton National Forest. It ends at Big Sandy Campground and Trailhead, an extremely popular entry point into the Wind River Range.

SIDE
TRIP

To reach the Big Sandy area, turn north on the BLM road and follow it uphill through a pine and aspen forest for 10 miles. The scenery at the end makes the narrow, winding road well worth the side trip (large RVs are not recommended). Beautiful mountain peaks, verdant meadows, and a clear mountain river make this a truly scenic part of Wyoming. There are numerous 4WD spurs that you can take to get off the main route.

Lander Cutoff Road continues westward, cutting through the trees at the edge of Little Prospect Mountain. From this higher ground, it drops to intersect Big Sandy-Elkhorn Road (CR 118) near mile 32. Turn right and drive north for a mile to the beautiful Big Sandy River at Buckskin Crossing. A roadside interpretive sign explains the significance of this conifer-lined river to those who were here in the 1800s.

The backroad now turns northwest keeping the mountainous terrain in view. Follow the course another 7 miles to another major junction near the banks of Muddy Creek. Turn right to stay on CR 118 and drive northward to reach paved HWY 353 in less than a mile. This highway leads 19 miles to the town of Boulder and HWY 191. From there, you can continue another 12 miles on HWY 191 to reach Pinedale.

If you want to further explore this area, consider a drive into the Scab Creek area. To get there, continue along HWY 353 toward Boulder for 12.5 miles and then turn north on Scab Creek Road (CR 122/BLMR 5423). Drive 1.5 miles to a fork, bear left, and drive another 7 miles to reach the recreation area consisting of a trailhead and campground.

9: Wind River Range Lakes
Drives to a half dozen lakes

☒ **Backcountry Drive**
Most vehicles

☒ **4WD Route**
4x4 vehicle or ORV

☐ **ATV Trail**
ORV less than 50" wide

Location/Map	North and east of Pinedale; Page 362
Roads	New Fork Lakes: CR 162 Willow Lake: CR 119 Fremont Lake and Half Moon Lake: CR 154, FR 743 Boulder Lake, Burnt Lake, Meadow Lake: BLMR 5106, CR 125
Distance	See below
Managing Agency	USDA Forest Service—Bridger-Teton National Forest
Starting Coordinates	New Fork Lakes: N43° 4.67' W110° 1.16' Willow Lake: N42° 52.25' W109° 52.29' Fremont Lake and Half Moon Lake: N42° 52.0' W109° 51.28' Boulder Lake, Burnt Lake, Meadow Lake: N42° 45.44' W109° 43.84'

Overview: When the glaciers receded from the lower foothills north of Pinedale, they left behind dozens of lakes and ponds as well as extensive wetlands. Easily accessed from maintained gravel roads (except Burnt Lake and Meadow Lake), the lakes are destinations that are worthy of both day trips and camping outings.

The Narrows at New Fork Lakes

All of these lakes reside within the Bridger-Teton National Forest, though barely. If you choose to explore some of the rugged two-tracks around some of them, be sure to first check a Forest Service map to make sure you are on public land.

Start: For the most popular destinations—New Fork Lakes, Willow Lake, Soda Lake, Fremont Lake, and Half Moon Lake—you'll start on paved roads from Pinedale. The last two, Burnt Lake and Boulder Lake, are accessed east of Pinedale near the town of Boulder (junction of HWY 191 and HWY 353).

Description (New Fork Lakes): The western-most (and furthest) route leads to New Fork Lakes. From Pinedale, head west on HWY 191 for 5 miles and turn north onto HWY 352. Drive 15 miles and turn right onto New Fork Lake Road (CR 162). The gravel road heads east a couple of miles to the Bridger-Teton National Forest where a pair of Forest Service campgrounds can be found within the aspen trees. Follow the road around the north side of the lake to find another campground as well as a good overlook of the lake. From this point, you can see the "Narrows," a small channel that connects two separate bodies of water.

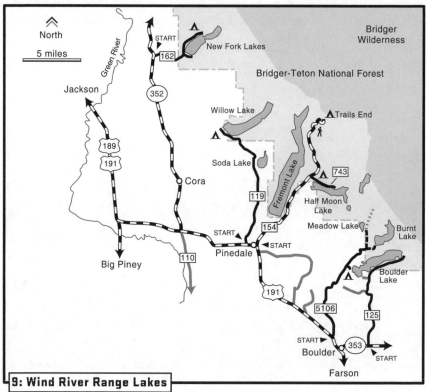

9: Wind River Range Lakes

Description (Willow Lake): To reach the next two lakes from the west side of Pinedale, drive north on Willow Lake Road (CR 119). Though rough and washboarded, the road is easily driven. Soda Lake and its surrounding wildlife habitat area are reached before mile 7. A viewing area here offers an excellent place to watch waterfowl. From Soda Lake, the county road continues north and then makes a steep climb over a rise to reach Willow Lake at mile 11. Treeless and barren, the views and the fishing are what lure campers to the shoreline.

Description (Fremont Lake and Half Moon Lake): To reach the area's largest and most popular lake, drive 4 miles north of Pinedale on paved Fremont Lake Road (CR 154). This lake features a large campground, marina, lodge, and swimming beach. When you're done at this lake, continue north another 3 miles and turn right onto FR 743. This gravel road drops down to Half Moon Lake, where you'll find a Forest Service campground hidden in a jungle of tall willows. A resort is located at the end of the road. Before returning to Pinedale, be sure to continue another 7 miles north to the end of Fremont Lake Road where you'll find big overlooks, trailheads, and another campground.

Description (Boulder Lake, Burnt Lake, Meadow Lake): The least accessible of the area's lakes is Burnt Lake. From the small settlement known as Boulder, drive north on HWY 191 a short distance to Burnt Lake Road (BLMR 5106). Follow this road north for 8 miles to reach a side road that leads to a primitive campground on the west side of Boulder Lake. Then continue northward along the lesser road for another 4 miles to reach the Bridger-Teton National Forest and a fork. Bear right onto a rocky 4WD road to reach Burnt Lake or stay left on the bumpy lane to reach Meadow Lake. An ATV trail continues north a short distance from Meadow Lake.

To reach the eastern, more popular side of Boulder Lake, take HWY 353 east from Boulder for 2.4 miles and turn north onto Boulder Lake Road (CR 125). It's another 10 miles along this bumpy lane to reach a secluded Forest Service campground as well as a privately owned lodge.

Other Nearby Drives

Pinedale Foothills—Four-wheeling opportunities in the foothills near Pinedale are very limited. Most routes are either very short (less than 2 miles long) or extend off known public lands. Aside from some of the spurs around the popular lakes, there are two Forest Service roads that are worth exploring.

Both of these routes begin at Kelly Park and wrap around the southeast flank of Fortification Mountain, which is covered with sagebrush, aspen, and pine. The shorter and steeper of these is FR 747, a rutted and rocky track that gains 650 feet in 1.7 miles. The road ends at a large meadow, but not before offering a memorable overlook of the region on the ascent. The other road, FR 746, is a very similar route, but has a few side spurs and is 4.2 miles long. To reach both of these roads, head north out of Pinedale on Fremont Lake Road and drive about 8 miles to separate turnoffs on the right. Parking for ATV unloading is available.

East Green River Road—To see an example of how water transforms a landscape, follow CR 110 as it parallels the mighty Green River. This waterway creates a lush swath of life where tall grasses, willows, and cottonwood trees all thrive. The result is a stark contrast from the surrounding dry terrain, where even sagebrush fails to offer much color. But it's not the plants that are said to have given this drainage its name, but green soapstone banks that give the water a green hue in places.

To reach the road from Pinedale, drive west on HWY 191 for 5.25 miles to the turnoff on the left (across from HWY 352). The driving is easy as the road cuts through the Upper Green River Basin and you'll enjoy generous mountain views in almost all directions. The Huston Access Area (public fishing and boating area) is reached at mile 4. Further south, the road passes the Pinedale Anticline Gas Field to the east, and then ends at 23 miles when it reaches HWY 351 east of Marbleton.

Warren Bridge Recreation Area—This beautiful recreation area provides access to miles of the Green River in the Upper Green River Valley. An 8-mile gravel road leads across rolling sagebrush hills where grouse and antelope roam. Along the way, you'll find more than a dozen places where you can access the river to camp, fish, picnic, or launch non-motorized watercraft.

To reach the recreation area from Pinedale, drive west on HWY 191 for a little over 20 miles and turn right after you cross the Green River. Drive north on BLMR 5201 (Warren Bridge Road) to reach the access point of your choice.

High Deserts And Shrublands

The high deserts of southwestern Wyoming are arid and expansive. Just in this corner of the state, the desert environment encompasses around 7,000 square miles of land that rise above 6,000 feet and receive less than 10 inches of precipitation per year. These parched wilds are painted in a variety of colors and have a rugged relief that includes buttes, basins, badlands, pinnacles, and isolated mountains that are sometimes lightly timbered. Covered extensively with sagebrush and short grasses, the area allows Wyoming to claim more of this type of habitat—and the pronghorn antelope that thrive in it—than any other place in the world. The outer fringe of the deserts is bound by semi-arid shrublands as well as the foothills of the region's larger mountain ranges.

There are two particular natural features that give this area distinction. The first is the Great Divide Basin where the Continental Divide splits and wraps around an endorheic bowl. Here, water evaporates rather than drains to a river and ocean. The second feature is the Red Desert, an area without official boundaries that is prized for its beauty, history, recreational opportunities, and natural resources. But how the desert is managed, and for what purposes, is the subject of many an argument. Perhaps no other area of the state is enshrouded in as much controversy as those who want to use the land for grazing, wind power, and drilling compete against those who want to preserve its uniqueness.

Land worth fighting over is land worth visiting, and there are many reasons to explore these hinterlands even if you're not seeking the solitude of wide open spaces or stargazing of unsurpassable quality. Among the treasures you may discover are the striking beauty of the Flaming Gorge, ancient petroglyphs, herds of wild horses and desert elk, an old volcano core, fossils from a subtropical era, and the largest active dune field in North America.

Land Ownership

Much of Wyoming's southwestern desert is managed by the BLM and there is no better place in the state to wander without concern of trespassing onto private property. However, a deal that the federal government made with the Union Pacific Railroad in the 1800s still continues to complicate management and recreation along a corridor that extends roughly 20 miles on both sides of I-80. Within this corridor, each square mile alternates between BLM and private ownership, creating what is known as the "checkerboard." As of this writing, the majority of these private allotments were held by the Rock Springs Grazing Association and Anadrako Petroleum Company. Historically and currently, these organizations allow public access to these lands for recreational activities such as hunting, but take note that you have no specific legal right to use them. Local BLM offices are located in Kemmerer, Pinedale, and Rock Springs.

Roads and Trails

Interstate 80 offers easy driving through the area. Aside from the remote stretch between Rawlins and Rock Springs, you'll find numerous highways off I-80 that head north, including HWY 191, HWY 372, HWY 30, and HWY 189. South of the Interstate, you can use HWY 150 at Evanston or HWY 414 at Mountain View, to reach the areas near the Utah border.

The primary backroads, which are county roads, are generally well-maintained and graveled, but they are prone to getting puddles that cover the entire width of the driving surface. The secondary roads and tracks are quite primitive and it's not difficult to get stuck in deep soil, a washout, or sand.

Seasons and Conditions

Many of the roads in southwestern Wyoming cannot be easily driven until May because melting snowdrifts leave them too sloppy. Even then you can encounter mud holes and ruts on the best routes. When summer arrives, days are often hot and nights are cool, if not cold. With an average elevation of 6,800 feet, temperature swings can be drastic here and seemingly perpetual winds also influence conditions. Many consider September and October to be ideal months to visit as roads are dry and temperatures are mild. On the fringe of the driving season, remember that a frozen roadway in the morning may become impassable when temperatures rise and the wet road thaws.

Fuel

Even though I-80 slices through this region, you'll discover that it's a lonesome stretch of road where services are scarce outside of the major towns. Fill up when you can and be wary of outdated billboards that can point you to gas stations that have long been closed. Along the Interstate, reliable stations are found in Evanston, Green River, Rock Springs, a trio of towns near Exit 39, and at Little America—an all-service complex at Exit 68. Stations are abundant in the western towns, places like Big Piney, Cokeville, and Kemmerer. On the north end, you can fill up in Pinedale, Lander, or Farson. There is nothing to the east but a vast desert.

Maps

Statewide atlases work well for navigating the main backroads of southwestern Wyoming. Two of the best include the DeLorme Wyoming Atlas & Gazetteer and the Wyoming Road & Recreation Atlas published by Benchmark Maps. However, if you're going to be on secondary roads and tracks, you'll be better off obtaining more detailed maps from the BLM. Even then, you'll need to carefully track your whereabouts. Many roads are not signed, especially within the mazes that have been developed in the gas and oil fields.

10: Red Desert
A tour of the desert's features

☒ **Backcountry Drive** Most vehicles	☐ **4WD Route** 4x4 vehicle or ORV	☐ **ATV Trail** ORV less than 50" wide

Location/Map	Northeast of Rock Springs; Page 370
Roads	CR 17, CR 83, BLMR 4102, CR 21, CR 74, CR 445
Distance	98 miles
Managing Agency	BLM—Rock Springs Field Office
Starting Coordinates	N41° 43.6' W109° 16.43'

Overview: The Red Desert and Great Divide Basin hold many Wyoming icons, such as the Killpecker Sand Dunes, Boars Tusk, Oregon Buttes, and the White Mountain Petroglyphs. This long drive visits all of these features, as well as a few others as it crosses through the vast landscape. In good conditions, this route can be driven with any vehicle. However, large mud puddles, sandy patches, and rough side roads are reasons to consider taking a 4WD vehicle.

Start: To reach the southern end of the route from I-80 at Rock Springs, drive north on HWY 191 for 9 miles. The turnoff for CR 17 is on the right. This point can also be reached from Pinedale by driving south on HWY 191 for 90 miles.

The northern end of the area can be reached from Lander by driving southward for 43 miles on HWY 287/28. The turnoff for CR 445 is on the left, across the highway from Lander Cutoff Road.

Description: The trip begins by following Chilton Road (CR17)—sometimes marked as Tri-Territory Road—east across a high plain of sagebrush and clump grass. After a couple miles, the county road swings north and reaches a side road that leads to a pair of rugged draws named Long Canyon and Crooked Canyon. The main course continues north and parallels an abandoned railroad that runs along the east flank of White Mountain—a steep, treeless rise. At mile 12, a fair-weather dirt road heads west to the base of the mountain and ends at the White Mountain Petroglyphs site.

SIDE TRIP

The Indian carvings found at the base of White Mountain are impressive and worth the 4 miles it takes to reach them from the main county road. The sketches in the sandstone cliff include many stick figures as well as horses and large game animals.

At 15 miles, Chilton Road reaches a junction at Fifteenmile Knoll. The more primitive-looking road headed left returns to HWY 191 after 16 miles to create a 31-mile "short loop." To continue on the main route, stay right and follow the road as it turns to the northeast.

The captivating landmark now seen to the north is Boar's Tusk—an old volcano core that is often the symbol of the Red Desert. The best views of this towering spire are found between mile 16 and 18.

SIDE
TRIP

Two unmarked dirt tracks, one near mile 16 and another off a trunk road near mile 18, can be used to drive to the base of Boar's Tusk and encircle it. This is not a maintained route and you may need a 4WD vehicle to make the drive, depending on conditions.

After 18 miles, a secondary road that heads north into an oilfield also provides access to the Killpecker Sand Dunes, North America's largest active dune field. Up to 150 feet tall and about 100 miles in length, the dunes are constantly changing shape as winds shift the sand. A better access point for the dunes comes in mile 20.

SIDE
TRIP

A 2.3-mile side road leads to the Sand Dunes Recreation Site, also known as the Sand Dunes Off-Road Vehicle Area. Here, several sandy paths connect a parking area to the dune field. The area is wildly popular with ATV riders, who have motorized access to nearly 11,000 acres of sand.

From the sand dunes turnoff, Chilton Road continues east and enters rougher terrain. At mile 26, the route passes north of two blunted mesas, North Table Mountain (7,931 feet) and South Table Mountain (8,287 feet). Freighter Gap Road (CR 83) is reached near mile 31. Turn left onto this gravel lane and follow it north. The Chilton Road, by the way, continues to the southeast and can be used to reach I-80 at Point of Rocks, nearly 30 miles from the junction.

Traveling north, the backroad passes the edge of a sand patch and then travels below the sheer southern face of Steamboat Mountain (8,683 feet), one of the most significant mountains in the Red Desert. At 34 miles, turn left onto BLMR 4102.

ALTERNATE
ROUTE

If you have any qualms about steep drop-offs or if you're driving this road in the off-season (when snow covers the top of the mountain), stay on CR 83 and follow it through Freighter Gap. Both of these roads converge farther north.

A single lane, BLMR 4102 climbs steeply to scale the mountain's rim. Magnificent views of the desert are attained as you look out to the east and southeast. Features that can be spotted include a band of sand dunes, Spring Butte, Black Rock (the smaller flat-topped butte), and the tall stacks of the Jim Bridger Power Plant.

Steamboat Mountain is topped with aspen groves and small brooks. A number of secondary roads (mostly two tracks) can be taken across the

Gravel lane near Steamboat Mountain

mountain and you can use these to reach the west rim to see the Killpecker Sand Dunes and Boars Tusk. These roads are closed between May 10 and July 1 to protect elk calving areas.

Veer right at an intersection at mile 36 and drive northeast another mile to reach the Tri-Territory Historic Site. Situated along the Continental Divide, this signed point marks the common boundary of the Louisiana Purchase, the Northwest Territory, and Mexico. An interpretive sign explains the historical timeline of the territories. This pulloff also offers a vantage point from which you can see the Wind River Range as well as the Oregon Buttes on the northern horizon.

From the historic site, continue driving north along the BLM road for another 5 miles to rejoin Freighter Gap Road (CR 83). Turn left (northwest) at this junction, which is signed as the Tri-Territory Loop. The escarpment north of this intersection is Bush Rim.

Follow the backroad as it heads northwest to a junction at mile 49. Then, turn right to assume a northeast bearing near the confluence of Jack Morrow Creek and Rock Cabin Creek. The road reaches CR 21 just a few miles farther. A left turn here would take you 16 miles through the Jack Morrow Hills, a well-known area of the Red Desert that has been locked into an environmental dispute over oil and gas drilling. Instead, turn right at the junction and follow Bar X Road (CR 21) to the east. This road soon climbs atop an elevated bench where it stays for several miles before descending into a pair of drainages. It then continues east along the backbone of a ridge that breaks ruggedly into Alkali Draw.

At mile 70, turn north onto Oregon Buttes Road (CR 74). While this road receives some maintenance and is easily driven in dry conditions, its driving

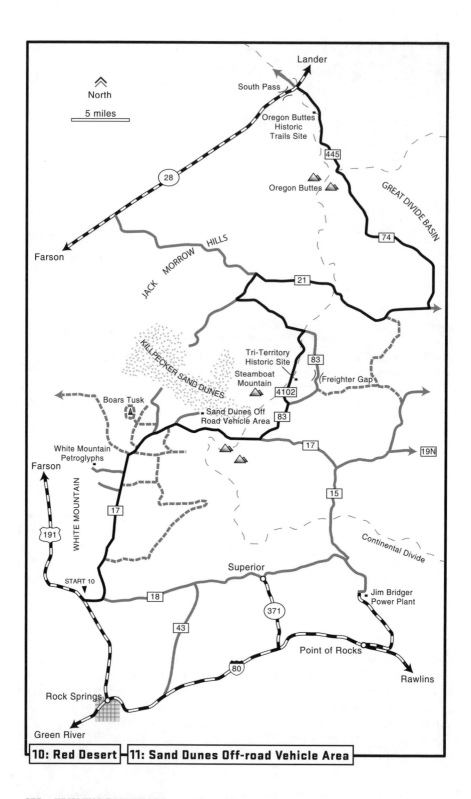

North

5 miles

Lander

South Pass

Oregon Buttes
Historic
Trails Site

445

28

Oregon Buttes

GREAT DIVIDE BASIN

Farson

JACK MORROW HILLS

74

21

KILLPECKER SAND DUNES

Tri-Territory
Historic Site

83

Steamboat
Mountain

Freighter Gap

4102

Boars Tusk

Sand Dunes Off
Road Vehicle Area

83

White Mountain
Petroglyphs

17

19N

Farson

WHITE MOUNTAIN

15

191

17

Superior

START 10

Jim Bridger
Power Plant

18

371

Continental Divide

43

Point of Rocks

80

Rawlins

Rock Springs

Green River

10: Red Desert — **11: Sand Dunes Off-road Vehicle Area**

surface has its share of bruises. After wet weather, the low points sometimes turn into huge puddles; mud and ruts can make driving difficult.

Follow the roadway northward as it cuts across the varied desert floor, crossing over Bush Creek before mile 73. The two looming Oregon Buttes are seen ahead and the road passes beside these high points in another 13 miles. Highly visible landmarks rising from the desert floor, the lightly-timbered buttes served as a sort of milepost to Oregon Trail pioneers as they measured their progress.

As the road continues north toward the Wind River Range, watch for the Oregon Buttes Historic Trails Site, which has a marker and interpretive sign. This site marks the Oregon Trail where it crossed the Continental Divide and summit of South Pass. The backway ends nearly 3 miles farther when it reaches HWY 28 at mile 98.

11: Sand Dunes Off-Road Vehicle Area
Play in the sandbox

☐ **Backcountry Drive** Most vehicles	☒ **4WD Route** 4x4 vehicle or ORV	☒ **ATV Trail** ORV less than 50" wide

Location/Map	Northeast of Rock Springs; Page 370
Roads	Not applicable
Distance	Not applicable
Managing Agency	BLM—Rock Springs Field Office
Starting Coordinates	N41° 57.67' W109° 4.93'

Overview: The Killpecker Sand Dunes comprise the largest active dune field in North America, though they are rarely seen for their remote location. The sand stretches intermittently across 100 miles of Wyoming's desert, but at the core is a continuous dune field about half of that length that tops 150 feet in height. The western side of this field consists of two wilderness study areas—these are non-motorized sections that are under Congressional consideration for permanent protection. On the eastern side, the BLM has set aside the Sand Dunes Recreation Site (also known as the Sand Dunes Off-Road Vehicle Area), a 10,500-acre allotment where you are free to drive on the sand. This playground is found on the active dunes, which are always shifting.

Start: From I-80 at Rock Springs, drive north on HWY 191 for 9 miles. Turn right onto Chilton Road (CR 17). This point can also be reached from Pinedale by driving south on HWY 191 for 90 miles. Drive north, and then east on this well-maintained gravel road for 20 miles and watch for the signed turnoff to the left (north). Turn onto the side road and follow it 2.3 miles to the recreation area.

Riding over to the Killpecker Sand Dunes

Description: From the recreation site (just a parking lot with vault toilets), you can take several paths to cut through the tall sagebrush and reach the dunes. On the sand, you can almost ride wherever you want, exploring the many summits and valleys of the area. One exception is the freshwater ponds that are formed at the base of some dunes. Fed from ice that melts from under the sand, these riparian areas are critical to area wildlife and are off limits to motorized users.

Many of the dunes are very steep with sharp crests, making for fun, but potentially dangerous, riding. Use caution on the slopes and also keep watch for other potential hazards in the area, such as cattle and partially-buried pipelines.

To best traverse the sandy terrain, your ATV should be equipped with paddle tires, though many riders do fine without them. Also consider using an orange whip flag to help alert others to your whereabouts—especially important when topping a blind ridgeline. As always (but more so here with the wind-whipped sand), a helmet with a face shield or goggles is in order.

12: Quaking Aspen Mountain
Travel to a high oasis

☒ **Backcountry Drive**
Most vehicles

☐ **4WD Route**
4x4 vehicle or ORV

☐ **ATV Trail**
ORV less than 50" wide

Location/Map	South of Rock Springs; Page 374
Roads	CR 27, CR 32
Distance	36 miles
Managing Agency	BLM—Rock Springs Field Office
Starting Coordinates	N41° 32.54' W109° 8.24'

Overview: This backcountry drive samples the scenic bluffs and rangelands of southwestern Wyoming while attaining a high overlook at Three Patches Recreation Area. This is certainly a backroad that can help you develop a whole new appreciation for the region's unique beauty. A great time to visit is during late spring or early summer, when the grass is at its greenest.

Start: From I-80 at Rock Springs, take Exit 107 to access HWY 430. Drive south of town for over 3 miles and turn right on CR 27. The turnoff is across the highway from a phosphate complex.

Description: Begin by driving southward on CR 27. The first few miles are paved, but soon give way to a good gravel surface. Keep right at a fork for

Eastbound on Muddy Springs Road

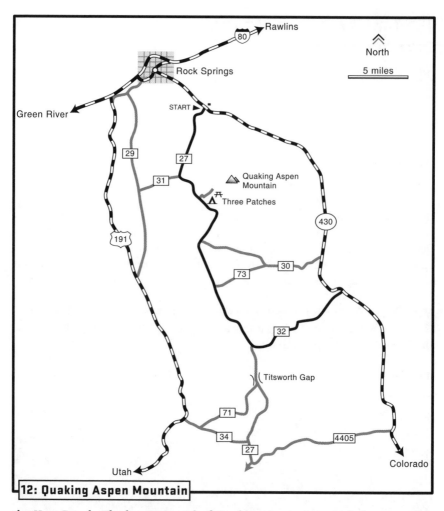

12: Quaking Aspen Mountain

the Kent Ranch. The large mound of Quaking Aspen Mountain looms to the south where communication towers jut from its bald top and bright pockets of aspen trees adorn the sides.

At 7 miles, the first BLM sign is encountered at a fork. Bear left for the Three Patches Recreation Area. The slightly washboarded road now steeply gains elevation on the northwest flank of Quaking Aspen Mountain. Before you pull to the top, be sure to glance to the sides where an entire panorama of southwestern Wyoming is revealed. The sharp peaks of the Wind River Range are visible along the northern horizon. Below the mountain range, you can see the Killpecker Sand Dunes and Pilot Butte standing over Rock Springs. In the other direction, you'll find miles of scenic bluffs and valleys below Utah's snow-capped Uinta Mountains.

Near the top of the climb, you'll pass a fork for Radar Towers Road. Stay right on the lower road, which bites into the edge of the mountain. The route soon makes its way around the hillside to reach a signed fork for the Three Patches Recreation Area.

SIDE TRIP

The recreation area is reached on a washboarded access road just 1 mile from the fork. Trees are precious commodities in this area of the state and the BLM has taken advantage of the aspen grove by developing a picnic area beneath the summit of Quaking Aspen Mountain. In the shade at nearly 8,500 feet, the picnic area offers an escape from the hot summer sun. Camping is also permitted and paved parking sites are available.

Heading south from the picnic area, the road gently descends to a high prairie of sage and native desert grass. There are good viewpoints along the way that reveal the region's many ridges and escarpments. Mining and mineral extraction have long been a part of Rock Spring's history and the occasional signs, poles, and pipelines along this stretch are reminders of how rich this land is with natural resources. Antelope and cattle are also found on this rangeland.

There are several routes that lead east to the highway. Pass the first few and turn left on Muddy Springs Road (CR 32), reached at 26 miles.

ALTERNATE ROUTE

If the scenery to the south is drawing you in, or you just want a longer drive, you can continue on for 12 miles through Titsworth Gap and then take east-bearing BLMR 4405 to return to the highway.

Muddy Springs Road travels for 10 miles between rocky bluffs and steep breaks in an arid land that barely receives nine inches of precipitation a year. The dryness can be realized in the rearview mirror where a dust cloud is likely to be lingering for a half-mile behind your vehicle.

The drive terminates at HWY 430 where you turn left to return to Rock Springs, some 30 miles to the north. The paved return route also travels through a rugged, desert landscape.

13: Adobe Town
Wyoming's badland labyrinth

✖ Backcountry Drive
Most vehicles

☐ **4WD Route**
4x4 vehicle or ORV

☐ **ATV Trail**
ORV less than 50" wide

Location/Map	Southeast of Rock Springs; Page 376
Roads	CR 19S, BLMR 4412
Distance	30 miles
Managing Agency	BLM—Rawlins Field Office
Starting Coordinates	N41° 33.02' W108° 33.15'

Overview: Adobe Town is a geological wonder that is located in the southern reaches of Wyoming's Red Desert. The prized badland formations you'll find here have been weathered over time by water and wind. Although the area only receives about six inches of annual precipitation per year, comparative to Africa's Sahara Desert, it still supports a spectrum of wildlife including the state's largest herd of wild horses. Deer and elk also use the fringe areas of Adobe Town as winter rangeland. Fossils have shown that the area was once habitat for some unlikely creatures too, such as turtles, crocodiles, and even the woolly rhinoceros.

Much of Adobe Town is designated as an 85,000-acre wilderness study area. For this reason, motorized travel is only permitted on designated roads. The BLM claims that the roads are marked on the ground as either open or closed, but I found few signs so use your own discretion.

If you go, take at least one good statewide map with you. I didn't, and I found myself driving for a couple of hours trying to navigate a maze of unsigned junctions and dead-ends. This is a very remote part of Wyoming, so be sure to pack plenty of supplies even if you're just driving in and back.

This drive doesn't take you through Adobe Town, but rather to the edge of it where you'll find an overlook of the Adobe Town Rim. There are a few rugged 4WD tracks at the rim, but I'd encourage you to explore this fascinating area on foot.

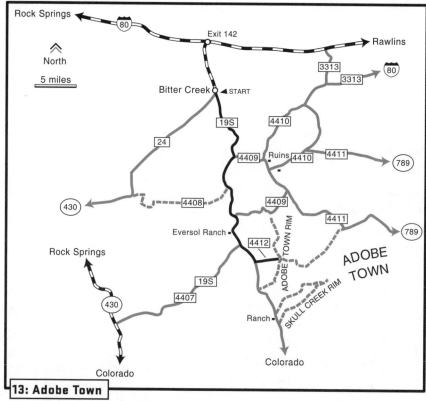

13: Adobe Town

Start: Take I-80 east from Rock Springs, or west from Rawlins, to Exit 142 (Bitter Creek). Turn south onto Bitter Creek Road (CR 19S) and drive 7 miles along a broken paved surface. Here the road crosses the railroad tracks and turns to gravel.

Description: From the end of the pavement, continue south by staying left at the fork after the tracks. Bitter Creek Road is wide and maintained here, but there are parts that get sloppy in wet weather. At mile 10, a side road (BLMR 4409) heads east.

SIDE TRIP

This narrow BLM road makes a worthwhile detour (and loop). Along the way you'll find the Fort LaClede Ruins, brick structures along Bitter Creek that once served as a fort and stage station in the 1860s. The historic Overland Trail parallels much of the road's course. Further east, on BLMR 4411, the road closes in on the northern portion of Adobe Town where you'll see the thousand-foot high formations known as The Haystacks.

Continue south on Bitter Creek Road where you'll find rugged land along Antelope Creek. At nearly 22 miles, the road rolls into the Emersole Ranch. Drive through the ranch, bearing left (southeast) onto a lesser road. Drive 1.7 miles to another fork and again stay left onto unsigned BLMR 4412. Follow this increasingly narrow road for 3.4 miles and then turn left onto a rougher track headed east.

Overlooking the Adobe Town Rim

From this point, only a few outcrops on the plain offer much hint that there is something special about this area. This quickly changes as you drive the final 3 miles. Park near the fenced pipeline station, and then walk over to the edge where the desert ground drops away. This is the Adobe Town Rim, one of three named rims in Adobe Town. It's among the most dramatic and accessible viewpoints into the remarkable labyrinth of sandstone badlands, spires, hoodoos, arroyos, and ravines.

To fully appreciate the area, explore the crusty, sun-parched formations on foot. For motorized touring, you can continue by taking one of the 4WD tracks, such as the one that runs north along the Adobe Town Rim. Another option is to head roughly 9 miles farther south to the Skull Creek Rim. You can also continue straight to drop down into the badland basin.

14: Pilot Butte Wild Horse Scenic Tour
Interpretive drive in wild horse habitat

☒ Backcountry Drive
Most vehicles

☐ **4WD Route**
4x4 vehicle or ORV

☐ **ATV Trail**
ORV less than 50" wide

Location/Map	Northwest of Rock Springs; Page 381
Roads	CR 14, CR 53
Distance	26 miles
Managing Agency	BLM—Rock Springs Field Office
Starting Coordinates	N41° 44.6' W109° 19.33'

Overview: The Pilot Butte Wild Horse Scenic Tour is a backcountry drive that showcases the wild horses that roam the rangelands of southwest Wyoming. The drive takes you along the rim of White Mountain and past Pilot Butte, making it a worthwhile tour even if you don't spot any horses.

Of the estimated 6,000 horses that roam Wyoming, hundreds of them live in the White Mountain Management Area, giving you good odds of viewing the animals. To increase the chances, the BLM recommends visiting the area between sunrise and mid-morning or in the evening hours. Even if your timing isn't perfect, you'll probably still catch a glimpse—I spotted over 30 horses on a blistery summer afternoon. Aside from the horse herds, you can spot rabbits, pronghorn, coyotes, and raptors.

Start: To access the eastern end of the loop from Rock Springs, take I-80 to Exit 104. Drive north on HWY 191 for 14 miles and then turn west onto CR 14. To start the loop from the west, follow I-80 to Exit 89 on the west side of Green River. Follow Flaming Gorge Way toward town and turn left at the first intersection onto Wild Horse Canyon Road. Follow this street under the interstate to begin the loop. Kiosks near the endpoints explain the scenic tour and give a map of the route.

Description: From the east end at HWY 191, drive west for 2.5 miles and then turn south on White Mountain Road (CR 53). This wide, easily-driven gravel route bends back to the east toward the edge of White Mountain. With the thousand-foot height advantage, you can look out a great distance. Try to find the Boars Tusk and Killpecker Sand Dunes—visible landmarks within the Red Desert—that are about 20 miles to the northeast. Another type of landmark has been proposed for White Mountain—wind turbines. Dozens of the white towers, potentially hundreds, may someday generate electricity from the wind that sweeps across this high desert mountain.

As you head south, you'll find numerous pullouts with interpretive signs that explain the area's natural environment, history, and development. At mile 13, two converging tracks depart to the west and lead to Pilot Butte, the dark, prominent landmark that is only 3 miles away.

SIDE TRIP

Follow the deeply rutted dirt path west to the base of Pilot Butte (7,932 feet), a mammoth mesa that crowns White Mountain. Drive as far up the slope as you dare, and then hike the rest of the way to the notch in the eastern rim. Here you'll find a metal ladder that leads to the broad, windy summit.

At mile 17, the road curves to the southwest while paralleling I-80, which runs just a mile and a half below the mountain's rim. Again, interpretive signs tell of the importance of this thoroughfare, both historically and currently.

By mile 20, the road descends toward Green River. The last mile of the drive is especially intriguing. Here, the road passes below huge rock outcrops with names like The Towers, Giants Thumb, Sugar Bowl Rock, and Teakettle Rock. The tour ends on Wild Horse Canyon Road at the edge of Green River.

A lone wild horse near Pilot Butte

15: Blue Rim

A cross section of the high desert

☒ **Backcountry Drive** Most vehicles	☐ **4WD Route** 4x4 vehicle or ORV	☐ **ATV Trail** ORV less than 50" wide

Location/Map	North of Green River; Page 381
Roads	CR 5
Distance	37.5 miles
Managing Agency	BLM—Rock Springs Field Office
Starting Coordinates	N41° 33.31' W109° 30.56'

Overview: Blue Rim Road cuts a north-south course through Wyoming's southwestern desert. The route loosely parallels the Green River along the southern stretch and then climbs to the edge of Blue Rim. There, you'll find terrific views of unblemished country.

Start: To reach the southern end of the road from Green River, take HWY 374 west for a little over 2 miles. Turn right onto Blue Rim Road (CR 5), which heads north under I-80. To reach the north end of the road from Farson, take HWY 28 to the southwest for 16.8 miles.

Description: From HWY 374 at the southern end of the drive, head north under I-80 and follow the road as it climbs above the lush Green River

High desert landscape along Blue Rim Road

drainage. At 3 miles, the road passes the Lower Green River Access Area, allowing for a short side trip to the riverbank.

The road soon crosses over Alkali Creek and then progresses north to reach a junction with CR 7 at mile 9. Bear right here and follow Blue Rim Road as it departs from the Green River watercourse and snakes its way across the desert plain. Watch for Pilot Butte (7,921 feet), the dark, flat-topped landmark to the east.

At mile 16, you can look west over the Green River Basin, a dried lakebed that holds the world's largest trona deposits. Trona ore is used to produce soda ash for products such as glass, toothpaste, and laundry detergents. The OCI chemical plant, where these resources are processed, can also be seen from this vantage point. According to the company, 90% of U.S. soda ash, and a quarter of the global supply, are manufactured from this basin.

At 18.4 miles, the road passes CR 14, a gravel lane that goes east to the Pilot Butte Wild Horse Scenic Tour and HWY 191 (route #14). A couple

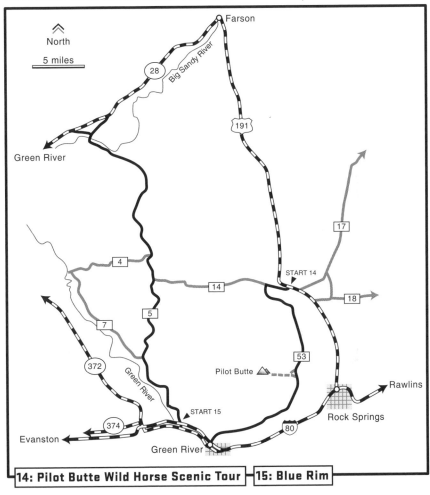

14: Pilot Butte Wild Horse Scenic Tour — **15: Blue Rim**

miles farther, you'll reach the edge of Blue Rim where the desert floor drops several hundred feet. The rim is crowned with photogenic buttes and ridges. On a clear day, you can see the Uinta Mountains in Utah from here, as well as the Wind River Range to the north. Across the northwest are the Badlands Hills, which stretch nearly a dozen miles.

The junction with Big Island Road (CR 4) is reached just shy of 21 miles. This road leads back to the Green River, but the bridge there is closed to motorized traffic. Blue Rim Road continues along the high crest for several additional miles and sometimes offers glimpses of the state's western mountain ranges. The most dramatic scenery is seen just before the road veers away from the rim and enters the badlands. These badlands are quickly passed and more gentle terrain is soon traversed.

The road now wraps to the northwest and soon crosses the Big Sandy River to reach a split on the other side. Turn either way (depending if you want to go east or west on the highway), and drive a short distance to HWY 28.

16: Flaming Gorge
A tour above the rugged eastern shoreline

☒ **Backcountry Drive**
Most vehicles

☐ **4WD Route**
4x4 vehicle or ORV

☐ **ATV Trail**
ORV less than 50" wide

Location/Map	Southwest of Rock Springs; Page 383
Roads	CR 33, CR 38
Distance	46.5 miles
Managing Agency	BLM—Rock Springs Field Office, USDA Forest Service—Ashley National Forest
Starting Coordinates	N41° 0.71' W109° 25.53'

Overview: When construction on Flaming Gorge Dam was completed in 1964 to hold back the Green River, it created a reservoir that stretches 91 miles across the Utah-Wyoming state line. Today, the Flaming Gorge National Recreation Area is popular for many different things, such as mountain biking, historical study (petroglyphs and geology), dramatic scenery, water sports, four-wheeling, camping, and trophy-sized trout fishing.

Most of the developed recreation sites, as well as two visitor centers, are located south of the border in Utah. On the Wyoming side of the recreation area, you'll find numerous backroads and 4WD tracks that crisscross rugged, semi-arid terrain. This backcountry drive follows Flaming Gorge Road, which is located on the east side of the reservoir. The route offers numerous access points to the lake while staying high enough to reward you with many terrific overlooks of the countryside. You'll encounter steep grades and loose gravel, but this road is fun and easy to drive (in dry conditions). The scenery continuously changes as you climb over ridges and drop into drainages. The road is best driven from June through November.

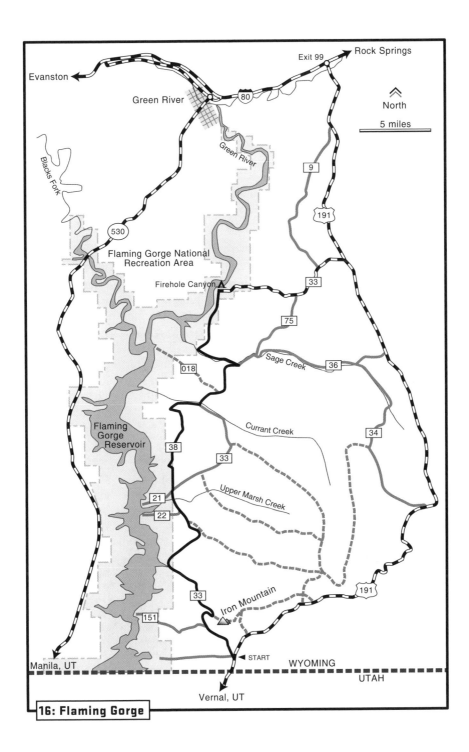

Evanston

Green River

Exit 99   Rock Springs

80

North

5 miles

Green River

Blacks Fork

9

191

530

Flaming Gorge National Recreation Area

Firehole Canyon

33

75

018

Sage Creek   36

Currant Creek

34

Flaming Gorge Reservoir

38

33

21

22

Upper Marsh Creek

33

191

151

Iron Mountain

START

Manila, UT

WYOMING

UTAH

Vernal, UT

16: Flaming Gorge

Start: On I-80, head east of Green River or west of Rock Springs to Exit 99. Then drive south on HWY 191 for 13.7 miles to reach the north end of the road, or 50.7 miles to reach the southern end of the road. The route described here begins from the southern end.

Description: The drive begins a mile north of the Utah state line by heading northward on CR 33, a gravel lane. The first couple of miles pass through tall sagebrush before climbing into a juniper woodland. This is a favored habitat for deer and elk during the winter months and mountain lions are common. Unique to this area is the midget faded rattlesnake, which grows to two feet long and has markings that fade with age. Other animals that reside within this broken terrain include antelope, grouse, badgers, coyotes, raptors, and feral horses.

At 2.9 miles, the road tops a rise on Iron Mountain and begins to descend into Wildhorse Basin. This point provides the first view of water as Flaming Gorge Reservoir is spotted 4 miles to the northwest. Follow the road as it curves to the east and reaches an unsigned junction at 4.5 miles. At 7,200 feet, this intersection is the route's highest point. Turn left here and follow the road downhill past burned trees. This is a long slope and you'll have wide views of the reservoir as you leave the woodland.

At 9.3 miles, the road reaches Middle Marsh Creek. This is the closest that Flaming Gorge Road gets to the reservoir and a short spur, FR 078, leads to the shoreline. Steer back to the northeast to pass another spur just 1.5 miles farther.

Looking north toward the Firehole Canyon area

The road now passes through rolling sagebrush terrain and then enters a level basin where you'll find a side road leading to Brinegar Ranch. The only thing that breaks this flat terrain is the steepness of the Upper Marsh Creek drainage, reached in mile 15. On the other side of the creek, you'll find a four-way junction. The road on the left is FR 021 and it heads west 2.3 miles to the water. The road to the right is CR 33. Stay northbound by taking CR 38. This road soon enters Lowe Canyon and then negotiates a series of stomach-turning rises and dips.

Staying on CR 33 by turning right at the junction takes you across Currant Creek Ridge, a lightly wooded mountain. You then follow Currant Creek to return to CR 38. It's a 9.2-mile road, but adds only 1 mile to the overall length of the trip.

ALTERNATE
ROUTE

Except where you top a ridge, the reservoir disappears from view over the next few miles. Multiple two-tracks are passed, but the next decent road that heads to the water is FR 018, reached at 23 miles. A mile farther, you'll reach another major intersection. This is where CR 38 and CR 33 rejoin. Bear left and follow CR 33 northward toward Sage Creek.

A marker for the southern Cherokee Trail is found at 26 miles. Round the next curve and you'll find additional markers, as well as the faint tracks of this historical wagon trail. Established in 1849 and used for more than four decades, the trail led gold-seekers to California.

North of the overland trail, you'll reach Lower Sage Creek Road (CR 36), which leads back toward HWY 191. Make a sharp left to stay on CR 33 and follow Sage Creek back to the northwest. The sagebrush found along the creek and adjacent hills become noticeably greener and thicker.

Continue around some bluffs to dip into Sage Creek Basin at mile 33. The top of the climb out of this depression comes with a surprise—awesome views of the Green River and Firehole Canyon. From this high point, you'll discover striking formations and rock chimneys that fill the skyline. Below a drop-off on the left, you'll find a number of tracks that follow the banks of the river. Continue north for another mile to reach pavement at Firehole Canyon Campground where there is also a beach and boat ramp.

To complete the drive, follow the paved road for nearly 10 miles as it travels through Firehole Canyon to HWY 191. If you're not ready for the highway, you can extend the backcountry drive by turning north on Little Firehole Canyon Road (CR 9), which is found on the left at 44.5 miles. This beautiful route follows a fair-weather road through Little Firehole Canyon.

Other Nearby Drives

Flaming Gorge National Recreation Area—If you visit the Wyoming side of Flaming Gorge, be sure to head into Utah and see the rest. Huge canyons with dizzying overlooks, visitor centers, and cool pine forests are just three reasons why the trip is worth the extra mileage. A 150-mile paved loop around the reservoir can also be made by combining HWY 530 (south of Green River), HWY 44 (in Utah) and HWY 191 (southwest of Rock Springs).

Black Mountain—The Black Mountain area, west of the Flaming Gorge National Recreation Area, is a barren landscape that is highlighted by gray, red, and green-tinted badlands. The most rugged and intriguing formations are found in the Devils Playground area on the east side of the mountain. To the south is Twin Buttes, a single mesa with two points upon its summit.

Bound on all sides by paved roads, the Black Mountain area allows for relatively easy four wheeling when conditions are dry, as they often are. With less than 10 inches of annual precipitation, the parched earth here is as arid as most of the nation's desert southwest.

Roughly 50 miles of primitive roads crisscross the area. The main routes include BLMR 4311, BLMR 4312, and BLMR 4313. Much of the area falls within two wilderness study areas that were set aside by Congress in 1983. For this reason, you must stay on designated roads.

There are three access points on the east side of the area. From I-80, take Exit 89 or 91 at Green River. Then drive southward on HWY 530 for 19 miles to reach McKinnon Junction. Continue on HWY 530 for 8.3 miles to BLMR 4311, a little over 12 miles to BLMR 4313, or 22.3 miles to BLMR 4312. These roads are unsigned.

For access points on the west side of the area, follow the same directions to reach McKinnon Junction. There, turn right onto paved CR 1 and drive 7.3 miles to BLMR 4311, 10.6 or 13.5 miles to the 4WD roads that lead to Pine Springs, or 13.8 miles to BLMR 4312. Some of these roads are unsigned.

17: Cedar Mountain/Burntfork
Visit a remote mountain and moonscape

☒ **Backcountry Drive**
Most vehicles

☐ **4WD Route**
4x4 vehicle or ORV

☐ **ATV Trail**
ORV less than 50" wide

Location/Map	Southwest of Green River; Page 388
Roads	BLMR 4314, BLMR 4317, BLMR 4315
Distance	53 miles
Managing Agency	BLM—Kemmerer Field Office
Starting Coordinates	N41° 4.41' W110° 9.52'

Overview: This loop drive begins by going up and over Cedar Mountain, which rises to an elevation of 8,580 feet. Topped with a broad, treeless summit that

A small aspen stand along Cedar Mountain Road

spans nearly a dozen miles, the mountain's steeps are peppered with juniper trees and aspen. For much of this stretch, you'll get a commanding view of the region, replete with badlands and Utah's mountainous skyline.

The second half of the loop travels through ash-colored formations and badlands on Burntfork Road. Even those who aren't easily impressed with the desert might appreciate the unique lunar-like landscape.

Burntfork Road has at least a dozen junctions and forks, some marked, most not. To stay on the main course, maintain a westerly bearing; any route that drastically departs in another direction is probably going to get you going the wrong way. Some of these side spurs dead-end at drilling pads, but others can be taken to further explore the badlands. If you venture off the main roads, be sure to take a 4x4 vehicle and carry extra provisions.

Start: To reach the western ends of the loop, take I-80 east from Evanston to Exit 34. Then continue east on the I-80 Business Route for over 5 miles to reach HWY 414 at Urie. Turn south on HWY 414 and drive to Mountain View. Here, turn east and follow HWY 414 for 7 miles to reach the northern end of the loop or 24 miles to an unmarked access road on the left (just north of Lonetree) to start at the southern end of the loop.

To access these roads from the east, take I-80 to Exit 89 or 91 at Green River. Stay on the main road when driving through town and turn south onto HWY 530. Follow this highway 19 miles to the southwest to reach McKinnon Junction. Turn right onto paved CR 1 and drive 8.7 miles to BLMR 4315 on the right.

Description: From the southern access point just north of Lonetree on HWY 414, drive east on the dirt lane along the willow-lined Henrys Fork drainage. At almost a mile, turn left onto Cedar Rim Road (BLMR 4314). This gravel course travels across a sagebrush steppe broken by badland outcrops and distant ridges. Just past mile 3, bear right at the junction and drive east to begin climbing the broad western flank of Cedar Mountain.

SIDE TRIP The fork that goes left at the junction is Sage Creek Mountain Road (BLMR 4316). This lane heads north for 3.5 miles to the foot of the mountain where it connects to more primitive roads.

By mile 6, the road passes Webb Spring, evident by the intermixed shrubs and aspen trees on the right side of the road. The splotchy grove of trees might not look like much, but in a desert like this, it draws an occasional weekend camper.

The gravel road parallels the steep slope of Cedar Mountain for a distance and then abruptly switches directions to make a steep 200-foot cut to the top. When the road levels off at the rim, turn left to the northeast. At 8,360 feet, this is the road's highest point and it offers a superb view. Looking back across the west, you'll see Sage Creek Mountain and the towns of Lyman and Mountain View behind it. To the south is a long horizon of tall peaks in Utah's Uinta Mountains. If the day is clear, you may also see the Wind River Range to the north and the Wyoming Range to the northwest.

Cedar Mountain presents easy driving across its broad summit. Along the way, you might spot antelope among the sagebrush, as well as cattle, which

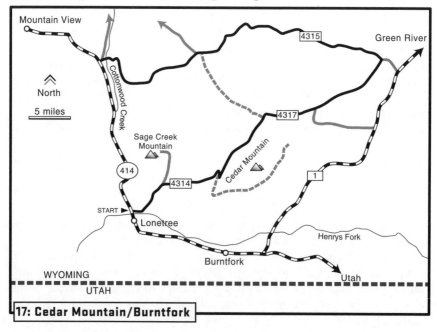

17: Cedar Mountain/Burntfork

are brought here to graze. Near mile 15, the road reaches an overlook at the edge of the rim. Here, it joins the lesser Cedar Mountain Road (BLMR 4317) and then turns east where you'll see the rugged terrain that surrounds Flaming Gorge Reservoir.

In less than a mile, the road begins to drop off the eastern side of the mountain, losing over 2,000 feet in just a few miles. The driving surface here is more prone to becoming slick, so use caution if there has been wet weather. The eastern slope is lightly timbered with juniper, but this soon gives way to the more barren flats.

At 19 miles, the road forks into separate paths, both of which end at paved CR 1. Stay left on BLMR 4317 and follow it to the northeast to strike BLMR 4315 near mile 26. Turn left here onto Burntfork Road (BLMR 4315) and drive westerly across the sagebrush steppe toward the northern reaches of Cedar Mountain.

After 30 miles, the road dips into a band of white and gray badlands with only isolated clusters of grass. Devoid of life as it seems here, you can spot antelope, prairie dogs, and raptors.

SIDE
TRIP
Watch for a pair of primitive tracks on the left between miles 33 and 35. If you want to explore the badlands further, turn onto one of these roads. The first leads up Cattail Draw along the southwest side of the formations. The second connects to several other 4WD tracks within a few miles.

Driving through badlands on Burntfork Road

Near Cattail Draw, the road intersects the historical southern route of the Cherokee Trail. This old trail was used by wagon trains—and many Cherokee Indians who had also caught gold fever—between Oklahoma and California between 1849 and the 1890s. Past this draw, there are a number of well-maintained spurs on the south side of the road, but these only lead to drilling sites.

The main course turns southward near mile 40 and begins to climb out of the badland basin. Views of the Uinta Mountains return as does the sagebrush-carpeted desert floor. A few miles further, Burntfork Road converges with Cedar Mountain Road in a bend. Keep right at this junction to stay on the well-traveled gravel road. A short distance later, Hank Hollow Road is passed on the right. Stay left and continue west.

At mile 52, the road fords Cottonwood Creek, but an underlying concrete base makes the crossing an easy one. A little over a half mile farther, the road reaches Cottonwood Bench Road. Turn left at this junction and drive a quarter mile to end the trip at HWY 414.

18: Piedmont/Muddy Creek Historical Backway
Return to the old west

☒ Backcountry Drive	☐ 4WD Route	☐ ATV Trail
Most vehicles	4x4 vehicle or ORV	ORV less than 50" wide

Location/Map	Southeast of Evanston; Page 391
Roads	CR 173, CR 204, CR 202
Distance	24 miles
Managing Agency	BLM—Kemmerer Field Office, other mixed ownership
Starting Coordinates	N41° 8.45' W110° 50.57'

Overview: This drive makes a historical tour in the southwest corner of Wyoming. The route travels along overland trails from the western migration, visits the ghost town of Piedmont, and incorporates the main segment of the Muddy Creek Historical Backway. These backroads can be very difficult, even dangerous, to drive when they're wet.

Consider visiting the Fort Bridger State Historic Site in Fort Bridger. This complex began in 1843 as an outpost for the various emigrant trails but was later turned into a military installation. Today, it's comprised of a trading post, museum, restored buildings, and a gift shop. It's a great place to learn more about the region's rich history.

Start: From I-80 at Evanston, take Exit 5 and turn south onto HWY 150. Drive 10 miles and turn left onto CR 173, just south of Sulphur Creek Reservoir. To reach the east end of the route, take I-80 further east to either Exit 24 or Exit 28.

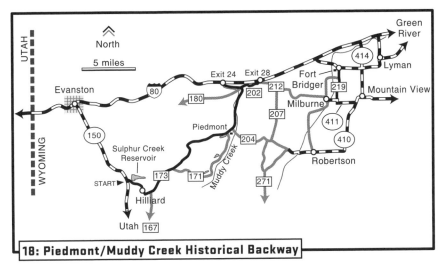

18: Piedmont/Muddy Creek Historical Backway

Description: Starting from the west end at HWY 150, paved CR 173 heads east along the southern shore of Sulphur Creek Reservoir. A recreation park here includes a boat ramp, picnic shelter, and picnic tables. The paved road continues past a spattering of homes and then turns southeast to Hilliard, a small, rural community.

After 2 miles, the county road changes to a gravel surface, passes through "Rock Cut," and then passes CR 167 on the right. Stay left at the junction and follow what is now called Piedmont Road to the northeast. This section of the road utilizes an old elevated railroad bed that stands high above the surrounding plain. Get too close to these edges and the result will be disastrous. Continuing northeast, the road passes Piedmont Aspen Road (CR 171) by mile 7. Again, stay left at the junction and continue through increasingly rugged terrain.

At 10.5 miles, the road enters Horseshoe Bend. In the middle of this curve, you'll pass the historic California Trail that led emigrants west. This wagon track merged with the Mormon Pioneer Trail just a half mile to the west of the curve. Portions of these are still visible today.

The road now heads east again and becomes more interesting as it passes through a colorful land of elevated benches and ridges. A reservoir is passed in mile 18, followed by another junction with Piedmont Aspen Road (CR 171). Again, stay left at this fork to reach Piedmont, a classic example of an old western ghost town. Remains can be found on both sides of the road, but much of the old site is located on private ranch land so it must be viewed from the public roadway.

The Union Pacific Railroad was the catalyst for Piedmont's growth. After building a station here in 1869, the town grew to over two hundred people. All the amenities of a functional town in that day were found here: a general store, post office, newspaper, hotel, school, saloons, and possibly a church.

Charcoal kilns at Piedmont

The most eye-catching feature at Piedmont, and certainly the most photographed, is a number of brick beehive kilns located on the east end of the site. These ovens were used to produce charcoal for silver smelting. Three of the five kilns have been restored while the other two lie in ruin. From this point, continue driving east a short distance to reach a three-way junction.

ALTERNATE ROUTE

Instead of following the Muddy Creek Historic Backway, you can turn right onto CR 204 and continue east on Piedmont East Road. Over the next few miles, the roadway begins to climb over more rugged terrain. The steepest ascent comes at 20 miles when the road gains the top of Bigelow Bench. At over 7,900 feet, this perch stands higher than the tallest point in 36 other states. As a result, you get outstanding views of the surrounding countryside, which is highlighted by exposed white sandstone. To the south, you'll find Utah's northern mountains.

To finish the drive, continue east on CR 204 and stay straight at the last three junctions. The road drops into a unique coniferous forest called Pine Grove outside of the town of Robertson. Here the road changes back to a paved driving surface as it turns into HWY 410.

Stay left on CR 173 and drive north toward I-80 along the Muddy Creek Historic Backway. Not much is published about this unsung backway, but the significant portion of it is here along the banks of Muddy Creek, a curvy stream that was a favored camping spot for emigrants who followed the Mormon, Pioneer, and California Trails. Around 70,000 Mormons are believed to have come through the campsite. An interpretive sign on the west side of the road marks the crossing and campsite. Further yet, you'll find a sign marking a "Historic Trail Site View Area."

The road continues a short distance north while paralleling Meyers Ridge and Bigelow Bench, which is lined with wind turbines. When you reach an unsigned four-way junction, you can continue straight along CR 173 (headed northwest) or bear right onto CR 202. Both of these roads lead to I-80 in about the same distance to end the drive. Be sure not to turn onto the road that heads southwest, which is CR 180 (unless you want to, of course).

Southwestern Mountains

Southwestern Wyoming includes numerous mountain masses such as the Salt River Range, Wyoming Range, Hoback Range, Tunp Range, Commissary Ridge, and the northern end of Utah's Uinta Mountains. The most substantial of these is the Wyoming Range, a sedimentary chain that ranks among the state's largest. Though it only measures 10 miles wide in many places, the range stretches north to south for nearly 100 miles and rises to a height of 11,378 feet at Wyoming Peak.

On a statewide popularity scale, these mountain ranges rate near the bottom of the list as they are trumped by the nearby Grand Tetons and Wind Rivers, both of which have captured global fame. However, the southwestern mountains have received political attention. When the Wyoming Range Legacy Act was signed in 2009 to withdraw more than a million acres from gas and oil development in this area, the spotlight came on and the curtains of obscurity were lifted. How this may change the area is yet to be known.

Dividends of scenery and solitude are paid to those who take the chance to explore this region's high country. The mountains not only hold a raw beauty that is unspoiled and luring, but they are also prized for their big game habitat. The Wyoming Range in particular is rich with wildlife. Moose, black bear, and elk are common here and the range has historically produced trophy mule deer. While lynx prowl the forests and bighorn sheep roam the higher summits, grizzly bears may also hold an unknown presence. One such bear was killed here in 2002 when it preyed on domestic sheep, which graze the range during the summer.

Land Ownership

The Wyoming and Salt River Ranges are managed by the Bridger-Teton National Forest, while the Uinta Mountains are managed by the Wasatch-Cache National Forest. Forest Service offices are located in Kemmerer, Big Piney, Afton, Evanston, and Mountain View. The fringes of these mountains, including the smaller ranges of the area, are mostly under BLM jurisdiction (Kemmerer Field Office). Most private properties are ranches adjacent to the major roads and are well marked.

Roads and Trails

Interstate 80 makes it easy to access this part of Wyoming. From this expressway, you have your choice of north-bearing highways such as HWY 189 and HWY 30. Along the Idaho border, use HWY 89 to travel through the multitude of towns in the Star Valley. South of the Interstate near Mountain View, you can use wide county roads to reach the Uinta Mountains on the Utah border.

Backroads in the mountains are often found in excellent condition, especially those managed by the Forest Service. BLM-managed roads are rougher, but still easily traveled in good weather conditions. The area's 4WD roads rate from easy to moderate with only occasional sections that are overly challenging. Mud, more than rock, presents the most problems for drivers. Designated ATV trails vary greatly in quality, but most range from easy to moderate. Of the motorized trails in these mountains, many of them are designated as single track for dirt bike use.

Seasons and Conditions

Mountain roads at lower elevations (6,000-7,500 feet) are mostly accessible by the middle of May. Roads that are higher or deeper in the backcountry are accessible by June. However, it's not uncommon to encounter roadside snow in July, especially within the shadowed canyons. September and the first couple of weeks of October present terrific conditions for touring these mountains, though the first chills of winter can't be ignored. Seasonal closures begin in October and go through December, depending on elevation and the Forest Service's management plan.

Fuel

Near the western mountain ranges, you'll find that gas stations are abundant in towns like Afton, Alpine, Big Piney and Kemmerer. Closer to the Uinta Mountains, make your stops along I-80 in Evanston, Green River, Rock Springs, and the towns near Exit 39.

Maps

For the Salt River and Wyoming Ranges, use the Bridger-Teton National Forest map for the Big Piney, Greys River, and Kemmerer Ranger Districts. This map includes the various regulations of the Forest's extensive travel management plan. Further south, along the Utah border, refer to the map for the Wasatch-Cache National Forest (Salt Lake, Kamas, Evanston, and Mt. View Ranger Districts). Free copies of these Forests' ORV maps or Motor Vehicle Use Map (MVUM) should also be used, especially if you'll be exploring the plethora of side roads and spurs.

For the smaller mountain ranges that are not within the national forest, you'll want a statewide atlas that shows county roads, such as the DeLorme Wyoming Atlas & Gazetteer or the Wyoming Road & Recreation Atlas published by Benchmark Maps.

19: Monument Ridge
Surmount a scenic overlook

⊠ **Backcountry Drive** Most vehicles	⊠ **4WD Route** 4x4 vehicle or ORV	☐ **ATV Trail** ORV less than 50" wide

Location/Map	Southeast of Jackson; Page 396
Roads	FR 30530, FR 30531, FR 30533
Distance	18 miles (last 11 miles may require 4WD)
Managing Agency	USDA Forest Service—Bridger-Teton National Forest
Starting Coordinates	N43° 14.91' W110° 29.7'

Overview: This beautiful drive travels across the northern end of the Wyoming Range. The trip offers several miles of easy and scenic backcountry driving followed by a 4WD road that climbs to the top of Monument Ridge. The high point offers a panoramic view of the surrounding mountains including the Gros Ventre Range to the north.

Start: From Jackson, drive south 11 miles to Hoback Junction. Turn left onto HWY 189/191 and drive east 15 miles to the turnoff on the right. If you're making the trip on an ATV or are more interested in the rougher portion of this road, continue to the Clarks Draw parking lot by continuing east on the highway for another 8.3 miles.

Description: From the western starting point, gravel FR 30530 heads south along Cliff Creek, a curvy stream that flows through a valley. Steep forested ridges rise in all directions above the drainage, but occasional low points reveal monstrous mountain peaks in the distance. If you like what you see, there are dispersed campsites along the way where you can pull off for an extended stay.

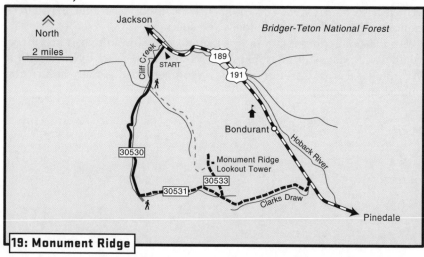

19: Monument Ridge

Descending eastward from the top of Monument Ridge

A foot trail leading to Monument Ridge is passed near Little Cliff Creek, and then a picturesque overlook is attained at a bend in the road near mile 4. From here, the valley widens for a couple of miles before the road squeezes through a gap to reach a junction at mile 7. This is the end of the backcountry drive segment, and the nearby trailhead makes for a good place to turn around.

To continue the drive with an ATV or 4WD vehicle, turn east at the junction and follow FR 30531, a secondary road that climbs along Sandy Marshall Creek. This track stays along the base of an open south-facing hillside rather than the opposing one that is heavily timbered. Continue along the creek and past some ponds for 3.5 miles to reach a junction. Turn left on FR 30533. This side road heads north for 1.5 miles and climbs to an elevation 8,257 feet—a gain of 530 feet. At its end, you'll reach the abandoned Monument Ridge fire lookout tower. From this splendid high point atop what is sometimes called the Hoback Range, you'll find a mountainous diorama—the Wyoming Range to the west and southwest and the Gros Ventre, which sprawls across the northern horizon.

From the lookout tower, follow the path back to FR 30531 and then turn left to resume an easterly course. The road is at its steepest here and a handful of narrow switchbacks return you to gentler terrain by mile 15. When wet, this is a daunting, muddy stretch that will have you grappling for traction.

The final 3 miles traverse cattle-grazing country covered in aspen, willows, and sagebrush. Traveling through Clarks Draw, the badly rutted dirt and grass pathway has few rocks and is quickly crossed with an ATV, but full-sized vehicles will take a beating from an onslaught of potholes and dips. Near the end, the road veers to the north, away from Clark Butte (7,154 feet) and ends at a large parking lot along HWY 189/191.

Other Nearby Drives

Lower Hoback Canyon—To access this shallow canyon on the northeast side of the Wyoming Range, take HWY 191/189 east from Bondurant for less than 4 miles and turn south onto FR 30700. For the first 10 miles, a gravel surface follows the Hoback River past numerous ranches while advancing toward a gorgeous ridgeline of snow-capped peaks. The roadbed then transitions to a good dirt surface, though it gets slippery during wet weather. As the route climbs above the pastures, it enters the narrowing terrain of Lower Hoback Canyon and is further enclosed by a forest of aspen and conifers. The road ends just shy of 14 miles at a turnaround near a beaver-dammed pond. From here, foot trails lead deeper into the backcountry; one continues west along the Hoback River and another heads south along Grizzly Creek.

20: Salt River Range
Short routes from the Star Valley

⊠ Backcountry Drive
Most vehicles

⊠ 4WD Route
4x4 vehicle or ORV

⊠ ATV Trail
ORV less than 50" wide

Location/Map	Southwest of Jackson; Page 401
Roads/Trails	Strawberry Creek: FR 10083 Willow Creek and Grover Park: FR 10080, FR 10081 Swift Creek: FR 10211 Dry Creek: FR 10079, FT 3182, FT 3037 Cottonwood Lake: FR 10208
Distance	35+ miles of roads and trails
Managing Agency	USDA Forest Service—Bridger-Teton National Forest
Starting Coordinates	Strawberry Creek: N42° 54.0' W110° 54.21' Willow Creek and Grover Park: N42° 50.87' W110° 53.62' Swift Creek: N42° 43.56' W110° 54.81' Dry Creek: N42° 41.02' W110° 54.8' Cottonwood Lake: N42° 36.68' W110° 53.59'

Overview: The Salt River Range parallels the Wyoming-Idaho state line. Rising to nearly 11,000 feet, its snowcapped summits create a beautiful backdrop over the small towns that line the Star Valley. While good gravel roads wrap around the range's northern and southern ends, only a few motorized routes—mostly single-track motorcycle trails—traverse the mountain's crest. There are, however, numerous roads that penetrate the thick, lush vegetation on the range's western side by following a creek through a tight canyon. These heavily traveled roads are narrow and dense brush often obstructs visibility; use caution as you proceed around blind corners and keep watch for places where you can pull over to pass oncoming traffic.

Start: From Jackson, drive south on HWY 26 for 11 miles to Hoback Junction. Bear right at the junction and drive 23 miles to Alpine. Follow HWY 89 southward until you reach the road of your choice.

Description (Strawberry Creek): To reach the northern most route from Alpine, drive south on HWY 89 for 21 miles and turn east on paved Strawberry Creek Road (CR 126) to Bedford. Continue east through town until the road begins at the Bridger-Teton National Forest boundary. The 3-mile backroad is paved until it reaches a power plant, and then has a gravel surface as it snakes through a brushy drainage below towering cliffs. The last stretch gets rocky as you pass below scree slopes—a 4x4 or other high-clearance vehicle is suggested. The road ends at a popular parking area at the edge of a small lake and dam. A single-track trail continuing east from this point is open to motorcycles and snowmobiles.

Description (Willow Creek and Grover Park): To access the next two routes from Bedford, turn south onto the paved Bedford-Turnerville Road and follow it nearly 5 miles to Turnerville. Turn east onto FR 10080 for Willow Creek or continue straight to reach FR 10081 for Grover Park.

The 6.3-mile Willow Creek road travels through a narrow canyon and is easily driven to a trailhead located at 2.1 miles. Here, a foot trail heads north to McDougal Pass. Past the trailhead, the road gets rougher with more rocks, mud, and washouts. However, the upcoming view is worth the bumps as the road slips through the canyon toward the snowcapped peaks that line the crest of the Salt River Range. Toward the end, the lane kinks and bends its way up a lush mountainside to reach a fork. The left road descends into a photogenic valley where it ends at a foot trail. The road on the right wraps around a small, unnamed lake that you might find dry.

The Grover Park area is bisected by FR 10081, a 4.5-mile gravel road. Beginning just south of Turnerville, the route gently climbs 2 miles to a saddle between higher summits to the east and west. Several rougher side roads branch off the main route and are used by dispersed campers and ATV riders. From the 7,000-foot high point, the road descends moderately along Phillips Creek until it ends at the small community of Grover.

Description (Swift Creek): To reach the heralded Periodic Spring at Swift Creek, drive south from Alpine for 33 miles to Afton. Watch for a sign for the spring at the north end of town. Follow this road east to the national forest boundary to reach FR 10211. This gravel lane makes for an easy 4.5-mile cruise. It begins by passing Swift Creek Campground on the right, and then follows a large water supply pipe through a narrow, deep gorge cut only by other side canyons. The drive ends at a trailhead where a foot trail continues less than a mile to the Periodic Spring, a geological wonder. Working much like a geyser in Yellowstone, the stream flows for about 18 minutes before it "dries up" and briefly stops altogether. This is a continuous cycle that is best viewed during the middle to late summer.

Periodic Spring near Afton

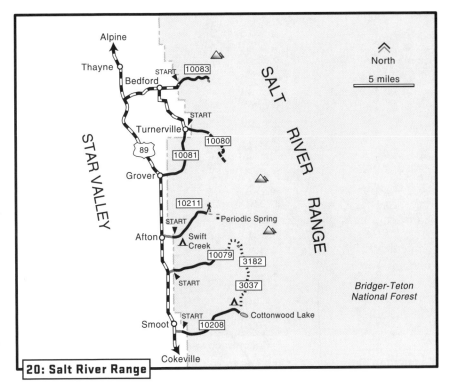

Alpine

Thayne ○

Bedford

START ▢10083

SALT

△

⌃⌃ North

5 miles

START

Turnerville ○

89

▢10080

10081

Grover ○

STAR VALLEY

RIVER

△

RANGE

10211

START ▼

Afton ○

Swift
▲ Creek

■ Periodic Spring

△

10079

3182

START

3037

Bridger-Teton
National Forest

Smoot ○

START

▼

10208

▲

Cottonwood Lake

Cokeville

20: Salt River Range

Description (Dry Creek): The most challenging route in this group is FR 10079, which runs along Dry Creek. To start, drive south from Alpine for 36.5 miles and then turn east on a paved access road that leads less than a mile to the national forest boundary. The first several miles are easily driven as the road parallels Dry Creek through a steep canyon. At the time of this writing, full-sized vehicles can only drive through this lower canyon because the upstream bridges are condemned (ATVs and side by sides are still allowed). Continuing upstream on an ORV, you'll find an increasingly rocky path. A shallow ford of Mill Creek is reached near mile 6.

From the ford, the track gains larger rocks and ruts. Higher still, the route passes through patchy meadows (watch for sheep and aggressive guard dogs) and then makes a distinct U-curve with a pair of fords of Dry Creek.

By mile 8, the old road ends near tiny Dry Creek Lake under the high summits of the Salt River Range. From this point, a 6-mile ATV route (comprised of Dry Creek/FT 3182 and Trail Fork/FT 3037) continues southward through a beautiful valley. The track takes you through high, lush meadows to reach a fork where a single-track motorcycle trail heads east. At this point, stay right on FT 3037 and continue a couple miles further through the timber to reach Cottonwood Lake on FR 10208. Take note that snow can be found along this trail even into July.

Cottonwood Lake

Description (Cottonwood Lake): The most southern route, FR 10208 provides access to gorgeous Cottonwood Lake where you'll find a trailhead (both foot trails and FT 3037) and a campground. To get there, drive south of Alpine for 41 miles to a road that runs east for a mile to the national forest boundary. Then follow FR 10208 up a tight, forested canyon along a fast creek. The lane is especially narrow, made worse by willows and other shrubs that lean over the roadway. A well-maintained gravel surface takes you 6 miles to the lake.

Other Nearby Drives

Jensen Creek—A short 4WD road and ATV trail can be found on the west side of the Star Valley in the Caribou-Targhee National Forest. From Thayne, drive south on HWY 89 for about 6 miles and turn right onto HWY 238. Follow this highway for 1.6 miles and then turn north for .7 mile to a gate at the national forest boundary. From the gate, FR 506—a rugged but easy track—bends northwest across open rolling terrain before reaching trees in a small section of private property. Ignore the first spur that is passed on the right and stay left to climb up a wooded hill. The road then descends the backside of the hill and soon narrows into a muddy deciduous woodland along Jensen Creek. The road ends a short distance after emerging from the trees, but continues on for another 3.5 miles as FT 025, an ATV trail. A couple of other short ATV trails (FT 26 and FT 27) also cross this area. Check the Caribou-Targhee National Forest Motor Vehicle Use Map (MVUM) for this route and others in nearby Idaho.

21: Greys River/Smiths Fork
Follow a river between mountain ranges

☒ **Backcountry Drive**
Most vehicles

☐ **4WD Route**
4x4 vehicle or ORV

☐ **ATV Trail**
ORV less than 50" wide

Location/Map	Southwest of Jackson; Page 405
Roads	FR 10138, FR 10072
Distance	83 miles
Managing Agency	USDA Forest Service—Bridger-Teton National Forest
Starting Coordinates	N43° 9.8' W111° 1.0'

Overview: Few backroads in Wyoming are as worthwhile as Greys River Road. This route follows the entire length of a river that flows between two remarkable mountain ranges—the Salt River Range on the west and the Wyoming Range on the east. The trip never bores. You get glorious views while passing through an area that is rich with history, wildlife, and recreational opportunities.

The northern half of this drive receives heavy use and is therefore very well-maintained. Further south, you'll find a narrower roadway that doesn't hold up as well in wet weather, but is still suitable for any vehicle. Generally, you can make this drive in its entirety from July through September.

Start: From Jackson, drive south on HWY 26/89 for 11 miles to Hoback Junction. Bear right at the junction and drive 23 miles to Alpine. Look for the signed Greys River Road on the north end of town.

Description: Starting from the not-a-secret-anymore town of Alpine, follow the access road past a small subdivision. Less than a mile from the highway, Greys River Road (FR 10138) enters the Bridger-Teton National Forest.

Steep hillsides soon crowd the road with wooded, north-facing slopes on the right and drier, south-facing slopes on the left. Some of these mountains rise more than 2,000 feet higher, creating an unnamed gorge. Before mile 3, the road crosses over the Greys River at aptly-named Bridge picnic area. From here, the road runs above the river affording picturesque views. At 8.4 miles, the road forks with Little Greys River Road (FR 10124), which is also worth a drive.

SIDE
TRIP

Little Greys River Road heads deep into the Wyoming Range. Nearly 14 miles in length, the course runs along the verdant Little Greys River drainage. This is practically a wildlife sanctuary and quiet visitors may score sightings of large game such as moose, elk, and deer. The waterway is also habitat for an abundance of bird life including blue herons and sandhill cranes. The road ends at a pair of trailheads where foot trails lead further into the mountains.

From the fork, FR 10138 turns south and bears a course through a coniferous forest of pine, spruce, and fir. A pair of Forest Service campgrounds is passed: Lynx Creek at mile 12 and Murphy Creek 2 miles farther. Deer Creek Guard Station is also soon passed; watch for osprey along this stretch.

SIDE TRIP

A short distance south of Deer Creek Guard Station, FR 10002 leads west toward Murphy Lakes—one of very few named lakes in these mountains that can be reached by motorized vehicle. The marshy ponds are pooled below the north side of the Star Peaks in the Salt River Range. A 4WD road continues past the lakes for a few more miles. There is also a lengthy ATV trail (FT 3183) that starts near this point and ends at Greys River Road near the Bridge picnic area.

Continuing south, the wooded banks of the Greys River are replaced with a lush, shrubby channel that stretches a quarter mile wide in places. The road keeps along the east side of the drainage and offers some of the best river access along this tour. Anglers will find a variety of trout in the stream's clear waters; brown, rainbow, cutthroat, and brook are all present.

Moose Flat and a campground of the same name are passed at mile 23. Now aligned with the mighty snow-creased summits of the Salt River Range, this stretch of road is among Wyoming's most beautiful. These peaks are made of sedimentary rock layers—similar to the Canadian Rockies—that give them unique hues and shapes that differ from the granite ranges found elsewhere in the Rocky Mountains. You'll find a pullout here, the Henderson Overlook, where you are rewarded with a view of several mighty peaks: Man Peak (10,326 feet), Visser Peak (10,015 feet), and Virginia Peak (10,141 feet). Visser Peak was named after a fallen Wyoming State Trooper who was killed by a drunk driver in 1981.

A short distance past the overlook, the road bends around a curve named The Elbow and then resumes a southern bearing. After passing a parcel of private property and the Meadows Guard Station, the road reaches a junction with FR 10125 at mile 32.

ALTERNATE ROUTE

A 46-mile road (FR 10125) connects Greys River Road to HWY 189 and makes a terrific alternative route out of these mountains. The bumpy road climbs over the Wyoming Range by passing through McDougal Gap at 8,430 feet. From this high point, it's a long, steady descent across the eastern front of the mountain range and into the distant Upper Green River Basin.

Driving a few miles farther along the Greys River, you reach Forest Park Campground, which is the last developed camp along this drive. This is also the location of an elk feeding ground that supports up to 2,000 animals in conjunction with the winter range near Alpine. But it's not only elk you might spy here. Watch the willow-lined river bottom for moose and deer. Beaver are common, too.

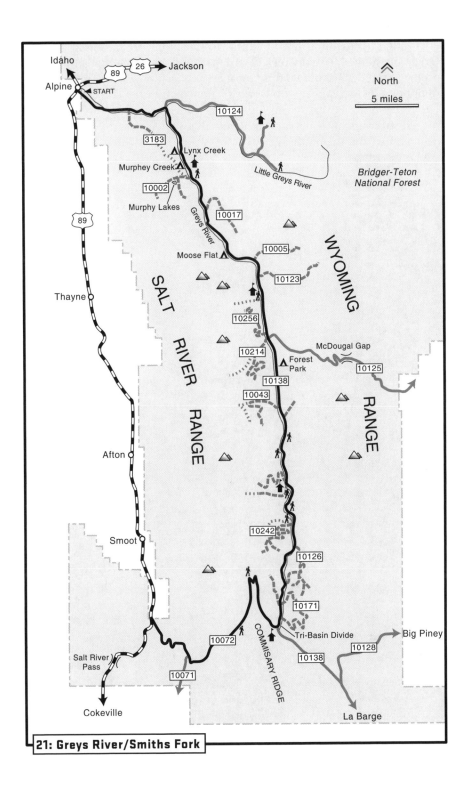

21: Greys River/Smiths Fork

Heading upstream, the road climbs to Cazier Guard Station at mile 46. Originally named Corral Creek Guard Station—the name that still appears on the Forest Service map—this Forest Service facility was renamed in 1984 to honor a district ranger who worked here. The location couldn't be better. The historic site is situated in a gorgeous valley bound to the east by the rugged summits of the Wyoming Range that rise 3,000 feet higher, barely over a mile from the roadway.

Greys River Road

While Yellowstone burned in 1988, wildfires also swept across this valley. Today you'll find that the slopes around Corral Creek are sprung with young conifers that are growing between spindly snags of lodgepole pine. Even decades later, it'll be a long time before this forest matures to any resemblance of that time.

If you're drawn to further explore this area—and it's hard not to be—you can continue your adventure on foot. There are four trailheads a few miles north of Corral Creek and another three just to the south. Some of these climb to the Wyoming Range National Recreation Trail, which mostly traverses the crest of the Wyoming Range over the course of 75 miles.

Several miles south of Corral Creek, the slightly rougher road crosses over the Greys River at Shot Hole Spring. An interpretive sign near the crossing explains that an exploring petroleum company created the spring with explosives in 1961. From here, follow the single lane as it threads through a narrow canyon and climbs to Poison Meadows where the headwaters of the river are drawn.

Past mile 58, the road reaches the Tri-Basin Divide at 8,679 feet. This is the geological point of three separate watersheds: the Great Basin, the Columbia River, and the Colorado River. This is also where the road splits with Smiths Fork Road (FR 10072). Steer right onto FR 10072 and follow the curve past another guard station. You're now following La Barge Creek upstream between two ridges.

ALTERNATE ROUTE

Staying on FR 10138 will take you out of these mountains on La Barge Creek Road. Over the course of 40 miles, the gravel road first travels through meadows where flyfishing is common along the creek. This is also where the historical Lander Cutoff of the Oregon Trail passed through the area. Although the shortcut trimmed off about 100 miles from the main route, it crossed arduous terrain; trail markers and emigrant graves can still be seen today. Further downhill, where the forest transitions to sagebrush country, the road endures some rough stretches as it passes through a mix of private, state, and federal land. The journey ends at HWY 189 south of La Barge.

After 63 miles, the road turns abruptly and attains the top of Commissary Ridge, a long rise. This tail of the Salt River and Wyoming Ranges continues dozens of miles to the south toward Kemmerer and reaches heights of 10,000 feet and higher. Here, the road tops the ridge at 9,240 feet, which is the highest point along the drive.

The road descends the steep western face of Commissary Ridge and settles into a different drainage system where the Smiths Fork flows southward to the mighty Bear River. Continue along this course to a reach a bridged crossing of the creek near mile 70. A trailhead located near the bridge offers access to the historical Lander Cutoff of the Oregon Trail. Open to foot travel, this segment of the trail offers the opportunity to labor across the same rugged terrain that thousands of emigrants did in the late 1800s. But you don't have to hike in to visit the actual route—the road intersects the trail at mile 73 and follows it for the remaining distance of the drive.

Leaving the Smiths Fork drainage at mile 75, the road turns northward and passes FR 10071, which travels 32 miles to Cokeville (12 miles are paved). From this point, the backway begins a series of downhill curves and turns as it descends.

The conifer-covered slopes of the high country gradually give way to drier hills where aspen trees are more prominent. The road ends at HWY 89, just a couple miles north of Salt River Pass. A quick drive to this high point will reveal a nice perspective of where you've just been.

Other Nearby Drives

Murphy/Squaw ATV Trail—The longest ATV trail in the Greys River area begins off FR 10001 near Bridge picnic area. After a few miles, a 4WD road transitions into FT 3183, which then continues southward toward Murphy Lakes. Together, the two paths form an 11.5-mile route that runs across high, lightly-wooded ridges. The route is open from July 1 through September 10. Room to park and unload ATVs can be found at either end.

Greys River Side Trips—While there are many intriguing side spurs that sprout off the Greys River Road, few lead to any notable destination. One of the longer 4WD routes is FR 10017, which travels 7 miles through the timbered hills above the Greys River.

Further south at Deadman Creek, FR 10005 is a rutted path that leads to an old mining site where ruins and equipment still remain. Today the road is primarily used by sheepherders, hunting outfitters, and for access to two single-track motorized trails.

Other roads in the area include FR 10123, which heads uphill several miles to Blind Bull Lake, a marshy pond. For impressive mountain scenery near Meadows Guard Station, turn onto 4WD roads FR 10256 or FR 10214 that lead up Cabin Creek and Bear Creek, respectively. Closer to Tri-Basin Divide, there are numerous 4WD roads that zigzag through logged forests that provide motorized rambling.

Dry Creek Road—Also referred to as Dry Fork Road, FR 10071 is a 20-mile dirt and gravel route that connects Smiths Fork Road to the end of HWY 232, 12 miles north of Cokeville. The road descends steadily from the Salt River Range and rolls out into the Smith Fork valley, where the Dry Fork-Smiths Fork is flanked by green rolling hills. In the lower valley, you'll pass by beautiful hayfields and a roadside grave for Emma Button that dates back to 1893. Though passable by most vehicles when dry, it can be a tricky route when conditions are wet.

22: Wyoming Range

A tour of the eastern front

☒ **Backcountry Drive**	☐ **4WD Route**	☐ **ATV Trail**
Most vehicles	4x4 vehicle or ORV	ORV less than 50" wide

Location/Map	Southwest of Pinedale; Page 411
Roads	CR 315, CR 138, FR 10138, FR 10128, FR 10046, CR 129, CR 117
Distance	87 miles
Managing Agency	USDA Forest Service—Bridger-Teton National Forest
Starting Coordinates	N42° 14.53' W110° 11.68'

Overview: This backcountry drive utilizes seven county and national forest roads to traverse the eastern flanks of the Wyoming Range. The route includes many places to stop and numerous side trips. Unhurried travelers can make this a full-day excursion. While the main roads can be driven with any vehicle, high clearance is desirable if you're planning on getting off the main route. Due to high elevations, the upper sections of this route may not be accessible until June.

Start: To reach the southern end of the route, head south from Big Piney on HWY 189. Drive 22 miles to CR 315, located just a mile south of La Barge on the west side of the road. To reach the northern end of the route, drive north from Big Piney for 13 miles to paved Cottonwood-Ryegrass Road (CR 117).

Description: From the turnoff south of La Barge, drive west on La Barge Creek Road (CR 315), a paved roadway that cuts through a gas and oil field and then parallels La Barge Creek. The pavement ends at Viola in 11 miles, but the road continues uphill as CR 138. Continue driving upstream along the creek and you'll find that the terrain becomes much more rugged. The gravel road is easy to drive, though a few rough spots are encountered where it passes over land that is not managed by the BLM.

After passing FR 10103 on the left (a road headed south to Kemmerer), La Barge Creek Road enters the Bridger-Teton National Forest at mile 24 and becomes FR 10138. Trees are still not plentiful on the surrounding slopes, but that soon changes as you ascend to higher, wetter country. Numerous side roads are passed along these first few miles in the forest, but few of these lead to any notable destinations. One exception is FR 10013, which accesses the Scaler Cabin Guard Station, a reservable Forest Service cabin that was built in 1937.

At 30 miles, bear right onto FR 10128 and drive to Thompson Pass at 8,752 feet (some maps show this as Witherspoon Pass). The road is now in line with a section of the Lander Cutoff, a shortcut of the historic Oregon Trail. The backroad then descends into Snyder Basin, a scenic valley where you should plan a stop. Here, you'll find interpretive signs that describe the pioneers' difficult passage and their graves that prove it.

Continue eastward a short distance to a junction and turn left onto FR 10046. The road here wraps around the southern end of the Wyoming Range and heads north along Mount Darby (10,651 feet). This distinctive mountain ridge, along with Coal Creek and the lush meadows below it, are sure to have you reaching for your camera. The scenic views are relentless as you continue north past Fish Creek Mountain to the next junction.

At mile 46, you reach Middle Piney Road (CR 111) which heads east to Big Piney. Turn left here to stay on FR 10046 and drive to the northwest. A must-do side road to Middle Piney Lake, FR 10024, is soon reached on the left.

SIDE TRIP

The 3.8-mile side road (FR 10024) to Middle Piney Lake comes about halfway through this backcountry drive. This is a steeper road and trailers are not allowed. The lake makes a good picnic destination or camping spot and there are two Forest Service campgrounds from which to choose. The mile-long lake is surrounded by wooded slopes, but they are not high enough to obstruct the view of the Wyoming Range's highest summits to the west. A hiking trail leads to waterfalls 2.5 miles above the lake and also connects to the Wyoming Range National Recreation Trail.

Continuing northward, the curvy route travels through an evergreen forest to reach North Piney Creek. A couple miles further, FR 10370 on the left

Red Castles in the Wyoming Range

offers access to the North Piney ATV trail (route #23). Then, as the backroad gains Bare Pass (9,103 feet), the rising spires of a formation named Red Castles will steal your attention. It's an unexpected landmark that stands in sharp contrast to the surrounding mountains.

On the other side of Bare Pass, your interest will be captured by distant Triple Peak (11,127 feet) and the more pointed Lander Peak (10,450 feet). Continue downhill to find interpretive signs that tell of a forest fire that swept through the area in 1940. Further yet, you'll find ruins of a dam used by tie hacks—loggers who cut and hewed logs into railroad ties.

At mile 61, the road bends to the northeast, passing FR 10050 in a stunning valley. This short spur heads west 2 miles to small Soda Lake, and then continues another 2 miles along the drainage.

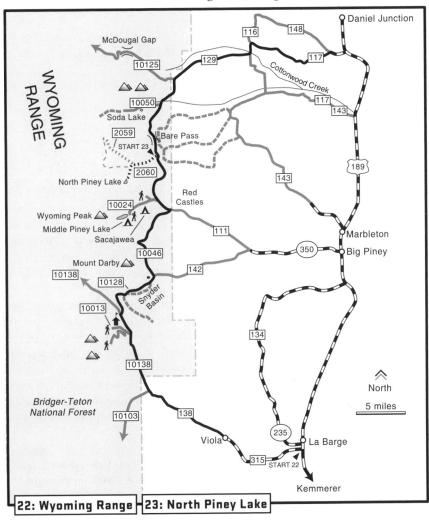

22: Wyoming Range **23: North Piney Lake**

Staying on the main route, you'll exit the national forest and turn north to a fork. A left turn here takes you 18 miles over the Wyoming Range to Greys River Road (route #21) on FR 10125. Instead, stay right and follow North Cottonwood Road (CR 129) east to another junction where the road intersects the creek. Turn north here onto Cottonwood-Ryegrass Road (CR 117) and drive a mile before the road curves to the east. It's now a 13-mile descent across increasingly dry terrain to end this trip at HWY 189. Don't be alarmed if you make the wrong turn and get on a different road; there are many routes along the last stretch that eventually return to the highway and most junctions are well-signed.

23: North Piney Lake
Paradise in the Wyoming Range

☐ **Backcountry Drive**
Most vehicles

☐ **4WD Route**
4x4 vehicle or ORV

☒ **ATV Trail**
ORV less than 50" wide

Location/Map	Southwest of Pinedale; Page 411
Trails	FT 2059, FT 2060
Distance	4.5 miles
Managing Agency	USDA Forest Service—Bridger-Teton National Forest
Starting Coordinates	N42° 40.948' W110° 30.83'

Overview: This outstanding ATV route follows the North Piney Trail through a gorgeous valley and then follows the Lake Creek Trail to reach North Piney Lake. Combined, these trails offer 9 miles of riding, but the lake is reached in just half of that distance. These are very narrow trails in places and passing can be difficult to impossible. With that in mind, keep watch for places to pull over if you spot another rider. Motorized use is allowed from July 16 to October 14. A Wyoming ORV permit is required.

The Wyoming Range offers terrific fishing, hunting, camping, and scenery; it's a special place that is revered by many sportsmen. Part of what contributes to the area's greatness is its unspoiled backcountry where motorized routes are few, at least compared to other national forests. Indeed, at the time of this writing, these two paths represented the only designated ATV trails on this side of the range. Please do your part to keep these routes open by staying on the trail to minimize resource damage and following posted rules. In return, you will not be disappointed at your experience in these mountains.

Start: From Big Piney, head west on HWY 350/CR 111 (Middle Piney Road) for 20 miles. Stay right at this junction and follow FR 10046 northward for 7.6 miles to FR 10370. Turn west onto this lesser road and follow it a half mile to the trailhead.

Lake Creek Trail near North Piney Lake

Description: The trail begins by descending through dark timber to reach the North Piney Creek drainage at a half mile. It then turns westward into a scenic, willow-lined valley and runs parallel to the creek. This is a narrow stretch with a few tight curves and a soft edge that falls away to the river. Watch your wheels, going off the trail here wouldn't be good.

At 2 miles, the trail undercuts a 550-foot scree slope, making for a short, but rocky stretch. A gate that will need to be opened and closed is reached a quarter mile further. Past this, continue west to a junction at 2.5 miles.

The right fork, FT 2059 (North Piney Trail) continues uphill through the valley for another 5 miles to North Piney Creek Meadows. Bear left onto FT 2060 (Lake Creek Trail) to head through the Lake Creek drainage toward North Piney Lake.

At 2.6 miles, the trail fords North Piney Creek through a wall of willows. Though the crossing isn't that deep, there are deep pools on the side that you can land in if you venture too far off course.

The trail pulls parallel to Lake Creek by mile 3. This timbered, roughening path gets more rocks and steeper inclines as it passes between small parks and a lusher forest of spruce and fir. You'll also pass a single-track trail (closed to ATVs) that connects this trail to the North Piney Trail.

The ATV trail reaches the mountain-enveloped North Piney Lake at 4.5 miles, but continues around the south shoreline to reach a trailhead. From here, a foot trail climbs to the crest of the range and intersects the Wyoming Range National Recreation Trail.

24: Big Spring Scenic Backway
Journey into the Tunp Range

☒ Backcountry Drive Most vehicles	☐ 4WD Route 4x4 vehicle or ORV	☐ ATV Trail ORV less than 50" wide

Location/Map	Northwest of Kemmerer; Page 416
Roads	HWY 232, FR 10062, CR 305, HWY 233
Distance	68 miles (96 miles with Hobble Creek)
Managing Agency	USDA Forest Service—Bridger-Teton National Forest
Starting Coordinates	N42° 5.16' W110° 56.67'

Overview: The Big Spring Scenic Backway offers a splendid tour of the lightly-traveled mountains that extend south from the Salt River Range. Officially known as the Tunp Range, the mountains are more commonly referred to by the creeks that run through them—Hams Fork and Hobble Creek—which also give name to two Forest Service campgrounds here. Commissary Ridge, a high divide that runs the length of the range, is a lesser-cited reference.

Simply stated, the backway climbs to a Forest Service picnic area and then returns to the lower country. But it's much more than that. Along the way, you'll find mountains that are replete with high overlooks and an abundance of wildlife and wildflowers. There is a side road that heads northward into remote backcountry near Lake Alice—a destination that is worth every step of the 1.5 miles it takes to hike to its shores. This is a backway that warrants more than a few hours to complete; plan on a longer outing.

A third of the backway is paved and you'll find easy driving if you stay on the designated route. But the mountains here beckon to be explored further and the numerous, tempting side roads demand good tires in dry conditions and four-wheel drive in bad. Depending on seasonal snow conditions, the backway is often accessible from July through October.

Start: The west end of the backway begins from HWY 30/89 at Cokeville, which is located 54 miles south of Afton. To reach the east end of the backway, drive north of Kemmerer on HWY 189 for less than a mile and bear left onto HWY 233.

Description: The official backway begins on HWY 232, which heads east from the town of Cokeville. The highway immediately swings around the abrupt, rocky spike named Big Hill and then heads northeast through the Smiths Fork drainage. This paved segment continues a little over 12 miles until it ends near a fork. Bear right onto gravel Hams Fork Road (FR 10062).

This road climbs briskly into short, sagebrush-covered foothills. A small stream, Coal Creek, parallels the roadway for a short distance but is lost when the road enters the Bridger-Teton National Forest. Evergreens can be found on the hills' wetter draws and northern aspects, but this is still exposed and dry country.

Near mile 18, the backway makes a sharp turn to the south and continues climbing to attain a ridge where you'll find a terrific overlook. A junction at the top requires a decision—continue to the right and stay on the backway or turn left onto FR 10193, which leads to Hobble Creek Campground and Lake Alice.

SIDE TRIP

> The 14-mile drive to Hobble Creek is not a quick jaunt, but is well worth the extra time and effort it requires. Rough and rocky in places, the road heads deep into the Tunp Range where you'll discover dense coniferous forests as well as wildflower-laden parks. The most exhilarating portion comes in the second half of the drive where the vast mountain vistas will convince you that the Tunp Range is Wyoming's best kept secret. Then, as if to prove the point, the road zigzags off a steep mountainside, offering a whole new vantage point of the Hobble Creek drainage and distant Salt River Range.
>
> When you reach the drainage, some 1,500 feet lower, you'll find a ford where the road crosses Hobble Creek. Though the stream can be found more than a foot deep by mid-summer, a concrete lining makes the crossing easier. Past the ford, you'll find Hobble Creek Campground, a remote Forest Service site that also serves as a trailhead for nearby Lake Alice. To reach the southern end of this natural reservoir, follow the foot trail for 1.5 miles through excellent moose habitat. Backcountry campsites can be found along the lake's shore.
>
> For your return to the backway, consider taking FR 10198. Though this narrow road is rough and not suitable for passenger sedans, it is easily driven in any 4WD vehicle. You'll pass through thick patches of wildflowers and cut across the top of Middle Ridge. This route rejoins the backway just a few miles east of where you left it.

Continuing along the backway, the road descends from the ridge and soon reaches FR 10069. Turn left at this junction and head east to the Big Spring Picnic Area. Here you'll find a pretty cascade that flows from the hillside and empties into the West Fork of the Hams Fork River.

From the spring, follow the road as it ascends a hill and turns northeast to reach a fork. On the right, FR 10151 diverts from the main route and travels several miles through the mountain range's high meadows. The scenic backway stays left and traverses Hams Fork Ridge where it rises above Basin Creek. The high point of this drive (8,525 feet) is reached at the top of this ridge where another junction awaits. Headed north is FR 10198, a rougher road that leads to Green Knoll and Hobble Creek Campground. Bear right here to stay on FR 10062.

From the high point near mile 26, the road curves through a coniferous north-facing slope and then switchbacks off the mountain to arrive in the Hams Fork drainage. Headwaters for this creek originate from springs and high terrain around Red Park, about eleven "river miles" to the northeast. From there, the stream flows southward for 30 miles before spilling into Lake Viva Naughton. It's a unique drainage that is lined with thick willows on both sides. The shrubs fill the valley bottom, a full quarter mile wide in most places. A bridge spans the waterway and the backway strikes a road on the other side that accesses the Elk Creek and Indian Creek Trailheads. Stay right and follow the road south to pass Hams Fork Campground and then the historic Elk Creek Ranger Station cabin, which was built in 1914.

The road now straightens out as it follows the natural course of the creek, but this isn't country that you want to travel through too quickly. The Hams Fork is known as one of Wyoming's best moose habitats. More than 300 of the large mammals spend their winter along this drainage. While they

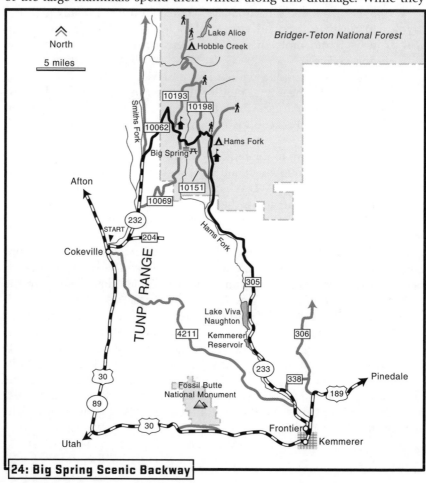

24: Big Spring Scenic Backway

are more dispersed during the summer driving months, your chances of spotting one of these animals are still tremendous. Not once have I toured this backway without spotting at least one moose. Elk, mule deer, and antelope are other big game animals that you might see.

The road steadily loses elevation and leaves the national forest by mile 35. Land ownership now transitions to a mix of BLM, state, and private. If you're looking to cast a line to the trout along this stretch, you're best off waiting until you reach one of the upcoming reservoirs or public river access points.

Overlooking the Hobble Creek drainage

Perhaps the most unusual feature you'll encounter along any Wyoming backroad is soon found as the road curves near a wooden post adorned with dozens of stuffed animals, mostly teddy bears. Known as Teddy Bear Corner, the oddity is said to have started by an elderly man as a memorial for a small girl who was killed at this spot. The collection has flourished over the last two decades and even the post has been upgraded.

At 50 miles, the scenic backway reaches Lake Viva Naughton, a reservoir that is popular for camping, fishing, and boating. The wetlands around this reservoir and its southern neighbor, Kemmerer Reservoir, are prime habitat for a variety of birds. On your way through, watch for sandhill cranes, grouse, geese, and great blue herons.

From the boat ramp at Lake Viva Naughton, the gravel backway turns into HWY 233, a paved course. Continue south a short distance and you'll intersect two paths of the historic Oregon Trail. Though the routes are not marked, you'll likely spot one of the deserted homesteads that were built by the settlers.

The highway crosses Hams Fork right before a turnoff for Dempsey Road (BLMR 4211), a backroad that is rich with emigrant history. The Big Spring Scenic Backway ends a short distance farther at HWY 189, just north of Kemmerer.

25: Hams Fork Plateau
Follow Dempsey Road along emigrant trails

☒ **Backcountry Drive** Most vehicles	☒ **4WD Route** 4x4 vehicle or ORV	☐ **ATV Trail** ORV less than 50" wide

Location/Map	Northwest of Kemmerer; Page 420
Roads	BLMR 4211
Distance	33.5 miles (3.5 miles may require 4WD)
Managing Agency	BLM—Kemmerer Field Office
Starting Coordinates	N41° 51.22' W110° 33.78'

Overview: This drive follows a historical wagon trail as it traverses the Tunp Range, a practically unnoticed uplift that connects to the southern ends of the Salt River and Wyoming Ranges. In the 1800s, many Oregon-and California-bound emigrants crossed this range as a shortcut that saved them about 85 miles and a week's worth of grueling travel. To complete this passage today, you'll need a vehicle with high ground clearance to tackle a steep and rocky section. Without adequate clearance, you can still explore most of the eastern portion of the route and simply turn back where the road roughens.

Start: To access the eastern end of the drive, take HWY 189 north from Kemmerer for less than a mile and bear left onto HWY 233 at Frontier. Head

Driving over Dempsey Ridge

north on this highway for 4.3 miles to the turnoff on the left. To reach the western end of the road from Cokeville, head east on HWY 232 for 2 miles and turn right at the turnoff.

Description: Starting from the east end at HWY 233, follow Dempsey Road (BLMR 4211) as it rises above the Hams Fork drainage. The initial ascent of the sagebrush-covered slope is bumpy and there are some ruts, but this is a short stretch and the ride soon smoothes out as the road strikes the broad summit of Hams Fork Plateau by mile 4.

The next few miles parallel the Hams Fork Cutoff, which was a connector wagon trail that emigrants used to tie into the more popular Sublette Cutoff. A quick glance at a topographical map shows why the pioneers chose this route. The gentle flats on Hams Fork Plateau bisect an area of very steep and rugged terrain. This provided travelers up to 15 miles of relatively easy passage across an area dominated by north-south running ridges that comprise what is now Wyoming's energy-rich Overthrust Belt.

A modern-day rock memorial is passed near mile 5 and a mine is passed a mile later. The road continues to track across the top of the plateau, offering generous views of the surrounding region and mountain ranges. Along the way, you might see antelope, rabbits, and domestic sheep, which are brought here for grazing.

By mile 12, the road passes over Quakenasp Canyon to the right followed by a deep valley on the left, which is Schuster Basin. Tall evergreen stands begin to infiltrate the open sagebrush groundcover. The Hams Fork Cutoff

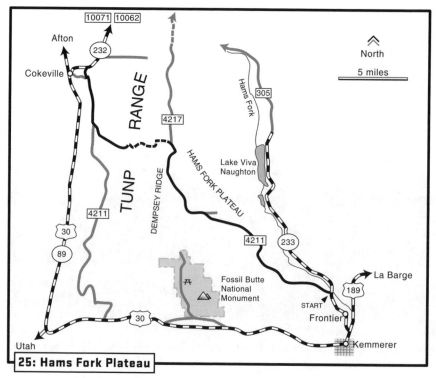

25: Hams Fork Plateau

converges with the Sublette Cutoff near mile 13.5. A sign here marks a side road that leads to two emigrant graves.

SIDE TRIP

Depending on conditions, a 4WD vehicle may be necessary to reach the gravesites about a mile to the east. One grave includes 20-year old Nancy Hill who died of cholera in 1852. The other holds several pioneers including Alfred Corum who died on July 4th, 1849 on his way to California.

Continue another mile to gain the top of Dempsey Ridge where you'll find Emigrant Spring, a favorite camping and trading spot for the emigrants. An excellent interpretive sign along the road tells more of their story. Further north, the road passes below a massive transmission line while weaving between stands of timber that dot the otherwise open plateau. The Tunp Road (BLMR 4217) is reached at 20.5 miles. Turn left at this junction.

SIDE TRIP

Tump Road (the sign shows Tump with an "m") heads north across the open crest of the range for 8 miles, topping Coke Mountain (8,890 feet) along the way. After that, the road drops into the timber and becomes a rougher, rutted, oft-muddy track that enters the Bridger-Teton National Forest by mile 14. A maintained road, FR 10069, can be reached a couple miles north of the national forest boundary.

If you're driving a low-clearance vehicle, this may be as far as you'll want to push it. From the junction, the route bears west and drops steeply along the edge of an evergreen stand. The road is rocky along this descent with a 13% grade. At the bottom of the hill, you'll find a grassy valley that holds a small pond. Drive around the pond, through a shallow ford of Rock Creek, and then up to the top of Rock Creek Ridge. If you're here before the hot days of summer, this last stretch of road through the valley may be muddy and troublesome.

A sign marking the Lost Creek Cooperative Management Unit, a 4,050-acre area managed for large game, is reached on the ridge. From the top of this rise—the last panoramic vantage point—the road descends steeply through Underwood Canyon. After dropping 1,200 feet in a little over 2 miles, you roll out onto the flats and pass a couple of unsigned junctions. Follow the main route through a couple of curves and then back to the north where it joins Stock Driveway Road (also signed as BLMR 4211). The next notable intersection, at mile 29, is signed as private property; stay right and continue north for 4 more miles across Stoffer Ridge, a shallow rise. The drive ends near Big Hill at HWY 232, just 2 miles east of Cokeville.

Other Nearby Drives

Fossil Butte National Monument—The Fossil Butte area was once a subtropical basin and the fossils recovered here include crocodiles, fish, and turtles. The visitor center has about 80 such fossils on display, as well as interpretive programs. A sole road takes you to the monument's attractions, including the visitor center, short hiking trails, a picnic area, and a scenic overlook. To reach this road from Kemmerer, drive west on HWY 30 for 15 miles and turn right on Chicken Creek Road (CR 300). Most of the road is paved as it accesses the visitor center and picnic area. After this point, it turns to gravel and becomes steeper and narrower as it climbs for a few remaining miles. Trailers and RVs are not recommended on the last section.

Overthrust Belt—Between Cokeville and Evanston, BLMR 4308 can be used to explore the Overthrust Belt, an uplift along the Wyoming-Utah state line that runs unbroken through the Rocky Mountains. This belt traps vast reserves of oil and gas. The northern half of the BLM road travels through isolated, unspoiled country. The southern half of the road, and the county roads south of it, runs through one of the largest natural gas fields in the Rocky Mountains, replete with wells, pipelines, stations, and two major gas plants. Signs along the southern half of the road warn motorists of poisonous gas conditions, hazardous material transport, and of potentially prohibited access at times. Take these risks and precautions into account before tackling this drive, or just drive the northern portion. To reach the northern end of the road, head south from Cokeville on HWY 30. Drive 19 miles to a curve in the road and turn right onto HWY 89 toward Utah. Drive just short of 4 miles and turn left onto the road.

26: Uinta Loop
A mountainous loop to Utah and back

☒ Backcountry Drive
Most vehicles

☐ 4WD Route
4x4 vehicle or ORV

☐ ATV Trail
ORV less than 50" wide

Location/Map	Southeast of Evanston; Page 423
Roads	CR 271, FR 058, FR 073, FR 072, CR 283
Distance	49 miles
Managing Agency	USDA Forest Service—Wasatch-Cache National Forest, other mixed ownership
Starting Coordinates	N41° 11.13' W110° 29.69'

Overview: Utah's snowcapped Uinta Mountains form a scenic skyline across southwestern Wyoming. This loop leads you to the north slope of these mountains where you'll discover the beauty of the Wasatch-Cache National Forest in Utah before turning back into Wyoming. Along the way, you'll pass a picturesque river, two large reservoirs, historical sites, and a number of campgrounds. A short section of this drive is not suitable for low-clearance vehicles, but any SUV or pickup truck should work fine.

Start: From Evanston, head east on I-80 to Exit 39. Drive south on HWY 414 for 6 miles to Mountain View. Turn west onto HWY 410 and follow this highway southward toward Robertson. The road reaches a junction after almost 7 miles; the gravel road headed south is CR 283 (shown on some maps as CR 246), the eastern end of the loop. To start the drive from the west end as described here, continue west along the highway for another 6.4 miles to CR 271 (shown on some maps as CR 208) on the left.

Description: Although the first few miles of CR 271 are paved, the road soon adopts a maintained gravel surface. Follow it south as it draws parallel to the Blacks Fork, a major tributary to the Green River. Being close to its headwaters, the river is much smaller here than when it empties into the Flaming Gorge Reservoir, some 50 miles to the east. The road passes two public fishing areas that give you access to the water.

The road climbs steadily toward the mountains and enters the Wasatch-Cache National Forest near mile 10. A few miles farther is the turnoff for Meeks Cabin Reservoir. Here, you'll find an attractive campground on the west shore, a historical site on the north side near the dam, and fishing opportunities for cutthroat trout.

Continuing south from the reservoir, the road, now numbered as FR 058, crosses into Utah, where you get a closer look at the mountain peaks within the High Uinta Wilderness area. The ruins of the Old Blacks Fork Commissary are soon reached. Starting in 1870, these log cabins were used as a government commissary, as well as a logging encampment, for some sixty years.

From the historical ruins, continue south another mile and turn left onto FR 073. This road, part of Utah's North Slope Scenic Backway, begins by crossing over the Blacks Fork. It then becomes a rocky, potholed lane that is not suitable for low-clearance sedans, but it is easily driven with a SUV or pickup truck.

More log cabin ruins are soon passed as FR 073 climbs out of the river drainage and into a predominately lodgepole pine forest. At 23.5 miles, FR 074 is passed on the north. This side road leads to Suicide Park, where three tiehack loggers are buried. Continuing east from this junction, the North Slope Scenic Backway gains a smoother surface and then bends south to pass the Forest Service's Hewinta Guard Station.

After 25 miles, the road enters a sprawling mountain park named Gilbert Meadow. Here, FR 075 goes north toward Mountain View. Stay straight and drive the meandering mountain road another 5 miles. The route climbs to nearly 10,000 feet and then drops into China Meadows, a riparian area where small ponds feed into the Smiths Fork River. A three-way junction is found as you enter the meadows. Turn right and you'll find a campground

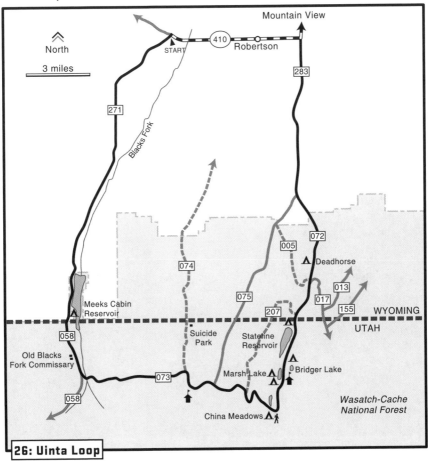

26: Uinta Loop

and wilderness trailhead. To finish the last leg of the driving tour, turn left onto FR 072 and follow it north.

The next 7 miles present many recreational sites. The first of these are Forest Service campgrounds—East Marsh Lake, West Marsh Lake, Bridger Lake, and Stateline—each of which are located in a lodgepole pine forest near a lake.

SIDE TRIP Almost 2 miles north of the Wyoming border, turn right onto FR 17 and drive south for 3.7 miles to FR 155 (Table Mountain). Follow this lane 1.7 miles to a scenic overlook of the Uinta Mountains on FR 403. At this viewpoint, you can survey the Bridger Lake Oil Field, but you wouldn't know it—and that's the point of the overlook, which is sponsored by several oil companies. What you see is a beautiful vista of ponds, forest, and the high, snowy peaks of Uintas.

A few miles after crossing back into Wyoming, you pass Deadhorse Trailhead, which provides access to ATV trails (route #27) and cross-country skiing in the snowy months. The trailhead also has a few campsites.

From Deadhorse, the road begins a steady descent from the Uinta Mountains by soon exiting the national forest and then traveling straight north to CR 283 (marked as CR 246 on the Forest Service map). Just shy of mile 50, the road reaches HWY 410 to conclude the backcountry portion of the drive. You can reach the town of Mountain View by driving northward on the highway for 7 miles.

Approaching Utah from the Meeks Cabin Reservoir area

27: Deadhorse Trail System
ATV trails on the Utah-Wyoming border

☐ **Backcountry Drive**
Most vehicles

☒ **4WD Route**
4x4 vehicle or ORV

☒ **ATV Trail**
ORV less than 50" wide

Location/Map	Southeast of Evanston; Page 426
Roads/Trails	FT 001, FT 002, FR 005, FT 005, FR 207, FT 600, FT 012, FR 370, FR 701
Distance	18+ miles
Managing Agency	USDA Forest Service—Wasatch-Cache National Forest
Starting Coordinates	N41° 2.02' W110° 22.03'

Overview: The Deadhorse ATV trail system straddles the Wyoming-Utah border, crisscrossing through a lodgepole pine forest on the northern slope of the Uinta Mountains. The ATV trails are generally short and segmented, but they connect with 4WD roads to create a decent off-roading network. The paths vary in difficulty, but most are relatively easy to drive.

A Wyoming ORV permit is required. Bear in mind that Utah has its own ATV laws and ORV permit requirements. If you cross the state line, you'll need to be registered in both states—there is no reciprocity. The trails are open to motorized use in their entirety from June 1 to October 31.

While well-signed when I visited the area, these entwined, twisting trails and roads could be very confusing if the markers were missing. A GPS unit that records your tracks could be useful. Also, be aware that trail numbers on the signs do not match the trail numbers shown on the Forest's MVUM. The best map available is the one that is posted on a board at the trailhead.

Start: From Evanston, head east on I-80 to Exit 39. Drive south on HWY 414 for 6 miles to Mountain View. Turn west onto HWY 410 and follow this highway southward toward Robertson. Drive nearly 7 miles to a curve, and continue south by taking CR 283 (marked as CR 246 on the Forest Service map). Drive 11 miles to Deadhorse Trailhead on the right.

The trailhead has a large parking area with four campsites. Other points of access include the intersection of FR 072 and FR 005 to the north, along FR 017 to the east, and from FR 207 near the Utah-Wyoming state line.

Description: From Deadhorse Trailhead, there are two starting options. Heading north you can ride the easy Warm Up Loop or any of the smaller connected loops. There is also the more moderate-rated FT 001, which cuts northwest to reach aspen-lined FR 005 in about 2 miles. This road can then be taken north out of the trail network, or south to tie into other trails. Besides some tree roots and small rocks, these northern routes are fairly easy.

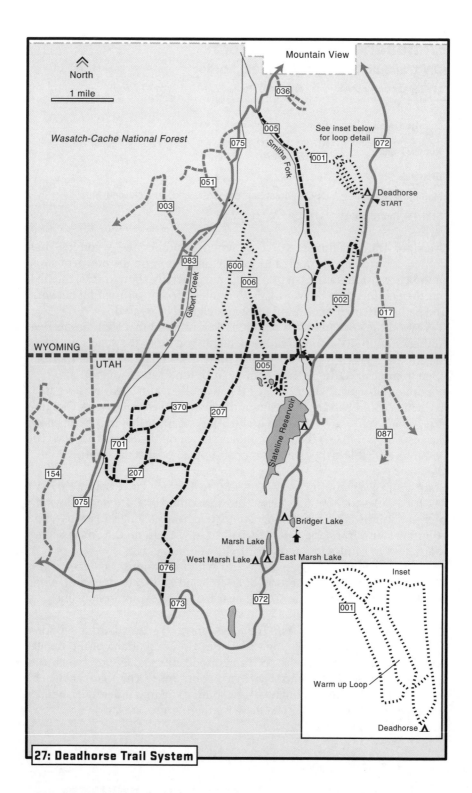

North

1 mile

Wasatch-Cache National Forest

Mountain View

036

005

075

Smiths Fork

See inset below
for loop detail

072

001

Deadhorse
START

051

003

083

Gilbert Creek

600

006

002

017

WYOMING

UTAH

005

370

207

Stateline Reservoir

701

207

154

087

075

076

Bridger Lake

Marsh Lake

West Marsh Lake

East Marsh Lake

073

072

Inset

001

Warm up Loop

Deadhorse

27: Deadhorse Trail System

An ATV trail within the Deadhorse Trail System

Headed south from the trailhead is FT 002, which is part of the Lake Trail. This is a more interesting route that includes rougher segments with more elevation change. Passing first through a lodgepole pine forest and then through parks along the East Fork of the Smith Fork River drainage, the trail reverses direction near Grahams Reservoir. Here, you can drive north and incorporate FR 207 and FT 600 into your trip.

Contacts

National Park Service
http://www.nps.gov

Grand Teton National Park
P.O. Drawer 170
Moose, WY 83012-0170
307-739-3300

Yellowstone National Park
P.O. Box 168
Yellowstone National Park, WY
82190-0168
307-344-7381

USDA Forest Service
http://www.fs.fed.us

Medicine Bow National Forest
http://www.fs.usda.gov/mbr

Laramie District -
Supervisor's Office
2468 Jackson Street
Laramie, WY 82070
307-745-2300

Brush Creek - Hayden
Ranger District
5556 State Highway 130
P.O. Box 249
Saratoga, WY 82331
307-326-5258

Douglas Ranger District
2250 East Richards Street
Douglas, WY 82633
307-358-4690

Bighorn National Forest
http://www.fs.usda.gov/bighorn

Tongue Ranger District
Supervisor's Office
2013 Eastside 2nd Street
Sheridan, WY 82801
307-674-2600

Medicine Wheel/Paintrock
Ranger District
95 Highway 16/20
Greybull, WY 82426
307-765-4435

Powder River Ranger District
1415 Fort Street
Buffalo, WY 82834
307-684-7806

Shoshone National Forest
http://www.fs.usda.gov/shoshone

Supervisor's Office
808 Meadow Lane
Cody, WY 82414
307-527-6241

North Zone Ranger Districts
203A Yellowstone Ave
Cody, WY 82414
307-527-6921

Wind River Ranger District
1403 W Ramshorn
Dubois, WY 82513
307-455-2466

Washakie Ranger District
333 East Main St
Lander, WY 82520
307-332-5460

Black Hills National Forest
http://www.fs.usda.gov/blackhills

Supervisor's Office
1019 N. 5th Street
Custer, SD 57730
605-673-9200

Bearlodge Ranger District
101 South 21st Street, Box 680
Sundance, WY 82729
307-283-1361

Hell Canyon Ranger District
1225 Washington
Newcastle, WY 82701
307-746-2782

Bridger-Teton National Forest
http://www.fs.usda.gov/btnf

Supervisor's Office
340 N. Cache
P.O. Box 1888
Jackson, WY 83001
307-739-5500

Big Piney Ranger District
10418 South HWY 189
P.O. Box 218
Big Piney, WY 83113
307-276-3375

Kemmerer Ranger District
308 Highway 189
Kemmerer, WY 83101
307-828-5100

Pinedale Ranger District
29 East Fremont Lake Rd.
P.O. Box 220
Pinedale, WY 82941
307-367-4326

Greys River Ranger District
671 N. Washington Street
P.O. Box 339
Afton, WY 83110
307-886-5300

Blackrock Ranger District
Highway 26/287
P.O. Box 278
Moran, WY 83013
307-543-2386

Jackson Ranger District
25 Rosencrans Lane
P.O. Box 1689
Jackson, WY 83001
307-739-5400

Caribou-Targhee National Forest
http://www.fs.usda.gov/ctnf

Supervisor's Office
1405 Hollipark Dr
Idaho Falls, ID 83401
208-524-7500

Teton-Basin Ranger District
515 South Main
P.O. Box 777
Driggs, ID 83422
208-354-2312

Ashton-Island Park Ranger District
46 South Highway 20
Ashton, ID 83420
208-652-7442

Wasatch-Cache National Forest
http://www.fs.usda.gov/uwcnf

Supervisor's Office
857 West South Jordan Parkway
South Jordan, UT 84095
801-999-2103

Mountain View Ranger District
321 Highway 414
P.O. Box 129
Mountain View, WY 82939
307-782-6555

Evanston Ranger District
1565 Highway 150, Suite A
P.O. Box 1880
Evanston, WY 82930
307-789-3194

Ashley National Forest
http://www.fs.usda.gov/ashley

Flaming Gorge Ranger District
25 West Highway 43
P.O. Box 279
Manila, UT 84046
435-784-3445

Bureau of Land Management (BLM)
http://www.wy.blm.gov

Wyoming State Office
5353 Yellowstone Road
P.O. Box 1828
Cheyenne, WY 82009
307-775-6256

Rawlins Field Office
1300 N Third Street
P.O. Box 2407
Rawlins, WY 82301
307-328-4200

Buffalo Field Office
1425 Fort Street
Buffalo, WY 82834
307-684-1100

Lander Field Office
1335 Main
P.O. Box 589
Lander, WY 82520
307-332-8400

Pinedale Field Office
1625 West Pine Street
P.O. Box 768
Pinedale, WY 82941
307-367-5300

Newcastle Field Office
1101 Washington Boulevard
Newcastle, WY 82701
307-746-6600

Casper Field Office
2987 Prospector Drive
Casper, WY 82604
307-261-7600

Cody Field Office
1002 Blackburn Street
Cody, WY 82414
307-578-5900

Kemmerer Field Office
430 North Highway 189
Kemmerer, WY 83101
307-828-4500

Rock Springs Field Office
280 Highway 191 North
Rock Springs, WY 82901
307-352-0256

Worland Field Office
101 South 23rd
P.O. Box 119
Worland, WY 82401
307-347-5100

Wyoming Game and Fish

http://wgfd.wyo.gov/

Wyoming Game and Fish
5400 Bishop Blvd.
Cheyenne, WY 82006
307-777-4600

Green River Regional Office
351 Astle
Green River, WY 82935
307-875-3223

Casper Regional Office
3030 Energy Lane, Suite 100
Casper, WY 82604
307-473-3400

Jackson Regional Office
420 North Cache
Jackson, WY 83001
307-733-2321

Cody Regional Office
2820 State Highway 120
Cody, WY 82414
307-527-7125

Lander Regional Office
260 Buena Vista
Lander, WY 82520
307-332-2688

Laramie Regional Office
528 S. Adams
Laramie, WY 82070
307-745-4046

Sheridan Regional Office
700 Valley View Drive
Sheridan, WY 82801
307-672-7418

Pinedale Regional Office
432 Mill Street
Pinedale, WY 82941
307-367-4353

Wyoming State Parks and Historic Sites & Trails

http://wyoparks.state.wy.us/

Wyoming State Parks and Historic Sites & Trails
2301 Central Avenue
Cheyenne, Wyoming 82002
307-777-6323

Wyoming Division of Tourism

http://www.wyomingtourism.org

Wyoming Office of Tourism
5611 High Plains Road
Cheyenne, Wyoming 82007
307-777-7777

Wyoming Counties

This list includes Tourism Boards, Chamber of Commerces, Information Centers, and Recreation & Parks Departments.

Albany County: 800-445-5303
Bighorn County: 307-568-2381
Campbell County: 307-686-3851
Carbon County: 800-228-3547
Converse County: 307-358-2244
Crook County: 307-283-2440
Fremont County: 800-645-6233
Goshen County: 800-577-3555
Hot Springs County: 800-786-6772
Johnson County: 800-227-5122
Laramie County: 307-777-2883
Lincoln County: 888-300-3413

Natrona County: 307-235-9311
Niobrara County: 307-334-2950
Park County: 800-393-2639
Platte County: 307-322-2322
Sheridan County: 307-672-2485
Sublette County: 888-285-7282
Sweetwater County: 800-354-6743
Teton County: 307-733-3316
Uinta County: 307-789-6540
Washakie County: 307-347-8900
Weston County: 307-746-2739

Wyoming Department of Transportation

http://www.dot.state.wy.us

WYDOT Headquarters
5300 Bishop Blvd.
Cheyenne, WY 82009
307-777-4375

Road Conditions: 511 (local) or 1-888-WYO-ROAD

Wyoming Highway Patrol

http://www.whp.dot.state.wy.us

Wyoming Highway Patrol
5300 Bishop Blvd.
Cheyenne, WY 82009
307-777-4301

Road Number Index

BLM Roads

BLMR 1109, 139
BLMR 1111, 139
BLMR 1113, 118
BLMR 1117, 109
BLMR 1129, 145
BLMR 1404, 136, 143
BLMR 1410, 143
BLMR 1411, 142
BLMR 1435, 142
BLMR 2107, 259
BLMR 2302, 278
BLMR 2324, 275
BLMR 2411, 273
BLMR 3115, 265
BLMR 3117, 267
BLMR 3123, 263
BLMR 3127, 263
BLMR 3129, 263, 264
BLMR 3137, 263
BLMR 3144, 264
BLMR 3147, 272
BLMR 3404, 311
BLMR 3423, 315
BLMR 3429, 291
BLMR 3431, 291
BLMR 4102, 367
BLMR 4105, 359
BLMR 4108, 275, 359
BLMR 4113, 360
BLMR 4211, 418
BLMR 4217, 420
BLMR 4308, 421
BLMR 4311, 386
BLMR 4312, 386
BLMR 4313, 386
BLMR 4314, 386
BLMR 4315, 386
BLMR 4316, 388
BLMR 4317, 386
BLMR 4405, 375
BLMR 4411, 377
BLMR 4412, 375, 377, 386
BLMR 5106, 361
BLMR 5201, 364
BLMR 5423, 360
BLMR 6214, 124, 127
BLMR 6217, 124
BLMR 6409, 251

County Roads

CR 102, 265, 272
CR 104, 130
CR 105, 127, 130
CR 109, 130
CR 110, 130, 364
CR 111, 127, 410
CR 111A, 127
CR 117, 134, 409
CR 118, 358, 360
CR 119, 361
CR 121, 272
CR 122, 360
CR 125, 130, 361
CR 129, 42, 409
CR 132, 358
CR 135, 232
CR 138, 409
CR 14, 96, 378
CR 146, 227, 229, 346
CR 154, 361
CR 160, 227
CR 162, 361
CR 17, 50, 227, 250, 367
CR 173, 390
CR 176, 134
CR 18, 250
CR 193, 346
CR 19S, 375
CR 2, 263
CR 201, 259, 260
CR 202, 259, 260, 390
CR 204, 232, 390
CR 208, 230
CR 21, 367
CR 211, 318
CR 212, 259, 346
CR 214, 230
CR 22, 277
CR 235, 341
CR 24, 249
CR 268, 114
CR 27, 373
CR 271, 422
CR 283, 422
CR 291, 268, 272
CR 295, 134
CR 3, 99, 100, 121, 132
CR 300, 421

Forest Roads

FR 868, 45
FR 870, 335
FR 874, 329
FR 875, 42
FR 898, 312
FR 933, 47
FR 942, 47
FR 973, 49

Forest Trails
FT 001, 425
FT 002, 425
FT 008, 76
FT 011, 71
FT 012, 425
FT 025, 402
FT 028, 58
FT 085, 76
FT 100, 103
FT 101, 58
FT 1041, 38
FT 1042, 38
FT 1043, 38
FT 1044, 38
FT 1101, 38
FT 1102, 38
FT 1103, 38
FT 1104, 38
FT 1105, 38
FT 1106, 38
FT 1107, 38
FT 117, 93
FT 1201, 38
FT 1202, 38
FT 1203, 38
FT 1204, 38
FT 1281, 38
FT 1282, 38
FT 1350, 50
FT 1351, 50
FT 1352, 50
FT 1353, 50
FT 1357, 50
FT 1358, 50
FT 159, 76
FT 187, 93
FT 201, 75
FT 2059, 412
FT 2060, 412
FT 211, 299

FT 2146, 220
FT 2149, 220
FT 222, 93
FT 26, 402
FT 27, 402
FT 3037, 398
FT 3182, 398
FT 3183, 404, 408
FT 33, 56
FT 359, 113
FT 360, 113
FT 361, 113
FT 38, 56
FT 402, 111
FT 4202, 199
FT 4204, 199
FT 4209, 194
FT 4210, 194
FT 4211, 194
FT 4212, 194
FT 4213, 194
FT 4215, 201
FT 4216, 201
FT 430, 68
FT 600, 425
FT 602, 238
FT 604, 245
FT 610, 245
FT 615, 245
FT 618, 247
FT 624, 243
FT 628, 65
FT 655, 245
FT 657, 245
FT 66, 111
FT 680, 230
FT 7699, 213
FT 82, 56
FT 849, 113
FT 907, 354
FT MT01, 348
FT MT10, 207

Index

Open Space Publications

Looking for more information on Wyoming or South Dakota? Check out these other titles:

- **Hiking Wyoming's Medicine Bow National Forest** covers several mountain ranges and hundreds of miles of trails in east-central and southeastern Wyoming. This trail guide will lead you to adventure in the Snowy Range, Sierra Madre, Medicine Bow, Pole, and Laramie Mountains.

- **The Wyoming Camping Guide** is the most comprehensive camping book you'll find for the state. With over 400 pages, this complete guidebook describes hundreds of public campgrounds so you can find the perfect place for your next outing. The campgrounds' descriptions include trails, picnic areas, and natural attractions. You'll also find where to fish, boat, view wildlife, or rock climb. The guide is complemented with an 8-page color insert as well as scores of photos and maps. All of the details that campers want to know, such as elevations, costs, parking spur lengths, and operating seasons are included to make your trip easy to plan.

- **Black Hills Camping** is a trustworthy guide for finding the perfect campsite in the Black Hills of Wyoming and South Dakota. You'll find dozens of public campgrounds that are located in the area's national parks, national monuments, national forests, and state parks. Each camp description includes a photo and map. You'll also find a 4-page color insert and descriptions of the Black Hills' most popular attractions.

Contact us for more information:
www.OpenSpacePublications.com

Open Space Publications, LLC
PO Box 50133
Casper, WY 82605-0133

About the Author

Marc Smith has been driving the dusty backroads of Wyoming for over 20 years. As a technical writer, he works on forest management projects with the USDA Forest Service. While much of his spare time is spent exploring Wyoming and the wilds of neighboring states, he also stays busy by serving on a Search and Rescue team.

Marc's other books include Hiking Wyoming's Medicine Bow National Forest, The Wyoming Camping Guide, Black Hills Camping, and Rocky Mountain National Park With Kids.

Updates

Updates to this guide can be found at www.OpenSpacePublications.com. If you discover an update that is needed or just want to share your trip notes, please forward the information to us at:

Open Space Publications, LLC
P.O. Box 50133
Casper, WY 82605-0133

info@OpenSpacePublications.com

Open Space
Publications

Casper, Wyoming